Praise for
Maxwell Taylor Kennedy's *Danger's Hour*

"A fast-paced, almost novelistic account of suffering and heroism."

—*The Washington Post*

"A chilling and captivating story of horror and heroic self-sacrifice . . .
Why no scholar or historian has told this story before is a mystery, but it's
hard to imagine anyone could have written a better book about it than
Maxwell Taylor Kennedy has."

—*Chicago Tribune*

"Extraordinary. . . . Remarkably complete and compelling."

—*The New York Observer*

"This book is a triumph—an original conception, a dramatic narrative
superbly told, with lyrical portraits of brave men on opposite sides of a
titanic struggle and impeccable research masterfully rendered. With *Danger's Hour,* Maxwell Kennedy's talents as a first-rate historian, an intrepid
interviewer, and a wonderful writer are on full display."

—Doris Kearns Goodwin, author of *Team of Rivals*

"One of the little-known aspects of World War II was the role played by
Japan's suicidal kamikaze pilots and their devastating impact on the U.S.
Navy in the Pacific. Maxwell Taylor Kennedy tells their story in a detailed,
vivid, credible, highly readable narrative."

—Stanley Karnow, author of *Vietnam: A History*

"This is a riveting, thought-provoking, superbly written history that unfolds and surprises like a novel. What we are permitted to participate in is nothing short of hell: a glimpse into the most asymmetrical warfare we Americans have ever faced—the kamikaze pilot."

—Ken Burns, filmmaker

"Maxwell Kennedy has written a spellbinding book about one of the most frightening developments of World War II—the rise of suicide attackers, the dreaded Japanese kamikaze pilots who were persuaded to become human bombs. This is the story of one of the most devastating attacks— on the USS *Bunker Hill*—and the Japanese pilot who carried it out. It is a story of courage, desperation, loss, and, most of all, a story that reminds us again of the madness of war."

—Tom Brokaw

"This fascinating story of the deadliest kamikaze attack in World War II provides a vivid window on the war in the Pacific. But it also contains critically important insights for today's struggle against terrorists. Maxwell Kennedy shows how suicide bombers are recruited, the role they can play in asymmetric warfare, and how our military can be resilient in face of such attacks."

—Walter Isaacson, author of *Benjamin Franklin: An American Life* and
Einstein: His Life and Universe

"The author combines extensive archival research with interviews of American and Japanese participants in a spellbinding account showing that much more than geopolitics was at stake in the Pacific war."

—*Publishers Weekly*

"Elaborate study of one of the final naval battles of World War II, focus- ing on both Japanese and American participants . . . Kennedy writes well, if gruesomely, of the lives of the fighters on both sides."

—*Kirkus*

"Kennedy picks apart the terrible events of that day in remarkable detail . . . Highly recommended."

—Library Journal

"Solid in the disaster-at-sea department, Kennedy's book, with its original slant on Ogawa, will be of particular interest to the WWII readership."

—Booklist

ALSO BY MAXWELL TAYLOR KENNEDY

Make Gentle the Life of This World

DANGER'S HOUR

THE STORY OF THE USS *BUNKER HILL*
and the Kamikaze Pilot Who Crippled Her

Maxwell Taylor Kennedy

Simon & Schuster Paperbacks

NEW YORK   LONDON   TORONTO   SYDNEY

Simon & Schuster Paperbacks
A Division of Simon & Schuster, Inc.
1230 Avenue of the Americas
New York, NY 10020

First Simon & Schuster trade paperback edition November 2009

SIMON & SCHUSTER PAPERBACKS and colophon are registered
trademarks of Simon & Schuster, Inc.

For information about special discounts for bulk purchases,
please contact Simon & Schuster Special Sales at
1-866-506-1949 or business@simonandschuster.com.

The Simon & Schuster Speakers Bureau can bring authors
to your live event. For more information or to book an event,
contact the Simon & Schuster Speakers Bureau at
1-866-248-3049 or visit our website at www.simonspeakers.com.

Text and back endpaper designed by Paul Dippolito
Front endpaper by Paul Pugliese

Manufactured in the United States of America

1   3   5   7   9   10   8   6   4   2

The Library of Congress has cataloged the hardcover edition as follows:
Kennedy, Maxwell Taylor.
Danger's hour : the story of the USS Bunker Hill and the kamikaze pilot who crippled her /
by Maxwell Taylor Kennedy.
p.   cm.
Includes bibliographical references and index.
1. Bunker Hill (Aircraft carrier : CV-17)   2. World War, 1939–1945—Regimental
histories—United States.   3. World War, 1939–1945—Naval operations,
American.   4. World War, 1939–1945—Aerial operations, American.
5. World War, 1939–1945—Aerial operations, Japanese.   6. World War,
1939–1945—Campaigns—Pacific Ocean.   I. Title.
D774.B86K46   2008
940.54'252294—dc22   2008015863
ISBN 978-0-7432-6080-0
ISBN 978-0-7432-6081-7 (pbk)
ISBN 978-1-4165-9442-0 (ebook)

For Vicki
All my love

CONTENTS

PART II · RENDEZVOUS WITH DEATH

PART III · AFTERWARD

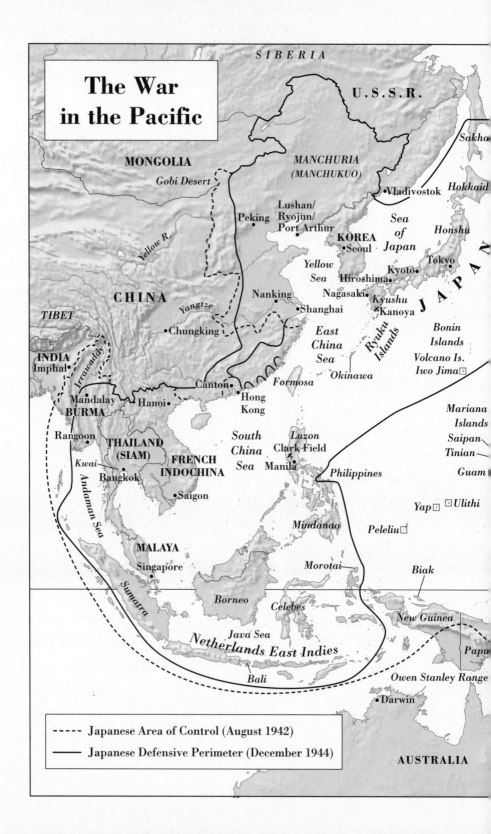

The War
in the Pacific

SIBERIA

U.S.S.R.

Sakha

MONGOLIA

Gobi Desert

MANCHURIA
(MANCHUKUO)

•Vladivostok

Hokkaid

Yellow R.

Peking

Lushan/
Ryojun/
Port Arthur

KOREA

•Seoul

Sea
of
Japan

Honshu

CHINA

Yangtze

•Chungking

Nanking

•Shanghai

*Yellow
Sea*

Hiroshima•

Nagasaki•

Kyoto•

Tokyo
•

Kyushu
Kanoya

JAPAN

TIBET

Irrawaddy

INDIA
Imphal•

•Mandalay

BURMA

Rangoon•

Hanoi•

Canton•

Hong
Kong

Formosa

East
China
Sea

*Ryukyu
Islands*

Okinawa

Bonin
Islands

Volcano Is.
Iwo Jima ☐

THAILAND
(SIAM)

Kwai

Bangkok•

FRENCH
INDOCHINA

•Saigon

Andaman Sea

South
China
Sea

Luzon
Clark Field
Manila

Philippines

Mariana
Islands

Saipan•
Tinian—

Guam

Yap☐ ☐Ulithi

Mindanao

Peleliu☐

MALAYA

Singapore•

Sumatra

Borneo

Celebes

Morotai•

Biak

New Guinea

Java Sea

Netherlands East Indies

Bali

Owen Stanley Range

Papu

•Darwin

- - - -   Japanese Area of Control (August 1942)

———   Japanese Defensive Perimeter (December 1944)

AUSTRALIA

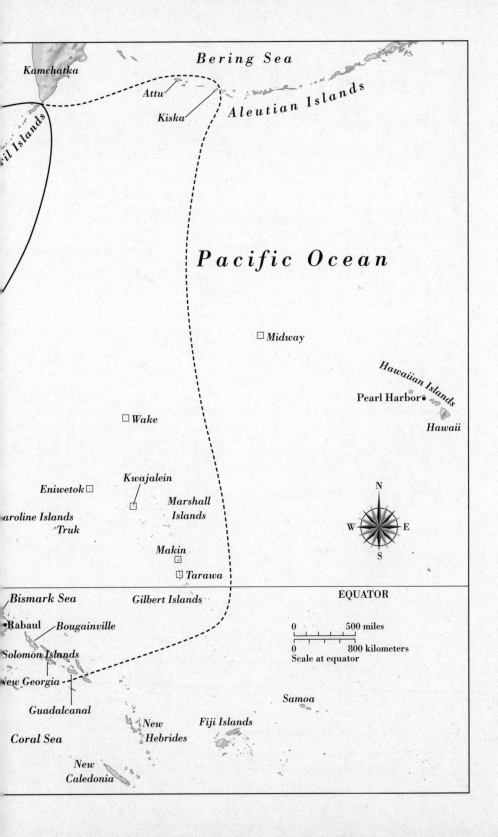

Kamchatka

Bering Sea

Attu

Kiska

Aleutian Islands

...il Islands

Pacific Ocean

□ Midway

Hawaiian Islands

Pearl Harbor •

Hawaii

□ Wake

Kwajalein

Eniwetok □

□

Marshall Islands

...aroline Islands

Truk

N

W   E

S

Makin

□

□ *Tarawa*

EQUATOR

Bismark Sea

Gilbert Islands

• Rabaul   *Bougainville*

Solomon Islands

New Georgia

Guadalcanal

Coral Sea

Samoa

New
Hebrides

Fiji Islands

New
Caledonia

0   500 miles

0   800 kilometers
Scale at equator

INTRODUCTION

The U.S. Navy's struggle against kamikaze pilots off the coast of Japan in the last months of World War II was the last great naval confrontation of the war. This is the story of what happened on May 11, 1945, aboard the USS *Bunker Hill*, during the worst kamikaze attack on American forces. Historians have ignored this confrontation for over half a century. Eclipsed by the surrender of Germany three days earlier, the attack has become a mere footnote even in detailed naval histories of the Pacific war.

Two cultures, American and Japanese, collided aboard the *Bunker Hill* that day. It was and is almost impossible for Americans to comprehend cultural forces that would obliterate the will to live. How could so many young men train for months for a mission whose success necessarily meant their own death? Particularly when the suiciders knew Japan was going to lose the war. As America struggles to come to terms with a global war on terror, and the reality of suicide bombings around the world, it is vital to understand the cultural forces that can overcome the basic desire to survive.

This is also the story of the men, both American and Japanese, whose lives intersected that day on the *Bunker Hill*, an icon of the Second World War. The *Bunker Hill* was the flagship of the American naval air forces that carried the Pacific war to the Japanese. Among the officers aboard her that day were two of the most important naval strategists of World War II and postwar U.S. naval doctrine: the father of carrier battle group strategy and the fast carrier forces, Admiral Marc Mitscher—who skippered the *Hornet* in the Doolittle Raid and at Midway and often sat in the bridge at night, wearing a long bathrobe and a lobsterman's hat over his bald head—and Mitscher's

1

equally brilliant chief of staff, Arleigh Burke.* Burke later served an unprecedented three terms as chief of naval operations and is rightly credited with building the nuclear Navy.

Histories usually are written about men like Mitscher and Burke—the military leaders who determined the course of the war. But the great lessons of World War II may be learned by passing on the stories of the "ordinary" men who were dragged into the conflict, who fought with and for each other. These men are dying now at a faster rate than they were killed during the war itself. It is vital that we record their stories, their hopes, and their wisdom to hand along to our own children.

This remains essentially a story about ordinary men—laborers, factory workers, college students—who were thrust into an extraordinary situation and performed many exceptional acts of bravery. But for Pearl Harbor few of these men would ever have joined the armed forces. The war, though, became their own.

Few *Bunker Hill* crewmen had been aboard ship before they joined the Navy. Most did not know how to swim. Many had not seen the ocean. Only a small portion could have found Japan on a map. By 1945, they had been tired for the nearly two years since she left Boston, because it was nearly impossible to sleep in the crowded quarters of a carrier where aircraft were always taking off and landing, and where the threat of enemy attack remained omnipresent for weeks on end. Yet at the critical moment, the time of decision, each had the particular quality to say, "I will do this."

"I will fight the fire."

"I will remain in the smoke-filled room, though it will kill me, because that is what it will take to save this ship, and my shipmates' lives."

---

* On the anniversary of Paul Revere's ride, April 18, 1942, Admiral Mitscher steered the carrier *Hornet* to within 600 miles of Japan—just close enough to launch sixteen specially modified Army B-25 medium bombers against targets in Tokyo and Nagoya. The aircraft, led by Lieutenant Colonel James H. Doolittle, carried just enough fuel for a one-way trip. After dropping their bombs, the pilots were to continue to U.S. airfields in China. It was the most daring American raid of the Pacific war up to that time, boosting American morale and deeply embarrassing the Japanese Navy and government. Mitscher's raid showed the Japanese that they were not safe from American attack.

Caleb Kendall and Al Turnbull—college students from dissimilar backgrounds—served aboard the *Bunker Hill* as Navy pilots. Turnbull was the son of an immigrant sign painter attending a state school. Kendall's ancestors fought in the Revolution—in the Battle at Bunker Hill—and, like him, attended Harvard. The chief engineer, Joseph Carmichael, joined the Navy in the 1930s. The son of a mining engineer, he kept the engines running. Edmund Skacan was a regular crewman—he joined the Navy to avoid getting drafted into the Army.

The war and the *Bunker Hill* brought all of these men together. But it was the kamikaze attack on May 11, 1945, that has held them inextricably intertwined since that day.

In 1943, the Japanese drafted a young, gifted university student and trained him to fly his plane into enemy targets. His name was Kiyoshi Ogawa. Kiyoshi was among the first men to use suicide as a tactic and to use aircraft as a suicidal weapon. His sacrifice was the only effective defense the weakened Japanese military could muster against overwhelming American matériel superiority. Kiyoshi's death dive changed the life of every man on the *Bunker Hill*; it also left Americans uneasy about the postwar world.

Americans in the middle of the twentieth century spent a huge amount of time avoiding the fact of death in their daily lives; not really accepting the capriciousness of the universe. They were taught that by improving their own individual lives, citizens would improve America. The Japanese, on the other hand, strove daily to accept their own limited individual lives, and to live instead *Bushido*, the warrior ideal of individual sacrifice in favor of the collective society. The kamikazes epitomized this warrior ideal, and its clash with American values.

Perhaps the most basic cultural value, the role of an individual within society, set Americans apart from Japanese during the middle of the twentieth century. Americans were schooled in the ideal of rugged individuals on an errand into the wilderness, hewing with a broad axe a new nation carved from a new continent, raised to believe that their nation was not subject to limits. The manifest destiny of the United States was to expand westward, and any difficulty could be overcome by an individual willing to work hard to solve the problem. American ability, ingenuity, and success, like the Great Plains, appeared to have no limits. Japanese understood more deeply that their individual lives remained fundamentally limited, and that the only thing that might last would be their contribution to Japan, which remained eternal.

In Japan the essence and continuance of society was preeminent for a thousand years. In medieval Japan *samurai* safeguarded the social fabric. Any threat to the *samurai* system was seen to threaten the whole community. Every Japanese knows the story of the 47 *ronin*: *samurai* whose master had been put to death. Duty required that they kill the man responsible. But the law dictated that if they murdered the culprit, they, too, must die. The *ronin* determined nevertheless to honor their social duty and avenge their master's death, even though revenge meant they all must commit suicide. It took the 47 *ronin* two years to carry out their plan, each day knowing they were that much closer to suicide. In the end, they cut off the head of the lord who caused their master's death. Then, together, they went to their master's grave and committed *seppuku*, a highly ritualized act of suicide. Each *ronin* thrust a nine-inch dagger into his own belly.* Then with both hands, he drove it up, tearing his chest cavity open. These suicidal *ronin* who put the group interest above their own are still revered by virtually every Japanese.

A basic tenet of Western culture is aversion to suicide. But this distaste is a relatively recent phenomenon. Romans, like the Japanese, considered suicide an honorable solution to personal failure. Greek and Roman civilizations revered the suicides of Socrates and Seneca, just as failing Japanese leaders during World War II saw suicide as a rational, even praiseworthy act.

Christian dogma, too, has not always held that suicide is a sin. Christians have always maintained that killing oneself in order to accomplish a greater good is acceptable. When a dangling mountain climber cuts his line so that the rest of his group might make a safe return, he is not committing a sin. The determination of righteousness lies in intent. If one is killing oneself to avoid pain or misery, it is forbidden, but if one is putting one's life on the line for a greater good it is heroic. This is not terribly far off from the Japanese point of view.

---

* A single *ronin*, probably the youngest, was allowed to survive.

The rub, of course, lies in determining what constitutes a legitimate interest and a legitimate death. Winston Churchill, when he saw news footage of the bombing of Berlin, asked, "Have we become animals?" But he continued to burn women and children alive throughout the war. Moral lines blurred. One of this book's objectives is to enable us to understand, through the power of a story, how an individual's desire to live can be so successfully suppressed that he is willing to train for months to kill himself in the perpetration of a mass homicide. The answer is as complex as human belief.

By the spring of 1945 Japan was devastated. They had almost no fuel; their air force and navy had been decimated by American forces. Their cities had been completely bombed out. Their army was retreating in Asia, and beyond the help of the Home Islands. Japanese civilians were starving. More than anything, the brutality of this war seemed to harden the will of combatants on both sides. Americans resolved that the Japanese war machine had to be utterly destroyed. The Japanese military hierarchy knew that the United States military would eventually annihilate them, and so in the war's desperate last nine months, they finally made suicide attacks state policy and turned increasingly to the kamikazes. The Japanese leadership came to see these young pilots as not merely a solution to their dwindling military aircraft, bombs, and fuel supplies, but also as a means of revitalizing the *Bushido* fighting spirit of the entire nation, the warrior ethic that it was better to die than to submit.

The kamikazes were the first men to use suicide as a matter of state policy. They used only marked military vehicles and always attacked in uniform. They never targeted civilians. Nevertheless the Japanese military leadership well understood the evil they were converting into state policy. "Such an inhuman thing will have to be answered for in heaven," Rikihei Inoguchi* said in March 1942 when he heard that Admiral Isoroku Yamamoto had organized midget submarine attacks in which the pilots were not expected to survive.

---

* Inoguchi was Senior Staff Officer of the First Air Fleet.

Desperation born of Japan's imminent destruction distorted Japanese values. Two years later, Inoguchi planned and organized the Imperial Japanese Navy's kamikaze program. The kamikazes moved Japanese policy an important step beyond the tactics of self-sacrifice. Pilots and crewmen of midget submarines had not been expected to survive. But it was at least theoretically possible for these submariners to both succeed in their mission and remain alive. A few did. A successful kamikaze mission, in sharp, appalling contrast to historic military policy in Japan and the West, absolutely necessitated the pilot's death. None who succeeded could survive.

Japan had not faced invasion since the thirteenth century when Kublai Khan sent 40,000 men to attack the Home Islands. The Khan's overwhelming force appeared certain to triumph against the paltry Japanese armed forces. But a severe typhoon struck the Khan's fleet and sank more than 200 of his ships. This storm became known in Japan as the Divine Wind. The wind appeared a clear indication of the divine protection of Japan as God's chosen culture. The character for Divine Wind may be pronounced as "kamikaze." Thus, the young men who served as kamikazes were a human realization of God's saving grace on the Japanese. Just as the first Divine Wind saved Japan at its darkest moment and ushered in a victory that would preserve the emperor's line for a thousand years, so the young kamikazes would again save the nation.

The kamikazes were more formally called *tokkotai*—"Special Attack Corps." So the kamikaze *tokkotai* was the Divine Wind Special Attack Corps. The term "special attack" was a euphemism for self-sacrifice or suicide. Today, the pilots who survived their assignment to the *tokkotai* corps refer to themselves interchangeably as kamikaze or *tokko* pilots. I will use both these words to describe them in this book.

Choosing death was a complex issue in Japan even during the war. Veteran Japanese fighter pilots serving in the Philippines volunteered in great numbers to be kamikaze in late 1944. When these front-line pilots were killed, it became more difficult to get newly trained conscripts to replace them. Many of the young draftees, like Kiyoshi Ogawa, were simply ordered to kamikaze duty in the last months of the war.

But it is clear that most of the kamikaze pilots were not mere fanatics, happily dying for the emperor. Few if any felt they would be rewarded in heaven for their martial deaths. Japan's decision to order widespread suicide missions upset and astonished many of the conscripted pilots. Flying Officer Ryuji Nagatsuka, who survived his kamikaze mission, wrote that when he bowed down before his final flight he saw flowers at his feet and thought, in outrage and amazement at his death sentence and imminent mortality:

> They still have the right to live, whereas I shall be dead in two or three hours! My life will have been more fleeting than that of a humble blade of grass.

The *Bunker Hill* functioned essentially as a protective shield for the men who fought aboard her—a steel holding environment from which to launch assaults. She was too valuable to take part in most forward engagements. But when the war finally moved to Japan itself, the carriers had to remain in harm's way, within easy striking distance of Japan's kamikaze bases. And so, suicide transformed the *Bunker Hill* from a place of safety in the vanguard of attack to the disquiet and anxiety of being America's largest target, waiting, it seemed, mainly to be bombed or crashed. It became obvious to the men on the *Bunker Hill* that the kamikazes were a new weapon, which like today's suiciders could come anytime, day or night, and from which no amount of aircraft, ammunition, training, or technology could protect them.

This is a story about men, but it is also a story about the world being remade, as it has been every fifty years or so since the Age of Reason. Japan, the last great warrior culture, was destroyed and then reborn as a peculiar bourgeois democracy, while the American triumph at the end of the Second World War marked the beginning of what Henry Luce called "The American Century." It has been more than fifty years since that victory, and the world is again beginning to change in vital ways. We cannot hope to understand those changes without knowing how Americans as a people won that victory.

Not since World War II has this story been more relevant. For the first time in sixty years the United States again is confronted by the actions of groups of people driven to sacrifice their own lives in order to harm us. Once again, the most effective weapon being used against American armed forces today is suicide. Aircraft carriers remain the backbone of U.S. naval ability to extend force beyond American borders. American carrier battle groups have sailed back and forth to the Persian Gulf for the last several years to support American troops in Iraq and Afghanistan. The carriers are still the safest, most flexible forward operations base in the U.S. arsenal. They have proved since the close of the Second World War to be immune from suicide attack.

"Horatius at the Bridge" was young Winston Churchill's favorite poem. This epic, a celebration of what bravery, determination, self-sacrifice, and moral authority may accomplish in battle over a foe with grave numerical superiority, could have been written by any of the poets of Japanese Shinto, and echoes the strategy of the kamikaze defense.

"Horatius at the Bridge"

Then out spake brave Horatius,
The Captain of the gate:
"To every man upon this earth
Death cometh soon or late.
And how can man die better
Than facing fearful odds,
For the ashes of his fathers,
And the temples of his Gods,

"And for the tender mother
Who dandled him to rest,

And for the wife who nurses
His baby at her breast,
And for the holy maidens
Who feed the eternal flame,
To save them from false Sextus
That wrought the deed of shame?
"Hew down the bridge, Sir Consul,
With all the speed ye may;
I, with two more to help me,
Will hold the foe in play.
In yon strait path a thousand
May well be stopped by three.
Now who will stand on either hand,
And keep the bridge with me?"
—THOMAS BABINGTON MACAULAY

Young men willing to sacrifice their lives, each to stop a single ship, could as individuals achieve more in Special Attacks than a thousand men in conventional battle. Churchill's hero Horatius gave his life to delay Sextus's shameful attack—and gave the city time to destroy the bridge and mount an effective defense. The kamikazes would sink enough carriers and other ships of the American invasion force to enable the Japanese to recover their military forces, or compel a more honorable peace. The war, however, had been decided long before the young men of the Special Attack Corps were called to their tragic mass self-sacrifice, and long before the men of the *Bunker Hill* were called to give so much to put an end finally to the long war.

But Horatius's self-sacrifice at the bridge remains important not merely because he held the bridge. Rather it is the fact that so many Westerners have been inspired over generations by individual martial sacrifices, similar to Horatio's, which must alert us to take note. American youth are taught that the sacrifice of servicemen in every American war was worthwhile to protect American freedoms. Japanese military leaders well understood they had lost the war when they forced so many young men to die as kamikazes. But they knew, too, that thousands, even millions, may be inspired to sacrifice by the moral example of a young man willing to give his life even to a desperate cause. Their last hope remained that Japanese of future generations would take heart and resist in the spirit of the special attackers. It is this alluring and ennobling aspect of suicide attacks that everyone living now must try to understand.

PART I

LOOMINGS

Circumambulate the city of a dreamy Sabbath afternoon . . . what do you see?—posted like silent sentinels all around the town, stand thousands upon thousands of mortal men fixed in ocean reveries. Some leaning against the spiles; some seated upon the pier-heads; some looking over the bulwarks of ships from China; some high aloft in the rigging, as if striving to get a still better seaward peep.

—HERMAN MELVILLE, *MOBY-DICK*

1. THE PATH TO PEARL HARBOR

But she goes not abroad, in search of monsters to destroy.
—JOHN QUINCY ADAMS ON AMERICA, 1821

Looming is an old sea term—it describes the result of peculiar atmospheric conditions that occur rarely, but most often at sea, in which ships far beyond the furthest horizon may be clearly seen long before they are within visual range. When this happens, sailors and landsmen near shore are treated to a view over the horizon—a look forward into time. Rural Americans were shocked by the bombing of Pearl Harbor. Easterners thought the war would begin in Europe, but students on the West Coast, and those Americans who followed events in Asia more closely during the 1930s, saw war in the Pacific looming over the not so far horizon.

In 1939, America and Japan were on a collision course. Both their economies were recovering. Defense spending was lifting each nation's economic potential. Shipyards in both nations were being expanded. All the while, a noose in the form of an economic blockade was tightening as America brought increasing pressure on Japan to end its expansion in Asia. Japanese militarists who controlled their government determined they would be overthrown if they capitulated to American demands. These leaders, including Hideki Tojo, realized, too, that they could not defeat the United States in a fair fight. The Japanese concluded that they had one chance: if they could severely damage the American Pacific Fleet—especially America's carriers—

then the weakened United States, more concerned about the war in Europe, would make peace with Japan.

It is difficult to rationalize the Japanese attack on Pearl Harbor, and much easier to write it off along with the kamikazes as the irrational act of a fanatical nation gone awry. However, it is important to try to understand the Japanese point of view leading up to the war in the Pacific, and the reasons behind the attack on Pearl Harbor. A detailed analysis is far beyond the scope of this book, but a broad outline may be drawn.

From the time of the first European settlements in America, a frontier line, descending north to south, separated civilization from wilderness. This line can be seen clearly on maps through the decades, beginning first on the Eastern Seaboard, and moving steadily westward. By the mid-nineteenth century, the western frontier began to merge with American settlements founded on the West Coast that were expanding eastward. By 1890, the census announced that the American frontier no longer existed. For a time, though, America continued to advance westward, beginning a period of colonization and imperialism that directly threatened Japanese hegemony in Asia and the Pacific. America's west, for the first time, did not end at the shores of California.

This expansion continued an extensive history of confrontation over control of the Pacific. Marines had been sent to Sumatra in 1831. In 1853, Commodore Matthew Perry landed in Japan and forced Japan to open trade with America. In the midst of the American Civil War, President Abraham Lincoln sent a U.S. naval vessel to the Sea of Japan to shell the Home Islands and teach the *Shogun* a lesson about American power and interest in Asia. In the 1870s, when Japan was wresting control of Korea from China, President Ulysses Grant sent naval forces to Korea to burn coastal forts.

Japanese and American expansion were poised to collide, each determining, as the nineteenth century ended, how to get the most of what was left of Pacific Asia. The de facto annexation of Hawaii in the 1890s put Washington, D.C., 5,000 miles from its farthest borders. Control of the Philippines in 1899 extended American territory westward even beyond Japan.

Before Perry's visit, Japan knew little of the outside world and considered itself the preeminent nation. But once Japan opened itself to the West, Japanese leaders were shocked by the power of industrialized countries, and determined to force 200 years of economic development into a single generation under the Meiji emperor. Remarkably, they largely succeeded and set their sights on becoming not merely an island nation, but a power on the mainland of Asia.

Japan fought China in 1894–1895 and won Taiwan and parts of Manchuria. Yet they were forced by the colonial powers, particularly the United States, to take a limited profit from their brutal China war. The Japanese people were told by the emperor that they must "endure the unendurable." (These words were echoed fifty years later by his grandson, Hirohito, when Japan surrendered.) The newly industrialized Japanese devastated the Russian fleet in the Russo-Japanese War in 1905. But the United States brokered peace, and again forced the Japanese to lose face—accepting less than they had won.

Although Japan was an ally of the United States against Germany during the First World War, the Japanese were insulted when the white Western powers refused to allow a racial equality clause in the peace treaty at Versailles. They again felt slighted when the victorious powers divided up the world and gave Japan only a few island chains considered to have little value—the Marshalls, the Carolines, and the Marianas. In 1922, again under American pressure, Japan signed a naval treaty in Washington, D.C., which limited the size of its navy to about two thirds the size of the American fleet.

It wasn't long before the United States and Japan were looking down each other's throats.

Japan, like the United States, was torn by the Great Depression. Families that had prospered for generations within the traditional Japanese economic system were suddenly undone by new competitive realities as Japan became integrated into the world economy. Japan's leadership grew alarmed at the paucity of jobs and economic possibilities for the growing and increasingly restless population. They feared that Japan would be unable to compete without controlling land beyond the Home Islands, so the military regime continued and extended a foreign policy of aggressive territorial expansion.

In 1931, the Japanese invaded Manchuria and established a puppet regime called Manchukuo. The subjugation of the Chinese population in the 1930s required an enormous political, economic, and military commitment. Japan sent thousands of otherwise unemployed youths to Manchuria to make it Japanese. They built railroads, roads, bridges, and schools—especially teaching schools to indoctrinate Chinese into the Japanese system. The Japanese government, like Adolf Hitler's in Germany, began a large-scale buildup of its military financed through deficit spending. This spending lifted the Japanese economy out of the depression and created an alliance between Japanese capitalists and Japanese military cliques. This coalition in turn determined a great deal of the country's national policy—a policy that led inexorably to war.

The League of Nations refused to recognize Manchukuo, so Japan withdrew from the League, and refused to sign the new Geneva Convention. Two years later Japan withdrew from the Washington Naval Treaty, which had set proscriptions on the size of the signators' navies. Japan then initiated a rapid expansion of their fleet. By August 1937, Japan was conducting a full-scale war against China, committing violent atrocities, including what is now known as the Rape of Nanking. The world was outraged, but Western powers, hoping to avoid war, did nothing aside from putting forth weak protests. This policy of appeasement emboldened the Japanese militarists.

By 1940, the Far East and the Pacific were controlled by the great European colonial powers and Japan. The British controlled Australia, India, Burma, northern Borneo, the east coast of New Guinea, the Bismarck Archipelago, the Solomon Islands, and the Gilberts. The Dutch controlled much of what is now Indonesia and southern Borneo. The Vichy French controlled Indochina (now Vietnam).* The United States controlled the Philippines, Hawaii, Midway, Wake, and Guam.

---

* Vichy France is the common term used to describe the puppet regime that ruled France during the Nazi occupation.

In addition to the Home Islands, Japan controlled Manchurian China, Korea, Okinawa, Taiwan, much of Sakhalin Island, and the Caroline, Marshall, Bonin, Ryukyu, and Marianas island chains.

The Japanese island chains in the Pacific were almost unknown to most Americans. Their names now have a deep resonance for anyone with knowledge of the Pacific war. Micronesia includes the island battlegrounds of Palau, Yap, Truk, and about 550 other small islets, including Ulithi Atoll. The Marianas chain includes Saipan, Tinian, and a dozen or so other smaller islands. Guam is part of the Marianas, but it was controlled by America via a small, extraordinarily brave contingent of Marines until the start of the war. The Marshall Islands became known for the battles on Kwajalein, Eniwetok, and Majuro—they include about thirty other coral atolls located halfway between Australia and Hawaii. The Ryukyus, the island chain hanging south of the Japanese Home Islands and sweeping down to Okinawa, was the battleground of the kamikazes. The Bonins are most famous for a small island called Iwo Jima.

Perhaps the most salient factor in Japanese territorial acquisition was that the Japanese, who had a relatively small military, were able to accomplish so much with so little. Radical nationalists had developed a pattern of brutal, lightning attacks against enemy strong points, followed by aggressive territorial acquisition far exceeding anything they could reasonably be expected to acquire, much less to hold. After these initial gains, the Japanese would enter into peace negotiations, in which much of the original territory would be divested, though still leaving Japan with enormous new territories, "legitimized" by the new peace treaty.

The United States, through a combination of economic sanctions and diplomatic pressures, determined to end Japanese expansion in Asia and the Pacific. This conflict between America and Japan was intensified repeatedly in a series of diplomatic moves by both countries that eventually made war inevitable. Each time the Japanese increased their territorial expansion, the United States ratcheted up pressure on Japan to withdraw.

America became particularly alarmed when the Japanese government, at the urging of General Tojo, formally aligned itself with Nazi

Germany and Fascist Italy in the Tripartite Pact. The Japanese pressured the French government in Indochina into concessions for naval bases in North Vietnam. In 1941, the Japanese forced the French to grant additional bases in the South. The United States feared that these would be used as a jumping-off point for a push through the Philippines toward the southern resource areas of the East Indies.* In reaction to this expansion, President Franklin Roosevelt froze Japanese assets in the United States and immediately put a halt to all oil shipments to Japan.

Roosevelt then made two demands upon the Japanese: that the Imperial Japanese Navy (IJN) withdraw from Vietnam and that the Imperial Japanese Army (IJA) withdraw from northern China. The IJN, which had entered foreign policy politics for the first time with its foray into Vietnam, could not afford to lose face to the domestic population by backing down.

The IJA, which was significantly more politically powerful than the IJN, was even more reticent to accept a result that ended in the army losing face. But if Japan could not ensure a reliable petroleum supply they could not hope to stand up to the United States. The American fuel embargo put the Japanese in an untenable position. They had only a year to a year and a half's supply of petroleum reserves.

The Japanese war machine, its economy, and its military regime were entirely dependent on imported oil. Radicals in the Japanese government began to look southward to additional violent territorial acquisition to solve their resource problem. The Dutch East Indies was full of oil then, as it is today, and the Japanese militarists determined to take control of these reserves. The only force left in Asia that could stop them was the American fleet at Pearl Harbor.

---

* There were many in the United States who felt that the Philippines were not worth fighting for. The islands were not necessary for the defense of the United States, and therefore there was no reason to maintain them as a colony. It was, in the words of the time, a "dangerous neighborhood," and the United States, for the most part, wanted little to do with it.

The Japanese generals knew that the United States would soon be at war with Germany. American leaders were vastly more concerned about a unified Europe controlled by Hitler, and so Japanese leaders reasoned that the war in Europe would take precedence over anything going on in Asia. But they also knew that it was possible for the Americans to fight on two fronts so long as the powerful U.S. Pacific Fleet remained ready.

The two nations had been furiously building warships since the middle of the 1930s, and both sides now had navies of nearly equal size. When the Japanese bombed Pearl Harbor they had ten aircraft carriers to America's eight, ten battleships to America's twelve (although the Japanese had the two most powerful battleships in the world), thirty-six cruisers to America's fifty, and only ten destroyers to America's one hundred seventy-one. Each side had a little more than 100 submarines. Nevertheless, the war-making *potential* of the United States vastly outstripped that of the Japanese.

According to the United States Strategic Bombing Survey (USSBS),* the successful Japanese history of use of force with limited commitments counted more in the minds of Japanese military planners than the relative war-making potential of Japan and the United States. The unfortunate pattern of Western appeasement, probably more than any other single factor, led the Japanese to believe they could attack America's largest naval base in the Pacific with relative impunity.

The Japanese armed forces decided on a complex, bold, but reckless plan to attack the United States fleet without warning. They would utilize carrier-based planes to deal such a crippling blow to America's naval forces that Japan could sue for a relatively benign peace that would end America's blockade and leave Japan in control

---

* The United States Strategic Bombing Survey was initiated by President Roosevelt in 1944 to study the effects of the American strategic bombing campaigns in Europe and Japan. Some of America's most brilliant economists and foreign policy experts, including John Kenneth Galbraith, Paul Nitze, and George Ball, directed the survey. They sent men to factories that had been bombed, recovered enemy government documents, and interviewed civilian and military officials to determine the impact of strategic bombing on the enemy's war effort.

of a steady supply of oil. After sinking America's Navy, the Japanese armed forces calculated they would be able to take, in relatively quick succession, the Allied-held islands of the Pacific out to Midway, north to the Aleutians, and south to New Guinea, along with the European colonial holdings in mainland Asia.

First, a Japanese carrier strike force would destroy or neutralize the American fleet at Pearl Harbor using a surprise attack on a Sunday morning. In order to ensure success at Pearl Harbor, Admiral Takijiro Onishi determined to send ten volunteers in miniature submarines, each about seventy-eight feet long and weighing nearly fifty tons. On the same day, Japanese troops would attack simultaneously in points throughout Asia. Their objective was to secure the "southern resource area," a group of mainly Dutch-held oil-rich East Indian islands. This oil would fuel Japan's economy and put off a major confrontation with the United States for half a century. But in order to succeed, the Japanese would have to destroy the American fleet at Pearl Harbor, especially the aircraft carriers, in a single, decisive battle.

The IJN fleet that attacked Pearl Harbor would then race back across the Pacific, refuel, and cover the advance of Japanese armies in Asia. Those forces would occupy Vietnam and use it as a launching point to neutralize the French in Cambodia and Laos, and British forces in Malaysia, Burma, and Singapore in order to gain complete control of the southern resource area. Half of the IJA divisions would be utilized in China to complete the conquest there, and to extend the Japanese empire into Burma. The islands of the Central and South Pacific would be occupied and then reinforced to become "unsinkable aircraft carriers" to defend against any attempted encroachment by the weakened American fleet, and to cut off the Philippines from American resupply efforts.

Then they would sue for peace.

Early on the morning of December 7, 1941, Japanese fighters, dive-bombers, and torpedo planes attacked the ninety-six ships of the U.S. Pacific Fleet at Pearl Harbor. American radar detected the initial Japanese sorties while still 200 miles away, but incredulous officers considered the blips erroneous or friendly. American ships remained anchored less than 1,000 yards apart. Nearly 400 American planes were lined wing to wing. American antiaircraft gunners did not have live ammunition.

Commander Mitsuo Fuchida, leading the Japanese aerial attack, radioed back to Admiral Yamamoto at 7:53 A.M., "Tora Tora Tora," confirming that the Japanese naval air forces had achieved total surprise.

The United States Pacific Fleet was devastated. The backbone of the American Navy in the Pacific, the battleships (BBs), were almost entirely wrecked at Pearl Harbor. The *Arizona,* the *West Virginia,* the *Oklahoma,* and the *California* sank at their berths after receiving multiple torpedo and heavy-bomb hits, and near-misses. More than 1,100 Americans were killed when the USS *Arizona* exploded and sank. The *Nevada* was struck by numerous bombs and at least one torpedo.

The *Pennsylvania,* the *Maryland,* and the *Tennessee* were damaged by bomb hits. The stern of the *Tennessee* buckled from the heat of the fires burning on the nearby *Arizona.*

American cruisers (CCs) were also badly damaged. The *Helena* was struck by aerial torpedo; the *Honolulu* was damaged by a near-miss from a large bomb. The *Raleigh* was struck by both torpedo and bomb and severely flooded.

The destroyers (DDs) were mauled. The *Shaw* was hit by a bomb that detonated her forward magazine. The *Cassin* and *Downes* were struck by three bombs in dry dock. A fourth detonated between the two ships. The *Cassin* rolled off her stands and struck the *Downes*—detonating torpedo warheads aboard the *Downes.* Fuel from the two ships then ignited and damaged both hulls.

Many auxiliary vessels were also badly damaged or destroyed. Some exploded against the sides of others. Many capsized before they sank, notably the *Utah,* which ended up almost precisely upside down.

The Japanese destroyed nearly every plane at the Army airbase at Hickham Field, and wrecked many naval aircraft at Pearl Harbor. Two thousand four hundred and three Americans were killed. In comparison, Japanese losses were paltry. Fifty-five Japanese airmen were

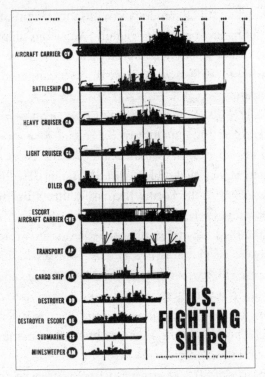

It is helpful to keep in mind the relative sizes of various American naval ships. The chart is reproduced from a wartime handbook for American sailors.

killed. They lost twenty-nine planes. All five of their suicidal midget submarines were lost; nine out of their ten crew were killed.*

America's Pacific Fleet was all but crippled by the Japanese attack. But far from being disheartened by the infamous assault, Americans

---

* Kazuo Sakamak, the lone submarine survivor, was one of the first Japanese suiciders of the war and the first American-held POW. He became intensely depressed during the long train ride to military confinement at Fort Knox. Sakamak, like most Japanese, had no comprehension of the size and power of America. Images of the well-developed United States rolling by day after day shocked Sakamak. He could not understand why Japanese leaders had attacked such a gargantuan nation. Even more surprised by the respectful, courteous, kind, and amiable treatment he received from his Army guards, the former suicider became a life-long supporter of the United States.

became set in their absolute determination to avenge Pearl Harbor and force the unconditional surrender of Japan. Nothing less would be sufficient. The American submarines and carriers, which were not at Pearl Harbor on December 7, were the only fleet arms to emerge from the Japanese surprise attack relatively intact. This fortuitous preservation led to a complete restructuring of U.S. naval strategy, based on carriers rather than destroyers. Ironically, loss of the fleet at Pearl Harbor forced the United States to create an entirely new, entirely modern fleet. American political will, incensed by the "dastardly" Japanese assault, allowed the president to immediately begin construction of the largest, most powerful navy in the history of the world, and to use the new carrier-based Navy as the principal means of destroying the empire of Japan.

The Japanese woefully underestimated the outrage, strength, discipline, and resolve of the American people and the war-making potential of the American economy. America may not have desired empire in Asia, but President Roosevelt never considered anything less than Japanese surrender after the attack on Pearl Harbor.

The Japanese leaders who initiated the assault on Pearl Harbor, especially Admiral Onishi, became increasingly desperate as the war moved closer to Japan and the magnitude of their error became manifest. Far from conceding, however, these men turned to increasingly fanatical measures to slow the American advance. In perhaps their most reckless undertaking, Japanese leaders drafted all of their most gifted university students in a single day. They taught the brightest of the student-conscripts how to fly, and in the final months of the war ordered these idealistic young men to crash their aircraft into the American aircraft carriers.

2. KIYOSHI OGAWA

Harmony is to be valued
—THE FIRST LAWS OF JAPAN (A.D. 604)

Kiyoshi Ogawa's life was typical of gifted Japanese children growing up between the wars. Japan was rapidly industrializing, but the educational system remained exclusive. Only the most talented young people and children of the oligarchs were able to attend Japan's few universities. But for those privileged scholars, life was almost easy. Japan's culture remained essentially feudal—individuals rarely were called upon to make choices regarding their own lives. Liberated from much of the burden of defining personal identity, Kiyoshi and his age-mates were freed to live a life that was chosen for them. But for the war, Kiyoshi and other privileged young men like him would lead lives of civic duty and contemplation. Military leadership was reserved for sons of officers. Enlisted men were drawn from Japan's poor.

Kiyoshi Ogawa was born at home at 433-1 Fujizaka, Yawata Village, Usui-gun, Gunma prefecture in what is now Takasaki City. Today, Takasaki is a modern metropolis with residential neighborhoods stretching out from a densely crowded city center. But when Kiyoshi was a boy, Takasaki was a small farming community, and Yawata Village a simple hamlet. All the homes were made of wood and paper and nearly everyone was a farmer. When Kiyoshi was a child, a row of centuries-old cedar trees, dark and forbidding, grew along the banks of the Usui River, which flowed forever westward toward Kare Mountain. An early shrine, built in the 1500s to honor Takeda Shingen, a local warlord, nestled in the dark trees. The river then was particularly prone to flooding, as dangerous to body as it was frightening to mind. The Jobu Road, a pebble-strewn street merely a few yards wide and used only for wagons—Yawata's only connection to the outside world—stretched into the distance. Children played safely. Life was slow. The huge coal-powered locomotives came through every now and then, but they never stopped.

There were no after-school activities, no organized sports, and of course no TV. Few villagers had radios. Children returned home from school and helped at farming. Each season the villagers celebrated a single festival that offered a short respite. The grown-ups organized games and contests. Takasaki drifted along, an isolated, provincial, but comfortable place to live.

Japan was struggling successfully to modernize their near-feudal economy. The businessmen in each of the towns worked hard, and risked much to improve their villages. Kiyoshi's family were members of an emerging rural merchant class. His father, Kinjiro Ogawa, was the chef at Kadoya, a small restaurant that the family owned and ran. He wore the typical chef's uniform of the day: a sushi chef's short smock-jacket tied with an *obi* sash and baggy striped navy blue cooking pants.

Gunma was far from the sea so the sushi Kiyoshi's parents served came mainly from freshwater fish like carp. The Usui River, which flows nearby their home, is famous still for its "sweet fish." The Ogawas served *makizushi* (fish rolled in nori seaweed) and *koikoku* (soup made with carp) or *koinoarai* (raw carp served as sashimi).

Mrs. Ogawa was unusually short, but spoke in a refined manner that impressed everyone in the neighborhood. She had an aura of elegance about her that the young people who grew up with Kiyoshi remember.

Kiyoshi's brothers and sisters were affable and bright, but he is recalled as more so than any of them. Kiyoshi was simultaneously the boy all the girls wanted to be with and the child every boy wanted as his best friend. Yet he remained unaffected by his popularity. And he was smart. His schoolmates recall that Kiyoshi raised his hand in class, but not in a way to show off—rather out of a joy and curiosity for learning. Everyone realized early on that he was special. They all knew he would probably end up going to college, an unusual thing in those days.

A photo taken of Kiyoshi in grade school. He was a skinny kid, but muscular, and seemed always to be smiling.

Kiyoshi had a flat nose, which gave him a slightly Caucasian appearance and makes him stand out in group photos. Everyone from Kiyoshi's childhood seems to remember five things about him: he was smart, he was funny, his face was pale and handsome, he was kind, and he had a *tsukitoota* voice, a vibrant, booming voice filled with joy. The people from Joshue (as Gunma was called in those days) are known around Japan for being outgoing. But Kiyoshi's openness and joyful nature were notable even there.

The future kamikaze pilot grew up in a military dictatorship in which information was tightly restricted by the government. Religion, politics, economics, and social order all converged and were controlled and defined by a single entity: the god-emperor.

It is difficult now to fathom the role the emperor played in the life of every single Japanese. The emperor was God; his word law. Even the calendar was changed to reflect the emperor's life. Each Japanese emperor takes a new name when he accedes to the throne. Emperor Yoshihito took the throne as Taisho from 1912 to 1926. Everyone born during Taisho's reign marks their life in terms of the emperor's rule.

Thus Kiyoshi was born on October 23, Taisho 11 (1922). The calendar begins with Taisho's accession, and ends upon his death. A new calendar is then initiated. Taisho's son, Hirohito, became the Showa emperor and led Japan during the war and through reconstruction, until his death in 1989.*

The emperor exercised his authority via a constitutional government controlled by the military. The only checks and balances among military and industrial leaders in Japan came from the emperor's inherent moral authority. But his actual authority and well-being rested in the military. Education, jobs, the press, all were controlled by the military. Japanese had no right to freedom of expression.

Authoritarian government in Japan, deeply enmeshed in duty and militaristic patriotism, was more subtle than that of other dictatorships. The constitution before the war stated specifically that the emperor was God. The Japanese called Japan *shinkoku nihon*: "God's country Japan." God and emperor were one, so when they fought for the emperor they were fighting for God.

They called him *daigensui-heeka*, the "Grand Admiral," and he controlled everything: the generals and admirals, all of the armed forces, the prime minister, and every single person. The emperor's authority far surpassed mere worship in the Western sense: it was religious, political, and social. Every Japanese always prefaced the word for "emperor" with *Chi*, "Our Fearful." *Chi* was a warning as well as an honorific. The word notified all in hearing that the emperor would soon be mentioned. This phrase was always followed by "*Kono tare! Kami goichi nin*," "Our Fearful and Only God."

Tatsuo Ono, a kamikaze pilot who trained with Kiyoshi, believes that the acceptance of the divinity of the emperor led to acceptance of the war. Ono cannot recall a time when he believed in *tensonkourin*, the belief that the imperial family is derived from *Amaterasu Omikami*, the Sun God. But he could never voice his doubts or his convictions. College students, more so than perhaps any other group, sensed the unreasonableness of the system, but they could speak of these things in only the most general and half-joking manner. They

---

* "Showa" means "Enlightened Peace."

lived a great strange lie that virtually every educated Japanese person knew to be absurd, yet none questioned.

The youngest of five children and his parents' favorite, Kiyoshi Ogawa was raised much like the other young people in his village. His best friend in school was Osamu Numaga, born one year behind him. They lived about 500 yards apart, separated by rice paddies and vegetable plots and bushy green mulberry fields—all easily crossed—and played together often.

After school, Kiyoshi and Osamu would stop at a little pond that had a small school of *koi* living in it. They would pause each day to sit and just look at the fish. Both would stare silently for fifteen minutes or so, in a sort of youthful meditation, and then resume their walk, children again. They fought epic battles with their classmates each day on the way home. But then they would see each other at school the next day and all were friends again. They were innocent and just playing games.

Children like Kiyoshi and Osamu all memorized the Imperial Rescript on Education during grade school. This text from the Meiji era defines the duty of all Japanese entirely in terms of their place in society. It is an extraordinary document and was read at every important event in school. The rescript taught children from the earliest age what would be expected of them at every stage in their lives.

Most, but not all, of the children in rural villages were able to complete primary school. Education for nearly every girl ended there. In the sixth grade, the boys were separated by intelligence, achievement, and gender. Kiyoshi was smart and able to move on to Takasaki Junior High School, which he attended from 1938 until graduation in March 1941.

Only one in five Japanese graduated from junior high school. Japan had just six major universities during World War II. Students were granted admission based partially on socioeconomic status, but because there were so few seats available, all had to prove themselves meritorious. The country could only afford to educate the brightest and most promising students and educators began weeding students out as early as grade school.

Kiyoshi, like every student who completed junior high school, took part in a national examination process that determined if they would go to a university, a vocational college, or end their education.

During *shiken jigoku*, the term for the examination period, which translates as "exam hell," young men would isolate themselves and attempt to create a wholly devoted frame of mind before the exams. They wore *hachimaki*, headbands reminiscent of those worn by the ancient *samurai*, symbolizing a complete dedication to a single task. Kiyoshi wore those bands only twice. The first was when he prepared to take the entrance exam for Waseda University. The second was during his time at Kanoya, preparing for his final mission.

Kiyoshi was tested in Japanese literature, language, *Kambun* (Chinese literature), English, math, politics, social studies, economics, physics, biology, and general education. The entrance examination questions could be almost randomly esoteric. Kiyoshi was required to sketch the *Kanji* Chinese character for *kappou*—a subtle and complex character drawing on the idea of cuisine.

Kiyoshi passed through *shiken jigoku* and on April 5, 1941, entered Waseda Second High School, a college preparatory school in the midst of the Waseda University campus. He was eighteen years old.

The day after Kiyoshi started university, Germany, which already controlled nearly all of Europe, invaded Greece and Yugoslavia. Both nations capitulated before the end of the month and Japan signed a neutrality pact with the Soviet Union. Three months later, President Roosevelt froze Japanese assets in the United States and cut off oil exports to Japan.

Waseda, though, remained an elite island of liberalism with fewer rules and restrictions than probably any other institution in Japan. Waseda students were able to wear clothes beyond the school uniform and attendance was not enforced.

Kiyoshi and his schoolmates were born during a sort of golden age of political liberalism in Imperial Japan that lasted only a few years. The liberal movement was led by Okuma Shigenobu, who founded Waseda University. Shigenobu was a nationalist intellectual who believed that Japanese success was tied to reconciliation with the West. He reasoned that liberalism was a vital component of West-

ern success, so he struggled to liberalize Japan. Shigenobu was backed
by Japanese corporations that flourished because of the liberalized
economy. For a time between the wars, Japan's leaders placed a high
value on freedom. Limited economic, social, intellectual, and political freedoms were taught then to be fundamental to the health of the
nation.

Japan's expansionist foreign policy in the 1920s that led to war in
China had shifted control of the nation from the liberals to a military
clique. This junta annihilated domestic political freedoms during the
Taisho dynasty. By the time the Second World War had begun, liberal
ideas had disappeared and were almost forgotten except by college
students isolated within the university environment.

Kiyoshi lived at a *geshuku*, a student boardinghouse, called Higashi
Gokenchou, in an area popular with students who did not receive
housing in one of the campus dormitories.

Waseda students awakened each day around 6:00 A.M., had a breakfast of rice, perhaps some dried fish, and *miso* soup. They walked to
school, where the first class began at eight. Classes were two hours long
and students attended two each morning and two in the afternoon.

Kiyoshi and all of the students were affected by the lack of basic
supplies, directly caused by the war with the United States. The cafe-
teria often served the same food for breakfast, lunch, and dinner: rice
with thin *miso* soup and a pickled radish. Sometimes they had *udon*
noodles. Meat was a rare treat. Though the food situation was tight in
1941, when they entered Waseda, it got progressively worse as the war
wore on. By 1945, Japan's lack of food would become critical.

Kiyoshi loved to eat *hinomaru bento*, an inexpensive white rice dish
served in a bento box. A sweet plum, pickled red, sat in the center of
the rice. The pickle juice radiated out into the rice in waving lines.
The rectangular box, with the red center and red lines in white rice,
was a patriotic dish formulated to resemble a waving Japanese flag
with the rising sun.

After class, many students returned home or to their rented rooms
to study or read. Radio programs were entirely state-controlled and

mundane. The military had inserted itself into all areas of life in Japan, including education, and Waseda, perhaps the most traditionally independent of the top colleges, was also affected. Waseda began teaching martial arts—a Japanese version of ROTC—to all students, and required a physical education course. The martial arts courses were taught by an officer of the IJA and included traditional work with swords, but the students also learned how to handle guns, basic military drills, and theories of ground combat.

Retired IJA officers ran the training, and in IJA tradition, they verbally and physically abused the college students, and often belittled the value of education. The students found the IJA to be boorish, locked in an old worldview that appeared increasingly irrelevant. Most col-

Japanese students were exempt from the draft, but in a symbolic show of patriotism they were required to aid in the war effort by carrying munitions along a narrow rail spur that ran through Waseda's campus.

Kiyoshi was strikingly fair-complexioned. He shaved before all known photographs. He is wearing the blue uniform of the Waseda Second Senior High School. Even sixty years later Kiyoshi's smile remains infectious. In nearly all of the photographs of Kiyoshi he is either bursting with mirth or seems uniquely aware of something terrifically amusing.

lege students were already aware of the differences between the services, but for those who were not, the negative ROTC experience with the IJA officers made most wish for an assignment to the navy.

This martial training was essential. Even before their attack on Pearl Harbor, Japan's military was too spread out. They had conquered far too much, too fast. Though the Japanese armed forces had excellent pilots and disciplined ground forces, the government had been fighting a war in China for many years and could not train new recruits quickly enough to replace seasoned veterans killed.

Kiyoshi graduated from the Waseda Second Senior High School on

September 30, 1942, and entered the School of Political Science and Economics at Waseda University the following day. The students at Waseda were gifted, and worked hard. They had passed through a grueling apprenticeship and challenging exams, and had been accepted into a university where the liberal ideas that they grew up with were still quietly and subtly acknowledged. The college students were held protected in this isolated intellectual environment, even as the war that had originally destroyed those freedoms closed in upon the country.

3. 1942: JAPANESE PRIMACY

You're in the army now

—SOLDIER'S SONG

With the attack on Pearl Harbor, Japan had begun the largest air, sea, and land assault in world history. And for a full year America struggled to halt the relentless Japanese onslaught.

In the days following December 7, Japanese forces expanded their wild, centrifugal assault, invading the Philippines, Malaysia, Guam, Burma, Borneo, Hong Kong, and Wake Island before Christmas. Japan took Wake on December 23 and the British surrendered Hong Kong on Christmas Day. General Douglas A. MacArthur had by then already begun withdrawing from Manila to the more defensible Bataan peninsula, which Japanese troops attacked on January 7. A few days later they began advancing into Burma and the Dutch East Indies, including British Rabaul.

The Japanese took the Borneo oilfield center at Balikpapan—which produced 70,000 barrels of crude each day, 90 percent of Japan's needs—on January 24, 1942. By the end of the month, British troops had withdrawn into Singapore. The Japanese invaded Java and Sumatra at the beginning of February, and the British surrendered Singapore at mid-month.* The victorious Japanese sent a large air force to attack the British base at Darwin, Australia, and invaded Bali.

---

* A disturbing pattern of Japanese abuse of Allied prisoners emerged during this fight. The Allies in Singapore suffered 138,708 casualties. Only about 9,000 of these died in battle. The rest suffered and died as prisoners of war in decrepit Japanese detention facilities. Japanese casualties were approximately 9,000.

America seemed plagued in the early part of the war by bad luck; the French ocean liner *Normandie*, which was being converted to transport troops, had burned at her pier in New York City and turned turtle. Ten days later, though, the United States received some rare good news: Navy Lieutenant "Butch" O'Hare, flying from the USS *Lexington* (CV-2),* had shot down five Japanese bombers in five minutes. He became the first American ace of the war, and the Chicago airfield later was named for him. The Japanese submarine I-17 shelled the Elwood oilfield near Santa Barbara on February 23.† President Roosevelt, in a tacit acknowledgment that the United States would lose the Philippines, ordered General MacArthur to leave. A couple of days later Japanese bombers sank America's first aircraft carrier, the USS *Langley*. The British evacuated Rangoon in early March, and the Japanese landed at Lae in New Guinea, about 200 miles north, across the Owen Stanley Range from the capital, Port Moresby.

On March 11, 1942, General MacArthur was evacuated to Australia by courageous PT boatmen who successfully ran the Japanese naval blockade. The men left behind by MacArthur in the Philippines were steadily crushed. The besieged soldiers slaughtered horses and mules for food. On April 9, about 2,000 Americans swam across a channel in Manila Bay to a small island called Corregidor. The 76,000 Americans left on Bataan surrendered the following day.

The Japanese were in no way prepared to deal with the great mass of American POWs, and almost immediately initiated a sixty-mile forced march to the Filipino village of San Fernando. Most of the Americans

---

* USS stands for United States Ship. The two letters CV signify the type of ship. The letters CV are unitary and denote carriers. The C stands for carrier and the V for the naval designator for heavier-than-air craft. The number following the letter designation is the ship's hull number designated by the Navy, usually in the order in which the ship's hull was laid down. Thus the USS *Bunker Hill* CV-17 is the United States Ship *Bunker Hill*, the seventeenth major carrier built by the U.S. Navy.

† The Japanese managed to attack the continental United States several times during the war. Fort Stevens, Oregon, was shelled on June 22, 1942. A Japanese submarine-launched plane dropped incendiary bombs on forestland in Oregon, hoping to create a gigantic forest fire. The fire quickly burned itself out.

were given no food or water and perhaps 11,000 of the prisoners were killed during the transfer, which became known as the Bataan Death March. Many were tortured by their captors and endured agonizingly slow deaths. A few days later, the desperate United States established the War Relocation Authority, which rounded up 120,000 U.S. citizens of Japanese descent and forcibly transported them to barbed-wire-encircled desert concentration camps.

Within six months Japanese troops conquered a huge empire including all of coastal China to the Soviet border, then arcing northward across the Aleutian Islands, and south across the Pacific just west of Midway, then arcing back across the midpoint of Guadalcanal and Papua New Guinea, then across Asia and the Indian frontier. Imperial Japan pulsed with a powerful sense of inevitable victory after Pearl Harbor. The near-complete destruction of the American Navy and the series of land victories against the European powers in Asia led to a sense of chosen invincibility. But thoughtful Japanese naval leaders knew that the American carriers had not been sunk and that a fight was coming.

Japanese leaders understood that Japan could not compete against the United States in a sustained conflict. Even a fully mobilized Japan could not possibly hope to construct a navy that could rival what the United States might produce over a period of years. As Japanese could not build sufficient numbers of their own carriers, they instead planned on creating a series of island bases that would act as "unsinkable aircraft carriers," which would allow the Japanese to project force thousands of miles from the Home Islands. The island bases would form a protective barrier through which the badly damaged American Navy would not dare pass.

These islands, stretching across thousands of miles of open ocean from the Bering Sea down to the Solomons, formed a sort of Maginot Line of heavily fortified fixed defensive positions. It also presented an almost insurmountable problem of logistics. Resupply quickly became Japan's biggest challenge in the Pacific. The Japanese island bases were effective only so long as they could fly their aircraft. Air groups required huge amounts of fuel and tons of spare parts, but supply ships traversing the 10,000-mile arc of the Japanese empire were imperiled by American submarines that could travel almost anywhere in the Pacific and already had begun a quiet campaign that severely curtailed and eventually all but eliminated Japanese resupply efforts.

Admiral Yamamoto wanted to finish the job begun at Pearl Harbor— to sink the American Navy. He realized, too, that Port Moresby of Papua New Guinea, the last Allied base between Imperial Japan and Australia, was a key to Japan's new line of defense. If taken, Port Moresby would offer the Japanese air and port facilities from which they could cut off sea lanes to and stage an invasion of Australia. But if the Allies continued to control Port Moresby, Japanese troops in Southeast Asia and Japanese oil supplies throughout the empire would be threatened. Yamamoto believed the small Allied force at Port Moresby could not hold out against a sea-based assault and almost blithely assumed that if the Navy carriers did show up for the fight, superior Japanese fliers would sink the American flattops.

The Battle of the Coral Sea was fought on May 7 and 8, 1942, entirely through air power projected by carriers. It was the first naval battle during which opposing vessels never visually sighted one another. Seamen everywhere began to realize that traditional surface ships were becoming irrelevant.

During the battle, Lieutenant John Powers, a carrier pilot from the USS *Lexington*, crash-dived into the Japanese carrier *Shokaku*. He was killed, but the *Shokaku* was disabled for more than a month. Her sister ship, the *Zuikaku*, escaped undamaged, but her air group was severely depleted. The Japanese called off their naval assault on Port Moresby when their carriers were forced to retire.

Soon after the Coral Sea, the course of the war began to change. A United States submarine sank a transport ship en route to the oil production areas in the East Indies and 900 skilled workers drowned; their loss seriously hampered the Japanese ability to manage oil production. Nevertheless, the Japanese assault across Southeast Asia continued and by the end of May, Japanese forces had taken all of Burma and crossed into India.

The Japanese won a tactical victory in the Coral Sea. The *Lexington* was sunk and a bomb badly damaged the USS *Yorktown* (CV-5). But the battle was an important strategic and moral victory for the United States. Robert Dixon,* the Avenger pilot who led the *Lexington*'s dive-bombers and who dropped one of the twelve bombs and seven torpedoes that sank the small Japanese carrier *Shosho*, radioed back "Dixon to carrier: Scratch one flat-top." This phrase, repeated in newspapers across the United States, became a powerful psychological boost. More importantly, Japan's naval assault on Port Moresby had been halted. Instead of an amphibious landing, the Japanese armed forces would have to slog southward over the Owen Stanley Range along the Kokoda Trail. This barely passable route slowed their advance until Allied reinforcements arrived.

Admiral Yamamoto understood that Japan could not compete against the United States in a war of attrition. Japan was then training only a few hundred pilots each year. Their veteran airmen were as good or better than the best American pilots, but they were dying much faster than they could be replaced. The United States was now engaged in the largest shipbuilding program ever initiated. Yamamoto knew that those ships would be larger, more powerful, and more numerous than anything Japan could hope to produce and that the new vessels would begin sailing against Japan in 1943. He reasoned that if the U.S. Pacific Fleet was not destroyed before the end of 1942, Japan would eventually lose the war. He decided therefore to try to lure the American Navy into a decisive battle, a trap for which the Americans would be unprepared. The *Lexington* had been sunk, and Yamamoto thought that the *Yorktown* was either sunk or so badly damaged that it could not take part in operations for at least a month. He wanted to use Japan's most powerful weapon, the *Yamato*—the largest battleship in the world—in a classic surface fleet battle to finally destroy the American Navy. But how could he force the Americans to fight so soon again after the Coral Sea?

Yamamoto decided to capture Midway, a tiny atoll 1,300 miles west

---

* Robert Dixon was later promoted to Rear Admiral and served aboard the *Bunker Hill*.

of Pearl Harbor. He knew that Midway had not been sufficiently reinforced to hold out against a major assault, and that the United States
could not allow the Japanese a land base so close to Hawaii. Once the
Japanese took Midway, the United States would have to send out its
still ill-prepared surface fleet to defend the island, and Japan could
sink the American Pacific Fleet in one final battle. Yamamoto had no
time to do the meticulous planning and drills normally required of a
large fleet action. For his plan to work, he had to rush to battle before
the Americans could repair their carriers. But the Japanese fleet had
dispersed across the Pacific. In order to get his fleet ready and into
position in time, Yamamoto sent his battle plan, in code, though on
open frequencies across the Pacific to his far-flung ships. They got the
message, but so did the U.S. Navy. Gifted code-breakers were able to
decipher most of the dispatch.

Yamamoto split his fleet; he sent six major carriers to Midway,
under radio silence, far ahead of his main force of surface ships, and
sent two light carriers, *Junyo* and *Ryujo*, to supplement a simultaneous
invasion of the tactically insignificant Aleutian Islands. He planned to
bomb Midway with carrier aircraft, then land sufficient forces to take
the island and await the Americans with his gigantic surface navy.
Yamamoto's defeat came about more than anything because he failed
to grasp the strategic value and tactical use of aircraft carriers. He
sought to end the war with a classic clash of battleships, the kind of
fight he had studied so often in the days before carriers.

Admiral Chester A. Nimitz, who had been promoted to commander-
in-chief of the Navy's Pacific forces after Pearl Harbor, was by then
commanding a carrier-based force. Nimitz understood that concentrated, well-protected carriers would win out in any battle against a
surface fleet.* Nimitz had only three carriers, and he knew he needed
all three together. But the *Yorktown*, badly damaged at the Coral Sea,

---

* Admiral Nimitz, who became commander of the Pacific Fleet after Pearl Harbor, fully understood that battleships were practically obsolete. He dismissively
ordered America's repaired battleships to return from Pearl Harbor to guard California against aerial attack. Only a year earlier battleships had formed the backbone of American offensive naval power. The new naval leader relegated them to
irrelevant harbor defense duty.

did not arrive at Pearl Harbor until May 27. Naval engineers figured it would take months to make the ship battle-ready. Admiral Nimitz personally climbed into the *Yorktown*'s dry dock, sloshing in knee-deep water to inspect the hull. He sent more than 1,000 dockworkers scrambling throughout the badly damaged carrier, and had her steaming out, still wounded, just three days later toward Midway. Nimitz sent the carriers *Enterprise* (CV-6) and *Hornet* (CV-8), together with the *Yorktown* (CV-5), to the back side of Midway, surrounded by surface ships that offered protection from submarines and aerial assault, and sharing the protection and offensive power offered by multiple air groups.

The opposing forces that met at Midway were roughly equal. Japan brought four major carriers; the United States had three. Both sides had about the same number of carrier aircraft (230 or so).

Despite the parity between American and Japanese forces, Admiral Yamamoto himself undermined his own strength. When the Japanese began their attack on Midway, he kept half of his aircraft aboard ship, in reserve. The major American counterattack came before the reserve squadrons were launched. All four of Japan's major carriers at Midway were sunk. Nearly all of their aircraft were lost along with more pilots than they could train in a year. In contrast, the United States lost fewer than 100 mostly obsolete aircraft, one already damaged carrier (the *Yorktown*), and a destroyer. Three hundred seven Americans died. More than 3,000 Japanese were killed.

Despite their victory, the American Navy made many serious mistakes at Midway. Though American admirals understood the strategic value of aircraft carriers, they still did not understand how to fight them tactically. Officers failed to communicate effectively with each other and even with their own air groups. The American carriers altered their intended course after an attack launch, but no one told the returning aircraft. Numerous pilots became lost and ran out of fuel before they could find their carriers. The *Enterprise* failed to inform the *Hornet* about battle conditions and so the latter ship launched her attack planes late for the attack on the *Hiryu*.

Unlike many military organizations, though, the Americans learned from their mistakes and even in victory revised and improved policies and procedures for carrier tactics, which carried the Navy to victory in later fighting. The Japanese attack on the *Yorktown* showed the American commanders the significant impact that a handful of skilled pilots could have, and the extraordinary survivability of American carriers.

Japanese dive-bombers, flown by some of the most highly skilled pilots in the world, scored three direct hits on the *Yorktown* and a second wave of torpedo bombers hit her with two "fish." In contrast, the Army bombers based at Midway released 184,000 pounds of explosives, and Marine torpedo planes dropped another 50,000 pounds, without hitting anything. The Navy planners realized that *skilled* pilots were an essential component of a carrier battle group, and the U.S. Navy vastly increased pilot training. While the best Japanese pilots were kept on the front lines where they could fight effectively, the finest American pilots were rotated home where they could teach thousands of other men to fight effectively.

Of equal importance to the skill of pilots was the Navy's failed damage control procedures. The *Yorktown*'s boilers were shut down after the strike. Without electricity, the ship had no light, and crews could not find their way through the hull to do damage control. Nor was there power to run the firefighting pumps. The *Yorktown* listed until its portside hangar deck was just above the waves, and her captain ordered the ship abandoned. Incredibly, though, she remained afloat. The ship was reboarded the next day and taken under tow. But the slow-moving carrier was attacked by submarine and hit by two more torpedoes. Her towing vessel was sunk by a third torpedo. Even then, the *Yorktown* remained afloat. American depth charges, loosed from the stricken tow vessel, exploded below her. Yet the stubborn carrier, which had entered the fight still damaged from the Coral Sea, did not sink for three days. She finally succumbed early on the morning of June 7.

Japanese strategic ascendancy dissolved in the American carrier victory at Midway. Japan lost offensive naval capability. Front lines were driven 2,000 miles back toward Japan. The IJN quickly became unable to resupply their far-flung island empire—they had no way of replacing lost ships and pilots. Their smaller shipyards, operating with few natural resources and limited fuel, could not keep up. America could afford to lose one carrier. But the Japanese could not afford to lose four.

At home, America was in the middle of the largest ship construction program ever undertaken, and was training 100,000 pilots, each of whom would have at least three times as many air hours as the few hundred pilots being trained in Japan.

America would build more than 100 carriers during the course of the war, a feat of naval shipbuilding never before contemplated. Such production would take time, however, and during the six months immediately following Midway, the United States Army and Marines suffered greatly due to America's lack of carriers.

By July 1942, battle lines in the Pacific war had almost stagnated. The Japanese controlled an arc extending from the Home Islands north through Sakhalin to southern Kamchatka, out to Attu and Kiska in the Aleutians, and south all the way to the center of the Owen Stanley Range in New Guinea. But the difficult thing about holding a great deal of captured territory is that the enemy can decide where to hit. The Japanese had only a small contingent establishing their base on the easternmost Solomon island, Guadalcanal. It was there America would strike.

Japan and the United States seemed simultaneously to grasp the importance of the Solomon Islands. If Japan controlled the Solomons they could protect their flanks, and harass sea lanes to Australia. If the United States controlled the Solomons, they could isolate Japanese troops in the south, especially at Rabaul, and cut Japan off from the southern resources.

The dogged resistance of American forces at Bataan and Corregidor played an important role in the Solomons fight. Fresh Japanese air and artillery units had been moved to Bataan so as to strike the stubborn American garrison on Corregidor. The Japanese had intended to use those units to secure a new airfield they were constructing on Guadalcanal. This left a small force of 2,000 Japanese building the airstrip on the tiny island that was to be the southeast cornerstone of their planned impregnable island battle line.

In August 1942, each side increased their commitments incrementally, seeming to hold their breath, watching to see who would win, knowing that somehow the ferocity of this fight—Guadalcanal—would determine the victor in the end. Neither side had sufficient carriers to commit to the battle and so reinforcement or resupply was difficult for both.

On August 7, 1942, with 10,000 men against 2,000 Japanese, Admiral Frank Jack Fletcher pulled the American carriers out of the landing force only two days after the American assault began. The naval supply effort, without carrier air support, was halted, and the Marines were left on their own. The Leathernecks often had only a few days' supply of ammunition, and only enough food for two sparing meals each day until October.

The islands offered a brutal, ugly, stultifying, but strangely even fight. The difficult, bloody combat there and in New Guinea established the horrifying pattern that would make the Pacific conflict so different from the war in Europe.

James Swett was born June 15, 1920, in Seattle, Washington. His striking blue eyes bespeak the joy he radiates each day at being alive. Colonel Swett loves to fly. He got his pilot's license while putting himself through college in California. He gained more flying hours through his private training than he received in the Navy Flight School. Swett graduated at the top of his class and opted for flying the Corsair for the Marines. He headed for the Solomons to defend the beleaguered Americans on Guadalcanal.

Admiral Yamamoto sent 200 planes on April 7, 1943, more than had been used at Pearl Harbor, to try to dislodge the Americans at Guadalcanal's Henderson Field. Swett's first combat mission was against this Japanese onslaught. Swett, with only three other American planes, intercepted a group of fifty Japanese Val dive-bombers. Most pilots would have returned to base, saving their aircraft for a more even fight. But Swett led his small squadron in to attack. He quickly shot down seven Japanese planes, making himself an "ace in a day."* Swett fired until his guns ran out of ammunition and his

---

* A pilot must shoot down at least five enemy aircraft to qualify as an "ace."

engines seized up. His canopy was shattered by enemy bullets, and he broke his nose on the fragments when his plane crashed into the sea. Swett survived, though, and his commander, Admiral Mitscher, recommended him for the Congressional Medal of Honor, which Swett received.

The Solomons were not all bad for Swett. The PT captains would take the pilots fishing on off days, and they would bum eggs from the Sea Bees, the Navy's engineering and construction corps. One day a couple of Sea Bees "accidentally" ran over a cow, and they all had hamburgers for a week. They fixed up a Japanese ice machine on Guadalcanal and made 700 pounds of ice each day. The men mixed the ice with powdered milk and added milk shakes to their hamburgers: "Man, that was really living." Planes started making "emergency" landings at Henderson Field for the burgers, but when a B-17 that was way too big for the 2,100-foot runway tried to land, "the Colonel said that's the end of the hamburgers."

Fighting in the Solomons was continuous through the end of the year. By late October, each country had about 22,000 men committed to the arena. By November, the Japanese had 30,000 men, slightly more than the Americans. But the Japanese resupply efforts were failing and their soldiers were beginning to starve. A month later there were 40,000 Americans and only 25,000 Japanese. On December 31, 1942, Emperor Hirohito gave permission to his men on Guadalcanal to withdraw. And by the beginning of 1943, it was clear that the United States would take the island.

Many of the Japanese military elites wrote off America's victory at Midway as an unfortunate result of Japan's lack of radar. When the United States defeated the Japanese at Guadalcanal, however, IJN leaders were forced to fundamentally reappraise their assessment of Japan's chances. Many Japanese naval officers realized then that the Americans could fight, and fight hard, and that they would fight to the end. Only then was Japan's economy placed on a war footing. Tight controls were established on the use of all strategic materials. But still the students were not mobilized.

Australia transformed. Rather than a trench to be defended, it became a point of departure for the Allies. The United States, no longer rushing to halt the Japanese, was given time to plan and rebuild its Navy, a fleet different in size and class from any that had been envisaged.

In one of the most far-reaching decisions of the war, full priority was given to construction of the Essex Class of carriers.

4. THE USS
BUNKER HILL
(CV-17)

What Price Glory

—TITLE OF LAURENCE STALLINGS AND
MAXWELL ANDERSON'S 1924 PLAY

A task force of fast carriers led America's assault across the Central Pacific beginning in the fall of 1943. By the end of the following year, these carriers had wrested control of the Pacific from the Japanese and had begun the attack on the Home Islands. The backbone of this Fast Carrier Task Force was the Essex Class carriers.

The massive carriers were designed with a war in the Pacific in mind—to confront Japan and project force across vast expanses of open sea. Before the Essex, navies essentially relied on battleships— dreadnoughts with gigantic guns that could fire huge shells for miles. But nearly the entire American Pacific battleship fleet was destroyed at Pearl Harbor. The loss of so much of the backbone of the Navy forced the Pacific arena to become a carrier war. By a fluke none of the American carriers had been at Pearl Harbor during the Japanese attack. Though many of the sunk battleships were refloated, repaired, and relaunched, airpower advocates such as Billy Mitchell, Admiral Marc Mitscher, and U.S. Navy Secretary James Forrestal argued that the great battleships were no longer relevant.

The U.S. Navy's continuing reliance today on carriers is due largely to the success of the Essex Class during World War II. The first Essex was authorized in 1939 after the expiration of the Washington Naval Treaty and was originally envisioned as merely a single ship. In 1940, when France fell, America began construction of a "Two Ocean Navy." Nine additional Essex Class carriers were ordered, including the *Bunker Hill*. Eventually twenty-four were constructed.

Probably no country on earth could have produced an Essex carrier save the United States. Certainly none could complete twenty-four. The construction of the massive ships was made possible because of the rapid development of the U.S. steel industry. The primitive Saucona Iron Company was founded in Bethlehem, Pennsylvania, just before the outbreak of the Civil War. It produced iron for the new railroads that were being laid down across the United States and structural steel for the U.S. Navy. In 1904, Charles Schwab, who had resigned from U.S. Steel, reenergized the company, renaming it Bethlehem Steel, and began producing the capital-intensive steel forms that enabled the construction of skyscrapers and eventually the giant Navy ships. Bethlehem Steel took over the Quincy Shipyard in Massachusetts and numerous others and built more than 1,000 Navy ships during World War II, including the *Bunker Hill*.

The Essex Class was a masterpiece of design work, especially considering that none of her architects could walk through her structure to make changes. For she was invented in their imagination, based on the successes and failures of the ships in two earlier classes of U.S. aircraft carriers.

Design and construction of the Essex Class was managed by the Navy's Bureau of Ships (BuShips). Their principal goal was to create a faster carrier that could operate a larger air group with heavier aircraft, stronger armor, at greater range, and with more guns than any carrier yet constructed. BuShips succeeded in all parameters. The *Bunker Hill* was so wide that some of the guns had to be taken off before she could slip through the Panama Canal.

Only thirty years before the *Bunker Hill* was laid down, the first American pilots landed on wooden platforms tacked to the stern of cruisers. The aircraft carriers' role in the First World War had been insignificant. The Essex Class carrier, under doctrine managed by Admiral John "Slew" McCain, allowed the United States to win the war in the Pacific and redefined naval warfare—and U.S. foreign policy—for two generations. International law recognizes naval carriers as sovereign territory, technically part of the United States. So an aircraft carrier is like an American military base that the commander-in-chief can move quickly to any hot spot on the globe. This mobility proved to be the undoing of the Japanese fixed defensive system.

Essex Class carriers were the most advanced and complex weapons systems employed by the United States during World War II. The *Bunker Hill* was made up of hundreds of millions of separate parts. She required 9,000 distinct sets of plans for her construction (in contrast, light cruisers needed almost a third fewer). Nevertheless, she can be understood fairly easily if one thinks of her simply as a floating naval airbase. Her purpose was to take American naval airpower anywhere necessary in the world to defeat Japan. She could attack just about any city within 200 miles of a coastline, which meant she could hit almost every important city and Japanese base during the Pacific war.

The United States fully mobilized the American economy for the war effort the day after Pearl Harbor. In 1942, FDR signed the largest tax bill in American history. It funded construction of war matériel, especially carriers and aircraft to fly from them. Every American industry was geared to the construction of the new Essex Class carriers (CVs) that would carry the war to the Japanese.

Before Pearl Harbor the United States lacked the desire or will to fight the Axis powers. After Pearl Harbor, Americans determined to destroy both Germany and Japan. But there was a special vengeful animosity reserved for the Japanese. The USS *Bunker Hill* was at the vanguard of this effort. She was a product of American economic strength, expertise, purpose, and resolve. And she brought retribution through the power of the American economy directly to the Japanese.

The United States began the war with four, mostly aging, carriers in the Pacific, the *Langley*, the *Lexington*, the *Saratoga*, and the *Enterprise*. Construction of the *Langley* and *Lexington* (which began as cruisers) started in 1911. The *Lexington* was originally a battle cruiser laid down in 1911, with a flight deck added later. The *Saratoga* also was laid down as a battle cruiser in 1920 and converted to a carrier. The *Enterprise* was launched in 1936. Of these, only the *Enterprise* and the *Saratoga* would survive the war.

The Essex Carrier forces ensured that American troops could be supported and supplied on the ground anywhere in the Pacific.

Carriers were primitive during the First World War—essentially they served as gimmicks merely to prove it could be done. But during the period between the wars carrier technology developed quickly. It took the United States half a generation to figure out how to use carriers effectively in war—they needed to travel in carrier battle groups with many other carriers, protected by large groups of surface ships, submarines, and especially their own aircraft. American carriers still fight in essentially the same way.

Carriers have always been extraordinarily difficult to build and maintain.* The Japanese empire had ten aircraft carriers when Pearl Harbor was attacked. The United States had eight. During the war, Japan was able to complete construction of fifteen additional carriers. In contrast, the United States built 141, including twenty-four Essex Class, and destroyed all of the carriers of Japan. The Essex Class played a pivotal role in these one-sided victories. Early in the war, American carriers were lucky to be able to travel in forces of two or three, but by the time of the Okinawa campaign in 1945 the Navy fielded multiple task groups of 300 ships, with ten or more carriers each. By the end of the war, Mitscher and his commodore, Arleigh Burke, had proved that with a well-protected carrier task force, the United States could extend its sovereignty thousands of miles beyond its borders and keep American cities well behind the battle lines.†

---

* The Soviet Union was unable to launch a single aircraft carrier until 1995. It was deployed only once.

† A task force is a temporary military unit established to perform a particular task. Thus the Fast Carrier Task Force was created to destroy Japan's navy and protect Allied forces attacking the Japanese in the Pacific. A task group is a particular subunit of the task force. The Fast Carrier Task Force, formally designated Task Force 58, was often made up of four task groups: TG 58.1–TG 58.4.

In Quincy, Massachusetts, in December 1942, a couple of months after Kiyoshi Ogawa began college and one year to the day after the Japanese surprise attack on Pearl Harbor, the USS *Bunker Hill* was launched at the Bethlehem Steel Company's Fore River yard. Joseph Carmichael, who would command the ship's Engineering Department, got a room at the newly requisitioned Harvard Club in Boston's Back Bay and began supervising the fitting out of her engine rooms and selecting crewmen to run her machinery. She had cost $53 million.

Joseph Carmichael, chief engineer of the *Bunker Hill*, was one of eight department heads and only four men aboard the ship who were authorized to command her. He graduated from the University of Washington and joined the Navy after ROTC because he expected a naval war against the Japanese empire and he wanted to be there.

Carmichael is one of the most tightly disciplined members of an American generation famed for its discipline. He is deeply and widely read. He has finished the full set of the Harvard Classics and the many hundreds of secondhand books on his shelves. He weighs the same 130 pounds he did when he was in charge of every moving part of the USS *Bunker Hill*. He drove himself to succeed in the wartime Navy and again when the war was over, competing at a saw mill and logging operation in British Columbia, and then returning to New York where he went to business school. Carmichael ended up at Irving Trust Company handling all of the real estate properties in fifteen countries for the Bank of New York.

In 1940 the Navy began writing to reserve officers, soliciting them to go on active duty in submarines. "Well, submarines seemed to me to be probably the most exciting duty you could have, which showed how little I knew about them." Carmichael volunteered for submarine duty and went to New London, Connecticut, to take the course at the New London Submarine Base. It was one of the rare instances in his life where he did not meet with success. He slacked off and ended up in the lower half of his class, "which turned out to be very fortunate for me. If I had been in the upper half of the class, I'd have gone in to submarines and I think my existence would have been fairly miserable.

"But me being in the lower half of the class, I was given the opportunity to volunteer for World War I destroyers which were being recommissioned." Carmichael ended up attached to the air tender USS *Clemson* (AVD-4). Her captain was an aviator, as the Navy required that all ships involved in naval aviation be commanded by pilots. The fast carriers' success resulted in more and more fliers managing the Navy after the war.

The Roosevelt administration was sending a lot of the old destroyers that had been headed for scrap to Central and South America. The *Clemson* took up station at various ports. Carmichael got to see Latin America. They worked out of Panama, Brazil, and for many months the Galápagos Islands. "There's probably no place in Central and South America that we didn't go. Partly it was showing the flag, as well as presenting a picture that the Navy was active to warn South America.

"Brazil had been taken over by General Eduardo Gomes*, a real Nazi sympathizer, one of those guys with a high collar, so sharp, if he turned his head, he'd cut his throat," he recalls with a laugh. The Navy was growing and Carmichael's work was not terribly dangerous.

About eight days after Pearl Harbor the officers of the *Clemson* were still living a fairly normal life in Brazil. They would go into town on weekends, meet Brazilian girls, go to the movies, restaurants, bars, and dancing. The big movie theater was advertising *The Disaster at Pearl Harbor* one night, so they all decided to go in and see what it was. "We were interested in the facts about what happened, because our promotions were all tied up with that, with Pearl Harbor." He laughs looking back at his own naïveté. The movie was very much the same film seen now in documentaries about the attack. Planes begin to come in, and then ships are blowing up, and the fires are breaking out—it was horrifying for the men of the *Clemson*. The officers left the theater shocked.

"These were filmed from the air, so I assumed they had been taken by the Japanese pilots, and then had been distributed by the Germans." Carmichael got his first taste that night of Japanese efficiency,

---

* Carmichael is apparently referring to President Getúlio Vargas..

The USS Bunker Hill *passes beneath the drawbridge of Route 3A in Quincy, Massachusetts.*

and as an engineer, he admired it. He could not believe they could take those films, develop them, copy them, ship them to Germany, cut them, and have them released in a movie theater in remote Natal, Brazil, eight days after the attack, all at a time when the world's oceans were active with warships on all sides.

The *Bunker Hill* was roughly the size of a modern skyscraper lying on its side. Her overall length was approximately seventy-three residential stories. If Rockefeller Center were laid out lengthwise on the deck of the *Bunker Hill*, it would fall twenty-two feet short of her bow. The distance from her flight deck to the bottom of her keel was nearly half a block and her maximum width was a full half block. She was 820 feet long on her waterline and from the waterline to her keel was close to thirty feet deep when fully loaded in wartime. She was so large that men who sailed on her recall the first time they saw her not realizing she was a ship at all—they thought she was part of the Boston skyline.

The *Bunker Hill*'s deck was crowded by the island structure so the flight deck at its narrowest point (between the 5-inch guns) was only ninety-four feet wide. Most of the time it was 109 feet wide. The flight deck itself was 862 feet long (plus four-and-a-half-foot-long ramps, slightly angled upward at either end).

From her keel up thirty feet to sea level, and then rising another thirty feet or so to her hangar deck, the *Bunker Hill* looked like an ordinary warship or a luxury cruise ship, perhaps, like the *Queen Mary*. But quite suddenly she bulged out in all directions like a Jersey highway barrier riding upside down in the sea. Her widest place at the waterline was only ninety-three feet, but above the waterline the flight deck bulged out 147 feet. The enormous island structure was built all on one side—it appeared almost ready to tip the *Bunker Hill* over. Yet she was one of the most solid ships ever built, practically unsinkable.

Structurally, the *Bunker Hill* is much like any other very large ship. Her hull may be thought of as a shell of steel that is kept from collapsing on itself by strengthening girders, like those of a skyscraper. The hull of a ship the size of the *Bunker Hill* must support the weight of thousands of tons of pressure from equipment on the inside and the force of the ocean on the outside.

The *Bunker Hill* was among the first ships built from the keel up to be aircraft carriers. Her flight deck, or runway, was a single, straight 870-foot platform from bow to stern, interrupted only by the island structure on the starboard side amidships. She was driven by four propellers powered by 150,000-horsepower steam turbines, run out of the four boiler rooms that were the heart-pump of the ship.

The island, on the starboard side flight deck, was her nerve center. It was a gigantic wedding cake structure, rising seven decks and more than eighty feet above the flight deck. It also proved to be a target for the Japanese and a significant impediment to landing planes. Aircraft had to stop short of the midway point. The planes then taxied or were towed past the island, and lowered down to the hangar deck on an elevator where they were repaired, refueled, and rearmed.

The *Bunker Hill* carried the normal complement of 104 aircraft, all stored below in the hangar deck. But during combat the *Bunker Hill* often had dangerously large numbers of fully fueled planes stacked up on her aft deck awaiting takeoff. The flight decks of the Essex Class carriers were highly vulnerable. They were constructed of steel deck plating a mere one-fifth-inch thick. Across that, a layer of four-inch-thick teak planking was laid down. The wooden decks were easy to repair, but made the deck and interior especially vulnerable to kamikaze strikes. Bombs and planes would tear right through into the hangar deck.

The designers at BuShips wished to create an armored flight deck, but determined that the cost in weight would be too high. The air group, which was its ultimate purpose and primary weapon, would have to be reduced by perhaps as much as two thirds. Diminishing the air group was not worth it. The men serving aboard carriers would have to fight with the risks involved in having almost no armor on their flight deck. The hangar deck could be penetrated from its sides above the armored belt as well as from above, through the flight deck. BuShips created a safe core, fully armored, within the *Bunker Hill*. They placed the most critical equipment and crew inside that armored box. Everyone outside the armored box remained highly vulnerable.

After Pearl Harbor, the international treaty restrictions on ship size had become moot, and the *Bunker Hill* was fitted with many more guns than her original specifications called for. Wherever designers could find space, they added another gun: the *Bunker Hill* carried at least fifty-two 20mm antiaircraft machine guns, sixty-eight 40mm Bofors antiaircraft guns, and twelve 5-inch guns—the latter so good that they remained in use through the Vietnam War. She fired the first proximity fuse shells in combat. These "smart" warheads used the bounce of radio waves to sense distance to incoming aircraft and then detonate.

Her sponsons, running like low balconies along the flight deck on either ship's side, were lined with double arrays of paired 40mm Bofors machine guns, which could throw tons of lead into the sky. Hung below and alongside the flight deck were long sets of 20mm machine guns.

The Navy was painfully aware of the explosive power of all the shells, ammunition, rockets, and millions of gallons of fuel, especially as they were packed inside the largest target within 3,000 miles of the enemy. As a consequence, emergency management was built into the design of the Essex Class. The boiler rooms that powered her also ran fire control pumps. These nine pumps could direct thousands of gallons of saltwater per minute anywhere in the ship. The greatest flaw, however, in the Essex design remained its vulnerability to fire. The two most significant defects were the location of the ready rooms and ventilator shafts. The pilots' ready rooms—standby compartments where the pilots could wait, nearby their planes, "ready" to fly—were suspended in a gallery deck below the highly vulnerable, mostly wooden flight deck and sandwiched between the flight deck and the hangar deck—two sources of prodigious amounts of fuel and ammunition with almost no means of safe exit for the pilots in an emergency. The only fresh air intake for ventilation of the entire ship came from amidships. If fires ever burned amidships, only foul air would be drawn inside—and the men would suffocate.

The engine and machinery rooms rose out of the ship's hold in the center of the *Bunker Hill*. They were so tall that they broke up the platform decks and had ceilings about twenty-five feet high. But these lofty heights could barely be glimpsed through the tangle of pipes, gauges, and ventilation trunks.

There was berthing and food storage space for 3,400 men tucked throughout the ship and stowage space for all the equipment necessary to run one of the busiest airbases in the world and one of the most powerful ships in the world, including 50-pound bombs, 100-pound bombs, 250-pound bombs, 500-pound bombs, 1,000-pound bombs, and 2,000-pound bombs. The bombs could be armor-piercing (AP), general purpose (GP), or incendiary. There were triggers, 5-inch, 40mm, 20mm, and .50-caliber ammunition, as well as small arms for the pilots. There was a jail, a ship's store, rocket motors, and fuselages, machinery rooms, engine rooms, boiler rooms, mess rooms for officers and men, repair equipment, a barber shop, butcher shop, bakery, hospital, dental offices, a general store, a tailor shop, tools, laundry, a post office, torpedoes, generators, radios, radars, weather gauges, elevators for ordnance and aircraft, hundreds of guns, hundreds of thousands of bullets, and hundreds of thousands of gallons of fuels, firefighting equipment, and life rafts, vests, and boats. Finally, the ship also had an ice cream stand for the treat the men called "geedunk."

The *Bunker Hill* as originally designed should have displaced 26,500 tons of seawater. But when she finally went to war her weight had become absolutely critical. She displaced 41,540 tons. Throughout her design process, engineers were careful to keep measuring the displacement and the import of each new system against its effect on the ship's overall performance. But when the war began, offensive and defensive systems were thrown in wherever possible and the carrier was forced to run at the edge of its design specifications.

The *Bunker Hill's* task became more complicated as the war dragged on. Aircraft became more numerous. The ship had to carry more fuel for heavier planes that carried more and heavier bombs, with more men, equipment, and spare parts required to keep the planes serviced. The original ship's plans called for an air group of ninety aircraft but by the end of the war, the *Bunker Hill* was flying more than 100, much heavier planes, and these aircraft all required their own specific repairmen and spare parts.

The extra guns, armor, radar, men, and matériel were taking a toll that endangered the ship's stability at critical times. A surprise examination showed that there were 800 rounds (at twenty-three pounds per shell) of 40mm ammunition stored topside, sixty feet above the water, at each of the 40mm guns. And an average of 4,076 rounds per 20mm gun. This added 250 tons of ammunition—about half the weight of a full ship's complement of unloaded aircraft—acting like pressure at the top of a lever. The extra weight caused her to sink lower in the water. It made the ship slower to respond and less fuel-efficient.

One can imagine the *Bunker Hill* at its core as an oblong strongbox 500 feet long and the full width of the ship. Solid STS steel formed its bottom, top, and sides. This box contained all of the most critical functions of the ship. The bow, stern, and island are all tacked on outside the box and the hangar and the flight decks are stacked on top of it. All of these outside-the-box areas remain highly vulnerable. The box top is the hangar deck floor. Its sides were Class B armor plating thick enough to protect against torpedo attack below the ship's waterline and 6-inch shells fired from six miles away above the waterline. The bottom of the box was the ship's bottom, triple-layered for protection against underwater mines and greatly compartmentalized against flooding.

Everything the ship needed to survive, and most of what it needed to continue functioning, including armories, fuel stowage, and engine and boiler rooms, was contained within the strongbox. All movement within the box was restricted by the need for full physical compartmentalization. The box, though, could not be impenetrable—hundreds of sailors had to enter and exit throughout the day. Therefore, a number of armored hatches pierced the box. Elevators to carry bombs, ammunition, and torpedoes pierced the box in heavily armored shafts up to the flight deck. Armored telephone, electrical, and other communication lines passed through holes in the box. The engine smokestacks also pierced the box. Because the idea of the box was that it could be perfectly sealed in an emergency—no fire, water, bombs, or torpedoes could pierce it—each hole created vulnerability. The greatest flaw in the design was that the men inside the box would require clean air brought through holes. In an effort to minimize the number of openings, the engineers left room for only two air passages into the nearly airtight box.

These two fresh air vent pipes, located beside each other amidships, were the *Bunker Hill*'s Achilles' heel. If the ship caught fire around this single ventilation system entry point no clean air could be carried to the men inside the protected box and the box would quickly fill with smoke from the fire. BuShips noted this defect and ventilation was improved in Essex carriers built after the *Bunker Hill*. But the immediate need to fight the Japanese with the new carriers outweighed the ventilation danger to the crews and air groups, and the *Bunker Hill* went to sea as originally designed.

BuShips moved several essential ship's activities to the vulnerable gallery deck, suspended from the flight deck and hanging above the hangar deck. Radio, radar, communication, and code rooms, which could not be squeezed into the crowded island structure, were relocated to this extremely vulnerable deck space. The blast-resistant hangar deck protected the pilots in their wardrooms, but the airmen had to be close to their aircraft when a mission was imminent, so the ready rooms were hung below the flight deck. The pilots, who formed one of the greatest assets of the U.S. Navy and represented thousands of hours of training and tactical knowledge, were left day after day to sweat out long waits for delayed missions in the exposed ready rooms.

As an airbase, the *Bunker Hill* required a landing strip, essentially a very long, straight, flat deck called the flight deck. The flight deck was narrow, barely wide enough at its widest point for six planes to sit abreast of each other with wings folded. She needed a hangar with a ceiling twenty-five feet high where she could store her squadrons when they were not in use and complete necessary repairs and maintenance on them out of sight of the enemy and protected from the elements. This was located immediately below the flight deck, and is called the hangar deck.

Aircraft were designed for highly specialized tasks during the Second World War. Carrier aircraft had the added restriction of needing to be able to land on a ship. Usually this meant they were slower, smaller, had less range, or could carry less ordnance than their land-based counterparts.

The *Bunker Hill* flew four different types of planes in 1945. On most days she carried about 104 aircraft: fifty fighters, about thirty SB2C Helldiver dive-bombers, and twenty TBF Avenger torpedo bombers, and three or four F6F Hellcats equipped with special radar for night fighting.

When the war began, carriers would almost randomly fire shells at incoming planes hoping to score a hit principally by sheer volume of lead in the air. As the war progressed, a more disciplined fire control was instituted in which all shells were set to explode at a predetermined distance from the ship. This created a wall of terrible explosions, through which it was hoped no enemy plane could fly. Finally, near the end of the war, proximity fuses caused shells to explode as they neared any object. When an American shell got close enough to damage an enemy plane, it detonated.

The aircraft were the ship's main battery. Everything depended on the pilots. The pilots had to be "at the ready"—prepared to fly at a moment's notice. But as we have seen, when BuShips put the ready rooms close to the aircraft, they also put them in harm's way. These rooms were located between the deck edge elevator and the ship's island—two prime targets for the kamikazes. Moreover, they were suspended beneath the unprotected flight deck and above the hangar deck, both of which were loaded with ammunition and combustible fuel. The pilots were terribly vulnerable as they waited for their missions.

Each of the four squadrons had its own shoebox-shaped, air-conditioned ready rooms (pilots and flight crews had separate ready rooms). These rooms were the places where the pilots tended to congregate most often, to hear the latest scuttlebutt* and news of upcoming and just returned missions, or awaiting duty, sitting for hours until they heard the words "Pilots, man your planes" and ran to the flight deck. The layout of each was identical. Flight gear hung from hooks along the walls.

The pilots had their own seats in the room. These were futuristic leather lounge chairs, designed for maximum comfort, with late-deco triangular head and arm rests and a triangular back. Below each seat was mounted a steel box where a pilot could keep his navigation clipboard and other more personal items. Al Turnbull, the squadron artist, had penned each pilot's nickname to his chair.

All the ready rooms had a chalkboard at the back where mission plans and communications information would be posted and illustrated, and from which the briefings would be given. The squadron officers had small offices to one side of the ready rooms so they could get work done and remain nearby.

---

* Seaman in the days of sail were given water from a barrel, called a butt, with a hole cut in it to withdraw the water. Holes in a ship that allow water to flow are called scuttles, so the sailor's water barrel was called a "scuttlebutt." Gossip was passed at these water fountains then, as it is now, and "scuttlebutt" became Navy slang for hearsay.

Atop the flight deck, and mounted in its center (amidships) on its extreme right (starboard) side, was the *Bunker Hill*'s island, or super-structure, the brains of the ship. From this tall, narrow pyramid the major operations of the ship and all her air groups were controlled. Her flag plot, navigation bridge, primary flight control, and all com-munications including radar, radio, and other signal stations, along with a host of other vital functions, were located or controlled from this structure. At a land airbase this island would be called the tower or command post.

Communication, command, and control, the three vital functions most heavily targeted by the enemy in every war, were centered in the island structure. The captain and his officers ran the *Bunker Hill* and the admiral and his staff ran the fleet air wing from their offices in the island. The island appears narrow against the hulking *Bunker Hill*, but it was sixty feet wide at its base. The island rose above the *Bunker Hill* visible, vital, and vulnerable. Though it was the ship's brains, it was not armored against bomb blast. The bridge was open; Captain George A. Seitz did not even have a windshield.

The first level served as the communication platform with radio and radar rooms, the boiler uptakes, and Admiral Mitscher's sea cabin. The second level contained the flag bridge and flag plot from which all of the ship's major decisions were made plus more rooms for communications equipment. When Admiral Mitscher came aboard the *Bunker Hill* and she became the flagship of Task Force 58, he was headquartered in flag plot. It became known as "Admiral's Country." The third level was the navigation bridge from which the ship was steered and run. It contained the pilothouse and was Captain Seitz's headquarters. It was "Officer's Country." The ship and all her crew were directed from this level.

The pilothouse was topped by air defense forward and the sky lookouts. Above that was the top of the stacks, covered with various antennas, a trash burner, and finally two more platforms with lights, flags, and various radio and radar antennas. At the very top, 150 feet above the sea, stood a lookout at the zenith.

The island structure also housed the uptakes, or smokestacks, for the ship's huge diesel-fired boilers. While a necessary construction, it impinged upon the flight deck at perhaps its most critical point. One of the biggest challenges in designing the *Bunker Hill* was figuring out how to make the island structure large enough to function with all of the necessary staff, while being protected against enemy fire, and still leave room for flight operations on the runway below it—all this without adding too much weight to an already weight-critical design. The island ended up the most crowded area on an overcrowded ship. In fact, the ship became so overcrowded that Admiral Mitscher and Arleigh Burke gave up their private cabins.

Hundreds of various-sized guns bedecked the *Bunker Hill*'s bow, stern, and sides. The threat of attacking enemy aircraft increased exponentially as the war moved closer to Japan's Home Islands and ground-based aircraft. Each time the *Bunker Hill* returned to port, additional antiaircraft guns were attached until she bristled with weapons on every quarter. Each new gun required additional gun crews and replacements to load it, aim it, fire it, and clean it twenty-four hours a day. The new guns also needed fire control radars to aim them. The guns added weight, so did their ancillary equipment, ammunition, and crews. Most of the ammunition was kept in heavily reinforced "fireproof" armories. But the gunners kept a large supply of "ready service" ammunition near their guns in case of aerial assault. The enormous weight of this supply became a problem on her later deployments, and, significantly, its explosive potential threatened the huge ships during kamikaze assaults.

The *Bunker Hill* was equipped with the most sophisticated radar at sea and could detect Japanese planes often when they were more than 100 miles away. Many historians credit radar more than any other single advance for the American victory in the Pacific. Arleigh Burke, though, complained about its limitations bitterly in his secret history when kamikazes began reaching to the heart of the fleet. A Combat Information Center (CIC) had to be designed, located, and manned to determine what to do with the flood of information coming from the various radars. CIC distilled all the information coming into the *Bunker Hill*. In CIC they read all the latest intelligence, received word of every radar contact, and reviewed each mission report. CIC was critical to ship's operations. It had been moved from the vulnerable and crowded island structure to the gallery deck and received a coating of armor to protect it from bombs. The men entered CIC through a steel blast door. A heavy steel hatch in the center of the floor of CIC led to the hangar deck as an emergency escape if fires blocked the blast door.

New systems constantly had to be integrated. On her first deployment, it was said that the radar operators had trouble distinguishing between low and slow "flying" destroyers and real-life enemy attack planes. But radar held the possibility of providing early warning of an enemy assault—it could save a fleet, so room was made for the new technology.

Radar was far from perfect in those days. Planes slipped through at times. They appeared on the radar and later disappeared. Whenever bogies (unidentified aircraft) showed on the screen the ship went to Torpedo Defense (TD), which meant the Gunnery Department was at General Quarters and the other departments were on alert. If the bogies got closer to the task group, the whole ship sounded GQ and everyone had to run to their battle stations.

Perhaps more than any other single development, radar put the greatest strain on the *Bunker Hill*'s weight and overcrowding, especially in the island structure. The radars left the island structure festooned like a Christmas tree. The radar operators further crowded the ship. Interior compartments of the ship were cramped with secret radar rooms where men wearing headsets sat glued to the monochromatic screens.

Three hydraulically powered elevators lifted aircraft up from the hangar deck. The number one elevator was located in the center of the flight deck near the bow, and the number three was in the same relative position, astern. A third elevator alternatively called the number two or the deck edge elevator extended on the port side amidships.

The *Bunker Hill* crew, using all three elevators, could bring a new plane on deck every eleven seconds. Japanese leaders figured that if the kamikazes could knock out even one of these elevators, the loss would so slow carrier operations that the stricken ship would have to return to Pearl Harbor for repairs, effectively removing that ship from the war for at least a month.

Engine rooms are nearly always the most crowded aboard any vessel and the more complicated the ship, the more the engine room becomes a mess of various apparatus and the ties that hold them together. The *Bunker Hill* had two engine rooms with two engines in each room. Each engine powered one of the ship's four bronze propellers. The engines were each powered by two boilers. The eight boilers were housed in four boiler rooms, each with two boilers.

The main engineering compartment was divided into six rooms. The aft engine rooms were closest to the stern. Then came the four boiler rooms, and finally the forward engine rooms. The propeller shafts were hardened steel, 220 feet long and eighteen inches in diameter. Normally the boilers in the number one and number two boiler rooms powered the engines in the aft engine room, and the forward boilers (numbers three and four boiler rooms) fired the forward engine rooms but the whole system was designed for maximum survivability, so that if even one engine was working and only one boiler would fire, everything could be cross-connected. That way, the ship could make way with only a single engine.

The engineers had to generate electricity to provide sufficient power for all of the equipment to run a small city and one of the busiest airports in the world. Just ahead of the forward engine room was the ship's auxiliary power plant. There were two 750-kilowatt steam-driven electrical generators that powered vital systems throughout the ship, including lighting. Steam from the generators satisfied all the ship's electrical needs. The blowers, giant fans that drove air through a central duct to all parts of the ship, were powered directly by the engine room.

Engineering comprised an enormously complex plant with almost unimaginable power demands, all cramped into an impossibly small space and all run by Commander Joseph Carmichael. The saltwater fire pumps alone consumed a large part of the boiler's theoretical power output. Those essential pumps were placed in secure rooms just forward and aft of the engine and fire rooms.

The boilers generated steam at enormous temperature and pressure, 850 degrees and 650 pounds per square inch. The engineers had to constantly open and close different valves to regulate the steam, making sure there was enough where it was needed, but not so much that an engine would overheat, or a dial, valve, vent, or pipe would burst. If the engineers could not maintain the pressure, they would have to take fire rooms off line. The machinery fell apart. The ship lost lighting. The blowers failed. Fire hoses lost their water supply. No air came inside the enormous hull for the men to breathe. The ship ended up dark, vulnerable, and dead in the water.

In designing the *Bunker Hill*, the General Board at BuShips had called for several improvements to the Essex Class over the previous Yorktown Class. The Essex ships would weigh 6,500 tons more than the earlier carriers. That weight was utilized principally for a longer flight deck, which allowed the *Bunker Hill* to put up much larger (four-squadron) deck load strikes, more and stronger bulkheads to isolate the effects of damage, and to rearrange the boilers and engine turbines into six separate rooms. These compartmentalized rooms could act completely independently of each other. The *Bunker Hill* could survive a direct hit to any engine or boiler room, and yet maintain speed and damage control functions.

BuShips added a protective triple bottom and the ship's wide protective belt around the box and increased engine horsepower. The *Bunker Hill* carried 25 percent more aviation gasoline (avgas—which was essential given the additional planes she would be carrying and the huge engines those new heavier aircraft flew). They also made the engines more powerful.

The USS *Bunker Hill* was an astonishing technical achievement, but it was extraordinarily complex, and relied on dozens of systems and thousands of men aboard the ship but also those scattered across the Pacific carrying fuel, supplies, and armaments, as well as those building aircraft, mining coal, and digging oil wells. The Navy utilized an extraordinarily rigid hierarchical system to ensure that all these groups worked together. Without them it would be impossible for the *Bunker Hill* to function. With their precise coordination, the *Bunker Hill* and her sister carriers could take the war all the way to Japan.

5. HOW IT WORKS

They Were Expendable
—TITLE OF BOOK BY LINDSAY WHITE

The naval battles of World War I had been fought and won by battleships. Naval admirals who had commanded those giant ships saw them as the naval weapon for all time. These men were opposed in the post-war years by a smaller group of mostly younger officers who realized that an aircraft carrier could launch its planes to sink a battleship long before the enemy battleship's guns could come within range of the opposing carrier. President Roosevelt, who had served as assistant secretary of the Navy, settled the issue.

Roosevelt fundamentally altered U.S. naval leadership after the successful Japanese carrier attack on Pearl Harbor, putting many naval aviators in top leadership positions. When the *Bunker Hill* sortied in 1945, the chain of command went from FDR to the Secretary of the Navy, James Forrestal—an aviator since World War I—then to the COMINCH-Navy, Admiral King, also an aviator, and who had skippered the *Lexington*, then to Admiral Chester Nimitz, who was a great proponent of naval air power, then to Admiral Spruance, who commanded the Central Pacific Force, designated as the Fifth Fleet. Marc Mitscher commanded the Fast Carrier Task Force delimited formally as Task Force 58. Fleet exercises had proven the need for "complete freedom of action in deploying carrier aircraft."* Thus the chain of command between Mitscher and Spruance is exceptionally vague. Mitscher had nearly complete tactical authority over his carriers

---

* *The Fast Carriers*, p. 17.

and so had effective control over a sizable portion of the fleet. The Fast Carrier Task Force included the Essex Class carriers, plus the sizable group of cruisers and destroyers deployed directly to protect the carriers.

To encourage naval airpower, Congress required that all commanders of aircraft carriers and naval air stations be pilots and ordered a quick, intensive twelve-to-fifteen-month training program for 6,000 additional naval reserve pilots.* When the Navy began construction of fleet carriers in the 1920s, ambitious naval officers of all ages began learning to fly. Naval air split into two groups: naval aviation pioneers like Marc Mitscher who had learned to fly a few years after graduating from the Naval Academy; and more senior officers who saw the potential of airpower and got their wings late in life—many in their late forties and early fifties—like John "Slew" McCain and Ernest King. By the time of the *Bunker Hill*'s final deployment in 1945, most of the top naval leadership were advocates of airpower.

Naval regulations required that air groups be commanded by airmen, but their second in command be a surface ship leader. Mitscher, the airman, was assigned Arleigh Burke as his second. The old admiral was irritated to have a "black shoe" foisted on him and made no effort to hide his annoyance. (Naval aviators wore brown shoes in part to distinguish themselves from the black shoe surface men.) Arleigh "31-Knot" Burke was the legendary leader of a destroyer squadron in the Solomon Islands campaign. Burke knew more about surface warfare than perhaps any other man in the Pacific. Eventually he proved his value to Mitscher, and the two became friends and worked together as well as any team in naval history.

Mitscher was known as "an aviator's aviator." He made the first landing on America's first fast carrier—the *Saratoga* (CV-3)—on January 11, 1928. Most Navy men regarded Mitscher as a tough, taciturn, fighting admiral. Up close, though, he had a remarkably benign, almost beatific smile. Mitscher spent his days in flag plot on the sec-

---

* In sharp contrast, the Japanese naval flight program remained elite. Only about 100 pilots were trained each year. After eight years of training, only the top pilots were given carrier duty.

Carriers were a new weapon during World War II. Few naval leaders grasped their full potential. Naval airmen in charge of the carriers were pioneers who learned to fly in primitive craft. Admiral Marc Mitscher (opposite) was one of America's first naval aviators. He attempted to fly across the Atlantic in a group of NC-1s. Mitscher survived, but did not make it to Ireland. The photo was taken of Mitscher taking off from Trepassey, Newfoundland, at 8:00 P.M. on May 16, 1919.

ond level of the island, watching the progress of the fleet and the war. Whenever his men were landing or launching, Mitscher would sit in a swivel chair two stories up, watching his men fly. He is renowned as well for caring deeply about his pilots. They knew he would do everything possible to bring them back alive, and it gave them the confidence to take the battle to the enemy day after day.

Mitscher had a standing policy of calling the first pilot to land directly up to his flag plot to question him about the mission. The admiral made it clear to everyone from his commanders on down that he expected them to speak their minds. He spoke with his pilots each day in small groups, often just one or two men at a time, wanting to know what had happened on each sortie at the earliest possible time. He liked to get it as straight as possible. No one was punished for being wrong, as long as they prefaced what they said by making clear it was an educated guess.

Admiral Mitscher was extraordinarily casual in his debriefings, not in terms of the factual information that he sought, which was detailed and demanding, but in the method that he seemed to prefer his pilots use in recounting the action. He usually gave them a cup of coffee and asked questions about conditions over the target, what it looked like, what it was like over the enemy position, what they would recommend doing next time, whether the gun that was reported silenced was really destroyed or merely had been pulled deeper into a cave.

Mitscher put the returning fliers at ease so quickly that the two would soon be speaking with their hands, like children playing with mock airplanes.

Dewey Ray talked with Mitscher only once, but it was a telling encounter. Ray had just returned from a bombing mission at Okinawa. The aircrew found a jagged piece of an American 500-pound bomb lodged in the bomb bay of Ray's fuselage indicating, he says, "that I flew too close to the target."

The officers were not angry about the damage. Apparently they were more amused than anything. They wanted Mitscher to know

how eager his men were, so they ordered Ray to carry the piece up to the flag plot to show it to the admiral. Ray said that Mitscher asked him "everything about the attack, the target, distance, his altitude, opposition—everything."

Part of the reason Mitscher made these interviews himself was to see how these men, who ran point for the whole carrier group, were holding up. He knew that they were under enormous pressure, holding the responsibility for their own lives, and their comrades', each day. Mitscher did everything he could to reduce the level of risk his pilots faced. He kept predawn launches, dark landings, and flying in heavy weather down to a minimum. If a pilot were downed he did everything he could to fish him out and bring him home. And if a ship were damaged he did everything possible to get it safely to port.

Wally Girts, a signalman new to Mitscher's staff, remembered entering Mitscher's cabin late one night to inform the admiral that bogies had penetrated the fleet's radar. Girts was shocked to see the gritty admiral, looking frail, and wearing a sissified nightshirt that went all the way to the floor. It looked to him like a woman's nightgown. But the next night he walked in while Mitscher was changing clothes. Wally was even more shocked when he saw Mitscher's body. The admiral was almost completely covered in aged tattoos. They went down his arms, even along the back of his neck below the collar. Mitscher wore the nightshirt so no one would know.

The *Bunker Hill* retained split commands. Captain Seitz commanded the ship, her officers, and crew. Admiral Mitscher commanded the task force—the air groups and the hundreds of ships surrounding the *Bunker Hill*. Mitscher was headquartered aboard the *Bunker Hill*, but he had no more specific control over that ship than any other in his fleet. Mitscher's mere presence aboard the *Bunker Hill*, though, made her his in a special way. Because she was the flagship of Task Force 58, all fleet orders emanated from the *Bunker Hill* and she was at the top of the chain of command of the task force.

Admiral Mitscher's flag staff ate, slept, and worked largely separated from the rest of the men of the *Bunker Hill*. The flag staff added more than 100 officers and enlisted men to the overcrowded carrier, from communications specialists to the Filipinos who served their meals.

Admiral Mitscher is welcomed aboard the Bunker Hill *by her captain, Commander George Seitz (shaking hands), and his executive officer, Commander Howell Dyson.*

The pilots on board the *Bunker Hill* were members of an air group, which took its orders directly from Admiral Mitscher, not Captain Seitz. They were neither officers nor crewmen of the *Bunker Hill*. The air group was housed separately, ate separately, and had no duties for the operation of the ship. This division became, at times, the source of a palpable tension between the surface officers of the ship who served under Captain Seitz, and those who served under Mitscher. The airmen acted almost independently of the ship, as though the *Bunker Hill* was merely their airbase.

The first air group embarked aboard the *Bunker Hill*, in 1943, was number 17. On her last deployment, the *Bunker Hill* carried Air Group 84. This was a new group, though many of the pilots were veterans of earlier Pacific battles, and a few, like Al Turnbull, had cruised aboard the *Bunker Hill* as members of AG-17.

America rushed to train hundreds of thousands of new pilots. After Pearl Harbor Al Turnbull trained as a torpedo bomber pilot. He had only six months of intense flight training before he was doing carrier landings.

Turnbull is a fairly typical pilot. He had two years of college, joined the Navy so he would not get drafted, and became a skilled flier.

Al Turnbull remains an incorrigible optimist. When he talks about how his family was affected by the Depression, his first thought was how lucky they were that he had a paper route that allowed him to have fine secondhand clothes to wear to school each day. Turnbull had a sense that he was participating in something monumental when he went to sea aboard the *Bunker Hill*. The Navy forbade all personnel from keeping any private notes during wartime. But Al Turnbull meticulously kept a secret diary, which was recovered from his personal effects after the *Bunker Hill* was hit.

Geoffrey Ernest Turnbull, Al's father, ran away from his alcoholic home in nineteenth-century London to seek a new life in Canada. He tried being a farmer in Saskatchewan. They had only ninety frost-free days each year, so after a few seasons, Turnbull emigrated to Pasadena, California, and found work hanging wallpaper. Turnbull raised a family in the growing town. All five of his children worked hard at after-school jobs to help their family make it through the Depression.

In high school Al majored in business and art. He took every possible class in sign writing, learning to draw with different types of paintbrushes. Turnbull later used this skill to keep score aboard the *Bunker Hill*, painting his unit's kill record on a board. He painted aircraft, surface ships, bombs falling on enemy emplacements, and symbols of Japanese flags. He became the torpedo squadron communications officer. Turnbull drew the mission plans and procedures on the huge chalkboards in the pilots' ready rooms before each mission, and kept the boards updated as weather, intelligence, and combat conditions changed.

The Naval Air Corps had all sorts of training devices that were supposed to weed out those who could not take the rigors of high-performance aircraft piloting. A sealed chamber simulated different altitudes by removing the amount of air available for the subject pilot to breathe. The altitude chamber trained pilots to recognize and deal with the effects of insufficient oxygen at high altitudes. The effects were linear. First, pilots' fingernails turned blue. Then the pilots became increasingly disoriented. Finally they would black out. The woman who ran the low pressure chamber was a looker named Harriet. They called her the Chamber Maid. Harriet tested various mental and motor capacities of the pilots and crew, especially their ability to use supplemental oxygen. They played tic-tac-toe or patty cake. Other tests were more rigorous. The story at the base was that Harriet took Al Turnbull up to 20,000 feet, and he never came down.

The Navy opened a specialized torpedo training field at Fort Lauderdale in late 1942. Turnbull's group was the first to train on the new TBF Avenger.* Isolated at Fort Lauderdale, Turnbull's squadron learned to fight as a group, practicing the tactics they would need to fight and survive as torpedo pilots. They remained together, training hard until they landed aboard the *Bunker Hill*. They were all keenly aware that nearly every torpedo pilot had been killed in the first run at Midway.

Turnbull flew several missions during which he was forced to employ the carrier's catapult, often to salvage aircraft from stricken carriers, ships that had been hit by kamikazes but not sunk. The *Bunker Hill* wanted the airplanes from these crippled carriers before they left the forward area. If their flight decks were badly damaged and the vessel could not make good headway into the wind, the only way to get the aircraft off the carrier before it left the combat zone was to use the catapult.

The plane crew would strap Turnbull in so tightly that it literally felt as though he had become a part of the physical construction of the aircraft. His shoulder harness pulled him back against the armor plate behind, and the seat belt yanked him firmly downward so that when they launched the catapult even its tremendous g-forces would

---

* The TBF and the TBM were the same aircraft, designed and built originally by Grumman. As war needs grew and the plane proved itself, General Motors began producing the additional aircraft that Grumman production facilities could not accommodate. The GM aircraft were designated TBM.

not move him back further; there was simply nowhere for him to go. He would set all his controls for the first thirty seconds or so of flight ahead of the launch because he would not be physically able to alter them. When the catapult fired, all the blood in his head would move back in his skull. The blood was even pulled out of his eyes and for a few moments he would be flying completely blind. Then there was an awful sensation as he came to and the plane slowed down rapidly and felt as if it were falling, about to crash into the water, and nothing could be done.

A moment later his senses would return, he could see, and he was in control of his airplane. But if he had not set the controls perfectly before the launch, the trim tabs, the rudders, and the empennage, when they hit the catapult he would be dead. Turnbull loved the thrill of catapult launches.

The air group was split into squadrons based around the types of aircraft they flew and included pilots, aircrews, and support staff. Fighter planes were in VF-84. Dive-bombers were VB-84, and torpedo bombers were VT-84. The letter V indicates they were carrier-based, and the second letter indicates their mission, i.e., B for bombers, T for torpedoes, and F for fighters. The number is their squadron number.

In January 1945, the *Bunker Hill* shipped out with a unique fighter group. Two small Marine squadrons, which are normally land-based, were attached to AG-84 during the 1945 deployment. These squadrons maintained their independent designations: VMF-214 and VMF-451, M for Marines.

Colonel Jim "Zeke" Swett commanded VMF-221. Blaine Imel, "Nick" Nicolaides, Joe Brocia, Fred Briggs, and Don Balch all flew in VMF-241.

Archie Donahue commanded VMF-451. Donahue became the Marines' first carrier-based ace in one day on April 12, 1945. He shot down three Vals and two Zeros off the *Bunker Hill*. Donahue had had nine kills in his previous tour of duty.

The *Bunker Hill*'s third fighter squadron was all naval fliers. VF-84 was commanded directly by Roger Hedrick. Hedrick had served as executive officer of the original VF-17 aboard the *Bunker Hill*. He was one of the Navy's highest scoring aces in the war, with twelve confirmed kills and four planes damaged, not counting the time he shot up his own CO's plane over the Solomons. Caleb Kendall, Wilton "Hoot" Hutt, and "Beads" Popp were members of Hedrick's squadron.

Wilbert P. "Beads" Popp was born on November 15, 1921, in Fresno, California. He is still the full six feet he was the day he was admitted to the Navy, May 7, 1942, but back then he weighed only 118 pounds. The flight program required that he weigh 122, so he ate "a whole lot of bananas" and made it in. Beads Popp joined the Jolly Rogers of Air Group 17 when it was first formed aboard the *Bunker Hill* and was transferred to the Solomons when the Navy decided not to use the Corsairs on carriers. Popp got his nickname because sweat beaded down his forehead during their first missions in the Solomon Islands. Mitscher, among the first men to land planes on aircraft carriers, was naval aviator number 33. Beads Popp was number 17,704. There were many more than 1,000 times as many aviators in the Navy in May of 1945 than there had been when Mitscher joined.

Hoot Hutt flew a fighter plane off the *Bunker Hill* in 1945. He was born in his granddad's home on December 15, 1922, in Norwood, Colorado, during a snowstorm. Norwood is nearly a mile and a half above sea level and the town's population still has not topped 500. Hutt volunteered after Pearl Harbor. He was one of the first twenty-five seamen with no college experience taken out of Great Lakes Naval Station for air officer training. Hutt became a fighter pilot and joined VF-3 aboard the Essex carrier *Intrepid* (CV-11) in 1943.

Squadrons VB-84 and VT-84 made up the *Bunker Hill*'s bomber and torpedo squadrons.

Captain George Seitz was the commanding officer, the top of the *Bunker Hill* chain of command. Seitz was a master administrator. He had studied at the Naval Academy and the Massachusetts Institute of Technology and brilliantly organized the supply efforts for the American takeover of Casablanca in North Africa. Commander Howell J. Dyson was Seitz's officious, by-the-book executive officer who ran the ship's day-to-day operations. Dyson was almost universally ridiculed for his careerist dedication to naval regulations and protocol—until the day the kamikazes struck.

The ship's command structure from commander to seamen was explicitly spelled out. When a ship's captain went off-duty, an offi-

An SB2C Helldiver comes in too far to starboard. A flight deck crewman is nearly killed as the plane careens along the deck. But emergency crews, dressed in white asbestos suits, do not hesitate to jump into the debris to pull the pilot to safety. The wrecked fuselage, stripped of radios and other electronics, is dumped into the sea moments after the crash.

cer of the deck, either Dyson, Chief Engineer Carmichael, or Commander King ran the *Bunker Hill*. Only the captain and these three men were qualified to command an Essex Class carrier. They would "share the night" throughout the war. Below these deck officers the command was split among the ship's departments: Air, Communication, Navigation, Supply, Chaplaincy, Medical, Gunnery, Hull, and Engineering. Each department's chief officer reported to Commander Seitz, usually through Dyson.

The Air Department was part of the ship's company, wholly separate from the air group, which was under the direct command of Admiral Mitscher. The Air Department was in charge of the flight deck. Their job was to launch, load, land, and rearm the planes, reload the bombs, cull out the duds, respot the deck, and then ready the deck for another launch.

The V1 division of the Air Department were the air traffic controllers. They ran the arresting gear and the catapults, handled operations on the flight deck, drove the jeeps and the tractors, and operated the elevators. Some were assigned white asbestos suits and were charged with braving the heat of exploding fuel to rescue pilots and crew from crashed planes. V1 cleared the wreckage, fought the fires, and made emergency repairs to the deck. They ran the hangar deck, too, releasing the planes from the arresting gear on the flight deck, pushing them onto elevators, and then hauling them intricately, like colors on a Rubik's cube, to fit each aircraft inside the confined hangar deck.

The Air Department's V3 division managed the operations, offensive and defensive, of the squadrons and the ship, melding them into a cohesive fighting unit. Aerology used weather prediction, then a primitive art—more conjecture than science—to hide the approaching American fleet beneath storm clouds. Air Plot acted as the tower at a modern naval airbase, utilizing radio and radar signals to maintain contact with the squadrons in the air, issuing flight plans, determining which type of armament squadrons should utilize, and guiding the squadrons and the Air Department synchronously. Air Plot kept the day-to-day plans of the Air Department flowing. The fighter director worked with the Combat Information Center (CIC) to launch the CAP—combat air patrol—for emergency intercepts. The photographic lab developed the film taken from the gun cameras and the spy cameras on American planes so that the Air Combat Intelligence (ACI) unit could determine, based on the reports of the pilots themselves and their photographs, what the next target and arming plan should be. In the tense, congested ACI compartment, it was said, visitors were as welcome as bogies.

The Communication Department transmitted and received all messages to and from the ship and managed the ship's administration. They created daily press briefings on the activities of the *Bunker Hill* and the task force, and ran the printing office. These men used a mixture of the most advanced communications technology and some of the oldest ways that man has communicated between ships at sea. They used radio facsimile, an early version of today's fax machines, and they were the signalmen who flashed messages with long-range lamps and the skivvy wavers who raised and lowered signal flags at the edge of the island.

The Navigation Department ensured the *Bunker Hill* did not get lost. They utilized sextants and the phases of the sun and moon, combined with accurate chronometers, to determine the ship's location. But they relied heavily on more modern techniques like radio beam tracking. They made the *Bunker Hill* arrive on time and location for every strike and brought her home along a safe route. They filtered all communications into the bridge and aided in the anchoring and docking of the carrier.

The Supply Department made sure the ship and all the men aboard had everything they needed. They maintained an account of all of the supplies, stores, and spare parts aboard. They handled the ship's payroll and aviation stores, including replacement parts for all the ship's aircraft. They were the cooks, the bakers, and the drugstore keepers. They made sure that the *Bunker Hill* had everything they would need to maintain 3,400 men for months at sea.

To give some idea of what this means, if the men were to eat only two eggs each for breakfast, two strips of bacon, two pieces of toast, one

The Bunker Hill's *post office was an astounding operation. It was run by the Communication Department. The ship's men mailed about 100,000 letters each month, and received nearly a quarter of a million. They filled $1 million worth of money orders and sold $75,000 worth of stamps each year.*

glass of orange juice, a slice of butter, and a cup of coffee, the *Bunker Hill* would require nearly 50,000 eggs, 50,000 strips of bacon, nearly 2,000 loaves of bread, 150 gallons of orange juice, and 3,000 sticks of butter, plus 150 gallons of coffee to provide breakfast for one week.

The Chaplaincy Department was in charge of the men's spiritual well-being. The department held services for Christians and Jews, had full oversight of the ship's patriotic and uncontroversial newspaper, *The Monument*, and performed last rites.

The *Bunker Hill's* Medical Department ran a small hospital with full dental staff in the sickbay. They took care of everything from minor injuries to major surgeries and serious battle wounds. Medical orderlies inspected the ship, especially living quarters and food preparation, for health and safety. They monitored every takeoff and landing aboard ship in case of accident.

The Gunnery Department kept the *Bunker Hill* protected from intruders twenty-four hours a day. The men were split into various divisions that manned the 20mm, 40mm, and 5-inch guns. Gunners under normal conditions worked four-hour shifts on their guns. They sometimes slept strapped in their gun tubs, or tied in the sponsons. When they were not in immediate danger, the men had other duties—swabbing the decks, keeping the life rafts and boats in order, and painting the ship's sides. But in 1945 there would be little time for any of that. They were rarely out of combat, and the gunners were often at their posts twenty-four hours a day for days on end.

Gunners ran the fire control equipment that found the targets and aimed the weapons. They maintained the torpedoes and surveyed the ship's ammunition stores to ensure sufficient ammo on hand. When the ship landed they manned the mooring lines and the gangway.

Emergency damage control was handled primarily by the Hull Department and the Engineering Department. The Essex carriers

Aircraft crowd the decks of the Bunker Hill *during flight operations.*

were so weight-critical by 1945 that they could not be sufficiently protected by their own armor, nor even by their own guns—the ships
simply weighed too much. In the end, the best protection the Navy
offered was probably the unprecedented level of procedural damage
control training offered constantly to every man aboard ship. The
Hull Department, led by Commander Shane King, managed construction and repair and kept the ship running efficiently. They made
sure that all of the hundreds of smaller machines were working. The
carpenters, fire marshals, painters, and shipfitters, all worked in Hull.
They were also the men who made her a small city—the barbers, the
mess cooks, the trash collectors. They ran the cobbler shop, the ship's
store, the tailor shop, the laundry, and the geedunk stand. They made
fresh water and organized repair parties and damage control.

When the Bunker Hill *was not in combat, the
men in Gunnery were given work all over the
ship.*

The Hull Department's shipfitters, like Al Skaret, were mostly experienced tradesmen, welders, carpenters, plumbers, and electricians before they joined the Navy. They could do or fix almost anything from a jammed aircraft elevator to a clogged garbage disposal. But their ultimate responsibility was damage control.

The Engineering Department kept the *Bunker Hill* moving. Joseph Carmichael ran Engineering and knew the names of all 500-plus men who served under him. They kept the boilers fired and the engine turbines rotating. They ran the large generators and the saltwater pumps used to make fresh water for drinking and showering, and to make steam for the boilers themselves, and for putting out fires if the ship were damaged.

Engineering's duties overlapped with those of the Hull Department outside of the engine rooms. The engineers were in charge of all of the communications equipment aboard ship, and of the thousands of miles of electrical wiring throughout. They maintained the ship's even keel by balancing millions of gallons of fuel oil, shifting it with pumps amongst various tanks and void spaces as it was used up by the ship's boilers. They worked regularly in the boiler and engine rooms, which remained at least 110 degrees Fahrenheit, twenty-four hours a day, for months on end. It was said that when Air or Gunnery men visited the engine rooms they would invariably step outside saying, "It *can't* be this hot all the time."

The main focus of Carmichael's efforts was to keep the boilers always running so that steam would be available to power the ship's massive 150,000-horsepower engines and its various generators and smaller motors and pumps. While in the battle zone, Carmichael would have a minimum of twelve men working in each boiler and engine room on all watches.

It is important to distinguish tasks aboard ship: engineers were men who worked with the engines; firemen were engineers who worked specifically in the boiler (fire) rooms; fire controllers were men who controlled the firing of weapons—aimed the guns; firefighters aboard ship were called damage controlmen. Virtually every crewman, though, received some damage control and firefighting training.

Carmichael was always amazed when he thought of the men in

Washington at the Bureau of Ships who designed the Essex Class and made this system work. These naval architects conjured in their minds the almost unimaginably cramped and twisted machinery and found a way for it all to work, in a manner that could be built and built fast. None of them had ever been on an Essex Class ship as no Essex had ever been built. Yet they designed a ship that could absorb enormous, almost unthinkable losses and survive, as long as the men aboard her, and especially the men in charge of her like Carmichael, remained to make her survive.

6. DRAFTED: JAPAN
1941–1944

There are two leaders among the traders, the one called Murashusa, and the other Christian Mota. In their hands they carried something two or three feet long, straight on the outside with a passage inside, and made of a heavy substance. The inner passage runs through it although it is closed at the end. At its side there is an aperture which is the passageway for fire. Its shape defies comparison with anything I know. Lord Tokitaka saw it and thought it was the wonder of wonders.

—*SOURCES OF JAPANESE TRADITION,*
RYUSAKU TSUNODA, WM. THEODORE DE BARY,
AND DONALD KEENE

Japan, at the beginning of World War II, had been controlled by a military junta for more than a generation. This cabal of mostly army leaders strictly controlled the press, radio, film, and, most significantly, the dissemination of ideology within Japan. Their chosen dogma was the only philosophy most Japanese people ever learned. The junta controlled every aspect of life in Japan, and enforced their ideology through absolute control over the laws, religion, governance, education, armed forces, and the economy, especially jobs. Their fundamental precepts stressed ultimate loyalty and ideal fealty throughout the lives of every citizen. Kiyoshi Ogawa and his fellow college students had known no other type of regime. These young men grew up steeped in the militarist ideology, which stressed adherence to an ideal of constancy, fidelity, dedication, and deference to a superpatriotism that required absolute obedience to family and nation.

These two institutions, family and country, were conjoined in the body of the emperor, who represented perfection of family and nation in God. In the militarists' view, the emperor was God, and any questioning or doubt in the government was heresy, an act of disloyalty and betrayal of family and nation. They succeeded to a remarkable degree in usurping freedom through their imposition of a form of social pressure that they enshrined in law and custom. The junta became the guardians of the emperor, and in his name, they enforced their will throughout Japan.

The Japanese military seemed to grasp Shigenobu's theory that individual freedom had contributed significantly to advancement, and hence power, in Western nations. They were leery, therefore, of obliterating all freedom of thought. Universities, separated from broader Japanese culture, were given a limited amount of freedom to teach various ideologies, not so much to be embraced, but rather to be utilized as theories to strengthen Japan. The college students thus were given more freedom of thought than any other group in Japan. Ironically, it was they in the end who were asked to sacrifice their own freedom far beyond what had been asked of fully inculcated Japanese.

Japan's ruling clique severely restricted information about the United States. Few Japanese college students had an accurate idea of the size and strength of the United States. The only reality that the students understood about America had come through state-controlled education and newspapers, which gave limited, almost universally negative, information. The term most often used to describe Americans was *kichikubei*. Roughly translated, it characterizes Americans as monstrous and bestial. The students did have one unrestricted source of information about America—Hollywood films. Remarkably, the junta allowed most mainstream American movies to play in Japan. The Japanese students loved these films, which seemed always to portray an America bursting with energy and material display. Every Japanese collegian knew John Wayne as the Ringo Kid in *Stagecoach*. They loved the danger and adventure of the westerns and the daring appeal of Spencer Tracy and Robert Taylor. It never occurred to most Japanese college students that Japan would go to war against the United States.

The students lived divorced from the realities of politics. After the Pearl Harbor attack occurred, most college students thought the war would be mercifully brief. Japan was winning and there did not seem to be any reason for it to go on long. Few had a clear idea of the causes of the war, and almost none understood the level and length of response the United States was prepared to muster after Japan's surprise attack.

Japanese college students seemed to be aware of the contradictions in their culture and yet were able to embrace those contradictions in thought and deed. Many detested the military regime that had controlled their lives, but all remained fiercely loyal to Japan. Ryoji Uehara, a college student who was drafted and trained with Kiyoshi Ogawa, wrote in his diary: "I could not care less about living *yūkyū no taigi* [forever quietly under the law of justice—living and dying for the emperor as an eternal, unchanging moral act], or things like that." Nevertheless, he continued: "I do truly love Japan. And I will fight for the independence and liberty of my fatherland."

By the fall of 1943, Japan's armed forces could no longer supply the periphery of her newly acquired, far-flung empire. The IJA was overextended on mainland Asia and the IJN task forces were outgunned. Perhaps most significantly, Japan was running out of every strategic resource. Incredibly, Japanese college students still had not been asked to sacrifice. Then, on October 1, 1943, Emperor Hirohito issued Imperial Order 755, which suspended liberal arts students' privilege of temporary exemption from conscription. Japan drafted Kiyoshi Ogawa and every single nonscience student in the country in a single day.

When Kiyoshi received his draft notice, he and all of the other drafted students returned to their homes for one final weekend with their loved ones. The Japanese cities and towns all held farewell ceremonies for their student-soldiers. While home in Takasaki, Kiyoshi met up with his childhood friend Osamu Numaga. After making their farewells to family and friends, the two students set out walking toward the train station. They stopped at a shrine where townspeople had gathered, and each spoke for a while with the local Shinto priest. Osamu was thinking how far they had come from the days when they would race each other home from school and play tag in farmers' fields.

Continuing on, they arrived at the station where a much larger crowd had gathered, waving flags, to see the students off. Someone made a speech about the destruction the Americans were causing, exhorting them not to be afraid. It had not yet occurred to Osamu that they *should* be afraid.

The newspapers were continuing to write stories about how Japan was winning the war. But everyone understood that supplies were running out and that if the nation were forced to draft its best and brightest then things must be terrible at the front.

The two young men traveled together by train to Tokyo, then down the Miura peninsula. From the station at Yokohama they marched south, passing by the Imperial Palace at Hayama (where Emperor Hirohito liked to collect and classify sea plants). Osamu had been attending Kokushikan University, an agricultural school. He looked up to Kiyoshi for attending refined Waseda and was keenly aware of the new difference in station between himself and Kiyoshi. His childhood friend was the most successful man Osamu had ever known. Kiyoshi appeared completely unaware that there was a difference in their social stations. They were friends, and chatted as they walked along, as though no time had passed, ambling for hours toward Takeyama, the new training base at the edge of Japan's sprawling naval facilities at Yokosuka. They talked about their schools and what it was like in college, and wondered what it would be like in the navy. Osamu had planned to be a farmer. Kiyoshi was preparing for a life in public policy. Neither was particularly nationalistic, and neither had ever considered joining the armed forces. It seems as though they had no idea that everything they knew and loved would change or be destroyed over the next eighteen months.

When the students first arrived, everyone felt lost. But Kiyoshi made new friends, *senyu* (wartime buddies), who helped him through this next difficult stage. His closest friend during basic training at Takeyama was Tatsuo Ono. Ono had attended Waseda and shared a major with Kiyoshi. The two boys were the same age and within an inch in height. They did not know each other at school, but had taken the same classes, shared the same examination challenges, eaten at the same restaurants. Ono felt alone at Takeyama until he paired with Kiyoshi. They became more dedicated and committed to each other than many brothers. No one could complete basic training without trusting in and working with their new comrades. But they were all so disoriented by their new environment that trusting anyone became a challenge, particularly because all felt constrained from speaking openly.

The students were technically in the Imperial Japanese Navy, but the Japanese had fewer ships with each passing day. Troops outside Japan could no longer safely return; those in Japan could not safely sortie. There was little chance that any of these liberal arts students, now naval cadets, would actually serve on a ship.

Kiyoshi began his training just as Japan began to lose the war on every front. The fast carriers increased the pace of their assault on outlying Japanese strongholds. They hit Kwajalein, Majuro, and Truk. British and American troops began to counterattack in Burma, and Japanese expansion in China fizzled. Land-based American bombers raided Japanese holdings in Thailand and Rabaul.

Kiyoshi entered the navy as a common seaman, but his superiors— the *tokumushikan*, noncommissioned officers—at Takeyama came from the less-educated and poorest, though reflexively patriotic, families. The noncommissioned officers had devoted their lives to their military career. The *tokumushikan* burned with a mixture of guilt and anger and shame that so many of their friends had been killed as Japan was losing the war. They felt demeaned to be training college students rather than fighting. The NCOs knew, moreover, that these spoiled students cared nothing for the traditions of the IJN, and worst of all, would soon outrank them.

The IJN encouraged random corporal punishment. Kiyoshi's instructors seemed to become more sadistic as their comrades on the front lines fell back, regularly beating the students bloody. They were pushed, slapped, punched, kicked, and repeatedly humiliated, verbally and physically. The students were cruelly hazed, worked to exhaustion, prevented from sleeping, dehydrated, and never given sufficient food. The physical abuse, meted out both individually and by squad, came to feel almost mundane.

Kiyoshi and his senyu *were sent out on a brief two-night infantry training. It turned out to be mostly a camping trip, and a welcome respite from the harsh routine they had become used to. They took a couple of photographs of their campsite in a pasture near what is probably Mount Tsukuba. Kiyoshi is furthest right in back row.*

One nasty torture was the *kyuu-kouka-bakugeki* or "nose-dive-bombing." Cadets were forced to stand awkwardly contorted for hours, decreasing the blood flow to their head, until they nose-dived, passing out. Another torture was "Valley Crossing of Nightingales" in which they had to crawl for hours while chirping like nightingales. The whole experience was surreal. "It was crazy," Ono said. A few recruits hanged themselves.

During their formal training, the student conscripts were studying all the same things as young men in the United States Navy. They learned how to fire various guns and studied meteorology and navigation. They learned to tap out Morse code and to signal with flags. But all of this seemed wholly peripheral to the real objective—indoctrination into the military. The whole training system of the IJN appeared more geared to destroying the cadets' humanity and sense of self than helping them gain any particular skills, beyond total reliance on each other.

In order to survive their brutal indoctrination the college students had to subsume all sense of self, in favor of their *senyu*. Military indoctrination destroyed the psychological self, amid abuse of the physical self. During basic training, many of the students came to feel that their lives meant nothing, were worth nothing. They were left without control or choice. Self-value was then rebuilt within an intense group dynamic that facilitated the ultimate sacrifice to protect those they loved. Dying in self-sacrifice came to seem a reasonable intention.

The cadets were united under the oppression of their instructor (*Honchou*). But their feelings were as convoluted as those of the millions of young men going through basic training in the United States, for they also deeply respected and desired the *Honchou*'s approval.

They were never allowed to do any action, no matter how slight, alone. Ono and Kiyoshi learned military life, discipline, and rules of behavior together. Their hair and uniforms matched precisely, they slept in identical hammocks, with identical blankets, in the same room. They were assigned to the same chores at the same time. Everything in their day was done together, in unison, from morning calisthenics to lights-out. They even were abused in the same manner by the same officers.

Ono describes their relationship as like husband and wife. They learned to rely on each other for everything. And each learned that he could always count on the other. Toward the end of their basic training, the two realized they even breathed in perfect syncopation. By sticking together absolutely, Kiyoshi and Ono endured the training and recognized they could survive anything by trusting in their *senyu*. Vicious training achieved a near-perfect union with these two men: they would die for each other.

The Imperial Japanese Navy sought to create a special cohesion and compliance in the new recruits, and rote memorization was thought to effect a united obedience. Kiyoshi and the other conscripts in the navy had to recite and meditate upon the *Gosei*—the five points of reflection—each night before lights out. The *Gosei* affirm the importance, as a guiding principle to the IJN, of the endeavor of spiritual and physical refinement. The U.S. Naval Academy adopted the *Gosei* after the war:

Hast thou not gone against sincerity?
Hast thou not felt ashamed of thy words and deeds?
Hast thou not lacked vigor?
Hast thou exerted all possible efforts?
Hast thou not become slothful?

Imperial rescripts were the expression and foundation of Japanese warrior culture extended into every aspect of life. The rescripts underpinned the emotional intensity, which led eventually to the extreme of sanctioned self-sacrifice tactics. Kiyoshi and the other students read this quotation from the Imperial rescript on the military just about every day:

> It is essential that each man, high and low, dutifully observing his place, should be determined always to sacrifice himself for the whole, in accordance with the intentions of the commander, by reposing every confidence in his comrades, and without giving even the slightest thought to personal interest and to life or death . . . always retain the spirit of attack and always maintain freedom of action; never give up a position but rather die.

Takeyama is famous for its blue azaleas. But the flowers remained dormant during Kiyoshi's instruction there. Cold days training outside were followed by colder nights in their unheated wooden barracks. Ono watched Kiyoshi endure strange pains in his leg each night at Takeyama. Exercise was the only way he could calm his knee enough to sleep. Kiyoshi would explain cheerfully to Ono, "My knee hurts if I don't move, so I'll go for a run." The NCOs forbade anyone from moving around the barracks at night. No one was ever allowed outside after lights-out. Nevertheless, Kiyoshi would climb out of the barracks window and take off into the darkness and snow. While Ono shivered badly under the single, thin woolen blanket, Kiyoshi would crawl back through the window an hour or more later, then slip under his blanket, drenched in sweat.

Kiyoshi could have avoided the grueling training period required

A photograph taken during basic training at Takeyama shows Kiyoshi, leaning forward, laughing, his arms around two friends, just above and to the right of the head of their terribly serious commander, who seems to have been caught up for a moment in their laughter. They all appear almost impossibly young.

of pilots simply by notifying his superiors of his medical condition—the Japanese did not want to train anyone unfit to fly. Because of his intelligence and education, Kiyoshi would have been assigned an office job. Yet he never told any of the superior officers about his leg pain. In fact, he risked brutal punishment merely to have the opportunity to be of service to his comrades and his country.

Ono was amazed that Kiyoshi would take such risks. He asked Kiyoshi every time he climbed back into their barracks where he had gone. Kiyoshi always replied, "I was just running." Ono wondered where he had been and what he had seen and still wonders at his running. No one ran back then. In a military that severely discouraged freethinking, and a society that valued conventionality perhaps more than any other individual trait, Kiyoshi remained a free spirit. He was a nonconformist, which makes his decision to crash-dive all the more difficult to understand or explain. Ono said later: "He was an original."

In January 1944, after about six weeks of near-constant abuse at Takeyama, each student was given an evening off to see his family. Parents and siblings of the student conscripts came to the base to see their loved ones and bring them food. All of the surviving students say it was their best night in the service. It proved that there was still sanity in the world. But as soon as they returned from the dinner, the misery and abuse began again.

Throughout their vicious physical training, Kiyoshi and the other students had to find time to study for the examinations to become pilots. Probably not a single Japanese cadet had ever seen the inside of a plane before he joined the navy. But virtually every man drafted in the student mobilization wished to become a pilot.

The student-cadets underwent a demanding set of written tests on various mechanical aspects of aircraft and flying. Kiyoshi and Ono,

Japanese student-cadets train in a sumo-style martial exercise outside the new barracks, heated with a wood stove at Yokosuka.

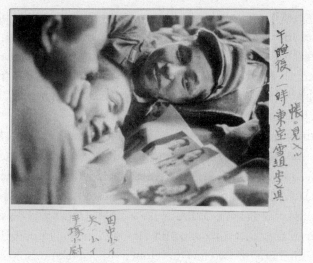

A photograph of student-cadets lying on their bunk dorm beds looking at pinup photographs.

miserable beyond imagining, took the tests seated next to each other. Both passed and were then subjected to an even more grueling series of physical examinations. First were the usual tests of vision and hearing. After he passed those, Kiyoshi was given a more idiosyncratic examination in which he was strapped to a whirling chair that spun rapidly, creating massive g-forces and dizziness, like a carnival ride run amok. Kiyoshi had to count the number of times the chair spun around and was tested on how well he could walk afterward.

The college-student draftees completed their basic training the day after U.S. Marines, protected by the fast carriers, landed on Kwajalein in the Marshall Islands in early February 1944. Kiyoshi had passed each assessment and transferred with a select group to the Japanese naval airbase in Tsuchiura, forty miles northeast of Tokyo, in Ibaraki prefecture, to learn rudimentary flying techniques. Kiyoshi and Ono made the long walk back to Echigo Station during the night in March 1944. There, they were assigned to different *buntai* (squadrons). Ono never saw Kiyoshi again.

The drafted students, now flight cadets, began learning to fly in small red biplanes called *Akatonbo* after a Japanese red dragonfly. The

Akatonbo were remarkably similar to the N3N Yellow Peril biplanes that the Americans used for training early in the war (named for their color and unreliability, not the threat they posed to Asia). That same month, March 1944, General Tojo, who became prime minister in the fall of 1941, ordered the Army Air Corps to begin preparations for suicide missions.

Japanese drill instructors organized everything by height. Kiyoshi was five foot three and one half inches tall—the second shortest man in his Tsuchiura platoon. He was paired there with Takeo Ayama, also a Waseda student, who was the next taller cadet. Kiyoshi and Ayama both felt lost at Tsuchiura. It was particularly difficult to be short in an environment that thrived on physical and mental humiliation and degradation. But the two men developed a *senyu* relationship of complete trust.

They spoke mostly about food, the little dishes they loved and missed from the restaurants surrounding Waseda, and about which shop had the best coffee. They talked about civilian life: going to Ginza at night, walking along the busy streets, wanting to go to the bars but not having enough money to get in. They talked a lot about movies, especially westerns.

Meanwhile, their superior officers continued their sadistic mistreatment. The cadets were worked to exhaustion each day. They were rushed from one grueling task, physically or mentally beyond their capabilities, to the next. Most say that the beatings were more brutal at Tsuchiura, but there was one great difference that made everything there better: they were learning to fly. No one was prepared for the joy of becoming a pilot. But compared with the American flight training program, the students received very little time in the air. They had to master all of the basic skills with less than ten hours flying. Those who did not, washed out. On May 25, the successful student cadets were graduated to flying officer status, and moved to intermediate flight training at Japan's great training facility at Yatabe.

Once the students became flying officers, their lot improved. Compassion for each other returned. Those that made it through felt a special bond that they have shared their entire lives. The Japanese military, though, still encouraged superior officers to beat the young officers. Their captain, Itekani-san, was particularly cruel and demanding. Many of the students came to loathe Itekani, but they developed, too, a fierce loyalty to him with a special intensity of feeling that approached love.

The barracks at Yatabe were relatively new when the students arrived. Kiyoshi's was a two-story building made entirely of wood, but with hundreds of small wood-framed glass-paned windows. The sunlight filtered in during the day. Bare light bulbs in enamel fixtures hung from the ceilings, casting shadows among the hammocks before lights-out. One hundred sixty men ate, lived, and slept on each level, separated by *buntai* into eight squads of twenty men. Each platoon had two rectangular wooden tables where the men ate in two groups of ten, five on a side.

The *Honchou* presided over the dinner table from a center seat, as he did over every single other aspect of their lives. The conscripted students were served atrocious food throughout their training. If they were lucky enough to procure some kind of fish, the military cooks invariably boiled it into a gigantic stew. They served the stew for each meal, breakfast, lunch, and dinner, often for ten days in a row. Each day the brew became more putrid. Their usual fare, however, was so disgusting that the men actually looked forward to the sickening slow-boiled fish. Brown rice mixed with cheap barley and a small piece of radish was often served every meal, every day, for months on end, without variation. The men, like navy men the world over, invented special labels for each dish. The Japanese students called the boiled fish *neko-matagi*: "a tasteless fish, even a cat does not take and steps over it."

At night the men strung their hammocks from rafters in neat rows, around and above the wooden dining tables. They stretched across the room, forming two even, nearly continuous planes, one above the other. It was hard at first learning to sleep in the swinging hammocks, but they soon got the knack of it. Each morning, in the cold dark before dawn, the students took down their beds to clear the room for study. They had no privacy and there was often no heat save that which emanated from the men's tired bodies.

Training was strictly regimented. No time went unaccounted for. But the students earned a small amount of free time at Yatabe. A short wooden bench and a long worn table sat outside their barracks and there the men gathered, playing cards, gambling, or smoking before the trumpet was played and lights were turned out at 9:00 P.M. It was during these times that the cadets got to know each other.

Each cadet received a pack of Hikari cigarettes every week. It was the only brand available, distributed free as a gift from the emperor to military officers. Hikari means "light," but these were nothing like the "light" cigarettes available today. "Light" was a more existential designation, the emperor's light shining upon his officers. The cigarettes came machine-rolled, in a hard pack, unfiltered.

Kiyoshi and the other cadets began each day with calisthenics at 0500. They should then have begun flying exercises, but because there was no fuel they ended up just doing more calisthenics—three times a day. Sometimes they fought vicious challenges of *bo-taoshi*, "topple the pole," in which one team tries to knock down a pole while the other team defends it. They studied air-to-air combat strategy, use of air-to-air weapons, and identification.

Day after day, as Kiyoshi and the other drafted students waited to fly, bad news arrived from every front. The farce that Japan was winning the war was destroyed when Tojo announced the fall of Saipan.

Standard military tactics were proving ineffective against the fast carriers. Military leaders in the Japanese army and navy determined at the same time there was only one way Japan could win the war. Rather than surrender, they would order thousands of newly indoctrinated students to become *tokko*—suiciders.

7. SAIPAN AND THE DESTRUCTION OF JAPAN'S AIR FORCES

The True Way is one and the same, in every country and throughout heaven and earth. This Way, however, has been correctly transmitted only in our Imperial Land.

—MOTOORI NOORINAGA ZENSHU, *PRECIOUS COMB-BOX (TAMA KUSHIGE) VI, 3–6*

The genesis of officially sanctioned suicide flights remains clouded. Most of the decision makers died during the war. Nearly every document surrounding the decision has been lost or was intentionally destroyed. Historians have pieced together some of what happened, but understanding the morality of those who ordered the kamikaze attacks remains a challenge. The pilots themselves were taught to mask their own feelings, and for a long time no one asked them what it was like to recognize and acquiesce to an order to commit suicide. The fast carriers' relentless drive across the Central Pacific in 1944, and America's astonishing edge in matériel, training, and technology, led directly, though, to Japan's desperate suicide tactics.

From mid-1942 through mid-1943, the American Navy had prevented Japanese expansion in the Pacific but failed to bring the war to Imperial Japan in any significant way. America, preoccupied with the war in Europe, spent the first six months of 1943 devising a strategy to destroy the empire of Japan and waiting for the Essex Class to arrive and execute that tactical plan.

The United States and its Allies determined to attack Japan on two fronts over the Pacific. The lion's share of American resources were directed at a drive by the U.S. Navy across the Central Pacific. A second prong, led by General MacArthur and the U.S. Army, would move north from New Guinea toward the Philippines. America requested that British forces open a third front against the Japanese in India, pushing them back into China. Russia, though America's ally against the Germans, remained neutral in the Pacific war.

The *Bunker Hill* departed Boston on September 4, 1943, passed through the Panama Canal, then on November 11 made her first assault—against Rabaul, Japan's most powerful base in the South Pacific. Japan's most experienced bomber and fighter pilots counterattacked the *Bunker Hill.* The ship remained under constant aerial assault for fifty-two minutes, the longest time under enemy fire, then, of the war. The *Bunker Hill,* though, escaped unscathed and earned her first Battle Star. Gunners aboard the *Bunker Hill* and the ships around her shot down dozens of enemy planes. The Japanese lost 150 aircraft in the fight.

The Bunker Hill *cruises through the Panama Canal, September 1943, on the way to war.*

The Bunker Hill *steams toward Pearl Harbor brimming with aircraft, men, and matériel for the war effort.*

When World War II began most naval planners thought that naval battles would be determined by surface-to-surface fire—that is, surface ships firing on each other with traditional guns. Planners knew that the great battleships were virtually immune to damage from surface-fired shells. Conventional wisdom held that the great battleships could only be sunk by piercing their hulls below the waterline. They thought that the best way for an aircraft carrier to sink a battleship was to have the carrier aircraft launch torpedoes at enemy surface ships. Both sides developed carrier-launched torpedo bombers.

These first-generation torpedo bombers were clunky, unreliable, unsafe, often defective weapons. Grumman's second-generation torpedo bomber, the Avenger, was better in every category than its precursor, the Devastator. The Avenger was probably the most rugged and survivable carrier aircraft, but torpedo bombing remained the most hazardous carrier combat duty. Six of the new Avengers were delivered to Midway just in time for the carrier battle there. Flown by inexperienced pilots (who had never flown out of sight of land until the day before), the Avengers launched from Midway Island and were the first to attack the Japanese carrier fleet. The Japanese combat air patrol devastated the Avengers. Five out of the six were shot down. Carrier torpedo bomber missions came to be thought of as suicide duty.

If a pilot dropped a torpedo a little too high or a little too fast, too low or too slow, it might "swim" too deep and pass beneath the hull of the target. If his aircraft bounced during the release, the torpedo might turn to either side before striking. The internal gyroscopes often failed, sending the torpedo in an endless circle until it sank. But probably the worst part of flying a torpedo bomber was lining up the target. The first planes could not be juked on their bombing run. They had to fly low, slow, and straight or their torpedoes would malfunction. They came in as ducks in a row, and on their first combat mission American torpedo bombers at Midway suffered casualties as high as any kamikaze mission. Of the thirty pilots and crew of Torpedo 8, only George Gay survived their single attack. The other torpedo bomber squadrons fared almost as badly. After the disaster at Midway the United States scaled back plans for torpedo bomber attacks. The Navy withdrew the TBD Devastator from combat and replaced them with the Avenger—a better aircraft in all respects.

There was no coverage in the American press about the poor American torpedo technology. But the pilots knew from experience that even if they dropped their torpedoes perfectly at 180 knots, from 200 feet on a straight and even run (which was nearly suicidal when hundreds of antiaircraft guns were firing at you), a great many of the torpedoes would be duds. The pilots never knew which ones would fail until they were fired in combat. After Midway, the Navy often used the torpedo bombers for close air support and as conventional fighter-bombers. But Al Turnbull got to launch a torpedo during the Rabaul attack.

Turnbull's first torpedo dropped straight and true. Turnbull watched his torpedo's thin white line streaming through the water as he banked away from the target vessel. Later aerial photos show its path leading into a Japanese naval vessel—but no explosion. The main problem seemed to be the complex gyro navigation and arming systems.

The pilots were rarely around to watch the explosions. Heavy anti-aircraft fire was severe throughout the first years of the war. The TBM Avengers were much slower than the Zero and the Japanese fighters seemed to be always on their tails.

Despite the torpedo's unreliability, the Grumman torpedo bomber was the most versatile naval combat aircraft in the Pacific war. Its standard complement was a pilot, a radioman who operated radar, and a tail gunner who fired a .50-caliber machine gun equipped with an electric turret that was more versatile, faster, and which could aim more quickly than its Japanese counterpart.

The Avenger's 1,700 HP engine had long-range capability. The aircraft could be armed with machine guns, rockets, and up to 2,000 pounds of bombs. It was originally designed to drop a single 2,200-pound torpedo, but the bomb bay had twelve shackles, making the aircraft ultraversatile. Each shackle could hold a bomb or a part of a bomb, thus the planes could carry twelve 100-pound bombs or four 500-pound bombs of any type, as well as general-purpose, armor-piercing, propaganda bombs filled with leaflets, practice bombs containing only sand, or the new terrifyingly effective napalm bombs. It could even drop up to four 500-pound barrel-shaped depth charges against submarines. The Avenger was a powerful plane, with an enormously powerful engine.

Even so, under a full load it often used every inch of the ship's flight deck to get airborne. When overloaded, aircraft could be launched from a carrier's catapult, or the TBM could use Jet Assisted Takeoff (JATO) tanks—essentially bottles of jet fuel mounted to the wings, which would rocket them off a short flight deck to cruising altitude. The JATO tanks were jettisoned after takeoff.

The Avenger often flew armed with 5-inch rockets that could be launched from beneath its wings and hit targets with approximately the same devastating impact as the 5-inch shells from the largest guns aboard the *Bunker Hill*.

The plane operated on 300 gallons of gas, more if it utilized auxiliary wing tanks. The Avenger burned a gallon of gas every minute, depending primarily on altitude and load, but it had roughly only five hours of flying time, and the pilots had to be very careful about timing missions.

The Grumman had special capabilities beyond strict combat operations. The TBM could carry up to six passengers in the "greenhouse" Plexiglas cockpit compartment, including a cameraman to photograph enemy installations. The Grumman could carry a smoke tank to lay smoke screens over the fleet, shrouding the ships from Japanese scouts.

The TBM operated target flights for the fleet where they strung a sleeve out the back end of the aircraft, like a plane dragging advertisements at the beach, and towed it around for antiaircraft practice. Days where other flight groups might have R&R during task force refueling, the TBM pilots would be working, towing sleeves.

The plane was nearly indestructible. The fuel tanks were self-sealing and the pilot's cockpit was protected by armored walls and a bulletproof glass cockpit canopy.

Planners code-named the American battle plan for the Central Pacific "Cartwheel." Led by the fast carriers, the U.S. Navy began, slowly at first, yet with an air of inevitability, to destroy the Japanese bases in the Pacific one by one. The fast carriers planned to roll over the Japanese Pacific island chains.

Rabaul was isolated after the November attack by the *Bunker Hill* and the fast carriers. Nearly 100,000 Japanese troops were stuck there, bypassed. They spent the rest of the war foraging for food. The *Bunker Hill* left a neutralized Rabaul and began a relentless assault driving westward across the Central Pacific without losing a single battle. Their tactical goal was to take Saipan, a small island in the Marianas, large enough to support a gigantic airbase that could operate a squadron of the new B-29 Superfortress bombers, which could make the massive bombing runs over the Japanese Home Islands—a strategy deemed necessary for victory. But before such runs could commence, America had to first destroy Japan's navy and naval air defenses. This could only be done through U.S. airpower. Fighters flown from the fast carriers would spearhead the U.S. war effort in the Pacific. In doing so, they would go up against one of the finest fighting planes ever made.

Japan began the war with one of the most battle-hardened armed forces in the world. They had fought in China for years. The Japanese naval air forces were arguably better than anything the Allies possessed in the Pacific up until 1943. And they flew one of the finest fighter aircraft ever made—the Mitsubishi Zero.

The Zero fighter's effectiveness shocked Army and Naval Air Force commanders. American planners had disdained Japanese technology and skill. But American pilots were consistently amazed at what the Zero could do when flown by experienced pilots.*

During the first year of the war, no one was certain how to counter the Zero threat. In 1942, Lieutenant Commander Jimmy Thach developed a tactic to fight the Zero. Two American pilots would fly in tandem, weaving back and forth when attacking. Then, as the Zero tried to dive right or left to double back on one of the Americans, it would have to pass broadside directly through the wingman's line of fire. No matter which way he turned, the Zero could not get behind the Americans without passing sideways through one attacker's line of fire. His only choice was to run. The "Thach Weave" worked so well it was adopted officially by the Navy and used throughout the war. Thach was sent home to train new pilots.

Perhaps as important as the Thach Weave was the improbable capture of an actual Zero. In June 1942, a lone Zero crashed on tiny Akutan Island in the Aleutians. The plane had been downed by a single bullet that severed its pressure gauge indicator line. The Zero's wheels caught on impact, flipping the plane and breaking the pilot's neck. The aircraft was recovered by American engineers, boxed up, and carried to California where it was studied, repaired, and flown.

Aviator Jim Swett, who would fly aboard the *Bunker Hill* in May 1945, flew the captured Zero in San Diego. He was shocked by its responsiveness and agility. The Zero felt impossibly light. It was exceptionally maneuverable, and flew "almost like a kite. I mean,

---

* The Mustang and Lightning, though powerful fighters, could not land on a carrier, and so were of limited utility in the Pacific.

it'd practically jump into the air." He loved the Zero's big fourteen-cylinder 1,200-horsepower radial engine on its light (3,920-pound) frame. The first time Swett gave it just a little stick, it nearly snap-rolled.

A new American weapon was perfected to destroy it: the F6F Hellcat, known to the Japanese by its maker, Grumman. The Zero was agile but extremely fragile—a handful of bullets could flame the highly combustible craft. The Grumman was not nearly as maneuverable, but it was rock-solid—very difficult to destroy.

The Hellcat flew in large numbers for the first time in November 1943 with the *Bunker Hill* at Rabaul. It demonstrated its vast superiority in June the following year during the struggle for Saipan. Hellcats flying disciplined formations could destroy squadrons of Zeros under virtually any flying conditions. The Hellcat was better at diving and climbing and was more heavily armed than the Zero. The Hellcat had self-sealing fuel tanks, better visibility, and superior guns that fired faster and more accurately—and were easier to aim. It carried more ammunition than the Zero, had greater range, and a bulletproof cockpit. Aided by ship's radar, the Hellcat could spot hostile aircraft 100 miles out.

Japanese pilots were not protected by armor and their tanks could not self-seal. This lightened the craft and made it so responsive it could throw an unwary pilot around in the cockpit. Lack of armor, though, made Zero pilots appallingly vulnerable to the machine cannons aboard the tanklike American fighters. The Zero's 20mm machine guns were almost completely ineffective against the well-armored American fighters. The Zeros carried a single 7.5mm cannon, which could do serious damage, but it was difficult to aim and carried few rounds.

Hellcats regularly returned to the carriers laden with bullets and holed throughout. Jack Bice's fighter from the *Bunker Hill* was jumped by a swarm of Zeros, which sprayed his aircraft with machine gun fire. He was shot in the arm and leg and his fuselage and belly tank were holed numerous times. Bice managed to shoot one of the Zeros down but did not have the strength to pull the heavy release to jettison his leaking tank. He could still guide the plane and pull the hair-light trigger on his machine guns, though, and he shot down two more Zeros before returning to the *Bunker Hill*. Gun crews determined that Bice had shot down three Zeros while expending only 200 rounds of ammunition. His own aircraft probably had at least that many holes.

Despite all these American improvements, and the lack of almost any Japanese innovations during the war, many veteran pilots maintain that nothing could beat a Zero in an even dogfight. American pilots had to come at it with altitude, make a single pass, fire hard, and then get out, counting on their wingman for protection. Swett says that his group would never dogfight them: "No way. That was suicide because they could just flip right over and be on your tail so fast. The only way we could fight them was the Thach Weave. With your wingman always protecting you, that worked out very nicely."

In addition to the Hellcat, a second impressive aircraft came into service: the improved F4U Corsair.

The gull-winged Corsair is perhaps the most recognizable fighter of World War II. It was also arguably the finest. The *Bunker Hill* was one of the few ships utilizing the improved Corsair as a carrier-based fighter plane in 1945. The Corsairs destroyed 2,140 enemy aircraft in combat, compared to a combat loss of 189.

The Corsair was the first American aircraft to break 400 miles per hour. It was built strong to power through turns with an incredible 2,250-horsepower engine. When it was first constructed, the Navy had intended to use the Corsair as a carrier plane. The Corsair's wheel struts (oleos) were extra long to hold its gigantic propeller off the deck. When they hit the short flight deck "it would bounce like a kangaroo." So the Navy moved all of the Corsairs off of the Essex Class carriers ashore to Bougainville where they were flown by Roger Hedrick, who was then executive officer of VF-17, and Marines like Jim Swett. The oleos also had a tendency to snap during hard landings. The United States gave many of the defective Corsairs to Britain. England solved the problem, and later in the war improved Corsairs were again flown off the *Bunker Hill*. When Hoot Hutt tried out the improved plane he said when you landed on the deck "it stuck like it had been glued."

The heavy Corsair formed such a steady gun platform that the American pilots could usually go full speed "downhill" in a steep dive that would destabilize the more fragile Zero. Even at the highest speeds, American pilots could give the Corsair full rudder and escape into a skid that the Japanese planes could not follow. But if the Corsair attacked at a low altitude where there was not enough room to escape, they could have a big problem.

Joe Brocia, a Marine pilot who flew with Swett aboard the *Bunker Hill*, tried diving solo on a Zero once. The Japanese pilot began a loop, and Brocia followed right behind him. But the Zero was almost unbelievably quick at changing direction, and while Brocia was still going up, the Japanese pilot had completed the loop and was now on his tail, firing. Brocia was in trouble. But he had altitude, so he put his nose down hard, and gave the Corsair full rudder and full throttle—100 percent RPMs, turning the Corsair to the right. He did not use his ailerons at all. This rotated the Corsair into a skid just like a car sliding sideways. He appeared to be heading to the right, but he was really just slipping sideways and falling steeply down. The pursuing Zero was firing everything he had at Brocia, but the tracers all passed just in front of him. The inexperienced Japanese pilot could not tell precisely what direction Brocia was falling in. Finally the Corsair started to violently shake, but Brocia could not pull out until the Zero ended its pursuit. The Corsair rattled so hard that rivets popped out of his wings. The Zero broke away at the last moment and Brocia was able to pull out of his fall before he hit the ocean.

During the last weeks of November 1943, the *Bunker Hill* launched strikes against Tarawa. The island was so obscured by smoke from exploding shells that the Navy pilots were of little aid to the Marines trying to get ashore. The poorly timed invasion had hung up on a reef at ebb tide. While the *Bunker Hill*'s planes continued to bomb the enemy positions, Japanese machine gun fire badly mauled the Marines pinned down on the reef. More than 1,000 Marines were killed in three days of brutal fighting on Tarawa. Nearly 5,000 Japanese soldiers were killed. Only seventeen were taken prisoner.

On December 8, two days before Kiyoshi Ogawa left his home in Takasaki to join the navy, *Bunker Hill* aircraft hammered Nauru in the

Gilberts. On Christmas Day 1943, the *Bunker Hill* penetrated further into Japanese-held territory than any carrier had since Pearl Harbor and attacked Kavieng, New Ireland, near Rabaul. She returned a few days later and again attacked the Japanese at Kavieng for New Year's.

The *Bunker Hill* began bombing Kwajalein in the Marshalls at the end of January 1944 to soften it up for an invasion. A week later, February 6, 1944, Kwajalein was declared secure. The Japanese had defended their positions suicidally. Their losses were 4,938 killed and 206 captured. The Marines lost 142 killed. Eniwetok and other smaller atolls fell shortly afterward. The Japanese countered the fast carriers with fighters, bombers, and torpedo bombers almost daily. The fighting was terrible, if increasingly one-sided, at least on sea and in the air. But the air remained a dangerous place for both sides.

Truk Island, in the Carolines, was Japan's largest and best-defended naval base in the Central Pacific. It became their Pearl Harbor. Most of the *Bunker Hill*'s veteran pilots who would go on to fight against the kamikazes in 1945 fought together at Truk in February 1944, albeit from different carriers. The *Intrepid*, the *Essex*, the *Bunker Hill*, the *Yorktown*, and the new *Lexington* were all there, along with a host of smaller carriers. The carrier air force blanketed the harbor and tore the island apart. The Japanese were so dominated that amidst the running battle an American Kingfisher float plane landed in Truk lagoon to pluck out the crew of a downed American aircraft. Japanese gunboats attempted to destroy the Kingfisher, but fighter pilots swarmed around it, protecting it through takeoff with bursts of machine gun fire.

Al Turnbull's plane was hit repeatedly by antiaircraft fire. Most of the bad hits to Turnbull's TBF Avenger occurred near the back of the plane. Unlike the hard aluminum of the rest of his TBF, the tail section—or empennage—was made of fabric and extremely vulnerable. The fabric would begin to flap and then peel off when it was hit. It snapped impossibly loud as they lumbered along. Bill Gerrity, Turnbull's gunner, was stationed near the shredded tail. They had trained and flown together on countless missions during the dangerous early days of the war.

Gerrity was badly shot up. Stuart, the radioman, climbed through the fuselage to help Gerrity. The plane was full of holes. Gerrity was lying against them, bleeding badly. Stuart wrapped him up in tourniquets and tightened down compresses, but it did not do any good. The Avenger's fuselage bottom was rounded but had a platform deck laid down on top to flatten it out for the gunner and radioman. Stuart lay down on the deck and held Gerrity tight as life flowed out of him. Gerrity bled the whole way back to the carrier. His blood seeped below the decking and into the fuselage bilge below.

When they reached the *Bunker Hill*, Gerrity was dead. Crewmen carried him out and air crews scrubbed out the aircraft. They got the cockpit well cleaned but could not reach the bilge area below the deck where Gerrity's blood had pooled. Turnbull still breaks down when he describes the death smell in that plane. It stayed with him forever: "You could smell it, and you couldn't forget it."

In the battle for Truk, the United States claimed 270 Japanese planes destroyed in the air and on the ground. They sank nine warships and thirty-four transports. A convoy with two troopships was destroyed with 1,200 Japanese aboard. The fast carrier operations at Truk and Palau destroyed about one third of Japan's tankers, which severely limited the maneuverability of the IJN. The *Bunker Hill* lost an Avenger, but sank a cruiser. The devastating losses sustained by the Japanese resulted in the resignations of the IJA and IJN chiefs of staff. They were replaced by General Tojo, who took complete control of Japan, serving as both the prime minister and minister of the armed forces. Tojo favored suicide before surrender. He had written the *Sen-jin kun* (code of battle), which transformed suicide from a right to a duty, and it was given Imperial imprimatur. At his war crimes trial, Tojo said: "From ancient times the Japanese have deemed it most degrading to be taken prisoner and all combatants have been instructed to choose death rather than be captured as a prisoner of war."

The fast carriers devastated Japanese defenses throughout the Pacific in the spring of 1944. Marines took the islands America wanted for bases and left Japanese soldiers isolated and starving in their strongest redoubts on islands that the United States did not need to occupy. Saipan was perhaps Japan's most powerful bastion. They had built complex defenses across the large island and garrisoned 30,000 troops there. Both nations realized that Saipan was the key to taking Japan. If the United States could take the island, American bombers could fly round-trip to Tokyo, bombing Japanese cities almost at will. The fighting on that island became more vicious and desperate than any yet experienced in the Pacific.

The fight for Saipan was really three separate battles, the first was against Japan's island-based aircraft, the second was a carrier confrontation now called the Battle of the Philippine Sea, and the third was the actual land battle for Saipan. Japanese forces were annihilated in each of these confrontations, and the one-sided American victories led to Japan's embrace of suicide tactics.

Mitscher did not want his carriers operating within range of Japan's island-based fighters, and no one wanted the Marines subjected to aerial attack. Therefore, before the Marines were landed at Saipan, the Navy had to neutralize all Japanese airpower on neighboring islands. One of Japan's largest island airbases within striking distance of Saipan was located on Iwo Jima. Nearly a year before the historically brutal land battles on Iwo Jima, the Navy destroyed Japan's air forces there. Japanese air forces on Iwo had about 300 aircraft at the beginning of June. The fast carrier air forces attacked Iwo on five occasions that month, each time destroying about half the Japanese air force, often without losing a single American aircraft. In the first attack, on June 11, 1944, fast carrier pilots flying the Hellcat destroyed 200 of the enemy's planes on the ground and in the air.

Early in the morning of June 15, 1944, the land battle for Saipan began. As thousands of Marines were landed, the Japanese retreated into caves, hiding during the day, and attacking in the dark. Marines used flamethrowers to burn out the defenders.

Admiral Soemu Toyoda, desperate to halt the U.S. assault, determined that the concentration of U.S. naval forces around Saipan presented an opportunity for a decisive battle in which the IJN could cripple the fast carriers. And so, in the midst of the ruthless land fight, the IJN made one final effort to destroy the American Navy with conventional tactics. Admiral Toyoda sent nine carriers and 473 carrier-based aircraft (aided by perhaps 200 island-based warplanes) against the Fast Carrier Task Force, which included fifteen carriers with more than 1,000 aircraft. It was a massacre. On the first day, June 19, Japan lost approximately 375 carrier planes, to U.S. losses of fewer than twenty-five aircraft. That same day, fast carrier aircraft destroyed sixty Japanese planes on the ground at Iwo Jima.

The battle began at 5:11 A.M. with a sibylline suicidal crash dive by a heroic Japanese dive-bomber pilot, flying from the giant Japanese carrier *Taiho*. The Japanese pilot saw the trail of a torpedo sent from the U.S. submarine *Albacore* headed for *Taiho*. He rolled his plane sideways and dove on the torpedo, detonating it 100 yards from the carrier. The *Taiho* turned sharply, but was hit by a second torpedo from the American submarine. The carrier sustained only minor damage. But her poorly trained damage control crews left the ship's air vents open. Fuel vapors saturated the ship. Several hours later, the vapors exploded and the giant carrier sank.

The Japanese lost nearly 500 aircraft and three carriers in two days. More than 90 percent of their carrier-based planes were destroyed. After this battle the Japanese naval air wing became a land-based force. The United States lost 130 aircraft during the two-day battle. More than 100 of these crashed after running out of fuel at night after a long search for the Japanese navy.

The loss of Japanese carriers and carrier-based aircraft doomed the Saipan defenders, who could no longer be resupplied. Their last hope was the land-based aircraft on surrounding islands. But these stood little chance against fast carrier attack aircraft.

The undertrained Japanese who took on the fast carriers during the Saipan battles had at most six months training and at best a few hundred hours flying. These Japanese replacement pilots stood in sharp contrast to the experienced Japanese veterans who flew at Pearl Harbor, Midway, the Solomons, and Rabaul. Those expert airmen had been well trained and seasoned in many battles. But most of those veteran pilots had been killed by mid-June 1944. All of the American pilots had at least two years of training and thousands of hours flying. On June 20, the Japanese managed to get thirty replacement Zeros to Iwo. And on June 24, a carrier air strike against Iwo was met by eighty Zeros. Half the Zeros were shot down. On July 3, the runway at Iwo was bombed and F6F Hellcats shot down twenty of the remaining forty Zeros. The next day, eleven of the twenty Zeros were shot down and other planes on the ground were destroyed. By the end of the day, only eight Jill bombers and nine Zeros remained to defend the island. The outpost had no hope of reinforcements or even resupply. The Japanese pilots, realizing they were doomed, determined to give their death some meaning.

Captain Kanzo Miura, the air leader on Iwo Jima, called his pilots together and told them that the situation was desperate and that ordinary methods would no longer suffice. Miura told them their only option was to dive directly into the enemy carriers *before* dropping their bombs. His speech was met by silence. It was the first time that Japanese pilots were ordered to commit suicide. But every pilot agreed to fly. They patched up and launched sixteen suicide attack planes. But Hellcats intercepted the suiciders en route, and shot down eleven. The five Japanese survivors hid in a powerful squall line. When they left the cloud, the inexperienced pilots could not find the American fleet. They returned to base before they ran out of fuel, expecting to be dishonored.

Commander Miura knew they were right not to waste their aircraft by crashing them into the sea and assured the surviving pilots that they would be given another chance. Instead, American bombers destroyed the remaining Zeros the next day.

This first kamikaze mission, conceived and carried out by tactical commanders, was not known to American intelligence until after the war. But it helped to open up the way for the beginning of sanctioned suicide attacks.

Desperate, the ground-based Japanese troops on Saipan also had resorted to suicide tactics. Three thousand Japanese remnants made a concerted suicide charge out of caves and mountain hideouts against American personnel on the night of July 7, 1944. Some carried only clubs. Horrified Marines had to leave their dugouts to clear piled Japanese bodies from their lines of fire. Japanese resistance on Saipan collapsed on July 9, 1944. Three thousand one hundred twenty-six soldiers and Marines had died. General Yoshitsugu Saito and his staff committed *seppuku* after giving the order for a final doomed charge. Altogether, 27,000 Japanese soldiers died or committed suicide during the month-long battle. Only a few hundred surrendered. The mortality rate for Japanese soldiers on Saipan was fairly typical of the island battles but the large numbers shocked American personnel. Perhaps most disconcerting, even many Japanese civilians killed themselves.

After the American victory at Saipan, the fighting moved closer and closer to the Japanese Home Islands. The "impenetrable barrier" of islands that the Japanese had called "unsinkable aircraft carriers" had been breached. Forces led by the fast carriers took the Mariana Islands. American troops recaptured Guam in late July 1944. In that battle, 10,000 Japanese and 1,400 Americans were killed. Fliers from the *Bunker Hill* bombed Tinian before two Marine divisions landed, also in late July. Japanese defenders fought tenaciously for nine days until all 5,000 were killed. Three hundred eighty-nine Marine and Navy men died.

A few days after the Tinian invasion, British and other Allied troops cleared all Japanese forces from India. This began a route through Burma into China from which land-based operations against Japanese holdings in the Western Pacific could be launched. The Japanese faced pressure from all sides of what they considered their sphere.

The last remaining island outposts would be starved slowly into irrelevant submission. The Japanese fell back to a new, secondary line of defense arcing through the Philippines, the Volcano Islands, and the Bonins. Both sides spent the summer devising tactics for the next phase of the war. American leaders argued over whether to immediately begin the attack against Japan, or to first retake the Philippines. The Army pushed for a Philippines assault, while the Navy argued that those islands should be bypassed, and the war taken directly to Japan. The *Bunker Hill* and the fast carriers, meanwhile, traversed the Pacific, taking on and destroying Japanese aircraft at scattered bases throughout their island empire and supporting Marine assaults.

American tactical success was due to the new, well-supplied American aircraft, flown by highly trained pilots and delivered through the mobility of the fast carriers. The Japanese knew their only way out was to disable the fast carriers.

Japan's well-known fighter pilot Captain Motoharu Okamura, the commanding officer of the 341st Air Corps, asked Admiral Shigeru Fukudome for permission to begin aerial suicide attacks against American ships. Such tactics were the only way their poorly trained pilots could damage carriers like the *Bunker Hill*. Captain Eiichiro Iyo, who had served at the Japanese embassy in Washington and been aide-de-camp to Hirohito, wrote to his superiors (in itself an extraordinary act in the Japanese military) with a dramatic proposal:

No longer can we hope to sink the numerically superior enemy aircraft carriers through ordinary attack methods. I urge the immediate organization of special attack units to carry out crash-dive tactics and I ask to be placed in command of them.

8. FIRST KAMIKAZES

In blossom today,
Then scattered:
Life is so like
A delicate Flower.
How can one expect
The Fragrance to last forever?
—"ONISHI OF THE *TOKKOTAI*"

Japan has a long history of the tactical use of suicide. Japan began the war with a suicide mission: miniature submarine crewmen sent to attack Pearl Harbor knew they would die.* Japan had refused to sign the Geneva Convention on prisoners of war in part because because General Tojo was concerned that it could be seen by his troops as condoning surrender. In May 1943, the U.S. retook for the first time a Japanese-held island: Attu, at the western end of the Aleutian chain. The Japanese ended the battle with a suicide charge. Many of their wounded blew themselves up with hand grenades. All but twenty-eight men died, and not a single officer surrendered. Dozens more islands were taken from the Japanese over the next two years. Each followed the same disturbing pattern of suicide charges and nearly absolute refusal to surrender.†

---

* Japanese minisubs were used in six raids: Pearl Harbor, Sydney Harbor (May 31, 1942), near Madagascar (May 31, 1942), in the Guadalcanal area (November 23, 1942, and December 7, 1942), and west of the Mindanao Sea (January 5, 1945). Twenty-eight submariners died and one was captured. All told they caused only insignificant damage to U.S. forces.

† The Japanese resisted to the death almost wherever they were confronted. At Aitape in New Guinea in April 1944, Allied soldiers under MacArthur killed 8,821 Japanese. Only ninety-eight were captured. The Allies lost 440 men.

Japanese society was based on the *Bushido* code, named for the *Bushi*, huge warriors who rode giant horses and lived by a challenging moral code beginning in the ninth century. Those that followed the code came to be called *samurai*. *Samurai* never attacked a fallen foe, and always protected those in need. Literature and poetry were as important to them as martial skill. *Samurai* centered their lives on the idea that they were always prepared to die. They could sit for hours barefoot meditating in the snow and carried at their sides eleven-inch daggers. Rather than being taken prisoner, they would use the dagger to disembowel themselves. The Japanese were mortified by the ignominy of being dictated to by foreigners when Commodore Perry arrived. The Meiji emperor determined to fully modernize Japan so that they could compete with Western nations. Meiji dismantled the *samurai* system, and instituted instead a professional, national armed service. All of Japanese society was reorganized, basing all social and economic rules in every sphere, from farming, to industry, to politics and the military using the *Bushi* code. Meiji's advisors felt that by using the disciplined principles of *Bushido*, Japan could accomplish in a generation the economic advancements that had taken the West hundreds of years to achieve.

Japanese culture was formed from a unique mixture of contradictory religious beliefs, often held simultaneously by the same individuals. Japanese Buddhism, Shintoism, Confucianism, and Taoism can all be held to some degree simultaneously. These belief systems are in a sense compartmentalized. Buddhism is the philosophy for managing one's self. Shintoism is the belief system used to relate patriotically to one's family, Japan, and the emperor. Confucianism is the philosophy used to manage government. Taoism is the Way that allows these to meld. Finally, *Bushido* is the interior code—the guide for one's internal force, the self-discipline that manages everything. Japan's decision to use *tokko* tactics, and the students' complicity in their own self-sacrifice, is to a great degree a product of the complex relationship among these beliefs.

By contrast, U.S. soldiers have always been willing to give up their own life for their brothers in arms. Sacrifice for comrades is a deeply held American value. American soldiers, sailors, airmen, and Marines are willing to give their lives for their country and their fellows. But suicide *tactics* have never been U.S. policy.

American soldiers under General George Pickett marched into withering cannon fire at Gettysburg. The British suffered 57,000 casualties on the first day of the Battle of the Somme in World War I. The Newfoundland Brigade sent 832 officers and men charging the German lines that day; 762 were killed or wounded. But the Japanese were the first to officially sanction tactics with no chance of survival. The *tokko* attackers were the first such assaults to continue for a protracted period of time. They were the first to use airplanes as suicide weapons.

Nevertheless, the Japanese were profoundly conflicted about the morality of suicide tactics. In July 1943, Rear Admiral Kameto Kuroshima asked the Japan War Preparation Examination Conference to sanction volunteer suicide attacks, which he called "Invincible War Preparation." The army and navy refused.

By the end of the war, suicide tactics would be used by all the Japanese armed forces. Frogmen carrying explosives trained to detonate themselves against American boats. Sailors rigged a fleet of speedboats with depth charges to ram American landing craft. The IJN utilized human torpedoes—extra-small miniature submarines. And in the spring of 1944, Japan began research for a manned suicide missile.

By 1945, American pilots were shooting down more than fifteen Japanese planes for every American plane lost. Japan turned to suicide "special attacks" with aircraft simultaneously in various theaters, at various levels of the military, in both the IJA and IJN. *Tokko* started at the bottom, among pilots who had seen most of their comrades die. Japanese pilots knew they stood little chance of survival and wanted their death to mean something.* Their commanders came separately to the same conclusion.†

---

* Two Imperial Army pilots in the 31st Fighter Squadron on Negros Island in the Philippines determined to launch a suicide attack. Two 100-pound bombs were rigged permanently to the wings of their fighter planes on September 12, 1944. They hoped to crash into aircraft carriers, but apparently their awkward loads made them easy targets. Neither returned and there is no record of any suicide attack that day.

† A single Japanese suicide pilot rammed a B-29 during a bombing raid on the Yawata iron works on August 20, 1944. The explosion of the first plane caused a second B-29 to crash. Japanese pilots were by then routinely receiving instruc-

Vice Admiral Teraoka controlled 500 Japanese aircraft prepared for the air defense of the Philippines in early August 1944.* After only one month of fast carrier attacks he was down to about 100 functional aircraft. Admiral Fukudome lost more than 500 aircraft in October battles with U.S. fast carrier aircraft. These losses obliterated Japan's chance for a serious aircraft presence during the upcoming land battle for the Philippines. Teraoka and Fukudome opposed suicide tactics but they were running out of influence as quickly as they were losing their aircraft.

Admiral Takijiro Onishi, an influential leader who had helped plan the Pearl Harbor assault, openly advocated suicide tactics in an editorial published on July 19, 1944. Onishi wrote:

> We have weapons called aircraft. If one is willing to crash a plane into the enemy, we need not fear the enemy's mobile units and B-29 bombers would not be able to intrude into the mainland of Japan. If an enemy aircraft carrier came into sight, we would be able to destroy it with a crash-dive attack. If B-29s came into sight we would be able to hit them with our body-crash attacks, we are sure to win the war. Numerical inferiority will disappear before the body-crash operation. And those who would make body crash attacks without heed for their lives deserve the name of godlike soldiers.

Admiral Onishi was ordered to the Philippines, replacing Admiral Teraoka, to reorganize Japan's defense of the islands. The Soviet Union, which had remained neutral in the Pacific war, informed the Japanese that America and her allies would attack the Philippines during the last ten days of October. The Japanese planned to respond to the American landings on Leyte with a decisive battle that they optimistically code-named Sho—"Victory."

When the *Bunker Hill* arrived at station off the Philippines to begin

---

tion on how to crash into American bombers. But *tokko* attacks remained isolated and voluntary.

* Prime Minister Tojo simultaneously announced his own resignation and the fall of Saipan on July 18, 1944.

attacking Japanese airfields to protect MacArthur's landing force at Leyte, she was part of the largest armada ever assembled, including more than 1,000 aircraft.* The American forces at Leyte dwarfed those of the Japanese in every category.†

The Battle of Leyte Gulf changed warfare, not because it was the largest fleet engagement of the war, though it was, nor even because the IJN was routed, but rather because a small group of fighter pilots for the first time in history were ordered to commit suicide as a battle tactic.

Admiral Onishi created the first official aerial suicide unit on October 18, 1944. Onishi officially named the new unit Kamikaze Special Attack Corps. During the war, though, the kamikazes were known as the *tokkotai*—the Special Attack Corps. *Tokko*—special—became a euphemism for suicide.

Onishi was a *samurai* in the old tradition. He was a ruthless military leader, and a skilled calligrapher-poet. He created a calligraphy to mark the initiation of *tokko*:

> *The wild cherry blossom* [Yamazakura]
> *falls without regrets after it scatters its perfume*
> *in the light of the rising sun* [Asahi]

---

* The *Bunker Hill*, though, missed the Battle of Leyte Gulf. Admiral William "Bull" Halsey mistakenly determined that the Japanese would not bring out the main carrier fleet so late in the battle. He sent the *Bunker Hill* to Ulithi to pick up more aircraft on October 23 and the following day sent out all of Task Group 38.1—*Wasp, Hornet, Hancock, Monterey,* and *Cowpens*—for a break from the battle. They could not be recalled in time to join the fight against the remaining Japanese carriers. The Fifth Fleet fought under Nimitz in the central Pacific. The Third Fleet fought in the western Pacific under Halsey. Whenever Task Force 38 fought in the Philippines, it was redesignated Task Group 38, indicating it was under operational control of the Third Fleet.

† COMPARATIVE STRENGTHS AT LEYTE GULF

	SHIPS					AIRCRAFT	
	Fleet Carrier	Escort Carrier	Battleship	Cruiser	Destroyer	Naval	Land-based
U.S.	8	26	12	29	111	1400	
Japan	1	3	9	19	35	116	300

Onishi ceremoniously divided the new corps into four groups: *Shikishima* (Beautiful Island), *Yamato* (the Japanese people), *Asahi* (Rising Sun), and *Yamazakura* (Wild Cherry Blossom). These names came from an ancient Japanese poem:

> *If you ask me what is the soul of the Japanese* [Yamato]
> *The people of the Beautiful Island* [Shikishima]
> *I will tell you that it is the Wild Cherry Blossom* [Yamazakura]
> *That scatters its perfume in the light of the rising sun* [Asahi]

Onishi concluded: "Thus these pilots should be willing to give the flower of their youth to their country without regret as the ancient poem suggests."

Onishi inherited from Teraoka only about thirty functioning Zeros flown mostly by the 201st Air Group at Clark Field. Twenty-seven pilots, now hardened veterans, survived. In the evening after creating the kamikaze unit on paper, Onishi drove 40 miles northwest of Manila to Clark airbase, which the Japanese had renamed Mabalacat, seeking pilots.

Onishi arrived at their field as night was falling. He was met by Acting Commander Assaichi Tamai near the landing strip in front of a cream-colored, Western-style house with green trim. The home had been confiscated from a Filipino, who lived with his family in the back.

Onishi told the gathered pilots that they would play a vital role in the outcome of the war. Then he explained Japan's strategy for the Sho operation. The Japanese had essentially no naval aircraft for their remaining carriers and not enough pilots who had the skills to land at sea, so the carrier planes were transferred to land bases. Onishi explained that if these gathered fighter pilots could disable the remaining American light carriers, then the *Musashi* and the *Yamato*—the two largest battleships in the world—could enter Leyte Gulf and destroy the smaller remaining surface fleet and the relatively fragile American landing and supply craft. The Americans could not stop the giant battleships without carrier-based aircraft. The invading American soldiers and marines already landed would be cut off and annihilated by Japanese ground forces. The whole operation hinged on stopping the carriers.

The fighter pilots already knew the details of the Sho operation. They realized, too, that the commander of the Philippines did not drive to Clark Field simply to brief them. Everyone knew that Admiral Onishi favored suicide attacks. They probably guessed the real reason Onishi was speaking to them. Finally, Onishi concluded: "In my opinion there is only one way of assuring that our meager strength will be effective to a maximum degree. That is to organize suicide attack units composed of Zero fighters armed with 250-kilogram [550 pound] bombs with each plane to crash-dive into an enemy carrier. . . . If you are going to die anyway, it is good to make maximum effect on enemy . . . maximum effect of your life. . . . What do you think?"

His grim words were met with profound silence.

Commander Tamai finally broke the silence by asking Chuichi Yoshioka, a pilot in the 201st, how effective a kamikaze attack by a Zero with a 250-kilogram bomb would be against a carrier.

Yoshioka said that it would have a good chance of succeeding and that it would put the carrier out of action for "several days." Left unsaid was that Onishi asserted that in order to succeed the carriers would have to be put out of action for one month.

Tamai responded by claiming that he did not have the authority to make this kind of decision and that he needed to ask their air group commander for permission. It was extraordinary for an officer to put off a request from the commander-in-chief of the Philippines.

Onishi responded curtly: "As a matter of fact, I have just spoken on the phone with [your air group commander] in Manila. He said that I should consider your opinions as his own, and that he would leave everything up to you."

The pilots all waited for Tamai's response.

Eventually, Captain Tamai asked for time to consider the matter. He left the room with another pilot. The two men returned a short while later and volunteered their pilots for the suicide mission.

Onishi was both relieved and sorrowful.

After committing them to Admiral Onishi, Captain Tamai gathered the twenty-three surviving NCO pilots in a room lit by a single, bare, incandescent bulb. He summed up the dismal war situation. Then he asked for volunteers for the suicide mission.

All agreed to fly.

The officers knew that the first mission had to be a success. They needed a leader with enormous character and ability. They determined on Yukio Seki. Seki was a highly skilled pilot who had graduated from the Naval Academy but had been with the 201st for only a month. His mother was widowed, and Seki had recently become engaged. Inoguchi, Onishi's aide, had taught Seki at the academy. As Tamai left to awaken the young pilot, he wondered what Seki's dreams were at that moment.

As Captain Tamai, his eyes welling with tears, explained the plan, Seki did not move. His face remained frozen. Then, in silence, he ran his fingers through his hair across his forehead. Finally, he replied: "I beg you to entrust me with this mission."

Inoguchi went to Onishi, who was lying on a cot in a small room, and told the admiral that Seki would lead the first group.

That night the pilots of the 201st all slept together. They were the first group of men in the history of modern warfare condemned to certain death as weapons by their own leaders. Onishi joined the men the next morning and spoke to them. His voice shook:

My sons, who can raise our country from the desperate situation in which she finds herself? Not the ministers, not the political advisors to the Throne, nor the Naval Chiefs of Staff. Still less a humble Commander-in-Chief like myself!

You alone who have souls as pure as they are steadfast.

You alone hold this power.

That is why I have dared to ask you, in the name of 100 million Japanese, to carry out this mission.

I hope with all my heart that you may be successful.

You are already gods, without earthly desires. But one thing you want to know is that your own crash-dive is not in vain. Regrettably we will not be able to tell you the results. But I shall watch your efforts to the end and report your deeds to the throne. You may all rest assured on this point.

Onishi's eyes welled with tears as he concluded: "I ask you all to do your best."

Onishi presented a calligraphy to his staff after the organization of the kamikaze *tokko* Special Attack Corps:

> *In blossom today,*
> *Then scattered:*
> *Life is so like*
> *A delicate Flower.*
> *How can one expect*
> *The Fragrance to last forever?*

He signed it: "Onishi of the *tokkotai*."

Three days after accepting his mission, Yukio Seki departed Mabalacat in a Mitsubishi Zero bearing a 500-pound bomb at 0725 hours in the *Shikishima* unit. Just before he left, Seki wrote a note of explanation:

It is not for the Emperor, nor for Japan that I undertake this suicide attack, but solely for my beloved.*

They were five kamikazes with bombs escorted by four Zero fighters. The escorts had planned to protect the ungainly overburdened Zeros, and to report on the results of the mission. It appears that several of the escorts decided to crash their Zeros as well. They flew in low, below the radar coverage of the American light carrier task group code-named Taffy 3, and snuck past the CAP. The nine planes of the

---

* Seki's fiancée remained unmarried for the rest of her life.

Shikishima unit were sighted at mast level almost simultaneously by the five light carriers of Taffy 3. The American ships sounded General Quarters, but it was too late. Seki crossed the bow of the *Kitkun Bay* (CVE-71), then climbed rapidly and banked over as a signal to his squadron to complete their attack. He dove directly at the *Kitkun Bay's* bridge, strafing the island as his plane fell.* Though Seki missed the bridge he managed to drop his bomb, which penetrated the deck before exploding. Seki crashed into the port catwalk, before sliding into the sea. This attack killed sixteen men and took the *Kitkun Bay* out of the war for two months.

Seki's squadron continued their suicidal mission without him. The group climbed quickly to about a mile above the American carriers. Each plane selected a target and initiated their dives.

Two Zeros (possibly escort aircraft, not carrying bombs) dove immediately on the *Fanshaw Bay*. Both were shot down. Two *tokko* aircraft, carrying bombs, dove on the *White Plains*. The 40mm gunners blasted hard and forced the kamikazes to break off their attack a few hundred feet above the carrier. One of the kamikazes was smoking as it pulled away. It dove directly through the flight deck of the *St. Lo*, detonating stored bombs and torpedoes. The *St. Lo's* elevator exploded hundreds of feet into the air and disintegrated. It would sink less than an hour later, killing 126 men.

Another kamikaze circled back to the *White Plains*. American gunners slammed it along the fuselage and wings, but the plane kept coming. A moment before impact, though, it rolled and fell, missing the ship by inches. Pieces of the plane rained down on the carrier's decks wounding eleven sailors.

The fourth of Seki's kamikazes also attacked the *Kitkun Bay*, from astern. Its wings were shorn off by the tremendous fusillade of American guns, just before the plane crashed. Its bomb exploded twenty-five yards aft of her stern. Debris damaged the ship and killed one sailor on the stern.

---

* It is impossible to know for sure which plane was Seki's, but by matching the accounts of his escort plane, which survived, and those of the Americans in Taffy 3, it appears highly likely that this first strike was Seki's.

Four Zeros dove on the *Kalinin Bay*. Two were shot down, but one exploded on her flight deck, and the other crashed her aft stack. It remains unclear which of these Zeros carried a bomb as *tokko*. The *Kalinin Bay* steamed to San Diego for repairs and never returned to battle.

The Americans were horrified. The gritty temerity of the attack was like nothing they had ever seen. Most staggeringly, one Japanese pilot, determined to die, had single-handedly sunk an American aircraft carrier. The sailors knew that they were witnessing an entirely new era of the war.

Leyte was one of the greatest battles in the history of naval warfare. American aircraft sank the super-battleship *Musashi*, killing 1,000 Japanese sailors. The IJN lost two additional battleships, four carriers, ten cruisers, thirteen destroyers, and five submarines. The American Navy lost the light carrier *Princeton*, two escort carriers, two destroyers, and a destroyer escort.

The only meaningful Japanese aerial success in the disaster at Leyte was the achievement of Yukio Seki and the Kamikaze Special Attack Corps. The suiciders damaged six escort carriers and sank the carrier USS *St. Lo* (CVE-63).*

Yet Onishi's kamikazes, though spectacularly successful, had failed in their mission. The tactical goal of the first Kamikaze Special Attack Unit pilots was to put all the U.S. carriers out of commission for a month—at least long enough to allow Admiral Takeo Kurita to pen-

---

* The IJA organized a *tokko* squadron just after Onishi initiated the naval *tokko* program. Early in the morning of the 25th, the IJA aircraft located and attacked a task group of naval escort carriers code named Taffy 1. The first official kamikaze crashed through the flight deck of the *Santee* (CVE-29) at 7:40 A.M. Fifteen minutes later the *Santee* was struck by a Japanese torpedo. She was taken out of the war for five months. A few minutes later, the *Suwanee* (CVE-27) was crashed forward of the aft elevator. The kamikaze's bomb blew a twenty-five-foot hole in the hangar deck. The *Suwanee* managed to continue operations but was hit by a second kamikaze the following day, which destroyed ten aircraft and forced the carrier to withdraw for repairs for five months.

etrate and attack landing forces at Leyte. But even the badly damaged *Suwanee* was able to continue flight operations the same day she was hit.

The Battle of Leyte Gulf was a rout. The IJN, which less than three years before commanded the entire Western Pacific, was destroyed. Initially, the *tokko* assaults were to be used for one purpose, in a single battle. After Leyte, Inoguchi, who had opposed suicide assaults, said to Onishi, "Shouldn't the *tokko* tactics now be ended?"

Onishi responded: "These young men with their limited training, outdated equipment and numerical inferiority, are doomed even by conventional fighting methods. It is important to a commander as it is to his men, that death be not in vain."

Onishi held a conference with Vice Admiral Fukudome after Leyte. Fukudome was despondent. His poorly trained pilots had mistaken dolphins for enemy submarines. Many could not tell the difference between cruisers and destroyers. It was Yukio Seki's striking success that convinced Fukudome that Imperial Japan's only hope for the defense of the Home Islands lay in *tokko* tactics.

Onishi convinced Fukudome to merge their two fleets. They would all be kamikazes—*tokko*. Onishi would serve as Fukudome's chief-of-staff but would wield the real authority in the new *tokko* corps.

Once the kamikaze corps was formalized, Onishi presented a new calligraphy to the pilots at Clark Field: "The purity of youth will usher in the Divine Wind." And so the kamikaze force which had begun as a temporary tactical expedient amidst a desperate battle became the guiding policy of the air forces of Imperial Japan.[*]

The *Bunker Hill* struck Manila and other parts of the Philippines from November 11 through 14 of 1944 and then returned to Bremerton, Washington, for much needed rest for the crew and repair and

---

[*] During the course of the Philippines campaign, Onishi sacrificed 378 aircraft in kamikaze missions. An additional 102 escorting planes were lost. The *tokko* pilots sank sixteen ships and damaged eighty-seven. Many of the damaged ships were not able to return to fight in the Philippines.

modernization of the ship. Kamikaze attacks in the Philippines intensified while the *Bunker Hill* was away. But the American advance could not be stopped.

One hundred eleven U.S. B-29s attacked Tokyo from Saipan on November 24, 1944. For the first time since 1281, Japan's Home Islands faced imminent invasion.

9. THE *BUNKER HILL* DEPARTS FOR ENEMY TERRITORY

Let's RE-MEM-BER PEARL HAR-BOR
As we go to meet the foe.
Let's RE-MEM-BER PEARL HAR-BOR
As we did the A-la-mo.

—"REMEMBER PEARL HARBOR," SONG
BY DON REID AND SAMMY KAYE

In 1945, no one doubted the Allies would win the war. It was reasonably certain that Nazi Germany would be defeated before the empire of Japan. This presented the United States with two colossal issues. The first was whether the Japanese Home Islands would have to be invaded—with a predicted cost of perhaps more than one million American casualties and some scenarios predicting more than a million American deaths, more than twice as many American lives as were lost in both the First and Second World Wars combined.

The second concern was that the Soviet Union, if free from the threat of Nazi Germany, would bring her forces to bear on the Asian-Pacific theater. The Russians could take the Japanese puppet republic of Manchukuo in China and probably the former French colonies of Indochina. The Soviet Union could then occupy and demand a permanent division of Japan. If the war lasted another six months to a year as was contemplated in the Allied war plans, the Soviets would be in a position to argue for such a division because they had sacrificed so much blood and resources in Europe and had destroyed two thirds of the German Wehrmacht. If the West was allowed to control most of Germany, then it would be only fair that the Soviets be given a share of Japan. Such an outcome was not to be chanced.

So the big question for the *Bunker Hill*, and the fast carriers, was how quickly they would be able to move up the chains of islands outlying Japan. America hoped to force the Japanese to capitulate early, without the necessity of fighting, yard by yard, across the mountains of Kyushu and Tokyo's Kanto Plain against a suicidal home guard.

The Navy had planned to use the fast carriers to cross and recover the Central Pacific from Japan. The carriers completed this task fully a year ahead of schedule. By 1945, the big ships were venturing more and more frequently within range of Japan's Home Islands. Carrier tactics evolved as hard floating Japanese targets disappeared. As more and more land-based bombers could reach Japan, the need for carrier torpedo and dive-bombers lessened. Land-based fighters, however, could not at first follow the B-29s all the way to the Home Islands. So the Navy decreased the number of bomber and torpedo planes on carriers and increased the number of fighters—which could go the distance—while simultaneously squeezing aboard every additional plane they could fit into the hangar spaces.* Every Japanese knew when they saw the smaller American planes that the American ships must be close. And they knew that the Japanese government could no longer protect them.

Strategic bombing began in the fall of 1944 against the Home

---

* The lack of fighter pilots in January was so critical that pilots who had served less than two months in the combat area on their current deployment, but whose air groups were being rotated back to the United States, were ordered to remain in combat. They were shifted to new air groups and helped to orient the newly arrived pilots.

Islands, peaking between March and August 1945. Meanwhile, attacks on conventional targets by the Navy and Army Air Force continued throughout the period.

Japan was deficient in supplies of almost every single strategic natural resource and relied on imports via merchant ships and tankers for nearly all raw materials: oil, bauxite, coal, iron ore, and a dozen other materials used to manufacture munitions. The United States, through submarine action and aerial bombing, made a great effort to destroy the ships that carried these raw materials to Japan for conversion into weapons. By 1945, Japan's merchant fleet had been almost completely destroyed, and importation of nearly every strategic raw material fell to zero.

Bombing of industrial and civilian targets in Japan, combined with the blockade, completely choked Japan's war economy and shattered the country's ability to wage conventional war.

The destruction of her air fleets and curtailment of construction operations contributed to Japan's decision to use its remaining aircraft as kamikazes. The strategic bombing had much less of an effect, though, than was initially thought. The U.S. blockade had already caused such severe matériel shortages that Japanese plants were operating well below capacity. Physical damage to military and production facilities by the bombing was negligible, but alarmed Japanese military leaders ordered dispersal of industrial production. It was the inefficiencies caused by dispersal, more than any direct bomb damage, that crushed Japan's production capability.* Even had aircraft production remained high, the great rate of loss of Japanese aircraft probably would have led to the same decision to disperse production facilities.

By 1945 Japan manufactured almost nothing. It was the most difficult year Japan had ever faced. The Naval Air Fleet had become

---

* Japanese factories were moved so far apart that they became totally inefficient. After a single Japanese truck plant was hit by only one bomb in 1944, the apprehensive Japanese initiated an immediate dispersal program for truck plants, which nearly ended all truck production in Japan.

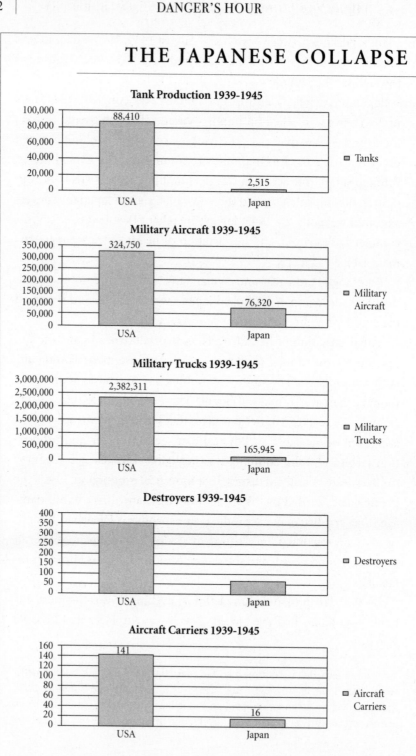

THE JAPANESE COLLAPSE

Tank Production 1939-1945

USA: 88,410
Japan: 2,515

Tanks

Military Aircraft 1939-1945

USA: 324,750
Japan: 76,320

Military Aircraft

Military Trucks 1939-1945

USA: 2,382,311
Japan: 165,945

Military Trucks

Destroyers 1939-1945

Destroyers

Aircraft Carriers 1939-1945

USA: 141
Japan: 16

Aircraft Carriers

IN THE PACIFIC, 1939–1945.

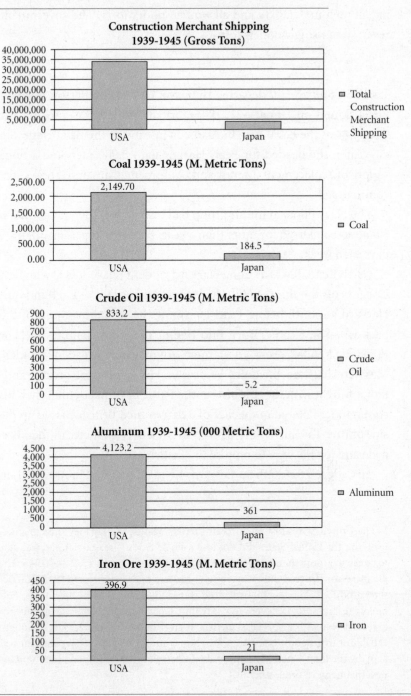

wholly land-based. Japan had no carriers and very few ships.* Its natural resources had dwindled. The High Command proposed drafting all men under sixty and all women under forty. The government reverted to using wooden coins.

The USS *Bunker Hill* departed the naval base at Bremerton through Puget Sound on January 21, 1945, for San Francisco to pick up Air Group 84 at the naval base in Alameda just inside the Bay Bridge. Six days later, she headed for Pearl Harbor with 5,000 men and a huge supply of replacement aircraft and equipment. Captain George Seitz commanded.

The Navy pilots in the air group had trained together at Coronado Island in San Diego for more than a year. They flew together, often six days each week.

Caleb Kendall was a young Harvard student (class of '43) who flew Corsairs off the *Bunker Hill*. He lived in Adams House E-11 and quit Harvard a month before Pearl Harbor so he would be ahead of the pack when war came. Born into one of the oldest families in New England, Kendall grew up at their original homestead in Holden, Massachusetts, northwest of Worcester. His great-great-great grandfather fought with the colonists at the Battle of Bunker Hill. When his commander faltered in the face of a determined British charge up the side of Breed's Hill, Kendall's forebear took over guidance of their brigade and led his men to repulse the British assault.

His great-grandfather, Edward Kendall, left the homestead in

---

* The United States lost ten aircraft carriers against the Japanese loss of nineteen. But the United States did not lose a single Essex Class carrier and was able to construct more than 100 carriers of various sizes between 1942 and 1945. The Japanese constructed only sixteen new carriers and lost virtually every carrier they produced. The few that survived were inoperable. The history of the *Shinano*, the largest carrier ever built, is telling. Japan launched *Shinano* on November 11, 1944, with a special cement and steel flight and hangar deck thought capable of withstanding any American bomb attack. Seventeen days later she was sunk by the lone American submarine *Archerfish*, with six torpedo hits. *Shinano* never launched a single aircraft.

Holden and traveled to East Cambridge, where the Longfellow Bridge now crosses into Boston. He found work as a day laborer at the Charles River Iron Works and rose quickly through the ranks. Within a few years, he became sole owner of the plant and changed its name to Kendall and Sons Boiler and Tank Company. The plant took up so much room that the subway station and surrounding area were renamed Kendall Square. Nearly all of the men in the family thereafter attended Harvard.

Kendall grew up on the family farm in Holden, with his younger brother Jimmy, dreaming of airplanes. Their early life was like something out of a Currier & Ives print—the colonial farmhouse was set back off the road on top of a hill on a couple hundred acres of old-growth forest, gardens, and orchards. They rode sleds down the long hill and then across the frozen lake at the bottom in wintertime, hiked into the woods with their father to cut a tree each Christmas, and swam and played with the animals and in the trees all summer long.

Kendall brought his future wife, "Brownie," the former Ellen Brown, from Newburyport, Massachusetts, to Harvard football games in the fall and then to the Christmas play at Adams House, where they drank rum and Cokes in paper cups, and fell in love. They married just before he volunteered to be a Navy flier.

Kendall knew war was coming and he wanted to be a pilot. He reasoned, correctly, that if he joined before war began he would be more likely to be admitted to a flight school, and get to the front faster. So he quit Harvard to join the Navy in November 1941.

Kendall flew bombers on his first tour. When he returned to the United States he switched to fighter training with VF-84 in Coronado. In September 1944, while the *Bunker Hill* was in the Philippines, Brownie wired to say she was pregnant. That afternoon, he had to go up in his Corsair for target practice on a towed sleeve. The average number of hits for a pilot on a single pass was six. That day Caleb hit the sleeve twenty-two times.

In a letter to his younger brother, who had just become a naval cadet, Kendall wrote: "Flying, like the sea, is not in itself inherently dangerous, but to an extent greater than the sea is unrelentingly unforgiving of carelessness." Eight ensigns in his unit already had been killed in the six months or so that they had been training at Coronado. At the conclusion of the concentrated training regime, Kendall transferred to the carrier *Takanis Bay* where more than 2,500 naval airmen received carrier qualifications. There, the pilots wrote up orders for Ensign John Sargent's puppy, Blackout, and brought her aboard with them as the squadron mascot. She took turns sleeping with different pilots, and they all snuck her hamburgers out of the ship's service. Even the captain seemed to love little Blackout—that is, until she urinated on the flight deck just below his watchful eye. She was ordered immediately off the ship.

Kendall began high-altitude training in mid-December. The Marine pilots arrived around December 21, and despite the loss of forty pilots in the main fighter squadron, and the addition of two disparate Marine fighter groups, the intense training continued to go well. Kendall was getting better and better at flying on instruments, and doing many night landings. On busy days, he would rise at 0430, take off in the dark, fly a long hop, sleep for a few hours in the afternoon, exercise, then practice night flying until nearly midnight.

On Christmas Eve, Lieutenant Commander Roger Hedrick, the skipper of the squadron, gave each pilot permission to fly his plane anywhere within a 1,000-mile radius of San Diego to celebrate. Kendall and his friend Lieutenant Ralph J. "Coke" Coconaugher headed out to Coke's home in Texas, but got lost along the way. They ended up spending Christmas in Stafford, Arizona, with their Corsairs stuck in the mud at the end of a small grass runway. The young pilots were treated like visiting dignitaries—plied with alcohol and fed home-cooked turkey dinners each night. They even went duck hunting. But all the while they worried what the Skipper would do to them when they returned.

When the weather finally cleared, the townspeople helped them dig out their planes. They got some gas and flew straight back to San Diego. When they finally arrived, still covered in mud, Hedrick just laughed at them. That week, Kendall watched *Thirty Seconds Over Tokyo* and wrote to his wife that he loved the movie. He found especially realistic the scene where the men get lost in the maze of tunnels belowdecks. He wrote to his wife, in a horrifyingly prescient passage, how often he still got lost in the carrier passageways.

Destroyer Squadron 23 officers at "Cloob Des-Slot," Purvis Bay, 1944. Arleigh Burke is third from left.

Just before he boarded the *Bunker Hill*, Kendall wrote again to Brownie: "My main desire in life is to come home and have a normal existence like everybody else. Let me put on a shabby suit, go to work every day and come home to my family every night to play with my children and love my wife."

Early in the morning of an almost unimaginably dark and cloudy January 29, 1945, the *Bunker Hill* left Pearl Harbor bound for Ulithi, accompanied at General Quarters by the *Randolph*, the *Saratoga*, the *Bennington*, the *Belleau Wood*, the *Alaska*, and seven destroyers. She entered Ulithi harbor just after noon on Wednesday, February 7, 1945. Ulithi, an atoll in Micronesia with less than two square miles of land area, had become the headquarters of the Pacific Fleet. There, the *Bunker Hill* would lie at anchor for three days, as battle plans and preparations were finalized for the next big push of the Pacific campaign: assaults on the Home Islands and the battle for Iwo Jima.

10. ULITHI: WAITING FOR BATTLE

Gosh, I'll be glad when this war ends.
—VAN JOHNSON, *THIRTY SECONDS OVER TOKYO*

At Ulithi in February 1945, Mitscher, Burke, and the other naval leaders met and developed the tactical battle plan for the first carrier assault on Japan since the Doolittle Raid. It was to serve as a huge psychological victory, and a successful diversion from the real target—Iwo Jima. This new plan became the template for carrier operations throughout the rest of the war. Though the Japanese had placed a circle of picket vessels around the Home Islands to serve as an early warning and protective system, Burke and Mitscher sent out a narrow line of destroyers ahead of the carrier task force to knock a hole in the enemy pickets. It was vital that the hole be just wide enough for the carriers to sneak through, but not so large as to alert the rest of the Japanese fleet as to their presence.

Planners used dummy ships on a board to create a disposition plan—"William"—which they ended up using for most of the rest of the war. They would go into battle with each of the task groups separated by about twelve miles, heading parallel to each other and perpendicular to the wind. That way, if any group needed to launch planes they could turn up into the wind and pass astern of the next group, then turn back into formation and catch up with the group. The aerologists, using primitive data-gathering equipment, had a great deal of trouble predicting wind behavior. The Navy had not maintained weather records from prewar Japan. Thus Navy weathermen had no long-term data on which to base suppositions.

Mitscher well understood that kamikazes would try to follow returning U.S. aircraft along safe approaches to the fleet. Planners decided to use specific return approach plans for American planes. American aircraft usually returned with or into the wind, perpendicular to the landing axis. This plan "saved our bacon" many times according to Burke, because the gunners knew that a plane approaching from some strange angle had to be enemy.

The returning planes also were vectored in low over the surrounding picket ships so they could be identified as friendly. The pickets confirmed, too, that there were no bogies attempting to hide behind their radar signal. The pickets were often hit hard by following enemy planes, but they rarely allowed any to pass through to the center of the fleet where the carriers patrolled.

Naval leaders also developed a new system for target coordinators. They sent out the air group commanders in rotation to the target area, a little ahead of schedule. The commanders would sight in the succeeding groups of attacking aircraft, directing them to specific targets using their own experience and the knowledge gained from long briefings based on photo reconnaissance and prior attacks. It made a great difference to have a trusted target coordinator who had seen the earlier attacks and who knew the enemy gun firing positions and the abilities of the American pilots as he directed the assault.

Planners created multiple target lists and new systems for dealing with the targets. They made complex configuration list plans that allowed leaders to call for "Plan X," which would encompass each plane and ordnance type and amount for a particular type of attack against a specific target. Thus everyone aboard would know precisely what their job would be as soon as the target was determined. It sounds simple, even obvious today, but it was done for the first time in preparation for the Tokyo raids, and the American Navy has done it the same way since.

Mitscher determined to bomb Japan from the task force for three days. The carriers, therefore, would be vulnerable to Japanese land-based bombers for at least seventy-two hours straight. He and Admiral Burke placed the night fighter carriers into their own separate task group, which would head in shore at dusk, launching as night fell.

Admiral Marc Mitscher and his chief of staff, Arleigh Burke, aboard the Bunker Hill *review battle plans before the first naval raid on Japan since Mitscher skippered Doolittle in the* Hornet. *An air chart of Tokyo is pinned to the bulkhead behind them.*

The night fighters would patrol Japanese bomber bases around Tokyo throughout most of the night, keeping the enemy on the ground. The regular carrier forces could then launch before daylight taking over guard duty. The fighters patrolled in shifts all day. The carriers had to recover the daytime fighters before dusk to avoid the losses that would inevitably result from dark landings. This meant that during the critical twilight hours the carriers would have no fighter protection. They solved the problem by launching a skeleton crew of sixteen night fighters that patrolled the skies over Tokyo during the dusk hours. It turned out that these planes, combined with an eight-plane CAP flying over the task force, were sufficient.

Tension had built on the *Bunker Hill* since she left the protected shores beneath the Golden Gate Bridge and moved inexorably toward enemy territory. Now, as the *Bunker Hill* waited at anchor at Ulithi, she laid in supplies, hanging fire while Burke and Mitscher finalized their battle plans. The planes were ready. The admiral stood aboard. The men had studied how to rescue their comrades in the cold Western Pacific and how to avoid the Japanese in mainland Japan.

The fighters' briefings made clear the enormous advantage in technology and matériel that the Allies had over the remnants of the Japanese air and sea forces. Caleb Kendall wrote cockily that he expected it would all boil down to something like sport: "Like shooting fish in a barrel."

Still, he was so bored at times he felt like the Navy "was just fattening us up—like pigs for a slaughter. The only difference is, it is the Japs who get the knife."

Life aboard the huge Essex carriers could be almost surreal. On board, they lived, in many ways, as they had at home—except many had never eaten so well. Battle rations often meant steak and eggs for breakfast and turkey dinners for the entire crew, with mashed potatoes and gravy just like home. Only the largest ships in the Navy could afford that luxury. Pete Probo looks back and says, "We lived like kings."

And the men felt safe. They were surrounded by the most powerful American ships, and facing an enemy that had almost no navy left. But they knew, too, that each day they were getting closer to a fight.

There were many periods of calm and boredom aboard the Bunker Hill. *During breaks between flight operations the men gathered on the flight deck to sunbathe.*

The kamikazes were already having an effect on American war plans. The *Ticonderoga* was supposed to join their task force but had been struck by two kamikazes and forced to retire to the United States for repairs. She was out of the war until summer. Pilots on the *Bunker Hill* spent much of their time memorizing and reviewing as they moved closer to the war. They studied Bakelite models to learn to recognize all sorts of Allied and Japanese ships and aircraft—submarines, transports, freighters, oilers, float planes, fighters, and fighter-bombers. They passed time taxiing planes around the deck for the plane spotters, moving aircraft forward so others could land, or moving planes below to be refueled. They worked on navigation problems or censored the ship's outgoing mail.

The Navy had almost no programs to keep personnel physically fit while on sea duty. But the aircraft carriers were one of the few vessels that offered an opportunity to exercise for those who would seek it out. Fighter pilot Al Turnbull knew it was vital for him to exercise each day, if possible, and he sought out every opportunity. The Navy provided medicine balls and when Turnbull could find enough room to form a circle with a few squadron mates he would organize them to toss the ball around for a while, or to do jumping jacks and skip rope. If that failed, he would end up jogging the deck, sometimes by himself.

Jogging could be challenging. When the ship was traveling at 25 knots into a 22-knot headwind, it was like running into a 60-mile-per-hour wind and then circling back every 900 feet to have a light tail wind pushing you from behind. Turnbull had to remain constantly aware of the threat posed by friendly aircraft landing, taking off, or being respotted on the deck. Enemy planes might strafe or bomb the *Bunker Hill*. Sometimes Byron White, who was serving on Mitscher's staff, would join Turnbull in his jog, wearing his white exercise uniform.

The *Bunker Hill* was designed to carry 215 officers and 2,171 enlisted men. When they left Ulithi in 1945, though, she carried about 3,404 men. Several dozen reporters also clambered aboard.

Arleigh Burke recalled in his secret oral history that one of the great challenges of 1945 was dealing with all the auxiliary personnel and press who wished to ride aboard the *Bunker Hill* from Ulithi. Experts in every imaginable field, with valuable contributions to make, but many of whom were not really needed on the flagship, vied to sail aboard the *Bunker Hill*. These men strained the already severely overtaxed ship's systems. Overcrowded enlisted men were assigned to sleep in hammocks in the mess halls, but many mess halls had to run nearly twenty-four hours a day to feed all of the men serving long shifts—these unfortunate sailors were left to find bunking space wherever they could.

Bunk space for ordnancemen like Tom Martin had been usurped for some other use. Instead, they slept in the gallery deck armory, amongst the explosives, in cots stacked three high. The heat and humidity in the nearly airtight armory aggravated tensions. A small ventilation tube ran past Martin's bunk. He and the other sailors cut holes out of it with their bosun's knives to get a little extra air. The chiefs would come by and order them taped up. Instead, the men stuck pinup cards to hide the holes, then opened them up at night when no one was around.

Martin's cot left him only a few inches below the ceiling (which was the bottom of the flight deck). Every time a plane landed, he felt the ceiling slam just above his face, and the whole armory shook violently. Sometimes aircraft, landing hard, tore into the flight deck. Martin could not get the image out of his head of one of the huge propellers shearing through the deck boards above his head, and cleaving him apart. He often tossed for hours, unable to sleep.

A lot of time the heat became unbearable and the armers would go up to the deck to sleep. Tom Martin tied himself to the iron catwalk just below the flight deck so he would not fall overboard as the ship slowly pitched and rolled. The *Bunker Hill* was totally blacked out at night, and he had to feel his way onto the deck, always afraid that a misstep would send him falling into the sea.

Overcrowding aboard the *Bunker Hill* added to the frustration and tension. Many nights when he could not sleep (which was most nights in the war zone), Martin would go below to the black stewardsmates' quarters. He would step through the hatch, clap his hands together, and announce: "Who wants to have their ass kicked tonight?"

Some stewardsmate always volunteered to fight him. Bare-knuckled, they beat each other bloody for an hour or so. Afterward, he would trudge, bruised and bleeding but finally exhausted and able to sleep, back up to his bunk. Martin stepped down there night after night, knowing what he was walking into. He saw it then merely as "recreation." Only years later did he begin to recognize the stress that led him to go below to fight.

In 1945, Commander Joseph Carmichael was promoted to chief engineer and took control of the ship's internal systems. He was in charge of all of the ship's machinery and 528 men in the Engineering Department. Upon his promotion, he received a salary increase to about $175 each month.

Carmichael's life in many ways made him uniquely qualified to preserve the *Bunker Hill*. Many of the ship's company credit him with saving the ship and their lives. He was quick, extraordinarily tough, disciplined, directed, and well reasoned. If the kamikaze pilots showed an especial bravery in their willingness to give their own lives, Joseph

Men aboard the Bunker Hill *thought of countless ways to amuse themselves during the times they were out of the combat zone. In the photo, Commander Gilbert Fraunheim learns to lasso. He is standing at almost the precise point of entry just behind the aft elevator where Yasunori Seizo's bomb would crash through the deck.*

Carmichael displayed an equally impressive resolve to sacrifice his young men to save the lives of thousands of others.

Carmichael was a plankowner: he had been aboard the *Bunker Hill* since she left Boston. By the time she returned to Puget Sound, he had cruised more than half a million miles aboard her and was determined that, whatever happened, the *Bunker Hill* would never be abandoned.

The chief engineer occupies a special place in the shipboard hierarchy. He is given his own quarters, which are designated on the ship's plan. In his room, Carmichael had a solid Steelcase desk, a couple of reading chairs, a lounge, desk chair, a capacious bunk, and his own bathroom (head). The admiral, his chief of staff, the captain, the executive officer, and the air group commander are the only other officers granted their own rooms.

Carmichael worked efficiently with most of his co-chiefs, but he and First Lieutenant Shane King, who was in charge of the Hull Department, got along particularly well. They reorganized and modernized control of the ship between their units. Their innovations were a key factor in the survival of so many men after the disastrous attack on May 11, 1945. King was a Naval Academy graduate. According to Carmichael, he "knew his job well and was a first-class manager of men."

When the Navy began putting steam engines into sailing vessels, the ship's hull belonged to the First Lieutenant, and all the engineering systems and piping were in the charge of the chief engineer. Engines and pipes and the hull are intricately interconnected in a modern naval vessel, and this system caused debilitating confusion. The Navy altered command so that the chief engineer would be in charge of the piping until it went into a wall—at which point it became the responsibility of the Hull Department.

The same breakdown of responsibilities held true for damage control. The chief engineer was held responsible for every machine on the *Bunker Hill*: the elevators, the electrical lines, everything. First Lieutenant King, though, managed the damage control room and was required to remain in this location throughout any casualty. Telephone lines connected this control room throughout the ship, but it had no gauges, and was located in a highly vulnerable area of the hangar deck.

King and Carmichael came to an informal agreement that, in case of any damage, Carmichael would take charge of all the engineering on the ship and would run it from the forward engine room. Anything from the flight deck on up would be King's responsibility.

Carmichael also developed an independent battle plan to deal with personnel. The official battle plan called for Carmichael to send all his engineers and other men to central locations, from which they could be dispatched by phone to areas of the ship where they might be needed. In theory that is a good idea, but Carmichael realized that there may be times when communications would be down, or travel through the ship impractical or impossible. So, rather than have his men wait at a random central location, he ordered them all to report to their duty stations. Electricians would go to electrical jobs, boilermakers to fire rooms, and engineers to engine rooms, or to wherever their duty station was. Carmichael sent them where they would likely be of most use. That way, if something happened they would be on hand to respond immediately.

Some criticized his plan, and the breach in procedure in implementing it on his own. They asked what would happen if everyone died at their duty station. Carmichael's response was that if they all died there, then the duty station would probably be wiped out, so those men could not do much to save the ship wherever they were, and that was their primary function—to save the ship.

Carmichael spent most of his time at duller work: having the main engines stripped and repaired, restoring everything that could be mended at sea, and managing the promotions and morale of the men. He dealt with a range of issues, almost like the mayor of a small town. The men were stacked together for months on end, in a steaming ship. They faced constant health issues. Some would not see a doctor even after becoming seriously ill, potentially endangering their bunkmates, while others "will come to you each day with a new ache—those guys were easy to cure."

Carmichael told me: "I used to go through the ship every night about one, or two o'clock, the hour when the men's alertness is pretty weak." He would see all sorts of things: "You'll find a guy sitting on a bucket reading a comic book when he shouldn't be. I used to walk

Commander Joseph Carmichael aboard the Bunker Hill *during the first tour, probably early 1944.*

through the compartment where they handled the bombs. There were always some kids with hammers playing tic-tac-toe on the bottoms of them. I said sooner or later one or the other of those would set the bombs off. I knew they weren't supposed to go off but, nevertheless, there are violations of physical laws sometimes that you couldn't explain."

Carmichael grew a red mustache during the cruise and his men began calling him the "Little Red Fox." Carmichael had a lot in common with the wily animal. The men figured he grew the mustache to make himself look older. They were right.

His engineers had to keep the bomb elevators running. Several times various unfortunate sailors looked into the shaft to see whether the bomb-carrying elevator was coming, "And indeed it was coming." When the elevator arrived on the flight deck, it would be carrying both a bomb and the head of the hapless sailor. Carmichael would send a young engineer along with a ship's surgeon to dislodge the body. He patrolled through the engineering compartments several times each night, at odd hours. He knew that whoever he passed by would pick up the sound-powered telephones to warn the next group. So he would pick up the phones, too, amused, to hear his men complain: "Where is that son of a bitch? Doesn't he ever sleep?"

Carmichael said: "Well, I used to get a nap in the afternoons whenever I could but there's no sense in advertising that fact to anybody. And there's a little bit of play-acting involved in that stuff. The men want to focus on somebody. They love eccentric characters for one thing. They cannot see them any other way. They like to see that their boss is a bit weird. It gives them something to talk about."

He used to "share the night" with Lieutenant King and the air officer, Gilbert Fraunheim. As deck and engineering officers and lieutenant commanders, they were all three qualified to command an Essex Class carrier. They would share the night talking softly so the captain could sleep, "the presumption being that *we* did not need to sleep."

One night after a *Bunker Hill* attack against one of Japan's island fortresses, the three men watched a darkened plane approach for a landing. The pilot circled in and the landing signal officer (LSO) went forward and waved him in to the flight deck. No one could see any markings on the plane, and it had kept radio silence. Normally, any plane that could not be identified was fired on. The ship could not be risked for one plane and one pilot. But everyone figured he was an American because he was making a night landing approach. He was just a few feet above the arrester cables when, at the same moment, the pilot realized he was on the wrong ship, and they all realized he was Japanese, as the enemy pilot suddenly veered away. No one fired on him. Carmichael said, "I don't think anyone should have fired on him after he had made it in that close."

Early in the morning on Saturday, February 10, the ship's 28,000-pound anchor was raised. The *Bunker Hill* fell into line with the task group as they motored out through the channel at Ulithi atoll, and toward the capital of the Japanese empire.

A little after noon, Captain Seitz announced via the ship's public address system that they were going to hit Tokyo and would be in harm's way for a long time. The pilots reacted outwardly as though this were the best news they had ever heard. Then they walked to their ready rooms where Chandler Swanson briefed everyone again on the Tokyo and Iwo Jima operations, which would come in quick succession.

Their mission was to hit two heavily defended aircraft factories at the heart of Japan—Tokyo. Al Turnbull's bombers would strike the Nakajima Ota plant in Gunma prefecture located forty miles inland, and only about twenty miles from Kiyoshi's home in Takasaki. The pilots reviewed their recognition photos and were briefed in detail again on air-sea rescue for the Tokyo operation. They argued about which gear was best used for various situations and began to study detailed geography of the region around Tokyo. They were told that every pilot aboard the ship should be ready to fly at a moment's notice.

When the CAP and the ASP (anti-submarine patrol) landed, Turnbull noticed how stale and unpracticed they all looked. It had been too long since the carrier had been moving fast enough for flight training and now they were headed for their most challenging attack of the war. Their lack of practice showed. Everyone was changing speeds too often, trying to stay in formation, and having a hard time of it. The *Bunker Hill* towed a sled, and the pilots fired 5-inch solid fuel wing-mounted rockets at it and then strafed it. Nearly everyone missed.

When the planes returned, one crashed into the barriers. An F4U broke its hook after landing hard on the deck. Another had no hook and smashed through three barriers before stopping. Many others landed low on fuel.

Turnbull walked up to the forecastle and looked out to sea, talking with the other pilots as the Pacific sky darkened and then filled with stars that showed the ship's eastern movement.

Many of the men had never seen the ocean before joining the Navy. From the *Bunker Hill*, they rarely saw land.

The days leading up to the raid were a strange time. The Japanese people persisted in clinging to the lie that they might win the war. American pilots, who had never been to Tokyo, still feared Japan intensely.

The whole task group slowed to allow every ship to be refueled before they got close to Tokyo. The pilots spent the whole day in preparations for their assaults. J. Waite "Slabo" Bacon talked them through the latest intelligence reports. Everyone read recognition books. It became increasingly difficult for the men to fall asleep.

The night before the Tokyo mission (February 15, 1945), Caleb Kendall wrote to his wife and the child she carried:

> Tonight I'll dream of you and Tiny. I'll see you sleeping with your face bathed in moonlight and wish I could duck in for just a minute to wake you for a good luck kiss and a sleepy encouraging smile. I could really use 'em right about now.
>
> I love you Brownie, and always will. . . . As long as I have you on my team, there'll never be a tomorrow I can't face with my chin out. . . . My job now and my ambition for the future is clear cut. I wouldn't ask that the situation be altered by a hair. Hold down the fort, honey, until we can hold each other tight once again.

That evening the *Bunker Hill* continued her northerly course, getting into colder and colder weather, while the smooth Pacific, churned only by the ship's four heaving 28,000-pound bronze propellers, lay so smooth that the men could see the reflection of a million stars streaking along with them.

The *Bunker Hill* produced a huge wake. Seawater churning behind the ship agitated tiny phosphorescent marine creatures, causing them to light up a trail that followed the carrier through the night. The soft green light tracing behind the ship pointed their location to enemy search planes. So the destroyer escorts patrolled through the wake, laying thick smoke screens behind them as they traveled.

Smoke from the destroyers surrounding the ship plunged the *Bunker Hill* into a ghostly blue-blackishness that spooked many of the sailors, filling them with the same shuddersome sense that has dogged sailors at night for millennia.

11. TOKYO RAID

We have fought in every clime and place
Where we could take a gun.
—MARINE CORPS HYMN

Pilots hated waiting for a fight. Thursday, February 15, 1945, seemed to last forever. There was simply nothing to do but wait. The *Bunker Hill* trekked north, weaving to a point within striking distance of Tokyo. Turnbull puttered around the ship. He visited the armory and reviewed every recognition picture he could find. He listened closely to Captain Seitz's last message about the operation that afternoon: the torpedo pilots would have to wait one more day. Caleb Kendall, though, would fly out the following morning.

Protestant and Catholic chaplains spoke to the entire ship and gave prayers for all hands. Turnbull went to bed around 11:00 P.M. Reveille awoke him at 3:45 A.M. But he had not slept. Three hours later the first fighter sweep took off to assess and soften up the defenses around Tokyo.

The huge task force, made up of five individual task groups including sixteen aircraft carriers along with hundreds of support ships, had reached their initial strike point only eighty-nine miles from Cape Suno-saki at the entrance to Tokyo Bay and still had not been discovered. Sailors and pilots were shocked. The truth was that Japan had almost no navy left, no fuel, no radar, and no reconnaissance ability. The Japanese probably only learned that the U.S. Navy had arrived after the first task force fighters began strafing their airfields that morning.

Still, it was a tough flight for the first squadrons. The *Bunker Hill* launched three more strikes that morning. The wind was blowing hard and the seas were rough. The first fighters strafed aircraft and hangars at Japanese bases along the coast, and shot down one Betty. On their way back to the *Bunker Hill* they shot up coastal merchant ships near the shore. The Japanese navy, now mostly sunk, was unable to challenge them.

Caleb Kendall launched at 2:40 P.M. with twenty-one fighters, thirteen SB2C dive-bombers, and fourteen Avengers loaded with four 500-pound GP bombs each. Caleb rode shotgun for the bombers. The bombers would only survive if the fighters remained on top, below, in front, and behind them during their run on the target. The Japanese would try to tempt each fighter to break formation, then move in for a kill on the bombers. The lumbering, heavily laden bombers, left without escort, would not be able to fight a Zero.

When they got close to the factory, antiaircraft guns opened up all around them. The percussion bounced his plane around. Exploding AA ink dots turned the sky black. Caleb felt nauseating fear grip him and weaved at full throttle as the Japanese pilots ran at him from all directions through the flak. But the fighters could not leave the bombers.

It seemed almost impossible to keep an eye on the Japanese, dodge antiaircraft, hold his position in the weave, stay on top of the bombers, and make sure no new Japanese planes came in on his tail, all at the same time. Heavy antiaircraft fire increased as Kendall's squadron headed deeper and deeper over the mainland. The sky seemed to fill completely with enemy aircraft. Everyone was shooting in each direction at once. Kendall turned his nose down, following the bombers in their dive straight into the maelstrom. They entered their glide at about 13,000 feet. Antiaircraft fire streamed back up at him. He was in the lead, with just about every other plane in the task force covering him, and it occurred to him that there would be no one to cover the last pilot in. When he saw a gun nest that was pouring tracers up at him, he dove straight down on it, cutting loose with his six .50-caliber machine guns. The Japanese gun stopped firing almost immediately. Kendall stayed on top of the bombers, firing at anything that flared up, trying to keep the smaller caliber antiaircraft gunners on the ground ducking instead of firing at the squadrons above. The bombers finally dropped their ordnance at about 3,500 feet. Kendall looked back to see the plant dotted with explosions.

He pulled hard on the stick, "jinking like mad" as the bombers pulled out and headed home. Freed of his charge, he dropped down to rooftop level, screaming over Tokyo. Kendall now was free to seek out targets of opportunity. He raced over Tokyo's still intact, totally unprotected neighborhoods. A beautiful big building came looming up. It looked to him like a hospital or school, covered with plate glass windows. He felt "like a kid on Halloween" and shot out all the glass on one side of it. People were standing in the streets looking up at him and waving crazily. "I gave them a few bursts, too. This part was fun."

A moment later a Zero came straight at him out of nowhere, blasting away on his machine guns. Kendall fired back, although both pilots appeared so startled by each other's sudden appearance that there seemed little chance of either being hit. They were both content to allow the other to escape. Kendall rendezvoused with his squadron mates and took up the weave again, but the Japanese interceptors had disappeared, so the squadron headed back to the *Bunker Hill*. He waited until he was out over the water, and then checked his plane for damage. He pulled back on the throttle to save fuel (he had burned a lot while over the mainland) and then lit a cigarette, and tried to relax as the squadron headed back to base.

The weather closed in on them very quickly. Kendall dropped down to an almost impossibly low altitude, but still could not see the ocean. Finally he opened up his cockpit to look down and found he was only a few feet above the breaking waves. He was soaked and freezing cold as he winged his way seventy-five miles back toward the flattop and he almost hit the ship before he saw her. Other pilots straggled in for more than an hour.

Al Turnbull wandered around the ship that day, trying to keep his mind off what he was about to do, while simultaneously going through every aspect of the raid in his head. He launched the next day.

Turnbull flew the first plane to take off in the second strike, targeting weapons manufacturing and supply depots. Jack Weincek was his gunner and George Gelderman worked the radar and radio gear. They brought one passenger, W. Eugene Smith, a *Life* magazine photographer, who sat in the greenhouse atop their TBF Avenger number 307. They were some of the first American pilots to see Japan since the war began. From their vantage point of 14,000 feet, they looked out on the plains and rolling hills around snowcapped Mount Fuji.

The weather had been poor—overcast and raining hard all day. But when they came over the mainland, it cleared and the sun shone brightly upon their aircraft. Smith snapped a photo of Turnbull's squadron crossing from the sea over the Japanese mainland. The picture made the cover of *Recognition*, the U.S. Navy's classified aircraft journal. Skyward-pointing arrows on the tails, indicating that the aircraft originated from the *Bunker Hill*, are clearly visible in the photo.

Turnbull's plane shook when they hit the expected turbulence associated with the change in temperature as their TBF cruised in over the coast. At once, the Japanese antiaircraft guns opened up. Gelderman was tossed around like a cork inside the cramped cockpit. Their plane was protected by a primitive version of what the Navy now calls chaff—on that mission called "window"—a thin paper strip about half an inch wide, backed with aluminum foil cut to different lengths.

Recognition *cover, photographed by W. Eugene Smith.*

Each length was supposed to block or confuse a different wavelength of the radar that pointed the Japanese radar-controlled antiaircraft guns. Gelderman was carrying 10-centimeter strips and he was supposed to throw them out his hatch by hand every six seconds.

A squadron of Zeros cut in at their edge, shadowing the torpedo bombers, but either because the antiaircraft was so intense around the invading Avengers, or because the American fighter escorts never broke rank, the Japanese planes did not penetrate the bombing group. From their altitude, the pilots could see flooded rice paddies that sliced into every hillside below the Avengers, each its own shade of calm green. Fuel fires ignited by bomb explosions punctuated the countryside.

Ack-ack burst all around the plane, but somehow always missed them. Gelderman figured if tossing the window every six seconds was good, every three seconds had to be better and he threw the stuff out by the handful as fast as he could. He was supposed to secure the bucket of the confetti-like material and close down his cockpit window before they turned into their dive, but in the excitement he forgot.

The plane jerked violently on its side when Turnbull pushed the stick over. The TBF dove on a steep glide through the ack-ack toward the Nakajima airplane plant. Wind whistled through the cockpit and all of the window escaped into the fuselage of the plane, burying Gene Smith in the tinfoil tails.

Gelderman looked out the cockpit window and saw Ensign Richard Brothers's plane crossing beneath them, out of formation. His engine was smoking. Brothers came on the radio and said calmly, "I've been hit. I'm losing power. I've got two Zeros on my tail. Don't wait for me."[*]

Turnbull continued in and dropped all four 500-pound bombs. The plane jumped as the weight was jettisoned and he pulled hard on the stick, wrenching the aircraft from its dive.

At 4:17 P.M., Gene Smith looked up as they pulled out and smiled at Gelderman. Smith was covered to his chest with the window.

---

[*] Ensign Richard Brothers and his crewmen W. L. Paolissen and E. V. Androso were killed.

They flew back through the driving rain and found the *Bunker Hill* a little over two hours later. The ship was cruising into the wind, waiting to land the bombers. Turnbull caught the number three wire.

The raid came at a high cost. Turnbull's squadron lost two planes out of fourteen. Men were shot down, forced to ditch, or crashed on the barriers.

Gene Smith gave Turnbull a bottle of VO after they had landed. He carried only two bags the entire period he covered the war. One had a change of clothes and his photographic equipment. The other had only VO. He used it to trade rides between various ships and to various islands. Another bottle bought him a ride to Okinawa a few months later where he was severely injured.

The U.S. Navy claimed 341 enemy aircraft destroyed in the air and 190 destroyed on the ground during the two-day fast carrier raid. Japanese leaders received detailed reports of Japanese performance against the Tokyo strike as the *Bunker Hill* steamed toward Iwo. They were told that out of the 1,650 aircraft that attacked Japan over the two days of carrier raids the Japanese had shot down 200 American planes. The Japanese claims were, as usual, wildly inaccurate. Thirty-two American planes were downed by enemy action during the assault.

That day Tokyo was the most heavily defended city in the enemy-controlled Pacific. Yet in its first combat mission, Kendall's air group shot down eight Japanese planes without losing a single aircraft. Before they sortied, the pilots had been in awe of their target—Tokyo—but afterward Caleb wrote that they figured they could take "anything and lots more than the slant-eyed boys could give us."

That evening, Kendall drank with his squadron mates. They went first through the squadron's private stores, and then the ship's medicinal stores. As the *Bunker Hill* passed out of range of ground-based aircraft, Kendall staggered down to the ship's brig to check out three Japanese prisoners who had been captured after their picket ship was destroyed near the coast:

The poor little guys were scared to death when they first came aboard. Apparently they expected to be creamed right off the bat. After a bit of indoctrination into the American way of operation, they came around to being friends. They couldn't speak a word of English, but after our reception, couldn't help being friends. We smiled, chattered, offered cigarettes, and struggled with a few pathetic attempts with their language.

They were obviously pleased, but were still plenty bewildered. I guess the boys are all right at heart but came under the wrong leadership. They sure seem to be plenty frightened of us in every sense of the word. Our actions to date only help to prove to them that they are terribly beaten beyond all hope. The opposition they offered us was pathetic. I'm just plenty glad I'm on our side.

The strikes were like punching a boxer struggling to keep his feet. The Japanese were being hit hard, seemingly from all sides. And it was only going to get worse. But not without a staggering loss of life—both American and Japanese.

After two days of strikes over Tokyo, the *Bunker Hill* turned southeast and steamed straight for Iwo Jima, arriving in time to cover the American invasion force, set to launch on Monday, February 19, 1945.

Japanese leaders initially estimated that the U.S. Navy had succeeded in landing approximately 1,400 Marines on Iwo. In actuality, 32,000 Marines had landed.

Hundreds of Navy vessels—aircraft carriers of every size, battleships, cruisers, destroyers, hospital ships, provisioning craft, ammunition craft, infantry ships—surrounded the island. Giant battleships sailed close in, only a mile offshore. It seemed that every ship was firing. They unleashed the largest naval bombardment of the Pacific war. Exploding shells transformed Mount Suribachi into a pocked lunar landscape. Caleb Kendall flew in over Iwo Jima at about 8:10

that morning, just as the naval bombardment subsided. The Navy would give the fighters and bombers ten minutes to drop their bombs and strafe before beginning again the rolling bombardment, as the landings began.

The massive bombardment, though, was profoundly ineffective. Admiral Spruance had promised to leave two battleships with the bombardment force surrounding Iwo Jima. But he did not want his surface fleet to be left out of the first naval raid on Tokyo. The Marines had asked Spruance to shell for ten days. But Spruance shelled for just three. Instead he brought all of his eight battleships with him, plus a new battle cruiser and five heavy and eleven light cruisers to Mitscher's Tokyo raid. The battleships were irrelevant in this carrier fight. Worst of all, though, hoping to prove the value of his surface ships, he armed them for a fleet action, with armor-piercing shells, rather than shore bombardment shells. The Marines were met with an onslaught more terrible than anything they had yet faced in the Pacific. For the first and only time, the number of Marines killed and injured outnumbered Japanese casualties.

The first day, the Marines suffered 2,420 casualties. Despite the magnitude of America's losses, Japan's uncompromising defense of the island was doomed, so long as the Navy could resupply the Marines ashore.

Though the bombers and fighters fired rockets at the pillboxes and gunnery targets on the beachhead, Japanese defenders remained well hidden. The Japanese had changed tactics. They did not have a word for "retreat" so the commanders at Iwo Jima ordered their men to "charge backward." They ceded the beaches to the Americans and allowed the naval aircraft to fly largely unchallenged over their guns. The Japanese preserved their ammunition and the location of their hidden weapons. They defended only the most protected enclaves. Predetermined, precise settings for their artillery allowed gunners to rain down accurate mortar and artillery fire on the unprotected Marines.

Turnbull flew Commander Swanson's brand-new Avenger the morning of February 19, 1945, on its first mission, carrying a dozen 100-pound bombs. He rode the Avenger up from the hangar with

Admiral Mitscher's photographer, Chaney, riding in the greenhouse, carrying a giant Navy-issue Kodak camera ready to photograph the island. But the elevator jammed on their way up, and Turnbull missed his launch. Instead he flew up the Bonin island chain, taking pictures of enemy forces at scattered bases to ensure the Japanese did not have sufficient aircraft within striking distance to launch a counterattack.

With Chaney snapping away, Turnbull flew north 150 miles to the Japanese bases on Chichi Jima. No one fired on him. He then circled back, photographing the bloodiest battle of the Pacific war. Landing craft, some burning, many sunk, lay on Green, Red, Yellow, and Blue Beaches. Finally, Turnbull looped around to join his squadron at 12,000 feet a few miles out from the island. The American forward air controller ordered him to drop his full load on a single artillery post at the southwest corner of a hill above the beachhead. Observers had quickly nicknamed the Japanese gunner there "Pistol Pete," for his deadly precision. No one could find him. Every time an American landing craft arrived at the beach the gunner wheeled out of a cave, fired, and destroyed the landing craft before the men aboard could escape up the beach. He was massacring the Marines. The controller assigned every pilot in Turnbull's squadron to drop salvos on that one gun.

Turnbull led the second section of the strike, flying in steep and fast, with his wingmen in single file to hit the lone gun. At about 2,500 feet a 40mm AA shell hit Turnbull's starboard wing hard. The detonation slammed their big plane, jerking it sideways. It blew a hole in the wing bigger than their aircraft tire, six feet around. The shell ignited his hydraulic fluids, which began spewing flame and smoke that trailed black behind him. Turnbull, though, maintained his dive, dropped his load above the target, and then gently pulled out.

Smoke filled the cockpit as he scanned the low horizon, searching for a place to ditch amid the invasion force. Chaney's shoe caught on fire and he put a hole through the cockpit floor trying to stamp out the flames. Gelderman spent most of this time staring at the flames that licked about the starboard fuel tank, wondering when it would ignite. The Avenger's internal communications were out. Control wires, torn loose from the wing, whipped and banged against the metallic fuselage so loudly that verbal communication was impossible. Turnbull scribbled a note and passed it to Gelderman, warning about the wing tearing off. Weincek and Gelderman knew that they would have to climb out quickly after a water landing. The two crewmen kicked out their separate hatches and hung their feet over the edge, ready for a quick exit. Turnbull wanted to set the plane down in the water before the burning wing tore off, but the sea was so crowded with Navy assault vessels that he was unsure whether he could find a clear spot to put the plane down in time.

Turnbull scribbled another note to Gelderman: "Keep chute on in case wing comes off."

Turnbull could not communicate with Chaney the photographer, who had realized they were going to try a water landing. He was seated on a couple of oxygen bottles and knew he would be slammed forward when the plane hit the sea. Fearing that the bottles "would have given him a goose like he would never have wanted again," he removed his chestpack parachute and wrapped it around the valves to cushion their impact.

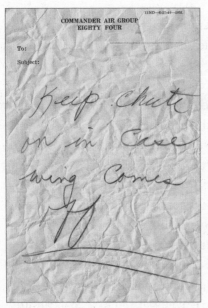

Al Turnbull's internal communications were destroyed when his Avenger was hit by a Japanese shell over Iwo Jima. He communicated with his crew by passing notes through the cockpit glass. At one point the hole in the wing seemed to be tearing away, and Turnbull wrote this note to George Gelderman.

While fire and smoke poured out of the wing, Turnbull began his descent. But Gelderman stopped him with a note: "Chaney isn't ready." Turnbull pulled up gently again and was shocked when his wing fires extinguished. The fire had worked through his rubber wheels and hydraulic fluids, but hadn't ignited his fuel. It had burned itself out.

Disbelieving their luck, Turnbull asked for and received permission to land. Hundreds of men crowded both sides of the catwalks to watch, scared, tense, but hopeful. They could see straight through the six-foot hole in his starboard wing. When controllers in the bridge saw the condition of his plane—and especially the metal stubs where the wheels had been—they ordered Turnbull to abort the landing and bail out: the *Bunker Hill* could not afford to damage her flight deck. Turnbull headed gingerly out to sea at 3,000 feet. He turned on the autopilot, opened his canopy, and climbed up and out. He sat for a moment, both feet planted firmly on the wing of his plane, his buttocks resting on the edge of the cockpit, and his hand holding tight to the metallic ridge across which the sliding glass windshield door opens and closes to the pilot compartment. Wind whipped past as he prepared to leap. And then he remembered Chaney, and looked into the greenhouse.

There, Chaney was frantically trying to stuff his parachute back into its pack. Stuffing a parachute so that it will open is a tricky business. Specially trained *Bunker Hill* crewmen carefully folded the chutes in a special parachute room equipped with sixteen-foot-long wooden tables. Unless a chute is packed perfectly it will not open. Without a functioning parachute, Chaney did not stand a chance in a jump and they all knew it, but the damaged aircraft could not survive a water landing. None of them understood, though, that the longer Chaney took packing that chute the better off they all were. The *Bunker Hill* by this time had retrieved all its planes and had no further missions scheduled that day. With all their aircraft safely aboard, she could risk landing a damaged Avenger.

Suddenly Turnbull's headphones, still plugged to his dashboard, crackled. "Gaucho 301, this is Gaucho Base. Return to land!"

Turnbull climbed back over the rail, sat down, and buckled himself in. As Weincek and Gelderman scrambled into their seats, he slowly, gently turned the Avenger back. He would be landing with a hole in his wing that he could almost walk through, torn control wires, no wheels, and no flaps.

After being waved off on his first pass, Turnbull managed to make another turn. But he was still flying too fast, and controllers waved him off again. They asked him how much fuel he had. Enough for one last try, he told them. Then Admiral Mitscher must have intervened. The entire task force was turned together, precisely, into the wind, and ordered to accelerate another 6 knots to maximum speed. They moved 100 ships in perfect unison to save the lives of one crew. Turnbull gave it a final try.

He knew now he could not make the usual carrier landing. So he took a wider turn, came in lined up much further out than usual and with more speed. He began easing back on the throttle as he caught up with the *Bunker Hill*. The Avenger began to drop as Turnbull used fuel flow to control altitude. The plane slowed, then started to settle down toward the sea as he pulled up along the stern. Then, as he passed over the stern, he flipped his wing over a little bit, cut the engine, fell straight onto the deck, and caught the second wire.

It was a perfect landing. Except that he had no wheels. The stubs where the burned wheels had been dug in hard to the deck and jerked the plane over on its side. The right wing bent up, as the Avenger skidded along sideways. But the fuselage settled back down, and the plane came to a stop, pinned to the deck on its metal wheel stubs. The crowd of relieved and cheering crewmen rushed forward as controllers in asbestos suits ran to evacuate Turnbull and his crew.

Mitscher had saved their lives. Despite the trauma, Chaney the photographer leapt out of the plane even before deck crews had climbed the wings. Gripping the film canisters tightly, he ran for the photo lab. He knew Mitscher needed his pictures.

Admiral Mitscher stepped out from his flag room onto the catwalk above the flight deck and gave Turnbull the thumbs-up. The torpedo squadron commander, "Skipper" Chandler Swanson, came running out and jumped on the remaining wing of the Avenger. He shouted sardonically at Turnbull, "You son of a bitch! Look what you did to my brand-new airplane!" and then cussed some more. Swanson was smiling, though. "Nice landing," he said.

Turnbull's controlled crash was filmed by Navy cameramen assigned to capture significant events in the life of the carrier so that analysts could later pore over the record to determine what could be done better to fight the war and historians would know more about life during the Second World War. But the films served other purposes. The squadron transcribed Turnbull's conversations with the bridge that day and read them out in the officers' mess room while they played the reel over and over of him flying around and around the *Bunker Hill* before destroying Commander Swanson's new plane. It was helpful for the men to know you could land an Avenger on a carrier, without flaps or wheels.

After supper, Turnbull stepped topside to watch the engineers and radiomen finish stripping his brand-new TBF and then push it over the side.

Turnbull rose early on February 21, D-Day plus 3 at Iwo, to watch the sunrise through a rainstorm. He flew that morning through rain so thick that he could not drop his bombs for fear of hitting Marines. The weather worsened on the way back to the task group. The pilots

Jack Weincek, George Gelderman, photographer Chaney, and Al Turnbull are here surrounded by the astounded crew of the Bunker Hill. *The hole in their starboard wing is about the size of Turnbull, who is standing just forward of it. The burned-out flaps on the port wing can be seen darkened at the edge of the fuselage.*

barely maintained formation and many of the planes narrowly avoided collisions. Turnbull jettisoned his munitions before landing, but the ceiling had dropped below 200 feet and when his bombs hit the sea three detonated, blowing holes in his wings, tail, and the gas lines to his center tank. But he had enough fuel to make it back to the ship.

Around 5:00 P.M., fifty Japanese aircraft, many of them kamikazes, attacked the carriers. They knocked the *Saratoga* out of the war, and in one of the most deadly attacks, sank the light carrier *Bismarck Sea*. The next day Mitscher pulled the fast carriers out of range of the kamikazes, and headed them back instead to raid Tokyo.

It is difficult, in hindsight, to justify the Iwo Jima battle. But the unflinching bravery of the Marines who fought there remains one of the greatest examples of American courage and resolve. Unfortunately, U.S. control of the island added little to the American war effort in the Central Pacific. Iwo could not have been used effectively as a naval base by the Japanese. The island's Japanese air force had been all but destroyed and proved only a nominal threat to the fleets of B-29s raiding from Saipan. Iwo never served as an essential base for the B-29s nor for the shorter-range Mustang fighters that escorted the Superfortresses.

Sortieing off mainland Japan, Al Turnbull, Caleb Kendall, and the other pilots were especially removed from the carnage of the war. Before they dropped their bombs, the Japan they viewed from their cockpits was a land of flooded rice fields and small homes with wisps of smoke drifting from narrow chimneys. They rarely looked back after detonation. In the evening they returned to clean sheets, a hot meal, and ice cream. When they killed people they rarely saw it. Nevertheless, the war they fought had grown intensely personal and intensely one-sided by February.

Caleb Kendall was shocked at how little protection the Japanese pilots had, but perhaps more so at their lack of training, which showed itself in their almost total lack of tactics. The poorly trained Japanese pilots fired their guns wildly, often when there was no chance at all of hitting an American. Their planes, too, were fragile. It seemed one only had to touch the unprotected Japanese fuel tanks with a few slugs and the whole plane would "blow up like a torch." The *Bunker Hill's* fighters annihilated the Japanese in every confrontation. One pilot even bailed out before Kendall's squadron could get close enough to fire.

In one run, Kendall jumped on the tail of a Zero above the Inubo peninsula, about fifty miles from Yatabe where Kiyoshi Ogawa was training, and fired a stream of tracers into the Zero's left wing. It flamed for a moment, then tore off. The Zero exploded. Kendall wrote home that he "flew through pieces of wing, tail, engine, fuselage and Jap." His first thought was, "Boy, won't Dad get a kick out of this when I tell him over a rum coke."

It struck him that the Japanese might as well have been committing suicide.

Like many other American pilots, Kendall had become infected to some degree by the American propaganda effort to dehumanize the enemy: "You'd think the little yellow boys would be only too happy to stay home with their sake, geisha gals, and what have you . . . [but] the General Quarters gong clangs like mad every 45 minutes and we all grab our life jackets and dash madly for the wardroom (nice safe spot)." He hated hiding out, bored, in the wardroom, waiting for "the bastards to go home." He got so sick of it that in the end he would often just stay in his less protected sleeping quarters, having a drink and writing letters home or reading.

A skilled and disciplined pilot, Kendall initially spent every moment in the air concentrating on his flying. He knew his weapons. He knew the proper setting of each instrument on the plane, his flap settings, RPMs, altitude, and ailerons at every speed, attitude, and altitude. And he kept a constant roving eye for threats from above, below, and all sides. He handled his radio and navigation at the same time and he made consistent kills. But after his son was born, his thoughts began to drift for the first time when he was in the air. The flights were long. Many missions lasted the full reserve of his fuel supplies. And on most hops they encountered few enemy aircraft. The lack of enemy fighters almost made the time in the air more difficult. It was a challenge to maintain concentration during those long periods, and though they did stay ready, the pilots' nerves became frayed through the difficult hours.

Scuttlebutt on the ship had them returning home soon. The *Bunker Hill* had spent more than her share of time in combat. Newly constructed Essex carriers had arrived to carry the fight. Kendall told Brownie that after this trip he would be coming back east for good "and never plan to take another look at the Pacific again as long as I live." He wrote lovingly, asking her "to get set for all of our dreams of the last five months to come gloriously true. It is horrible to wait, but it won't be long."

With their run on Tokyo and their bombing runs on Iwo, the men aboard the *Bunker Hill* had completed their baptism of fire. They worked well together. But they knew that the next battle, for Okinawa, would be more intense, and last longer than anything yet undertaken by the carrier battle group. After the Iwo landings, the Essex carriers returned to Ulithi where everyone thought they would be safe from the kamikazes. But the Japanese had appointed a new *samurai* to lead the kamikaze defense of Okinawa. It turned out that, even at Ulithi, more than 1,000 miles from Kanoya, the *Bunker Hill* was not safe from Admiral Matome Ugaki's kamikazes.

12. FRATERNIZATION AND RACE RELATIONS ABOARD THE *BUNKER HILL*

This land is your land
This land is my land
—WOODY GUTHRIE (1940)

Rote shipboard work no longer distracted the men. The stress and anxiety of approaching combat intensified every friction, ill feeling, and strain aboard ship. Each action, word, deed, and even glance potentially created conflict. The men reacted in different ways to the pressure. Tom Martin climbed below and boxed the black stewardsmates. Some pilots drank, others turned to books. Still others to religion.

All of the inconsistencies in the American Navy became exacerbated by the tension of danger. It was a challenge for all the men to navigate within the naval hierarchy. Relationships between pilots and their crews, the ship's officers and the flag officers, the crew and their chiefs, and men in different units were all complex affairs. The Navy had regulations for nearly every contingency. But they all had to figure out how to get along throughout an indefinite mission, fraught with danger, surrounded by men they did not know, and on whom they would have to rely for their lives. Insubordination toward any officer was a serious offense and warranted a range of punishments. Crewmen were put on bread and water for the most minor abuses.

167

More serious offenders were half starved and sprayed with stinging saltwater, then locked in darkened solitary confinement.

Most top Navy officers were Annapolis graduates when the war began. They did everything by the book. But as the war progressed, the Navy increased exponentially in size and more and more officers were reservists, "ninety-day wonders" who had volunteered and after only ninety days of officer training joined the Navy as officers. They changed the Navy. For the first time, the majority of naval officer ranks were filled with men who had no intention of making the Navy their life. They arrived with strikingly different values and imperatives from the naval careerists. The reservists and draftees loosened up the Navy. And they derided many of the regulations and traditions that the Annapolis men held dear. But even this influx did not break the barrier between officers and enlisted men.

The Navy absolutely forbade fraternization between officers and enlisted men under any circumstances. Al Turnbull thought this probably the worst rule of many senseless regulations. He worked best with the pilots he knew well. Turnbull wanted to know his crew, too.

George Gelderman, Jack Weincek, and the rest of the crewmen aboard the torpedo bombers were enlisted. They passed hundreds of combat hours with Turnbull in his small plane. Turnbull thought it ridiculous and dangerous that they were never allowed to speak socially together. They relied on each other on every mission. They faced countless emergencies together. He figured that the better he knew his crew, the more efficiently they could work together, but also that it was vital that they all get to know each other *before* they faced an emergency together. They were a team. The three men in Turnbull's bomber had to work together each day to get to a target, hit it, and return home. Their cooperation would become all the more essential if they had to ditch, to get out of the plane, to make it back if they bailed out over enemy territory, or to try to keep the plane flying if they were hit. Turnbull regularly had his crew look over the plane to aid him in inspecting it. They spoke together about what they would do if various emergencies occurred: if they were struck by antiaircraft fire, if certain controls were lost, if the radio went out. They planned together in detail what they would do in a water land-

Jack Weincek, Al Turnbull, and George Gelder-man pose in front of TBF number 26 on the tar-mac at Alameda just before boarding the Bunker Hill.

ing, who would be responsible for which tasks. Often their conversations drifted to other matters. What their lives had been like back home, and what they would do when the war was over. Naval regulations forbade those personal interactions.

Turnbull would sometimes be having a laugh with his crewmen as they climbed out of their Avenger. He would look up to see the ship's officers on the bridge looking down at him. The career Navy men would see Turnbull talking with his crew and put him on report to Commander Swanson. Swanson would call Turnbull in and ask him what he was doing talking with his crew out on the deck. Turnbull figured he could live with the reports—a lot of pilots who never discussed anything with their crew were no longer living.

The officers were treated very differently from enlisted men. The ship's bathrooms were a constant reminder of enlisted men's lower status. Most officers shared a head with just a small group. None of them ever had to clean their own toilets. Black stewardsmates did it for them. Some, like Carmichael, had private bathrooms.

In contrast, the crewmen's latrine was dirty and extraordinarily public. Most of the men shared a lavatory in the center of the ship. The foul room was open on both ends so that men could enter from bow or stern. Two sets of benches ran along each side. A trough ran below each of the benches. A constant flow of seawater streamed down the troughs. The saltwater was carried in by pipes at the bow end, then drained by pipes at the stern end of the communal latrine. Dozens of men sat on boards atop these troughs, facing each other, twenty-four hours a day.

The men sat crowded in their collective indignity, often reading the ship's newspaper *The Monument*. Al Skaret laughs as he recalls that sometimes men at the bow, where the seawater entered, would light their newspapers on fire and let them float down the trough, sending a whole line of their shipmates jumping off in mid-movement, with singed buttocks.

Few of the pilots developed close relationships with their fellows during the war. The Navy required men who were willing to die and willing to die for each other. But these highly trained men also had to be insulated from the loss of those closest to them. Much of the system of training and deployment actively discouraged the making of close friendships amongst men in combat areas. Turnbull rarely knew anything about the backgrounds of the men with whom he flew. He had no idea that J. A. "Cherry" Blossom lived in a penthouse that took up the entire top floor of the Knickerbocker Hotel in Chicago, waited on by liveried butlers, or that another Chicago pilot, Joe Neary, lived in a basement apartment in an ethnic slum in one of Chicago's toughest neighborhoods. Few onboard the *Bunker Hill* were aware that another pilot, Ensign Edward P. Stack, was the heir to an enormous chocolate fortune.

Those kinds of things never came up. They talked about flying, the enemy, and life aboard ship. They spent their time working out navigation and fuel problems for upcoming missions, writing reports of missions past, figuring out where they were going, how they would get there, and how they would find their way back to the base (unlike land-based planes, their "landing field" could have moved almost anywhere within 150 miles in the course of a single mission). They exercised physically and tried to keep up with their mail. Sometimes when mail arrived they talked about the girls they had left behind, but mostly it was about the performance of their aircraft and their duties aboard ship.

The pilots almost never spoke graphically about sex. They all passed around *Forever Amber*, a sort of Harlequin novel, in which many of them felt the author had, as one pilot explained, "sex on the brain."

Most of the men aboard the ship, who rarely saw an enemy plane, idealized the flying officers. They knew that the pilots were up against the enemy every single day. The crew saw their aircraft return riddled with shrapnel and bullet holes. They knew, too, that many did not return.

Most of the pilots on the *Bunker Hill* seem never to have left a very small area of the ship and almost none of the ship's company ever left their own unit's designated area. Units would go to their own mess, their own bunks, and maybe the geedunk shop, but had almost no contact outside their unit's region of the ship. Turnbull was different. He seemed eternally curious. He almost flaunted breaking the rules against fraternization with enlisted men. He was cited for this misconduct more than any other officer on the *Bunker Hill*.

Joe Gilbuena, a Filipino-American serving aboard the *Bunker Hill*, grew up in California and volunteered for the Navy. Gilbuena was shocked when he found out that the Navy was fully segregated—and he was on the wrong side of the line. He ended up at a training camp in Virginia. The southerners did not know what to do with him. They could not allow him in the white barracks. But they did not feel they could put him in with the blacks, either. In the end, they gave him his own lonely barracks of one. Finally, they transferred him out to become a stewardsmate and he ended up serving with a number of other Filipinos for Admiral Mitscher.

Gilbuena was required to live with the blacks aboard the *Bunker Hill*, to use their restrooms, and eat in their mess. Gilbuena had no problem living with the black sailors as long as everyone did. But he hated the badge of race that the segregation aboard the *Bunker Hill* created. Admiral Mitscher allowed the Filipinos who served him to set up cots in a small pantry in Officer's Country in the island, near the flag plot where Gilbuena spent nearly twenty-four hours a day. The blacks were kept bunking below. So the *Bunker Hill* ended up like old South Africa, with the blacks in one area, the whites in a second, and the Filipinos, like Indians, somewhere in between and separated from all.

African-American men were isolated more than any other group. They were cut off from the officers because they were enlisted men and they were cut off from the rest of the ship's company because they were black. Their bunks were completely separate. Disciplinary actions against blacks were often meted out by their own chiefs, off the books. A stewardsmate swore at Beads Popp in a hallway. The chief saw the incident and told Popp he would take care of it. Popp saw the man later. His commanders had beaten him in the face with a sock filled with nuts and bolts.

Many of the crew aboard the *Bunker Hill* on her first cruise were from Massachusetts. Everyone seemed to get along well. But when they left Bremerton in 1945, many of the experienced sailors were sent out to crew on the newer carriers, and other men were brought in to the *Bunker Hill*, many of whom were from the South. Jim Spence, a gunner, had almost no experience with blacks growing up. There was only one black student at his high school in Revere, Massachusetts. Spence never thought about what life was like for blacks in the South. There were several instances, especially during the tension of the kamikaze battles, when fights broke out between the black stewardsmates and the white crewmen. The Shore Patrol kept a watchful eye during crew changes when the blacks would have to file past the white sailors.

The stewardsmates worked the mess and took care of the officers. They cleaned their sheets, swept their rooms, picked up their laundry, and made them snacks. They served meals wearing white uniforms. The most powerful officers, like Mitscher, had individual black or Filipino sailors assigned for all of their personal needs.

During battles the stewardsmates passed ammunition. They

loaded it through the vulnerable armored compartments open to the flight deck. This put them in some of the most dangerous compartments, surrounded by live ammunition, when the *Bunker Hill* was under attack.*

Two stewardsmates remained with the torpedo squadron after training at Alameda. Neely cleaned their rooms, pressed their sheets, made the bunks, and cleaned their clothes. Munson took care of the mess sandwiches outside the ready room.

The pilots and their stewardsmates were stuck together in close quarters for months on end while in constant danger. But the fliers were strictly forbidden from talking with them about personal topics of any sort. Many of the pilots broke this rule. Turnbull became close with Munson, the stewardsmates who ran the little snack bar right outside their squadron ready room. Every time he would get fruit or sandwiches, the two men would talk for a little while about their lives at home and their families. Over the course of training at Alameda and combat aboard the *Bunker Hill*, Munson and Turnbull became, in a lopsided way, close. Every time Turnbull sortied, Munson would climb up to the portside flight deck catwalk, as far forward as he could go. Just before Turnbull would take off, Munson would salute him. Turnbull would wave back. Munson prayed for Turnbull each night and he told Turnbull that his mother and father were praying for him as well.

Munson was only fifteen or sixteen years old. The Navy often looked the other way to take young black men aboard to work in the mess. When the squadron flew to Alameda from San Diego to board

---

* Black sailors refilled ammunition magazines in the clipping room for the 20mm guns where Jim Spence worked. The loaded magazines had to be carried by hand across the mess deck and then up another elevator to the flight deck by his gun battery. Sometimes they would bring the bombs up via the mess deck as well, and if they were in a real rush, the ordnance men would fuse the bombs right on the mess deck so they could hurry the explosives to the flight deck ready to be hooked into the bomb bays. If GQ was called when the bombs were being readied on the mess deck, everyone scrambled to get them out of there as quickly as possible. The *Bunker Hill* was nearly indestructible. But if she took a bad hit while her own ordnance was susceptible to detonation, it could cause a chain of explosions that might destroy the ship.

the *Bunker Hill*, Munson, a talented illustrator, designed an image for each pilot and then painted it on the nose of their aircraft. He gave each flier a voluptuous woman to lead them into combat, and called Turnbull's "The Duchess." Wishing to be a part of the air group and separate from the denigrated stewardsmates shunted away below, near the ship's holds, Munson had moved his mattress into the small closet galley by the ready room and succeeded in gaining a special measure of closeness to many of the pilots. But he would never be fully accepted, and so in the end lived apart from everything.

13. STUDENTS BECOME *TOKKO*

Without shaking off
The dust of the last journey,
I must set out again on a new road.
—KAWAKAMI HAJIME

Admiral Matome Ugaki was one of the last great *samurai*. He was scrupulously well mannered. He loved his country, and his family. He was a poet and a military leader, and was always prepared to die.*

Ugaki had retired from service after the Leyte Gulf battle, but was recalled just before the *Bunker Hill*'s aircraft attacked Tokyo in mid-February. His new mission was to organize and lead the kamikaze air defense of Japan. Perhaps his greatest legacy, though, is the detailed diary, filling fifteen volumes, that he meticulously kept throughout the last seven years of his life. This remarkable book is probably the best source for Japanese actions throughout World War II. Ugaki chose the Japanese naval airbase at Kanoya on Kyushu to build his headquarters and run the largest suicide program in history. Most of the Japanese naval kamikazes, including Kiyoshi Ogawa, would sortie from the Kanoya base. Admiral Ugaki's diary details the misery of life at that grim terminus and is helpful in understanding the plight of Kiyoshi

---

* As Admiral Yamamoto's chief of staff, Ugaki flew beside the admiral from Rabaul to inspect forward bases. Both their aircraft were downed by American fighter planes in an ambush targeting Yamamoto. Ugaki, though, survived, clinging to wreckage.

Ogawa during his last days. Ugaki was not thrilled by the prospect of organizing the kamikaze defense—he knew that Japan would lose the war, and he wrote in his diary: "I'm resigned that the time for my last service to the country has come finally."

Ugaki arrived at the Japanese naval airbase at Kanoya in mid-February 1945, two and a half months before Kiyoshi Ogawa. He toured the newly constructed underground facilities that had been built over the previous six weeks throughout the Kanoya base in preparation for the aerial assault they knew was coming. Ugaki marveled wistfully that sailors' hands could build so well ashore. He soon was informed that a Japanese reconnaissance plane had just discovered nearly 100 American vessels heading toward Iwo Jima. This was larger than the extant Japanese navy but only a small part of the force that would attack the small volcanic island.

The IJN General Staff determined that approximately 450 suicide planes plus 100 Ohka piloted suicide missiles and 300 escort Zeros were required to sink sixteen American aircraft carriers. They planned to use the Yatabe students as a sacrificial diversion; flying an additional 150 *tokko* aircraft, the students would fly against lesser ships of the American fleet, sowing destruction, confusion, and terror amid the invading navy. Many Japanese after the war were particularly embittered that the military sent so many ill-trained students on suicide runs, while preserving well-trained pilots, militarists from the elite Naval Academy, for the reconstruction of Japan.

Kyushu is the southernmost of Japan's four major Home Islands. It is one of the most isolated and least populated regions of Japan. Most Japanese have never traveled there. Sharp mountains in the center are covered with deep, verdant foliage and dotted with steaming geothermal vents that leave much of the mountains clouded in thick mist that drifts about day and night. These vents exist in such great numbers that they are regularly used for cooking by the local Japanese, who place eggs in the water and steam other items atop it. Central Kyushu is pitted with green valleys perfect for hiding from American aircraft or dispersing planes to avoid destruction by raiding B-29s. Ground crews dragged the aircraft into hidden redoubts and jungle woodland surrounding the bases. Hundreds of small, well-camouflaged landing strips dotted Kyushu.

Kyushu is both geographically and socially distinct. The people of Kyushu more closely resemble those of Okinawa than traditional Japanese, and Kyushu was the first part of Japan opened to the West. When the Portuguese invaded Japan in the 1830s, the Kyushu authorities allied with the Europeans, and Portugal remained influential there. Perhaps as a result, Kyushu has been more receptive to the West than the rest of Japan. Before World War II, Nagasaki, in northwest Kyushu, was probably best known for its *castella*, a soft Portuguese cake they had perfected locally. Kyushu is famous for its pottery productions. Near the end of the war strategic metals had become so scarce that the artisans of Kyushu were employed making small ceramic hand grenades for the final defense of Japan.

Kanoya is a small town nestled in the tableland south of the mountains of southern Kyushu. The Kanoya naval airbase, just outside the town, is surrounded by rich rice land, well irrigated by quiet meandering rivers and streams. The IJN began to build up facilities in Kanoya during the 1930s because it was well protected and within striking distance of coveted Asia. The runways were laid out in 1936. In January 1945, they began to strengthen defenses at the base, digging tunnels and burying buildings in preparation for the coming homeland battles. Though the base had grown significantly in the 1930s during the war with China, it experienced explosive growth when it was used for kamikaze attacks. Perhaps 50,000 ground personnel worked at the base in the winter and spring of 1945.

The Kanoya naval airbase, according to the (accurate) U.S. intelligence estimates, was a 600-acre, irregular, five-sided field with several runways. Contained on the base were 250 air raid shelters and concrete revetments to hide and shelter aircraft and antiaircraft weapons. Traces of these revetments may still be seen. A couple of the *entaigo*, low-slung, protective hangars just large enough to slip a Zero inside, also remain. The nightingales, descendants of those heard by Ugaki and Kiyoshi, still sound in the late afternoon. During the winter of 1945, workers constructed a new command center in a heavily fortified bunker beneath the barracks. It had a narrow, low, reinforced cement entry, dimly lit by naked electric bulbs. The poorly ventilated space was dank, moldy, sticky humid and smelled badly of stale cigarette smoke. But it was safe. The senior officers and staff brought their bunks inside after B-29s began making their first reconnaissance flights over Okinawa.

At first the pilots slept in hammocks at the surface headquarters building. But it became a clear target for the American fighters and bombers. The structure still stood after several attacks, but the walls could no longer support hammocks. The *tokko* pilots moved into the Nozato school, a decrepit, nondescript elementary education building only a couple of hundred yards from the underground command center. The Japanese dug caves and trenches at the bottom of the hillsides that surrounded the plateau where the airfields were located. These battlements were used to store ammunition, house the makeshift hospitals, and hide the aircraft. These hollows can still be seen, marked only by thin police lines on the edge of the neighborhoods surrounding the base.

Kanoya base was struck often, at least four times each day, by carrier-based bombers and the much larger land-based, long-range bombers. Despite the terrible damage inflicted by American bombers—the runways were pocked with craters—829 kamikazes would fly from Kanoya before the end of the war.

Japan's empire was destroyed, one island at a time, while Kiyoshi Ogawa and his fellow cadets waited for fuel. Kiyoshi began training at Yatabe in 1944, after the cherry blossoms had fallen and long before Japan would embrace suicide tactics. It would be his second to last base. IJN leaders, preoccupied with their faltering war effort, paid little heed to training new pilots. Meanwhile, though, Japan's now irreplaceable experienced pilots died in combat, day after day. Through the winter and spring of 1944, Kiyoshi and the other trainees idled about at Yatabe performing drills or studying how to fly. But little actual flying was done.

Kiyoshi did not know that winter that the United States had taken Kwajalein and Majuro, nor that Japan's great airbases at Rabaul and Truk had been destroyed by American carrier-based aircraft. On May 25, 1944, when Kiyoshi arrived at Yatabe, Japan had not yet been subject to strategic bombing. Then everything changed. The fast carriers' success in June could not be hidden. The IJN lost its carrier planes in the Marianas, then lost Saipan. Tojo was forced to resign as prime minister. B-29s began bombing the Home Islands in the autumn of 1944.

The *Honchou* at Yatabe promoted Kiyoshi and most of the other students to the rank of ensign on Christmas Day 1944, and assigned them to the Konoike air force. Kiyoshi should have transferred to the base at Konoike, but there was no point in moving. None of the training bases had fuel. Kiyoshi remained at Yatabe. All the while the Japanese navy, now dominated by Admiral Onishi, moved inexorably toward a policy of suicide.

Admiral Ugaki traveled across Kyushu, in February, preparing secret bases large and small for the kamikaze assault that would begin when the Americans attacked Okinawa. His most important duty, though, was ensuring he would have thousands of pilots ready to crash their *tokko* aircraft.

Ugaki traveled from Kanoya to the nearby Kushira airbase on Wednesday, February 21, 1945. The Kushira commander was running a makeshift production facility, harvesting biofuels from pine trees. The Japanese were producing ethanol and methanol, which they utilized to power their Zeros. The fuel had serious drawbacks. The Zeros, especially under heavy loads, tended to stall and were nearly impossible to "hot-start." Ugaki sweated in the wet heat, listening to the bush warblers and larks. He seemed depressed at visiting underground facilities and dispersed aircraft at every base. The desperate pine tree fuel program was perhaps the worst sign of all. The United States produced 1.6 billion barrels of crude in 1945. The Japanese total national reserves had fallen to only 3.7 million barrels: less than the United States produced each *day.*

Ugaki was a subtly reflective man and illustrated his diary with poetry—short, dramatic lines that often tied images from his day to the current war situation. He was scheduled to move into underground quarters on the last day of February, but rescinded the order to try to keep his staff healthy—outside the dank, stale shelters.

Early in the morning of February 22, 1945, as the *Bunker Hill* steamed away from Iwo Jima, the PA system at Yatabe announced that all of the student cadets must report to the *koudou* (auditorium) and line up for an assembly.

Kiyoshi and his fellow students filed in together. They knew something big was happening. Every important meeting took place in the *koudou*. But they had no idea why they were all being called. Previously, they had always been split into two *buntai* (the Second [ni] and Fifth [go] Units). But this day, all of the students were brought together—500 young men in the single auditorium. The room was enormous, several hundred feet long. The ceiling was about sixty feet above them and all around the upper portions of the wooden walls rows of small wood-framed, paned-glass windows filtered sunlight to the hollow interior. The sun was setting and the falling rays glinted off the floor, but mostly it was dark and full of shadows. The light fell away as the assembly dragged on and the men increasingly were enfolded in darkness.

The *Hikouchou*, the leader of the Yatabe naval flight training program, stood up and stepped behind a thin podium raised on a low portable wooden stage. It had been carried over from the wall and set up just before the students arrived. He began to speak without a microphone, but everyone heard his words. Every man respected him. About ten years older than the students, he was an outstanding flier. The *Hikouchou* spoke for seven or eight minutes, announcing with devastating specificity how the tide of war had turned against the Japanese. He spoke of the American advantage in technology, resources, and training. But, he said, the Japanese could still win because of their unique spirit and self-discipline. The time had come when everyone must make the most supreme sacrifice for their nation, their mothers, and their brothers and sisters. The only way Japan could win now was to begin a series of Special Attacks—*tokko*. He asked who would be willing to give his life for his country.

The Japanese military government had tried to carefully control the flow of information about how badly the war was going. But with American planes attacking Japanese cities every day, there was little reason to continue the charade. Young men, like the students at Yatabe, were called together at military bases across the country. They were told that Japan had lost her carriers, that the Philippines had fallen, and that every ship and plane in Rabaul had been destroyed. America controlled Saipan and the Marshall Islands. An American invasion of Okinawa was imminent, they said. Nevertheless, they rallied the young men and announced that surrender was out of the question. These cadets were told that the essence of *Bushido*—the thing that gives Japan its unique quality—was "to fight on until one's sword is broken and one's last arrow spent."

Some student survivors from Yatabe, however, recalled that their *Hikouchou* spoke more enigmatically, saying that the war situation had become severe and that they would use *tokko* (Special Attack) methods to alter the situation. This was the first time they heard the term *tokko* to describe a method of attack. But everyone knew what their *Hikouchou* meant when he said "special." He meant suicide. The *Hikouchou*, concluding, said that no one had any choice but to complete their mission.

Orderlies passed around a simple bureaucratic form, normal and banal. Two sheets of rough, browned, inexpensive, standard Japanese writing paper were given to each pilot. The form began in a usual way. Students were required to fill out their full names and ranks, then their parents' names and the names of each of their siblings. The second page, though, was different. Formally, it appeared merely another "*daku-hi*" (yes-or-no) military form. But the questions overwhelmed. The students were asked to write whether they would join the *tokko-tai*. The form provided three possible answers, each printed in stark black ink. Each answer had a box next to it that could be checked. The last items stated, in order:

☐ I do not want to join the *tokkotai*.
☐ I would like to join the *tokkotai*.
☐ It is my fervent desire to join the *tokkotai*.

Every single superior officer left the room. Only the students were left. No one said a word. No one coughed. It seemed as though no one was moving. They all stood frozen, staring at the sheet in front of them in absolute silence.

Hisashi Tezuka was a gifted flight student drafted from Tokyo University, Japan's finest college. He had no desire to join the *tokkotai*. He felt, though, that he had no choice but to "obey the order of the country." Tezuka wrote down his parents' and siblings' names easily. Then he was left with the final question. He could not write. He could not even move. He merely stared at the paper.

Finally, he checked the middle box: "I would like to join the *tokkotai*." A few men remained writing when Tezuka left. He had no idea whether anyone wrote that they did not wish to join the *tokkotai*. But personally, he felt utterly constrained. "It was quite a special atmosphere in which they handed us these sheets."

Fumihide Kohari later explained: "We were under a serious pressure and we couldn't possibly acknowledge that we didn't want to go." Kohari felt that these types of attacks were going to be made no matter what he wrote and that if he did not agree to go, someone else would have to go in his stead. He did not want that person's death on his conscience. So, like nearly every other man in the room, he agreed to become a kamikaze.

Tatsuo Ono is absolutely certain that Kiyoshi had no choice but to join the *tokkotai* or that once that decision had been made, Kiyoshi had forced himself to accept it. Two of the pilots in the *daigobuntai* (fifth unit) signed their papers saying they did not wish to become kamikazes. But there is no evidence that this "choice" exempted them from the *tokko* squadrons.*

In mid-January 1945, the IJN and IJA chiefs wrote a joint order requiring all branches of the armed forces to use suicide tactics. The Japanese military had to train thousands of pilots immediately in Special Attack methods. The monumental organizational effort necessary to carry out mass kamikaze raids during the Okinawa cam-

* Volunteering for kamikaze missions became a mere formality. Leaders at each airbase had already determined and listed those who would become *tokko*.

paign precluded use of an all-volunteer force. Despite the appearance
of a choice, suicide became the official plan of defense. Kiyoshi and
the IJN pilots of the student draft were forced to join the *tokkotai*.
Japanese military leaders continued to implement the farce in which
cadets filled out their choice on rough paper.

The Japanese have a particularly strong attachment to the honor of
their mother, father, and ancestors. This feeling is probably somewhat
akin to the feelings of so many young Englishmen who went "over
the top" during World War I, straight into German machine gun fire
and death. Perhaps the best explanation was offered by an erudite student drafted into the Army Air Corps who became a reluctant kamikaze. He wrote, "Just because they forced me to do it, does not mean
I would not have volunteered."

The phenomenon was accurately described by Maurice Pinguet,
who taught French literature at the University of Tokyo. Pinguet
wrote in his study *Voluntary Death in Japan*: "Good son, good student, good soldier: The young pilot of the kamikaze special unit was
less the martyr of a fanatic faith than of his own good heart and good
will."

*Kiyoshi poses beneath the flowering
cherry blossoms at Yatabe during his
last days at the training base.*

It is difficult, perhaps impossible, to understand the complex nature of volunteering versus being ordered to do something in Japan during the Second World War. The governing system seemingly prescribed every behavior and specifically proscribed all that was unacceptable. This overweening, conservative system fostered a powerful atmosphere of passivity. Perhaps the best explanation of how Kiyoshi became a kamikaze pilot was offered, without a hint of sarcasm, by his Waseda classmate Maseo Kunimine: "He was volunteered for it."

Rikihei Inoguchi, who directly supervised the kamikaze program at Kanoya, refused to state that the kamikaze system was involuntary. But he did speak a lot about the kamikazes during his postwar interrogation, and co-authored a book with a member of the U.S. Strategic Bombing Survey on the kamikazes. Inoguchi wrote in classic enigmatic style that in 1945 the Japanese vastly increased the kamikaze program:

> In this circumstance the volunteer system of earlier days was plainly inadequate. So there developed a pressure, not entirely artificial, which encouraged "volunteering." And it is understandable that this change in circumstance would effect a change in the attitude of the men concerned. . . . Many of the new arrivals seemed at first not only to lack enthusiasm, but, indeed, to be disturbed by their situation.

Inoguchi claimed that this "disturbance" typically lasted only a few hours or days and eventually gave way to a spiritual awakening: "Then, like an attainment of wisdom, care vanished and tranquility of spirit appeared as life came to terms with death, mortality with immortality."

One naval official in charge of choosing kamikaze pilots told me proudly that no one refused to volunteer. But when every single person volunteers, perhaps the situation is not really voluntary.

"We were taught this from the time we were children—the Imperial

Rescript on Education was posted in every school," Tezuka explained. The rescript states in part:

> Ye, Our subjects, be filial to your parents, affectionate to your brothers and sisters; as husbands and wives be harmonious, as friends true; bear yourselves in modesty and moderation; extend your benevolence to all; pursue learning and cultivate arts, and thereby develop intellectual faculties and perfect moral powers; furthermore advance public good and promote common interests; always respect the Constitution and observe the laws; should emergency arise, offer yourselves courageously to the State; and thus guard and maintain the prosperity of Our Imperial Throne coeval with heaven and earth.

The student conscripts, now in their eighties, can recite this rescript word for word, despite the fact that it has not been used in official ceremonies for sixty years.

During the war, Tezuka never questioned whether he would die as a *tokko*. When he learned he would join the *tokkotai*, he knew his life was over. He felt empty. It was an order. It was for the country. It was his duty. He could not run away. He would fulfill his obligation. He would die. There were some students so devoted to the emperor that they genuinely would volunteer for a *tokko* mission. But they were the exception and even the most zealous students did not take that decision lightly. "We all have a natural desire to live," Tezuka stated.

After the presentation by their *Hikouchou*, Kohari, Iwama, Ono, Tezuka, Kiyoshi, and the others walked out of the gymnasium in total silence. They trudged together back to their barracks in the evening light, without saying a word. Each was absorbed by his own thoughts. Says Tezuka, "We were gazing into our own minds." The next day they went back to their old, fully regimented routine and everyone acted as though nothing had happened. The IJN did not encourage social reflection. The atmosphere at the base was suffocating. The Yatabe cadets slept in close quarters, side by side, usually touching each other. They all had nightmares for about a week after the meeting. All night long hundreds of students, cramped together in small hammocks, row upon row, swayed back and forth as the tortured men tossed and kicked violently, many of them moaning or crying out in their sleep. Some ran into the jungle, slicing violently through the bamboo forests with their swords. Others rampaged through the town, cutting their way through the *fusuma* doors of frail restaurants in the middle of the night. The cadets, Kohari stated, "were desperate to calm their tempestuous minds."

"But then the clouds disappeared from the sky and everyone picked up their spirits again." At about the same time, all of the students returned to their former selves. They seemed, as a group, to go through the various stages of loss together and to emerge prepared to accept their fate. They resolved to complete their missions and die for their country. None of the usual concerns mattered any longer. "My mind was spotlessly clear," Kohari said. "Everybody in the *tokkotai* seemed to have completely sorted out their feelings."

Aboard the *Bunker Hill*, the Navy censored letters sent home to preserve military secrecy. The IJN used censorship to enforce cultural and political conformity. Liberal ideas, thoughts about individual freedom, and antiwar beliefs held by some students could not be voiced. Love letters were deemed unconducive to the "soldierly spirit." The IJN strongly discouraged the students from establishing personal relationships with women and banned students from writing to any single women who were not family members. The atmosphere at the base simply did not allow for the kind of independence necessary to form a lasting bond with the opposite sex.

The IJN permitted Kiyoshi a special night away from Yatabe just before he departed for Kanoya, to spend the night with a "comfort" girl who met him at the base gate. Few Japanese of Kiyoshi's generation had sex before marriage, and it was virtually unknown among the students. Asahi Iwama was a young poet studying at Keio University when he was drafted with Kiyoshi. One evening before Kiyoshi's departure, when Kiyoshi and his friend Iwama were playing bridge and chewing tobacco, Kiyoshi talked to Iwama about the night he had spent with a woman. Iwama alluded to Kiyoshi's liaison in a poem he wrote for Kiyoshi. Sex was never normally mentioned, but Iwama felt that it was more important to speak the truth at the end of Kiyoshi's life. Kiyoshi carried this poem with him on his final mission.

The student-cadets had been born at a time when most Japanese worked as their parents had. Few felt the pressure of responsibility for their personal identity; it had been chosen for them. Educated Japanese, for the most part, did what was expected of them. During his naval training, Kohari was confronted with a disquieting uncertainty about his life. He did not think he would survive. But he no longer had any idea what life he would lead. He was not ready to kill, but neither was he ready to die.

Many Americans, upon entering the armed services, felt freed of the burden of accountability for their lives. The Navy made most decisions for them. For the kamikaze pilots, their experience in the IJN had been the opposite. Far from release, many seemed to comprehend for the first time the precious nature of their own lives, and the fragility of their future. These realizations filled them with anxiety for all that they had experienced and hoped to accomplish. Their final, certain death sentence paradoxically made living in the IJN much easier. The present no longer pressed upon them. Japan was falling apart. The generals were planning for trench warfare around Tokyo. Everything they knew would soon be destroyed. But after becoming *tokko*, the students no longer were troubled by the things that bothered others. Overwhelmed by a feeling of serenity, they were relieved by the certainty that they would die quickly in an airplane.

The students remained who they were, but became a sort of superversion of themselves. Kiyoshi had been "a high-spirited person with his funny, raspy voice. But he became even more energetic and cheerful to everybody," Kohari recalled.

They were ready to go to defend their family, their country, and their race, and, for some (though not many), their emperor. Even those who had been liberals and antiwar accepted their fate. If any had spoken out and determined not to go, they would be demoted from officer to private and would certainly be sent immediately to the front, where they still would be killed. Their family would be labeled *hikokumin*, "unpatriotic," a stigma of utmost shame.

The Yatabe *tokko* group was officially formed on March 5, 1945, as the *Bunker Hill* provisioned at Ulithi. Two weeks later, Iwo Jima fell. Japan was defeated but refused to surrender. The American Navy could not be stopped. But individual ships could be sunk, and thousands of sailors would be killed by Japanese airmen who killed themselves for their country. Together they would form a sacrificial onslaught unlike any previously fielded by an armed service.

14. KAMIKAZES STRIKE ULITHI

Along the borders of the fields
Following the bean plants
Go the fireflies.
—BANKO

The *Bunker Hill* floated undisturbed at Mog Mog, the largest island in the Ulithi archipelago. Ulithi's existence remained classified, but the Japanese were well aware of the gigantic American base. Nevertheless, the Navy considered Ulithi, like Pearl Harbor, one of the safest places in the Pacific. Hundreds of American ships filled the anchorage. They rested more than a thousand miles from any functioning Japanese base. The Navy had built a little USA at Ulithi. Officers ate grilled hamburgers and drank cold beer on the beach at Mog Mog. Pilots and crewmen played volleyball and football and swam in the clear, warm waters. They got drunk, argued, and fought each other. They dreaded going back to the war, but for a few days they knew they were safe.

On Sunday, March 11, 1945, the men aboard the *Bunker Hill* were treated to a rare performance by Commander Dyson, the ship's "Annapolis Navy" executive officer. Though he could not prove it, Dyson had surmised that a group of former Air Group 84 pilots had gone AWOL from Hawaii, faked orders, bummed their way to Ulithi, stolen a tender, then set it adrift after landing aboard the *Bunker Hill*. Those pilots had risked jail just so they could join their comrades to fight the Japanese. The rule breaking, though, infuriated Dyson. He officiously interrupted breakfast by ordering an officer's personnel muster, during which he lectured pilots about uniforms, shore leave, and how the whale boats and tenders should be used. Muster had not been called since cadet training, and it was offensive to the officer reservists.

Just after the officers' meeting, Dyson ordered a full hangar deck parade. The men had not tried one since they left San Francisco and, perhaps intentionally, fouled the whole thing up. Further enraged, Dyson marched throughout the ship during much of the day, making announcements such as, "Today there will *be no* liberty," and "Today there will *be no* dessert," and "There will *be no* gambling aboard this ship."

That evening the men began to call Commander Howell J. Dyson, "Beno" Dyson. All felt it to be a particularly appropriate nickname.

Admiral Ugaki had no reliable radar. His few search planes had little fuel and were flown by inexperienced pilots. Following the sighting of an American destroyer close to the Japanese mainland by one of his reconnaissance planes, Ugaki scrambled a major nighttime attack

Bunker Hill *crewmen sunbathing on the deck edge elevator at Ulithi.*

with heavy bombers, additional search planes, and a squadron of suicide attackers. Intelligence later determined that the recon plane had mistaken a small island for the American ship. Such was the state of the IJN air program.

Ugaki had to suspend training often and for long periods. He spent much of his days touring construction of underground defensive positions. He wished to die fighting, not buried in a dank shelter. When he learned the news of the gathering of the American fast carrier force at Ulithi, he saw an opportunity. Ugaki decided to sacrifice some of his best pilots and finest aircraft to demonstrate that the U.S. Navy was not safe anywhere in the Western Pacific. The Tan operation, he hoped, would show America that the Japanese were filled with a courageous resolve and could accomplish with bravura what the United States hoped to achieve through matériel and technological superiority.

The plan was intricate, brazen, ambitious, and tenuous. Ugaki determined to attack the American fleet at Ulithi with kamikaze pilots flying twenty-four long-range Frances bombers. Tan was the longest and boldest kamikaze mission ever flown. The bombers had to fly to the absolute edge of their maximum range; 1,360 miles from their base at Kanoya. Everything would have to go perfectly for success.

The mission began as scheduled. A Japanese flying boat was launched at three in the morning, on March 12, 1945, to test weather along the route. Four land-based bombers then flew from Kanoya at 7:30 A.M. to clear a path ahead of the main attack force. Finally, the main force of twenty-four Frances bombers, loaded with 2,000-pound warheads, joined the escort planes over Cape Sata and proceeded on a circuitous route, to avoid detection, toward Ulithi. Soon, though, the consequences of Japan's lack of spare parts doomed the mission. Thirteen of the bombers turned back because of engine trouble. Thunderstorms forced the remaining eleven bombers to take an additional detour. The kamikazes needed to arrive at Ulithi with sufficient fuel and enough light to see their targets. At dusk, and still many miles out, the bombers began to run dangerously low on fuel. The eleven remaining aircraft were forced to slow down to conserve fuel. By then, the thirty-three men flying the bombers understood that they might arrive too late to find their targets.

The Americans, however, felt so secure that at least one light had been left burning aboard a ship at Ulithi. The kamikazes saw the glow as night fell. But as they made their final approach, their engines began to splutter. The Japanese aircraft, each with a crew of three men, fell, one by one, harmlessly into the sea a couple of miles from the American fleet. Only two planes made it into the anchorage. But they arrived well after sunset, in near total darkness.

Arleigh Burke stood, as usual, in flag plot with Admiral Mitscher a little after 7:00 P.M. He looked out at the USS *Randolph* where a group of sailors were watching a film on the hangar deck. Burke noticed, irritated, that a cargo light had been left on in the aft portion of the ship. Then he heard a plane.

A single kamikaze, his tanks nearly dry, struck the stern port quarter of the *Randolph*. His fuel never exploded. But his bomb detonated and the concussion badly damaged the ship. Ammunition and other flammable materials ignited immediately, covering her aft section in flames. By the time the fires had been extinguished, twenty-five men had died and more than 100 were injured aboard the *Randolph*.*

It was the first time that Admiral Mitscher and Arleigh Burke had witnessed a kamikaze attack. But it would not be the last.

---

* *Randolph* was scheduled to sortie with the *Bunker Hill*, but was kept out of the war for more than a month. The *Randolph* could not take part in the initial attacks on Okinawa, and she did not cover the landing force on Easter Sunday. The second kamikaze apparently mistook the low-lying Mog Mog atoll for a vessel, and crashed into the beach. Fourteen American sailors were killed in his crash.

15. THE *YAMATO*

Revere the Emperor, Repel the Barbarian
—TOKUGAWA MITSUKUNI

In January 1945, when the *Bunker Hill* sortied on her third deployment, she steamed into a fundamentally changed Pacific Theater. Arleigh Burke, in his oral history of his time with the Fast Carrier Task Force, said, "Although there was always a possibility that we could be defeated, the probability was very slight." The Navy no longer was running shoestring operations in the Solomon Islands. The task groups were enormous, often around 100 ships, and "took up lots of ocean." By the time of the Okinawa invasion, the *Bunker Hill*'s task force numbered 300 to 400 ships and could attack the enemy anywhere in the Pacific. The Japanese could react, and they could damage the force, but they could not destroy it.

Even as the outcome of an American victory became more certain, the danger to the *Bunker Hill*'s crews became more severe.

The *Bunker Hill*'s air crews exclusively utilized "dumb" bombs that used only the speed, altitude, and location of the plane, plus the bomb's tailfins and shaped nose, to determine the location of the strike.

The warring countries employed two broad types of conventional bombs during World War II. Until 1945, the *Bunker Hill*'s aircraft used mostly unitary munitions, single units that came in all sorts of shapes—spheres, barrels, pills, teardrops, canisters—and created a single detonation. Unitary bombs were primarily directed against structures, equipment, and matériel. The other category was cluster bombs, which could carry hundreds of sub-munitions that would be dropped over a target area where they would spread and detonate separately. Cluster bombs, for the most part, were directed at people. In 1945, the *Bunker Hill* aircraft increasingly targeted people rather than structures. Perhaps the most devastating conventional bomb used by the *Bunker Hill* was the M-69 napalm cluster bomb.

In 1943, Dr. Louis Fieser* headed a team at Harvard that eventually mixed gasoline with sodium (which has the chemical symbol Na) and palmitrate to create napalm. The sodium palmitrate acted as a thickening agent that, when mixed with fuel, created a sticky gel that burned at high temperature and was virtually impossible to extinguish—it had to burn itself out. Each bomb contained thirty-eight clusters. Ordnancemen aboard the *Bunker Hill* never mixed the volatile chemicals until just before the bombs were loaded aboard the aircraft. If even a single napalm cluster exploded, it could be a disaster for the carrier.

The individual M-69 firebombs looked like a length of hexagonal pipe, with each tube weighing just a little over six pounds. The hexagonal pipes fit together like geodesic puzzle pieces into clusters of thirty-eight each. Fins were added to the rear of the cluster, and a nose cone to the front, to allow it to be guided roughly to its target. The bomb broke apart at a preset altitude and the individual M-69's pipes separated. Each pipe then deployed a strip of cloth to stabilize its fall, guiding it down nose-first. Impact with the ground caused the napalm inside the pipe to ignite. It fired out of the tube, shooting a sticky, burning gel 150 feet behind it.

Conventional explosives destroy structures by blowing them up. It is the shockwave caused by detonation that demolishes buildings. The M-69 created a relatively minor explosion. It could not penetrate most artificial structures. However, nearly all Japanese built their *homes* of wood, with walls of mere screening paper. To test their new weapon, the U.S. Army constructed a typical Japanese residential area and dropped an M-69 on it. The M-69 caused a conflagration that obliterated the entire mock neighborhood. The test confirmed what

---

* Fieser later developed antimalarial drugs and helped prove that cigarettes cause cancer.

every military leader had already guessed: B-29s, dropping incendiary bombs, could burn to the ground every major Japanese civilian center.

Army Air Force General Curtis LeMay ordered the American strategic bombers to begin night incendiary raids on Japanese cities rather than attempting daylight precision bombing of industrial centers. The Superfortresses honed their skills in three raids against Tokyo. A single bombing raid in February destroyed at least 25,000 buildings. But the most devastating attack of the war, more deadly perhaps than both atomic bombs together, occurred on March 9, 1945.

Two hundred seventy-nine Superfortresses, sortieing from Guam, Saipan, and Tinian, dropped firebombs from 7,000 feet on Tokyo's residential areas. The paper and wood city erupted in inescapable flames. Sixteen square miles were completely destroyed.

During this single raid, approximately 100,000 Japanese civilians were killed. Many died from being scalded as they tried to save themselves by crowding into the city's canals, which boiled. By comparison, 100,000 civilians died in the Hiroshima nuclear attack, while 35,000 died at Nagasaki.

Renowned as one of the most beautiful universities in Japan, Waseda was hit by American incendiary bombs. When Kiyoshi was attending, the gate to his college looked like this.

After the firebombing, the view into the university from the same gate looked like this. Kiyoshi's dorm was located about 150 yards straight down the path shown in the foreground. The gate to Waseda had been marked by two globes symbolizing the interconnectedness of the entire world.

The raid lasted three hours. American Superfortress pilots and crews in the last wave vomited in their aircraft from the stench of burning flesh carried to their mile-high altitude.

Kiyoshi could see the fires from Yatabe. Japanese AA, directed against the high-flying bombers, had little effect and Japanese fighters barely challenged the B-29s. The student pilots were powerless to protect their cities.

Over successive days, the B-29s progressed to other Japanese cities. The United States burned Nagoya, Osaka, Yokohama, then Kobe. Then the bombers moved on to the lesser cities. As Japan had few AA guns left, the B-29s could strike with virtual impunity. The United States began broadcasting the names of cities that would be destroyed in the coming week. Citizens were warned with leaflets that their neighborhood would be razed. But few had anywhere to go. By the end of the war, nearly 400,000 Japanese civilians would be killed, mostly in American bombing attacks.

Throughout her history, Japan had won most of her wars in single decisive battles. The destruction of the Khan's Mongol fleet by fortuitous typhoons in 1281 and 1284 saved Japan. The destruction of the Russian navy and the storming of Port Arthur brought Japan victory in the Russo-Japanese War. Similarly, the attack on Pearl Harbor was to cripple the American fleet and cause the United States to sue for peace in order to avoid a two-front war. When the United States refused to make peace, Japanese military leaders sought out a new decisive battle. Yamamoto attacked Midway, hoping to establish the Japanese line of defense so far forward that the Americans would have to give up hope of penetrating their lines. Failing that, Japan engineered a decisive engagement with the American Navy in the Philippine Sea. Then Leyte. Finally, Admiral Matome Ugaki, commander of Japanese forces in Kyushu, would write in his diary of the Okinawa campaign that was to be the final "Decisive Battle."

Ugaki was correct. Okinawa would be the final decisive battle of the war.

Okinawa was the turning point, the moment at which Japan became a suicide nation. Use of Kamikaze Special Attack Unit aircraft became central to their strategy for the first time in the war. Now, the Japanese made clear they would resist surrendering at all costs, even if it meant utter annihilation.

The *Bunker Hill* spent the time during the initial fire bombings, from March 4 through March 14, at Ulithi. The men relaxed between Beno Dyson's drills, and Admiral Mitscher finalized his plans for the invasion of Okinawa, which was scheduled for Easter Sunday, April 1, 1945. The plan was to use Okinawa as a staging area for the coming invasion of Japan.

Okinawa is the largest of the Ryukyu Islands, a chain extending in an arc south from Kyushu to Taiwan. It had been part of Japan since the 1600s. The battle for Okinawa would be the first time that Americans attempted to wrest control of Japanese soil from the Japanese.

The island was within range and protected by Japanese airbases on the Home Islands, and its defenders had stockpiled supplies and developed an extensive defensive plan. General Mitsuru Ushijima retired with his troops to fortified upland caves, with well-protected tanks and artillery pieces, and awaited the Americans. The U.S. Navy delivered the invasion force and provided virtually all close air support during the invasion.

The American assault on Okinawa was of historic proportions not seen since the Roman Empire. The Navy's phase of the attack on Okinawa was arguably more significant in terms of its scope—the nature of the invasion as an intercontinental assault by sea—than even the seaborne portion of the Normandy landings. More than 1,320 Allied vessels took part in the April 1 landings, including forty aircraft carriers. The Navy landed more than 60,000 American personnel on the first day. The American Navy fired 44,825 rounds of 5- to 16-inch shells (mostly high-capacity fragmentation shells that would detonate on impact) at the Japanese defenses. This was nearly 10 percent of the total number of shells fired in the entire three-and-a-half-month campaign. Tenth Army bombers and land-based Marine fighter squadrons and their personnel added an additional 368,000 men directly involved in the assault—a total of 548,000 Americans. By the end of June, around 300,000 American soldiers and personnel had landed on Okinawa, which would be the most costly battle in American lives in the Pacific Theater. It is the only battle in which more Navy men died than Army personnel ashore.*

---

* Total U.S. battle casualties: 49,151: 12,520 killed or missing, 36,631 wounded.
    Army losses: 4,675 killed or missing, 18,099 wounded.
    Marine losses: 2,938 killed or missing, 13,708 wounded.
    Navy casualties: 4,907 killed or missing, 4,824 wounded.
    (6,800 U.S. armed forces personnel died at Iwo Jima)
    36 Navy ships were sunk, 368 damaged.
    763 U.S. planes lost in the air from April 1 to July 1.
Approximately 110,000 Japanese were killed on Okinawa.
    7,400 were taken prisoner.
    7,800 Japanese planes were destroyed, 16 ships sunk.
Source: *The U.S. Army in World War II: The War in the Pacific, Okinawa: The Last Battle*

The U.S. Navy now was led by fifteen Essex Class carriers.

Probably no planner dared to think that they would prove themselves so well. The carriers were an almost entirely new weapon. No one was sure how to sink one. They would be very difficult to destroy by conventional ship-to-ship gunnery. Only once during World War II did an American carrier get close enough to fire its gun battery at an enemy ship. It had been contemplated that they might be hit by submarine-launched torpedoes or by an airborne torpedo bomber. Few ever contemplated that aircraft would be used as manned bombs.

Airpower during the First World War was largely an instrument of reconnaissance or of scaring an urban population. Between the wars, naval aviators like Marc Mitscher argued that aircraft—particularly naval aircraft—would be decisive in the next war and they tried to convince anyone they could. But in the early 1920s, even Mitscher still supported the strategy of an American Navy based on battleships. The visionary aviator Billy Mitchell argued forcefully that a $10,000 bomber could sink a $10 million battleship. In 1921, the Navy conducted its first bomber-versus-battleship trials. Relatively inexpensive bombers were able to sink obsolete battleships. This gave aviation enthusiasts an enormous lift in the armed services. Armed forces are often accused of planning for the previous war. Battleships largely carried the day. Churchill believed that the United States could not mount a successful offensive in the Pacific for two years after Pearl Harbor because of the loss of so many battleships. The argument was finally settled when the *Bunker Hill* and her task group sank the Japanese super-battleship *Yamato*, while the two ships were still hundreds of miles apart.

On the eve of the invasion of Okinawa, Ugaki emerged from his dugout as a fog was clearing from the landing field. He wrote a short poem:

Heavy fog clears up at last, revealing nothing. Regret still remains
for the daydream of spring.

Ugaki realized that a new spring for Imperial Japan would never
come. Japan would be defeated and occupied. He could not live in
Japan under those circumstances. Ugaki wanted the nation to fight
to the last man. The next day multiple formations of B-29s flew over
Kanoya. That night he had dinner with Vice Admiral Teraoka. They
merged the Fifth and Third Air Fleets, both of which were rapidly
running out of aircraft and pilots.

During the early days of the battle for Okinawa, the Japanese
launched, for the first time, a program of massive, coordinated IJA
and IJN kamikaze raids. Admiral Ugaki and his army counterpart had
scavenged all the aircraft they could get their hands on, and relocated
them to bases scattered across Kyushu. These planes were launched
together, in massive attacks of hundreds of kamikaze. Their aim was
to overwhelm the American defenses by sheer number. If even a small
percentage could penetrate the American fleet, their aircraft could
severely damage America's war effort.

Americans tend to code-name their assaults either matter-of-factly
("Plan Orange") or dramatically ("Shock and Awe"). The Japanese
nearly always chose more poetic names for their war plans. They
called these mass suicide attacks *Kikusui*, which directly translated is
"Chrysanthemum Water." Its true meaning is more subtle, and is a
window on the Japanese view of poetic self-sacrifice. Images of death
in Japan are often linked to flowers. There is an old Chinese legend,
repeated in Japan, about an isolated country stream. Flowering chry-
santhemums crowded its banks. The falling blossoms made the water
extraordinarily sweet, and all the villagers who drank from it lived
long lives of heavenly joy. The chrysanthemum became the family
crest of the emperor.

Kusonoki, a fourteenth-century *samurai*, was staunchly loyal to the
emperor Godaigo. He fought a battle at Minatogawa near Kobe for the
emperor against the vastly superior army of a usurper. *Minatogawa*
has come to mean "to fight a war out of loyalty to the emperor, even
though you cannot win." The emperor, grateful for Kusonoki's sacrifice,

offered Kusonoki the emperor's own family crest of chrysanthemum. But Kusonoki felt that the emperor's chrysanthemum crest was too graceful for him, so, in humility, and recalling the sweet stream, Kusonoki hid half of the blossom in water. This motif is called *Kikusui* (chrysanthemum water). Kamikazes frequently referred to their mission as their *Minatogawa*—a futile sacrifice made out of loyalty to Japan.

Each morning, Admiral Ugaki met the departing kamikaze pilots at the edge of the runway. Just before they took off, he promised them, "I shall follow you . . . We shall meet in Minatogawa."

The U.S. troops on Okinawa were wholly dependent on a supply line stretching all the way from the West Coast of the United States to Pearl Harbor and across the Western Pacific to Okinawa. The Japanese *Kikusui* mass kamikaze attacks were directed primarily against the U.S. line of supply. The primary tactical target of the Japanese was the Essex Class carriers that defended this supply line.

Admiral Ugaki launched the first *Kikusui* on April 6, 1945. He sent 355 aircraft on suicide missions over the course of forty-eight hours.* Ugaki hoped that the massive raid would disrupt American

---

* There were ten *Kikusui* raids between April 6 and June 22. But it is impossible to know the precise number of kamikaze attacks. The official naval history of the war written by Samuel Eliot Morison states that 1,840 *Kikusui* special attack sorties took place during the battle for Okinawa between March and the final *Kikusui* Number Ten in June. Nine hundred sixty of these were either shot down or crashed into American ships. An additional 185 planes were used in Ohka attacks. One hundred eighteen of these were destroyed. Four hundred thirty-eight Japanese died in the Ohka assaults. Three hundred sixty-eight additional Zeros were utilized alongside the Ohkas. Two hundred eighty-four of these planes and their crews were shot down or crashed into American ships. However, Japanese records recently discovered and translated for this book indicate many more aircraft were sent on kamikaze missions on May 11, 1945, from Kanoya than was previously known. It is reasonable to assume that a great many attempted kamikaze assaults remain unrecorded. The Japanese lost large numbers of planes due to accidents and mechanical failures that had sortied as kamikaze, but were not counted as suicide attacks because they were destroyed operationally.

In addition to the *Kikusui* and Ohka attacks, there were between one and twenty attack groups of kamikazes sortied against the American fleet each day. There were also numerous conventional attacks that often deteriorated into spontaneous kamikaze assaults. The numbers of these last two types will never be known.

naval operations sufficiently for the super-battleship *Yamato* to sneak through the carrier blockade around Okinawa.

Herman Melville wrote of the power of the sea to sap energy and loll sailors into languor. But probably no American naval ships ever faced combat day after day for as protracted a period as did the fast carriers during the opening phase of Okinawa. Piloting missions around the clock for weeks on end made combat flying during Okinawa feel, at times, commonplace, almost predictable. Despite the bromidic effect of being at sea for two months straight, crewmen faced the terrible reality that the carrier was in harm's way for the entire campaign. During that time, the *Bunker Hill* was attacked by kamikazes almost every single day. Since Midway, American combat pilots had believed themselves to be safe and secure once they returned to their carrier. For many, though, during the Okinawa campaign, life on the carrier seemed more fraught with danger than their own combat missions. The suiciders came close at least thirty times in sixty days. The banality of life on the carrier was particularly incongruous with the chilling phenomenon of watching multiple suicides, and the murder of comrades and friends, on *Kikusui* days. Crewmen aboard the *Bunker Hill* often watched, appalled, as other carriers, just as powerful and well defended as their own, burned.

On April 7, 1945, Mitscher received word from a submarine that the *Yamato* had sortied the previous night. He immediately launched 386 aircraft on a search-and-destroy mission. The IJN had commissioned the super-battleship *Yamato* one week after Pearl Harbor. She was the largest battleship ever built and weighed 68,000 tons—more than twice as much as the *Bunker Hill*. Her sides, top, and bottom were plated with unprecedented armor and her main battery of nine 18-inch guns fired a projectile the size of a Volkswagen forty kilometers. At first the Americans could not find the *Yamato*, so Mitscher sent his attack aircraft, including Air Group 84 from the *Bunker Hill*, to where Arleigh Burke reasoned the *Yamato* would be.

The fast carrier squadrons attacking the *Yamato* seemed doomed. The *Yamato* was the most powerful and well-defended ship in the Japanese navy, and the Americans had no precise idea where she was.

They were sent to the absolute end of their maximum mission distance. The weather was so bad that they had to fly below 1,500 feet nearly the whole way there and would not have the kind of angle of attack that they would need to have maximum speed and maneuverability over the target.

The saga of the Japanese super-battleship *Yamato* is emblematic of the war. Its construction represented the potential of Imperial Japan, its mission signified Japan's desperation, and its destruction embodied not merely the devastation of Japan, but also the hegemony of carriers and U.S. power. Japanese naval leaders planned to sacrifice the "indestructible" ship on a suicide mission, but instead, American carriers obliterated the *Yamato* before it could do any damage.

The *Yamato*'s orders were to run aground at Okinawa so as to become a stationary firing platform, then discharge all of her massive shells at the invading Americans. Any *Yamato* sailors who survived would swim ashore to join their army comrades as ground forces. She carried only enough fuel for a one-way journey, and was manned by a skeleton crew of 3,000.

Mitsura Yoshida, a Japanese lawyer graduated from Imperial University, had been drafted by the Japanese to work as a junior radar officer aboard the *Yamato*. He stood on the open bridge between the admiral and the captain, amongst twenty or so other sailors, briefing messages from all parts of the ship. He saw the chart of the American landing beach spread out on a table with a wide, forty-kilometer arc outspread from a central point on the beachhead where the *Yamato* was to run aground. The arc represented the maximum reach of *Yamato*'s largest guns and the area that she could control with them.

The *Yamato* was Ugaki's first major command. He dreaded her destruction, yet he had no aircraft left to protect her. What remained was more than 150 antiaircraft machine guns and dozens of antiaircraft cannon, in addition to her titanic anti-ship main and secondary battery. She was also heavily protected by the many antiaircraft guns aboard her screening destroyers and the light cruiser *Yahagi*. Moreover, the Japanese gunners were familiar with the flying characteristics of the Avenger and thus knew where to aim and how far ahead to lead the torpedo bombers.

Admiral Mitscher believed that sinking the *Yamato* would destroy the Japanese navy and prove once and for all that the future of the American Navy lay in airpower.

Turnbull and the other pilots of Air Group 84's torpedo squadron (VT-84) knew that the *Yamato* could only be sunk by torpedoes. Each knew when they awakened Saturday morning that some of their friends would not be alive by nightfall.

Dark clouds, heavy wind, and rain descended around the *Bunker Hill* just before takeoff. The weather deteriorated so much that the torpedo bombers flew at 1,100 feet nearly the full 250 miles to the *Yamato*. So many attack aircraft flew alongside the bombers that it seemed to Gelderman the fast carrier squadrons darkened the skies.

The Task Force 58 squadrons used a classic attack plan. Fighters came in first, firing all of their .50-caliber guns, trying to get the AA gunners on the *Yamato* to duck long enough for the dive-bombers to drop their ordnance. Their explosives could not penetrate the deck, but direct hits would knock out some AA weapons, and sow massive confusion.

The attackers from the *Bunker Hill*'s torpedo squadron determined to strike the *Yamato* at precisely the same moment, with each of the fourteen planes assigned to a specific 25-degree section of a 360-degree circle around the ship. If all the planes dropped a single torpedo at the same time from various slices around the target, then no matter how the *Yamato* turned, she would remain broadside to at least several torpedoes. Their hope was that these would slow her down enough that aerial bombers and further torpedo missions could finish her off. Theoretically, the *Yamato* could not escape.

Dick Walsh, from Phoenix, Arizona, sat in the back of the ready room. He and Turnbull had graduated together from flight school at Corpus Christi where they received their commissions and had flown together many times as cadets. Walsh was to be Turnbull's wingman when they flew against the *Yamato*. But Turnbull found Walsh sitting in one of the big lounge chairs in the back of the ready room, smoking a cigarette, with a terrible, solemn look on his face as though he was sick. Turnbull asked him what was the matter.

"Bull," Walsh said, as he leaned forward. "I am not going to make it back from this strike. I got that feeling."

Turnbull knew what Walsh was talking about. Turnbull had felt that same gut-wrenching sickness before a few bad missions and he tried to give Walsh some confidence: "Look at the board. I'm flying your section. I am your leader, and I am coming back. You hang in there with me, and I'll get you back, Dick."

Walsh said he knew that he would lead them well and that Turnbull would make it back, but he was certain that he himself would not.

A few moments later the intercom speakers in the ready room and throughout the *Bunker Hill* blared, "Pilots, man your planes!" Turnbull and the others hustled up the gangways and out to the decks into their waiting torpedo bombers, Corsairs, and dive-bombers.

The Corsairs in Beads Popp's fighter group each were assigned a particular torpedo bomber to escort in for the final attack. Popp was assigned to protect Dick Walsh. Dewey Ray could not get his wheels up after he took off. The increased drag made it likely that he would not have enough fuel for the return trip from the *Yamato*. The *Bunker Hill* radioed him that he could return. Dewey Ray knew that, broken, less maneuverable, and slower, his Avenger would be the easiest target in the squadron. Yet he determined to continue his attack.

They flew through choppy near-absolute overcast for a couple of hours until, using the primitive onboard radar, George Gelderman sighted the *Yamato* at 12:32 P.M. The giant battleship was still 200 miles from Okinawa.

Commander Swanson ordered the TBF pilots to drop below the last remaining cloud cover to prepare for the attack. A few moments later, he ordered the attack squadron to break up into the planned smaller formations of two or three planes each. Turnbull peeled off with his two wingmen, together covering 75 degrees of the *Yamato*'s port side aft. They broke out of the clouds low just above the water, skimming at the *Yamato* directly amidships. Turnbull dropped a little behind to her port quarter to take up his assigned attack position just as the *Yamato* executed a hard turn to port. Chandler Swanson led the squadron. The *Yamato* was cornered. By the time Turnbull dropped the torpedo he was almost dead abeam her port side. As they closed in on the massive ship, antiaircraft fire lit up the sky like a fireworks display. Every enemy ship was winking at them, their AA guns flashing white as the antiaircraft fire hurled upward. Turnbull flew in from north to south lined up on the *Yamato* flying only sixty feet above the wrinkled sea, traveling at 180 knots. Gelderman stopped praying long enough to look into his radar scope and announce their distance to the target through the ship's intercom to Turnbull. Turnbull, who was watching their altimeter and waiting for the precise moment of optimal range to release the torpedo, juked the plane back and forth wildly, trying to avoid AA fire.

The enemy knew that the Avenger would have to be traveling at 200 knots when it dropped the torpedo and that it would be flying within range, straight and level, at an altitude of fifty to 100 feet, an easy target. Every gun in that fleet would be trained on the Avengers. Perhaps the easiest plane in the world to hit was one flying straight and level at 100 feet.

Melvin Francis "Guts" Guttenberg's aircraft dropped in toward the *Yamato*'s starboard side forward, almost precisely opposite Turnbull, who was port side aft. In sync, they dropped low to release their fish. Tracer rounds tore past them on all sides. Guttenberg dropped the torpedo. As the plane jerked upward, a large shell tore through his starboard side. The shell entered his Avenger just above the hatch door at precisely the spot where Kelly, the radioman, had hung his parachute against the bulkhead. The hatch door disintegrated. Shrapnel tore into the fuselage. The shorn metal fragments ripped through Kelly's right arm, tore into his back, and across his right shoulder. The high-pressure hydraulic line beside him ignited, spewing burning oil around the cabin, like a child's water hose gone loose. The concussion knocked Duffy, the gunner, seated just above the hatch, unconscious. He began to slide out of the broken hatch, as the interior of the aircraft burned.

Burning oil seared Kelly's good arm as he reached across the cabin to grab hold of the spewing hose. He held the hydraulic line with his left arm extended through the flames, then stretched his right hand down to Duffy's shoulders, trying to hold his buddy from sinking out of the turret hatch. Duffy regained consciousness after a few minutes, and they put their section of the fuselage in order. The parachute had absorbed the brunt of bomb fragments, and saved them.

As Guttenberg and his crew struggled to maintain control of their aircraft, Turnbull slid his thumb over the small red "Fire" button on the top of his joystick, listening intently but with calm to Gelderman's distance pronouncements. Turnbull had practiced this run over and over since he had first signed up for the Navy after the Japanese bombed Pearl Harbor. It was not so much that he knew what to do. It had become automatic. His biggest concern was opening up the bomb bay doors. The antiaircraft fire was severe, from every kind of antiaircraft weapon the Japanese possessed, and Turnbull did not want to open the doors until the last possible moment. The increased drag from the twenty-five-foot-long doors made the Avenger feel as though it had stopped in the air, like running into a brick wall, then slogging through Jell-O.

As they came in closer, Clint "Mouse" Webster's plane was slammed by AA. So was Phil Wainright's. Webster's crew kicked out their side door to get ready to ditch. Buck Berry got hit in the starboard wing, and the explosion nearly knocked the plane on its back, but he recovered, and kept the TBF flying.

The *Yamato* appeared to be throwing their largest 18-inch shells at the Avengers point-blank as the TBF squadron stormed in for the final run. The *Yamato* gunners may have realized that the chance of striking a plane with one of the giant shells was unlikely. Instead, Beads Popp figured the Japanese gunners were firing the weapons into the sea in front of the onrushing TBFs, sending up huge buffers of water in hopes of disrupting their flight.

When they reached 1,300 yards off her port side, almost amidships, Turnbull straightened out his plane for the briefest moment possible. He opened the bomb bay doors, jamming the plane to a hard stop. Just as he was about to press the red "Fire" button he felt an explosion to his right, and looked out to see a ball of fire where Dick Walsh's plane had been. Walsh took a direct hit in the belly before he could release his torpedo. Everything exploded. Turnbull had lost one of his closest friends. But he straightened out for a moment, and pressed the red button. Turnbull dropped the fish in range and on target. The plane, freed of the 2,000-pound torpedo, jerked upward and Turnbull immediately pulled hard on the lever, manually closing the bomb bay doors so they could get out of there as quickly as possible. Then he threw the stick over, juking the TBF back onto a zag as he continued to head directly toward the *Yamato*.

Mitsura Yoshida, aboard the *Yamato*, was amazed: "These enemy planes managed to maintain [their] vulnerable position for only the briefest interval and then immediately shifted to zigzag flying." In agreement, the *Yamato*'s chief of staff remarked, "Judging from their skill and bravery, these must be the enemy's finest pilots!"

A bomb struck the *Yamato*'s radar room, and Yoshida was sent to make a damage assessment. Heavy steel walls protected the radar room, so Yoshida was hopeful. But when he arrived, he found the reinforced room split in two by a direct hit. All of the equipment was shattered beyond recognition. "A human torso was blown against one bulkhead and other fragments were scattered here and there. But these were all that was left of eight human beings!"

Gelderman, passing above the bow of the *Yamato*, could see the guns firing up at them and the sailors running across her decks. Jack Weincek sat at the stinger gun in the tail, firing .30-caliber bullets when the TBF turned, giving him an angle on the ship.

Yoshida noted: "This was most disconcerting for our gunners whose peaceful firing practice against sham targets had been quite different. Here were incessant explosions, blinding flashes of light, thunderous noises, and crushing weights of blast pressure."

Gelderman flew so close to the *Yamato*'s antiaircraft guns that he could see individual gunners firing up at him and he thought for a moment back to a hunting trip with his good friend Nick Roorda from Duvall, Washington. They had gone out into the fields behind Nick's dairy farm and scared up a lone mallard. The two young men opened up on that solitary duck with both barrels. Somehow the duck escaped the pasture fields and their weapons without a scratch. Gelderman figured he now knew how that duck felt.

His torpedo away, Turnbull banked wide and took a straight line back toward the *Bunker Hill*. He flew the Avenger over a Japanese destroyer on the way back and Weincek strafed it, watching, gratified, as crewmen topside hit the deck.

Recalling that afternoon, Yoshida wrote: "As though the very breath of the hostile planes were being puffed against us, the misty smoke of the explosions, the roar of the bursting shells, and the pillars of flashing flames all converged against the bridge windows with terrific force."

Half of the men on the bridge of the *Yamato* lay dead or dying. The ship began to list from the weight of water sloshing in through the holes made by the torpedoes of VT-84. The captain ordered the engine and boiler rooms flooded immediately. There was no time to warn the men working inside. They were incinerated by the steam of saltwater contacting the superheated boilers, or drowned when their stations finally filled. But, Yoshida wrote, "The sacrifice of the engine room personnel scarcely affected the ship's list."

Yamato's own magazines finally detonated, causing an explosion that could be seen on Kyushu.

A direct hit from a dive-bomber destroyed the dispensary, killing all the wounded and medical personnel aboard the *Yamato*. Her list increased to 80 degrees and her rudders were either jammed or their control rooms flooded so that she had lost all control and was stuck turning in a clockwise death-throe.

Finally, the *Yamato*'s own shells, shifted by her steep heel and shaken loose by reverberations, fell asunder inside her armories and began to detonate. She rolled over to port, her magazines exploding as she sank. A mushroom cloud rose thousands of feet into the air and could be seen in far-off Kagoshima on Kyushu. Fewer than 300 Japanese survived. Another 1,000 died aboard the light cruiser *Yahagi* and the sunken and damaged escort destroyers.

Task Force 58 had prevailed mightily. The world's deadliest battleship had been sunk. Nearly 300 Task Force 58 planes had attacked the ship, which was probably hit by fewer than a dozen torpedoes and ten bombs before detonation of her own magazines ultimately sank her. The devastated IJN never again sortied against the United States.

The TBFs headed back to the *Bunker Hill*, for the most part out of formation, feeling their way through near zero visibility. Caleb Kendall took his fighter down low, just above the waves, then opened up his cockpit and let the rain wash over him, grateful to be alive. Mouse Webster, with an open hatch, and Dewey Ray with his wheels down, were running dangerously low on fuel as they dragged their way home.

Ray set his throttle to 5,200 RPMs and hummed Count Basie's "One O'Clock Jump," whose beat syncopated perfectly with the Avenger's pistons and push rods. He tore out his radio and all of his radar gear, as well as everything else he could dislodge from the TBF, and pitched it all into the sea to lighten the load, and then he fired off every round of ammunition he had.

Normally each returning plane is required to enter a landing pattern and fly one circle around their ship before landing, but Webster and Ray came straight in. Their last turn had been at the *Yamato*. Mouse's engine conked out on the arresting wire. Ray landed, but his engines ran out of fuel before completing his taxi.

Guts Guttenberg, flying in with his injured crewmen, had to wait for all of the other aircraft to land so that he would not muck up the flight deck with his damaged craft. The men aboard ship gathered around when his plane taxied up. The radioman's compartment looked like a salt shaker. Later they counted more than 300 holes. The sailors were shocked to see Kelly step from the plane. No one thought it possible that anyone could be alive in the passenger compartments. The tunnel and greenhouse looked like a sieve. Guttenberg was credited with a torpedo hit on the *Yamato*.

VT-84's assault was the last great aerial torpedo attack of the war and the most successful. The *Bunker Hill* torpedo squadron was credited with nine torpedo hits on the *Yamato*, most on the port side. The attack on the *Yamato* probably marks the last time that torpedo bombers will be used in warfare.

Mitscher's planes had sunk the most powerful battleship in the world, along with an escorting cruiser and four destroyers. Two other damaged Japanese destroyers were later scuttled. Ten American planes were lost and twelve air crewmen died.

The Imperial Japanese Navy only three years before had commanded the entire Western Pacific, from parts of Alaska down to northern Australia and eastward nearly to Midway. Now, the Japanese fleet no longer existed.* Three thousand six hundred sixty-five Japanese were killed in the *Yamato* operation, perhaps more than all of the kamikazes in the battle for Okinawa. Vice Admiral Seiichi Ito and the *Yamato*'s commander, Kosaku Aruga, chose to drown with the crew. Admiral Toyoda ordered Aruga to receive a two-grade promotion—traditionally given to kamikaze pilots posthumously. Aruga became a vice admiral the moment he died.

The attack on the *Yamato* snapped Turnbull out of the depression he had been suffering. Americans on the ground in Okinawa continued slogging against the determined Japanese defenders, and the kamikaze pilots on Okinawa continued their *Kikusui* campaign against the carriers.

---

* The loss of the *Yamato* is considered by most historians to be "the end of the Japanese Imperial Navy." Ronald Spector points out in his book *Eagle Against the Sun* that a handful of cruisers, destroyers, battleships, and carriers of the Imperial Navy remained at the surrender, but they had no fuel and were incapable of offensive action. These last hulks were merely targets for Allied bombing.

The Army Air Force's B-29s were utilized largely to carpet-bomb Japanese cities and military-industrial targets. They could have been better deployed bombing strategic transportation hubs and the airfields used to launch the kamikazes that were devastating U.S. naval forces around Okinawa. But Army General Curtis LeMay could not be swayed. The Navy bore the brunt of that Army decision.

Most of the kamikazes probably realized by the time they sortied that it was unlikely that their families would ever receive their belongings. Most Japanese thought that if some part of their lost loved ones was returned for burial in their local cemetery, the soul of the departed would find rest, tended by their descendants. Many of the student kamikazes, having seen so much death, wrote at the time how silly they thought these "old beliefs" were. Many of the young kamikazes wrote home, trying to soothe their parents. One university student turned kamikaze pilot, raised as a Christian, wrote to his mother just before his sortie:

I will keep your picture in my bosom on the sortie, mother, and also the photo of Makio-san. Victory will be with us. Our sortie will deliver a coup de grace to the enemy. I am very happy. We live in the spirit of Jesus Christ, and we die in that spirit. This thought has stayed with me. It is gratifying to live in this world, but living has a spirit of futility about it now. It is time to die. I do not seek reasons for dying. My only search is for an enemy target against which to dive.

—*May 11, 1945*

Another wrote:

Dear Parents:

Please congratulate me. I have been given a splendid opportunity to die. This is my last day. The destiny of our homeland hinges on the decisive battle in the seas to the south where I shall fall like a blossom from a radiant cherry tree. How I appreciate this chance to die like a

*man. Think well of me and know that I so died for our country. May
my death be as sudden and clean as the shattering of crystal.*

> *Written at Miyazaki on the day of my sortie,*
> Isao

Often, the kamikazes carried one or two personal items on their
last trip. Yasuo Ishijima brought a French-English dictionary, a symbol of his desire to learn and improve himself. Ryuji Nagatsuka carried
a Japanese translation of French philosophy. He noted one French-
man's observation that "resignation is our daily suicide."

In the days following the *Yamato* debacle, *tokko* pilots could not take
off because of heavy rains. Ugaki was frustrated that they could not come
up with a way to fly in rain and low visibility conditions. It was doubly
irksome that American carrier-based aircraft continued to bomb and
strafe Kanoya in the bad weather. The news from Japan's ally in Europe
was even worse. Germany's western front had been deeply penetrated.
And then the Russians abrogated the Russo-Japanese neutrality pact.

American planners canceled all offensive missions and prepared for
another huge *Kikusui* assault on April 12 and 13. They de-gassed and
de-bombed all non-CAP aircraft. Mitscher then launched perhaps the
largest CAP of the war, with twenty-four planes flying above each task
group and another dozen cruising above the radar control destroyer
squadron stationed twenty-five miles out toward the Kyushu kamikaze launching fields. He sent twenty-four more carrier fighters over
Okinawa to support U.S. Marine Corps ground-based fighters there,
plus an additional twenty-four Corsairs to orbit Kikaigashima and
Amamioshima, 100 miles north of the task force.* Nevertheless, these

---

* Burke and Mitscher reasoned (correctly) that the kamikazes were using Kikaigashima and Amamioshima as navigational beacons to find their way to the task
force. They ordered the intercept squadrons to remain above these islands at
staggered altitudes, circling to prevent any flights from getting through without being challenged. If the first CAP line was engaged, the task force could still
launch more planes before the enemy arrived.

hundreds of fighter aircraft, assisted by radar and the thousands of AA guns in the fleet, were not enough to stop poorly trained pilots determined to die.

The task group had moved into antiaircraft formation so that their guns had interlocking fields of fire, providing the maximum amount of protection to every ship in the fleet. The antiaircraft fire of all the ships was coordinated for the first time through a single antiaircraft fire coordinator aboard the *Bunker Hill*.

The Japanese *Kikusui* planes came in about 1:30 P.M. They used every measure to harass and attack the American fleet. They made feinting attacks. They dove out of the sun and dropped window, and they came in very high, gliding along the radar voids or low, just above the waves. Eleven planes in the first wave penetrated the fighter sweeps but all were shot down by the task group. The *Bunker Hill*'s 5-inch gunners were particularly effective. Still, eight of these first kamikazes crashed within 100 yards of various of the big carriers. The assaults continued throughout the day, and by evening twenty-nine suicide planes had been shot down by the task force.

The *Enterprise* was near-missed four times. Debris from crashing planes raked her decks. Her aircraft caught fire. Though not hit, she suffered damage that took her out of the war for nearly a month. The *Essex* lost her radar; her forward fuel tank was pierced. The destroyer USS *Kidd* suffered a direct hit with thirty-eight killed. Three other destroyers were forced out of the war zone for repairs.

The *Kikusui* continued the following day. The Big E (*Enterprise*), the *Essex*, and the *Bataan* each had two close calls with kamikazes that were shot down just before striking the carriers. Fourteen ships were hit, and a destroyer was sunk by an Ohka missile. Kamikazes attacked the *Bunker Hill* numerous times.

Turnbull and the other pilots who were not flying that day spent most of it in the wardroom listening to the antiaircraft guns and tracking the enemy's proximity by the change in the type of guns firing at the kamikazes. On two occasions all of her guns opened up; two kamikazes were shot down within 150 yards of the ship. That night, Turnbull climbed to the deck and watched an American ship burn. No one aboard the *Bunker Hill* was sure which one it was.

The Bunker Hill *narrowly escapes a strike.*

Admiral Ugaki determined after the first *Kikusui* that "most of the enemy carriers had been crashed." He could not understand how it still appeared that the Americans had so many and decided that a great part must have been decoys. He still could not conceive of the size and scope of the American fleet. The trees around Kanoya had become vividly green and the wheat was getting tall.

Ugaki's diary painfully reveals a thoughtful man out of time, being torn asunder. He is at once deluded and intensely practical. It is easy to revile the stoic admiral for devotedly leading thousands of youths to needless suicide. Yet Ugaki was raised a *samurai*. His *Bushido* mores required him to follow all military orders and to sacrifice his own life. But his diary reveals a man uncontestably distraught at the squandering of so many young lives. Near the end, he ceases attempting to justify their deaths in military terms. Knowing Japan would lose, he rationalized the waste of the students' lives for the value of their example of selflessness, which, he told himself, would help sustain a hundred generations of Japanese after their defeat. Ugaki was certain that the personal sacrifice of the *tokko* pilots would always be remembered and honored. Following Japan's surrender, however, almost no one in Japan wished to discuss or even consider what came to be seen as the shame of sanctioned suicide.

That same evening, as Ugaki pondered his role and Japan's future, Turnbull and Lieutenant Bob Weir walked the flight deck at sunset, gazing out at the darkening horizon through field glasses. Turnbull sighted a twin-engine Japanese Frances bomber diving in to attack the *Sodak* (the USS *South Dakota*). One after another, the fleet opened up on the Frances, but the kamikaze drove its attack home. Antiaircraft fire ignited the plane, lighting the entire sky, but it pressed on toward the ship. Moments before impact, the bomber was struck hard and fell, exploding into the sea just aft of the *Sodak*'s stern. Two Corsairs parked aft of the *Bunker Hill*'s firing 5-inch guns were so damaged by the percussion that they were pushed overboard. A moment later, as the fleet zigged to starboard, another kamikaze came into view, but was quickly destroyed by an American night fighter.

Learning of President Roosevelt's death on Friday, the 13th of April, one kamikaze pilot at Kanoya wondered whether it would change the course of the war. Another countered: "Whatever happens, all of us will die in kamikaze attacks."

Admiral Ugaki, always a patrician, noted that the Japanese government should properly send a note of condolence on the death of President Roosevelt. The next morning, though, Ugaki continued the second *Kikusui*.

Despite the futility of their course, the Japanese were still able to put enormous pressure on the task force. Support strikes for infantry on the ground on Okinawa had to be canceled on April 16 while the CAP protected the fleet from Ugaki's third *Kikusui*. The Japanese attacks continued throughout that day and into the night. The USS *Intrepid* took a direct hit from a kamikaze that passed straight through her flight deck. She was forced to return to San Francisco for repairs and in effect was taken out of the war for good. Arleigh Burke said famously that the Navy was losing "a ship-and-a-half each day." Even America could not long survive those kinds of losses. The kamikazes had to be stopped. Navy brass convinced the Army Air Force to intervene and finally begin bombing the kamikaze bases. The following day B-29s from the 330th Bomber Group attacked Kanoya in six raids code-named "Checkbook." They dropped sixteen tons of high-explosive (HE) bombs, all around Ugaki's headquarters, and left the hangars burning. But the kamikaze raids did not slow.

16. KANOYA

Mei wo matsu, hei wa katarazu, kichi moyuru.
Soldiers who are waiting for orders did not say
anything, just watched their base burning.

—WRITTEN BY KENICHI WATANABE AT KANOYA
IN THE SPRING OF 1945. WATANABE WAS A
KAMIKAZE PILOT WHO TRAINED WITH
KIYOSHI AND LATER BECAME A
BUDDHIST MONK.

Just before Kiyoshi left for Kanoya, his friend Iwama gave him the poem he had written for Kiyoshi. It is actually a series of six short poems called *Tanka*. A thirty-one-syllable poem with the syllable pattern 5–7–5–7–7, *Tanka* are brief, and so rely on suggestive images to convey meaning. Iwama's language is archaic, though he maintains a powerful poetic sense:

Dedicated to my dear friend Ogawa, from Iwama

What an open-hearted man you are from Joushu!
I've been respecting you for that.
Now I am left behind.

Gazing upwards the dream is emptied
Violence boils in your stomach;
You are filled with flaming emotions but

You still smile
With an innocent face
Though you are down-hearted.

Iwama ended his writing by quoting Shouryou Yoshiue, a Japanese poet who lived from 1884 to 1958:

> *You, emperor's sons, did not depend on the time when divine*
>   *winds blow,*
> *you blew divine winds out of your souls.*

Emperor Hirohito assumed the name Showa when he succeeded to the throne. The students from Yatabe adopted his name for their kamikaze corps that flew from Kanoya.* Fifty-four students were transferred from Yatabe to Kanoya as *showa-tai*, including Kiyoshi Ogawa. Fourteen of these men survived the war. Seven are still alive.†

On April 7, 1945, the nineteen student-cadets of the first Yatabe group chosen for *tokko* missions were gathered together beside the airfield at Yatabe as the first *Kikusui* was commencing. Their *Hon-chou*, Hidakata, stood atop two wooden benches that had been placed side by side, and congratulated the young men on being chosen first for their mission. A long wooden table was carried to the tarmac, and covered with a white cloth. The commander of Yatabe airbase, wearing white gloves and his full dress uniform, stood at the center of the table. There were no chairs. Orderlies placed before each man a single small sake cup, filled with water instead of rice wine to symbolize the purity of sacrifice. Then the commander spoke for a few moments, explaining their mission as the other student-cadets, standing at attention, looked on from the side. Together, all of the men drank their cup, and then, together still, they boarded their Zero fighters, and flew to Kanoya where they were greeted by Admiral Ugaki. Most of these men were killed in the third *Kikusui* on April 15–16.

---

* Kiyoshi flew in the seventh Showa attack. *Nana* means "7," *tai* means "force," so Kiyoshi was a member of the *dai-nana-showa-tai*.

† I was able to speak with most of these survivors to gain an idea of what it must have been like for Kiyoshi at Yatabe. I also interviewed men from other kamikaze corps who were stationed at Kanoya and read accounts in the diary of Admiral Matome Ugaki, the commander of Kanoya, and the diaries and letters of students who had died in the *tokko* and in the Ohka corps.

Kiyoshi's flight training remained clandestinely surreal. Kiyoshi was there to learn to dogfight. Instead he learned to crash. Training resumed when he was chosen to be a *tokko* pilot, for only *tokko* training was deemed worthy of fuel consumption. He and all the kamikazes were given the new elite uniform of the *tokkotai*, which included a white scarf and *Kirin* insignia on his chest.

Tokko missions had become the principal aerial defense tactic, thus Kiyoshi and his fellow student-cadets never learned to fly combat. At Yatabe, Kiyoshi rode in the front seat of a modified Zero, with an instructor in the back, ready to take the controls if something went wrong. He taxied out, circled, and landed, over and over, but for at most one half hour a day. After less than ten hours, Kiyoshi soloed. Most of his comrades were barely competent fliers. They could take off and land but little else. Few could accomplish the demanding maneuvers required in dogfighting. Most would have trouble flying in formation. Probably none could navigate in bad weather.

The average kamikaze pilot had just two days to practice takeoffs. The next two days were spent on formation flying. And the last three days were used to practice approaching and striking a target.

Trainers developed crash methods based on the experiences of the first kamikazes in the Philippines. These first kamikaze pilots of the 201st developed, through trial and error, two proven methods of kamikaze attack. Each of the students at Yatabe was schooled in both. They would choose operationally which method they would use to end their life. The attack methods were designed to take advantage of weaknesses in American defenses, particularly radar coverage.

Kiyoshi flew to Kanoya on April 15, 1945. He had been served by the same ground crew for many months at Yatabe. The ground crews knew that the fighter each man flew from Yatabe to Kanoya would soon be their coffin. They prepared the aircraft specially, polishing and cleaning it thoroughly. The student cadets teared when they saw how much emotion the men had put into preparing their Zeros. The pilots took off a little before 7:40 A.M., on April 15, 1945, and circled up to 6,000 feet. It was Kiyoshi's last day to fly. He completed the drills quickly and then was allowed to take his plane across the skies above Tsuchiura, back and forth in all directions to his heart's content.

They landed again late in the morning, and at 1:00 P.M. lined up in front of the command post. His classmates had decorated his refuelled plane with cherry blossoms. Kiyoshi said goodbye to his friends, and they took a picture of him sitting on the wing of his Zero, smiling.

The departing students shared a *kanpai* (toast) and then ran to their planes at double-time. Kiyoshi's muffler fluttered in the wind as he took off with seven other students bound for death. They circled their base in formation. Kiyoshi looked down at the aerodrome that had become his hometown passing beneath him and knew that he would never see it again. They headed south over the little town of Tsuchiura and it receded quickly behind them. A series of decisions and events had led each of them to this place from which there now appeared to be no turning back. They passed by Mount Tsuchiura, then above Mount Ashigara. Some of the pilots threw cherry blossoms from the cockpit in offering as they passed by the sublime Mount Fuji. The group of *tokko* pilots continued west to land in Suzuka in the mid-afternoon, then flew on to Kanoya.

Prime Minister Kuniaki Koiso's cabinet resigned in mid-April. A new Japanese government was formed, now heavily dominated by the navy. Ugaki fought on, contemptuous of his colleagues, the sailor-politicians. He used his sardonic wit unsparingly in his diary: "The navy, now without ships, is going to fight at the critical time by forming a new cabinet . . . Ha! Ha!"

Kiyoshi arrived at Kanoya with forty-one new pilots flying in from various training bases near Tokyo. When their truck arrived at the hangar, the young men were ordered curtly to go to their sleeping quarters and prepare to die. They would sortie in the morning. American aircraft bombed Kanoya irregularly night and day. Bombers hit the base again a few hours after Kiyoshi landed. Kanoya and its men had deteriorated badly, both physically and psychically, under the month-long American onslaught. New recruits, no longer volunteers, were increasingly pained at their orders to die. Ugaki wrote that *tokko* pilots who remained long at the base were becoming "surly and disrespectful."

Kanoya had been hit the day Kiyoshi landed. B-29s from the 330th Bomber Group dropped nearly fifty tons of HE munitions. At first, the Japanese had been able to quickly repair torn runways. On this day, though, the runway lay unrepaired, pocked by bomb craters. American bombers had begun using random delays on some of the bombs, which might explode hours or even days after they were dropped, making repair work exceedingly difficult and dangerous.

One surviving kamikaze said that the Americans attacked Kanoya so often, and at such odd intervals, that no one there was ever safe. Kiyoshi likely saw his own friends killed by bombs and strafing raids.

One seasoned veteran of some of the harshest conditions in Rabaul and the Philippines said Kanoya was the most miserable base he had ever seen. While the first volunteer kamikazes in the Philippines were honored with sushi and rice wine, the young Japanese pilots at Kanoya ate the same spartan meals they had been served every day for years. The kamikaze sacrifice no longer merited celebration. Suicide had become banal. Many of the kamikazes departed for their final trip with a matter-of-factness that defied the comprehension of those around them. The morning of their mission came as grim relief to many pilots. They no longer had to wait in dreadful anticipation of their death.

The kamikazes at Kanoya were cut off from the outside world. Radios and newspapers, already heavily censored, were forbidden. Flight training throughout Japan was suspended often, and for long periods, because of lack of fuel; at Kanoya fuel existed for only one mission per plane. Kamikazes often departed on their final mission with their magazines half filled, as the base was running out of bullets.

Yet even at Kanoya there were students who, condemned like Kiyoshi, survived. The new arrivals were shocked to see six friends who had departed earlier. It was like looking at ghosts. Survival was accidental. Their friend Kitahara's plane was hit by a strafing F6F and exploded. The blast ignited five additional aircraft, so six *tokko* pilots were saved. Those six men were the last survivors of the first large group from Yatabe that had gone to Kanoya.

The pilots slept side by side on the floor of the abandoned Nozato grade school (earlier that year the resource-strapped Japanese had ended all public education). A bomb hole the size of a truck allowed light, wind, and rain to flood into their makeshift dormitory. The wind scattered cherry blossoms across the bodies of the pilots sleeping side by side, waiting for their turn to fly and die. Everything had been removed except for some desks and a few too narrow, recently arrived bamboo beds. One of the pilots had brought in flowers to decorate a desk—a rose, delicate oxalis, and a spray of Roger's bronze—which lent a touch of particularly Japanese loveliness to the graceless school. But even as they waited for death, they lived with it—the bones of two student pilots rested in one corner.

The young women of the *Seishintai* corps (teenage girls taken in 1945 from their farming families and drafted for clerical work) initially lived near the base with families. But American bombing quickly made above-ground locations too dangerous and they were moved into Admiral Ugaki's *Bakugo* (command center). The *Bakugo* was a fortress dug deep vertically and horizontally into the side of a hill. The men smoked inside, against regulations, fouling the dank, stale air. The young women slept on planks beneath coarse wool blankets and did not leave the base grounds until Japan surrendered. They answered phone calls from Japan's rudimentary radar stations and warned commanders of incoming American raids. But the primitive Japanese radar often mistook shadows for aircraft or missed the American planes altogether. Air raids sounded so frequently at Kanoya that they were widely ignored. Even the dedicated phone lines to the radar operators were often knocked out. Japanese commanders frequently could not speak to their counterparts on different islands. Every building above ground was badly holed, and often burned. Most had collapsed.

In the mornings when the *tokko* pilots were preparing for their missions, the girls of the *Seishintai* would sometimes come out and watch them. The girls would whisper "good luck" in low voices that did not carry, like a prayer. They were not supposed to know that the young pilots were flying suicide missions. But they all knew these young men would not return. The *tokko* pilots wore their rank insignia on their left arm and on the right a simple image of the sun, red but not rising. The pilots' uniforms, scarves, and helmets masked any emotion that may have betrayed them. The girls just watched them quietly, bowed, and left together.

That afternoon, April 16, 1945, eighty American assault aircraft bombed and strafed Kanoya for more than two hours. Although the Japanese received warning of their approach, the air raid siren was not sounded because the attendant did not know how to switch the circuit. Admiral Ugaki barely made it into his underground shelter in time. This was Kiyoshi's first full day at Kanoya. He and the other kamikaze pilots lay frozen for hours in ditches around the base. Admiral Ugaki launched more planes as soon as the American attackers departed, hoping to follow the carrier planes to their ships. Most of these *tokko* planes were shot down. It was the middle of Ugaki's third *Kikusui*. By the next day, he had sent 165 young pilots to die.

An inexperienced pilot taking off in a Betty bomber carrying a 500-pound bomb crashed on takeoff into the mulberry trees at the end of the runway. The bomb detonation was heard for miles around the base. The aircraft was completely destroyed. Other pilots ran along a trail of oil from the poorly maintained engine, leading directly down the runway to the smoldering wreckage. They picked up bits and pieces of the crew. The largest they could find was an ankle, and part of a spine with burnt flesh still clinging to it. Admiral Ugaki noted, "Night and day fighting combined with lack of sleep made us feel languid." He took a lonely walk carrying a stick, which he began speaking to.

Americans were shocked at the combination of ferocity and naïveté of this third *Kikusui*. The destroyer USS *Laffey* was attacked twenty-two times in eighty minutes, strafed, hit by six kamikazes and four bombs. But she did not sink.

Kanoya was struck again that same afternoon by B-29s and B-25s. Army P-51 Mustangs also attacked that day. Ugaki determined sadly that the short-range Mustangs must have come from Iwo Jima. They returned nearly every day and the demoralized Japanese base had no effective defense against the Superfortresses.

On April 18, 100 B-29s bombed Kanoya and other kamikaze bases, dropping 33.6 tons of HE munitions. Most of the remaining Ohka

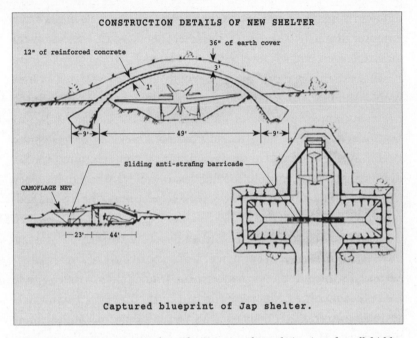

CONSTRUCTION DETAILS OF NEW SHELTER

36" of earth cover

12" of reinforced concrete

3'

1'

←9'→ 49' ←9'→

Sliding anti-strafing barricade

CAMOFLAGE NET

|—23'—|—44'—|

Captured blueprint of Jap shelter.

Japanese revetments at Kyushu. The Japanese kept their aircraft well hidden in caves and jungle hideaways. Planes awaiting takeoff were stored in individual reinforced revetments—low-slung, with narrow fitted openings that neatly matched the wings of the Zero. The openings faced different directions, so the Corsairs would have to come in single file, one revetment at a time. By the second attack the Japanese gunners would have them dialed in. It was almost impossible to avoid being hit. Joe Brocia lost his wingman at Kyushu. Thirty Japanese planes jumped his four-plane squad. Half of his Marine division flying that day were killed fighting over Kyushu. A couple of these shaped revetments survived the war, and remain, overgrown with sawgrass on the edge of the runway at Kanoya.

pilots were transferred away from Kanoya a few days later to safer ground. Kiyoshi Ogawa was left behind in the barracks at the now nearly empty Nozato school. Red flags flew throughout the base, marking the locations of unexploded bombs, which detonated periodically. The explosions kept everyone edgy. Aircraft that could not be salvaged were left out as decoys. The remaining operational aircraft were hidden in secret earthen caves dug into the hillsides at the edge of the base, far from the runways.

There were no large targets left for the bombers at Kanoya and it became unsafe even to sleep at the Nozato school. The pilots and other personnel eventually carried their blankets and mats into the dank hillside caves and slept in the dirt beneath the wings of the aircraft. The *Seishintai* girls would see them ambling, dirty, out of their sleep holes in the morning, taking walks by the little stream that still wends its way through the base.

Ugaki learned that Hitler had issued an order for every man to "defend their positions to the last." He knew that when such orders were given, an army would soon be destroyed. He wrote in his diary, "Sad indeed." Then Ugaki made himself "a whip and a fishing rod" and took some time off.

The next day, April 19, more than 219 B-29s bombed naval airbases across Kyushu. The shooting season ended that day and Admiral Ugaki turned in his hunting license. He wrote that hunting would be one of the nicest memories he had in this world. And added, "I don't know whether I will be alive when the shooting season comes again in the fall."

17. THE REAL THING

Men acquainted with the battlefield will not be among the numbers that glibly talk of another war.
— GENERAL DWIGHT D. EISENHOWER,
CHICAGO, JUNE 1946

Okinawa was the bloodiest battle by far of the Pacific war. More than twice as many Americans died there as at Guadalcanal and Iwo Jima combined. The battle seemed to begin well because the Japanese commander, General Ushijima, did not oppose the American landings. Ushijima gave up his two airfields and most of the northern portion of the island almost without a fight. Instead he concentrated virtually all of his forces in concentric lines of defense around an ancient fortress, Shuri Castle. Ushijima's large guns were protected in a series of natural and artificial caves, where he also preserved a large store of food and ammunition. The Americans determined to take the Shuri defenses by frontal assault. General John Hodge, commanding the Army's 24th Corps, said, "There are 65 to 70,000 fighting Japs holed up in the south end of the island, and I see no way to get them out except to blast them out, yard by yard."

In every other island fight during the Central Pacific drive, the fast carriers had been able to neutralize Japan's available air defenses before the invasion force landed. After the initial air battles, the carriers could operate with near-impunity, far beyond range of Japan's ships and aircraft. But on Kyushu, Japan maintained dozens of airstrips within range of American troops on Okinawa. Carrier aircraft were the only source of available air support for Americans on Okinawa for much of that battle. The carriers had to remain within range of Okinawa in order to support American troops fighting there, which meant that for the first time in the war, American carriers faced constant attack by land-based Japanese aircraft. Okinawa degenerated into a battle of attrition. Day after day, the pilots, aircrews, officers, sailors, and marines performed astonishing acts, which became routine during Okinawa.

On the *Bunker Hill*, Seaman Patrick King and the others in the Engineering Department were isolated four decks below where the fighting was taking place, and rarely saw it firsthand. Everyone made fun of the engineers because they were always so pale. Sailors topside glowed with healthy tans, but King had stood so long in the ship's dungeon that the Pacific sun pricked his skin like needles. By May, he was avoiding the deck entirely. The engineers had learned to understand what was happening on the decks above by recognizing the patterns of fire from the *Bunker Hill*'s guns.

When Japanese aircraft were sighted on the radar, the men in Engineering were called to their GQ stations. Most of the time the enemy aircraft never made it close to the ship, and after an hour or so the *Bunker Hill* would return to a standard readiness level. Usually, that was the end of it. But when the dozen 5-inch guns on the deck opened up, shaking the whole ship, the men in the engine rooms took notice. Still, they were not too concerned. They knew the 5-inchers fired at a screen at least three miles away from the ship. The enemy planes often either backed off or were shot down.

But when the 40mm guns opened up it meant the Japanese were making a concerted attack and had penetrated to within a mile and a half of the ship. A Zero could cover that distance in fifteen seconds. The last guns to begin firing were the 20mm machine cannons. When they opened up, everyone was scared. It meant that a Zero was only 1,000 yards out, and less than ten seconds away from striking the ship. Every gun on the vessel, hundreds of barrels, would then be blazing away, firing thousands of rounds per minute that shook the ship as the attacker launched forward toward them.

Fred Briggs flew a Marine Corsair off the *Bunker Hill*. Briggs had made only one carrier landing before the *Bunker Hill* sortied from California. His second landing was in the war zone. His third was returning from Tokyo.

Briggs's Corsair was badly torn up on a mission to Okinawa. He lost his starboard landing gear and all hydraulic pressure. He lost his flaps. His ailerons were completely out, and his tail hook had been blown away. He could barely control the direction she was flying. Briggs was ordered to bail out. Jim Swett, his wingman, was ordered to land, but feigned radio problems so he could stay with his mate. As Briggs parachuted safely into the ocean, Swett and his fellows circled, crushing their dye markers so as to paint the ocean around him.* Strong winds, though, blew their pulverized dye particles well beyond Briggs. Every man on the rescue destroyer stood on the deck staring in the wrong direction, looking for Briggs in the center of the other pilot's dye markers. He shouted and splashed as hard as he could as the 300-foot warship bore straight down on him.

Briggs, wearing his giant awkward life jacket, could not swim out of the way and it was too late to take it off. The shadow of the destroyer's bows passed over his head, and he quickly rolled onto his back. The ship's bow wave lifted him up briefly, and he fell against the ship's side. Briggs pulled his flight shoes up in time to brace them against the slick sides of the destroyer's hull. He pushed off as hard as he could, but was sucked right back against it. He began running along the hull—his back in the water, and his legs doing the fastest sidestep he had ever made. He marked the ship's passage

---

* The solid dye marker was a remarkable chemical invention, and a great aid in finding downed pilots. Each pilot was given two, attached to either side of their life jacket. Briggs made a small tear in the packages one at a time. As the seawater began washing in, it dissolved the solid, and a bright trail, about as wide as a pencil, began to trickle out. At first he thought no one would ever see it. But as it seeped away from him, it began to spread out. The dye could leave a trail more than two miles long, and hundreds of yards wide. It would lead a destroyer or search aircraft right to a pilot.

watching the forward torpedo tubes, then the top of the super-structure, then the aft torpedo tubes pass by. He knew the propellers were next.

The destroyer crew had deployed a cargo net over the side so they could pull up Briggs when they found him. He glanced aft and saw the netting dragging swiftly through the water. As it passed by, he flipped his legs down and jerked his arm through the netting to his elbow. The rough hemp ropes ripped him forward through the water. It felt as though his arm were going to tear out of his shoulder. He turned his head and got his mouth above the wake his own body was making, then raised his left arm and put it through another gap in the net, a little higher. Pull by pull, he climbed the net, then fell exhausted over the gunwale. Briggs lay on the destroyer's deck, unable to move, for several minutes before someone finally noticed him.

The next day, Briggs returned to the *Bunker Hill* and flew another mission.

The *Bunker Hill* had to turn into the wind before aircraft could land. This often meant that all of her escorts also had to turn into the wind, which meant that the entire fleet had to turn into the wind. To land just one solitary plane, 100 vessels might have to alter course. If they suspected a submarine nearby, they could not risk turning the fleet for the sake of a single pilot, so the flier had to keep his plane aloft—or crash.

Marine pilot Joe Brocia's engine broke down early on a mission, and he requested permission for an emergency landing. The controllers asked him how long he could stay in the air. Brocia figured twenty minutes, but he was wrong. When he lost his engine, it was too late, and he had to ditch in the Pacific.

It was not that hard to skid a Corsair upright into the ocean. Getting out was the trouble. The thrust of impact often jammed the canopy hatches shut. Several times Brocia listened helplessly to crashed squadron mates trapped in sinking Corsairs. The frantic pilots talked to him over their radios, saying goodbye as they worked to break out.

Brocia hit the ocean hard. The Corsair stopped short and immediately began to fill with water. He slid open the hatch, relieved, and floated gently out of the plane as it sank beneath him. A destroyer picked him up a few minutes later.

When Marines were pinned down by Japanese gunfire forward observers called the communications officers at their HQ, who called out to CIC on the *Bunker Hill,* which relayed the message to the CIC on an assigned carrier, which then sent the message out to aircraft that

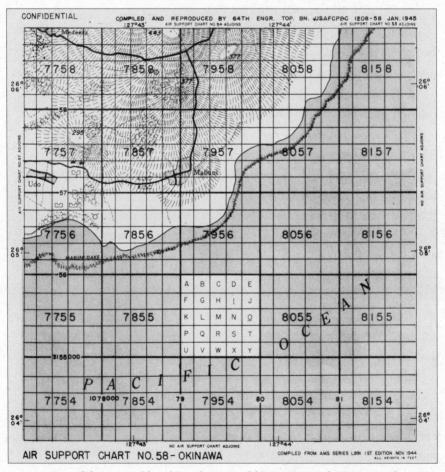

One of the sectored bombing charts used by Joe Brocia during ground support missions to Okinawa.

were hopefully nearby. But the naval aircraft rarely arrived in time to help. The system was revamped during Okinawa. The island was broken up into numbered squares like an AAA map. Each of those numbered squares was further broken into letters. Elevations showing ridgelines were clearly penned in navy blue. This way, close air support was greatly simplified. Men on the ground could communicate with pilots almost as though they were in the same platoon working together to take a ridge. Forward observers were chosen from men who had some air experience, and grasped some of the challenges a combat pilot faced. They were given special communications equipment that enabled direct communications with strike leaders in the air. The observer on the ground was given a sectored chart, identical to the attacking pilot's chart.

The fighters so dominated the air that they could usually come in first and make a dummy run so as to better determine the enemy's location. Armed with overlapping coordinates, the forward observer would then tell them to try it again, fifty yards to the right, say. The pilots then would circle around and make a firing run, usually with napalm.

The Navy seemed always to be testing out new ordnance. They changed the Corsair's guns, added extra fuel tanks, attached JATO bottles, and fastened all sorts of bomb racks to the fuselage and wings. Napalm perhaps was the deadliest. The Marines used it from the *Bunker Hill* for the first time on Love-Day,* at Okinawa.

That day, when the air assault was launched, Beads Popp was circling the *Bunker Hill*, watching curiously. The first Corsair, piloted by Lieutenant Rik Marble from VMF-451, launched and fell immediately into the sea. The *Bunker Hill* rolled over it. There was no time for the pilot to escape. The second plane, piloted by Captain M. L. Parks from VMF-221, also fell straight into the sea and beneath the *Bunker Hill*. The pilot disappeared. Admiral Mitscher stopped the launch.

---

* The day of any landing assault is normally called D-Day. But the name became so heavily associated with the Normandy landings that the Army and Navy decided to call the Okinawa landings, which occurred on Easter Sunday (and April Fool's Day), 1945, "Love-Day."

A Corsair attempting to launch on Love-Day—Okinawa. The fighter planes were outfitted with new napalm canisters that wrecked their aerodynamics. The first two crashed just ahead of the carrier, which drove over them before the pilots could escape.

The VF-84 chief, George Mallard, examined the aircraft. Guidance fins on the M-69 bomb, which had been newly installed on the Corsairs, hung out under the wing, corrupting the airflow. Mallard told the third pilot to decrease his flaps to 20 degrees from 50. They were all pretty sure the Corsair could not take off with so little flap. The next Corsair pilot knew that no one was sure. But he followed orders and launched. It worked. Eventually, it was determined that the cluster bombs were being dropped from such a low altitude that the fins did not really make much difference and they were removed.

Every combat air patrol was different. Generally, they would fly up to 15,000 or 20,000 feet, then circle the task group about thirty miles from the carriers at its center. If bogies were sighted, the CAP could be vectored out 100 miles or more to meet them. Most of the time they were not more than sixty miles from their carrier.

The Japanese would often try to follow the American planes back to the carriers. These followers could hide in the radar shadows created by the American planes, and use them as a guide to the fleet. The CAPs were supposed to make a 360 degree turn before returning to their carriers. The turn would bring the returning CAP back on the tails of anyone who was following them in. But often the patrol was not called back until they were low on fuel, without time to add an extra turn. Then the kamikazes could follow straight in.

The Navy developed an additional mechanism to guard against enemy intrusion.

The fast carriers in 1945 regularly launched raids of hundreds of aircraft of various types. Japanese kamikazes often followed home the returning raiders. In order to defend themselves without destroying their own air arms, the carriers had to differentiate enemy aircraft on their radar screens. But every radar contact looked the same. If radar operators were unsure, they marked the signal as a bogie. Bogies, whether friend or foe, often were fired on by the fleet. Allied engineers developed a radio frequency identification device called IFF—Identification Friend or Foe—to solve this problem.

Both sides in World War II tried to create methods of telling their own aircraft from the enemy. The Germans were the first to create an effective system. Allied forces fighting over Germany noticed that German fighters flying in formation would sometimes attempt simultaneous barrel rolls for no apparent reason. Eventually the British intercepted a ground radio signal that immediately preceded these maneuvers. The Allies realized that just before going into battle above German AA guns, the German aircraft, on a signal from German radar operators, altered their return profile for a moment by barrel rolling, in order to be tagged as friend through the battle.

The Allies quickly completed development of a more sophisticated system of identification based on the same mode. A carrier or ground station would send a query signal to all radar-identified aircraft. If the aircraft were equipped with an IFF transponder set to the frequency of the day, it could receive the signal from the *Bunker Hill* and send out a reply, indicating that it was a friendly aircraft. This system allowed the Allies to fight the Japanese in near-zero-visibility conditions, and to scramble accurate intercepts when Japanese fighters were more than 100 miles out. The IFF broadcast in a very narrow band—to the human ear it sounded almost like a chicken squawking.

The IFF system developed during the Second World War is the basis for the worldwide air traffic control system used today, still called IFF. It is rarely used any longer to prevent aerial suicide attacks, but aircraft are still ordered by ground stations to squawk on specific IFF frequencies.

The war aboard the carriers at Okinawa dragged on through April 1945, day after day, with more Essex Class carriers coming and going. When the Navy launched the first Midway Class aircraft carrier—the most powerful carrier ever built—everyone aboard the *Bunker Hill* wondered when they would finally be relieved.

18. GRIND

If it kills Japs, it's important; if it doesn't kill Japs, it's not important.

—COMMANDER ARLEIGH BURKE, USN,
CHIEF OF STAFF TO ADMIRAL MARC MITSCHER,
COMMANDER OF TASK FORCE 58

Despite the unprecedented influx of new ships, the kamikazes were hitting the fleet so hard the *Bunker Hill* could not be spared. The Navy iterates often that the kamikazes did not sink a single Essex, but this is misleading. Many major carriers were so badly damaged by the *tokko* pilots that they had to be taken out of the war for good.

The *Franklin* was hit by a kamikaze on October 27, 1944, and did not launch an attack again until March 18, 1945. The following day she was hit by conventional bombs. More than 700 men were killed. The *Franklin* never returned to war.

A kamikaze struck the *Intrepid* in the Philippines on November 25, 1944. She did not return to battle until mid-February the following year. Two months later, on April 16, kamikazes hit her again. The *Intrepid* returned to combat only in the last weeks of the war.

Two kamikazes hit the *Ticonderoga* on January 22, 1945. Her captain was killed and the *Ticonderoga* was taken out of the war until June.

The *Saratoga* was struck by multiple kamikazes on February 21, 1945, at Iwo Jima and never returned to war.

The *Randolph* was hit by a kamikaze at Ulithi on March 11, 1945, during the Tan operation, and did not return to battle until April 7.

A kamikaze hit the *Enterprise* on April 5, 1945. She returned on May 6, but was struck again on May 14. She never returned to war.

A kamikaze slammed the *Hancock* on April 7, 1945. She did not return to the war until July.

The kamikazes also damaged around twenty-five smaller British and American carriers. Admiral Spruance was forced to change flagships twice because of kamikaze strikes on his battleships.

For the men aboard the *Bunker Hill*, the war could seem incongruously far away in the morning, and then tragically close the same afternoon. One of the pilots died at least every few days. George Ottinger, the popular Air Group 84 leader, strafed in low over the Japanese positions by Yontan. Japanese AA gunners hit him just after he fired his rockets. George Gelderman watched from Turnbull's Avenger as Ottinger nursed his plane toward the *Bunker Hill*, smoking badly. Ottinger kept his plane up for nearly twenty minutes but eventually had to ditch. Everyone flying from the *Bunker Hill* circled Ottinger's plane, watching as it sank. Commander Ottinger made it out, and swam a couple of strokes. An SB2C dropped a raft to him. He was headed toward the raft, but a moment later stopped swimming and rolled over. He was dead.

AA shattered Marine Major Dickson's windshield the same day. Flying shards blinded him and the carrier told him to try to ditch in the Pacific. He never made it out. Lieutenant Wesley was hit that afternoon while flying low. He bailed out, too near the ground and his chute never opened.

The pilots understood that they were killing many others on a daily basis. Most never questioned the necessity of the war. Nevertheless, being close to so much killing and danger was taking its toll. By late April 1945, all were challenged by the guilt of homicide.

The *Bunker Hill* rearmed, refueled, and reprovisioned on Wednesday, April 18. The men aboard knew this to mean that they would in all likelihood remain at Okinawa without a break until the job there was done. They had now been at sea from Ulithi for more than a month. The days blended together, with long tedious periods of mind-numbingly boring activities punctuated by acute anxiety and the terror of the kamikaze attacks. Not knowing was much worse than anything else. Once in the air, every ounce of Turnbull's mental and physical energy was fiercely focused. If he relaxed for even a few moments, he knew they might well not make it back. Ironically, the missions were the only times for many of the pilots to live without anticipation. Amid their intense concentration on flying combat, all felt released from tedium. Fear, though, remained.

It was a privilege in many ways to be a flying officer aboard a fast carrier in the U.S. Navy toward the end of World War II. They had the best training, the finest mechanics, the best equipment, the best armament, and the best food. A steward did their laundry, cleaned their sheets, and served their meals. Many of the pilots lived more comfortably aboard ship than they had at home.

On Thursday, April 19, 1945, the men aboard *Bunker Hill* celebrated her 20,000th landing. This called for lemonade and cake with sandwiches in the ready room. Guts Guttenberg got the landing. The next morning, though, they all knew they would be flying support again over Okinawa.

Through the end of April, the American assault on Okinawa slowed. The whole island seemed encircled in a haze that had become a metaphor for the fighting on the ground. Front lines were confused. The pilots dropped their weapons, too, often unsure whether they were hitting enemy or friend. The ships never moved outside their sixty-square-mile operational area seventy miles southwest of Okinawa and about 350 miles from Kanoya. The weather was the only thing that seemed to change.

Oftentimes, out of boredom or denial, Turnbull and many of his comrades did not bother leaving the vulnerable ready room when General Quarters sounded. They had been through GQ too many times. Torpedo Defense interrupted Mass, but this time the priest continued through it. They were all getting used to the kamikaze routine. Turnbull strolled the flight deck at sunset during "darken ship" when the whole task force disappeared into blackout.

Combat pressures were overwhelming. Most soldiers in combat situations say waiting is the worst part. Pilots often felt that their whole lives had become a wait for their next mission. They flew combat at least every other day. And they spent much of their days waiting in ready rooms for delayed sorties. April 25 was typical. Turnbull rose at 3:30 A.M. to wait in the ready room for the first strike. By six the weather had socked in the ship and he returned to his bunk to try to read. He got up again at 9:30 and bumped around the ship, waiting for the weather to lift, without really anything to do. He wandered to the laundry, the bakery, and the galley. He prepared the plotting board for a late morning run on Okinawa and ate an early lunch. The squadron was continuously ordered to stand by for the weather to clear. At 3:30 P.M. he finally boarded his plane for the hop but ended up only taxiing around as the weather was still too squally. Finally, he went by the ready room, said good night, and headed to his room at 10:00 P.M. to try to catch up on his letters home. Scuttlebutt had them returning to the States.

Meanwhile in Kanoya, daily bombings from the American B-29s drove Admiral Ugaki underground into his damp, graceless shelter. Ugaki had grown up an aristocrat in a near-feudal nation, and as a naval leader was given every entitlement available in a nation renowned for its exquisite politesse and mastery of privileged culture. His life at Kanoya stood in sharp contrast both to his prewar upbringing and experience, and also to the relatively comfortable lives of the pilots aboard the *Bunker Hill*. The chief of the Naval Medical Bureau who inspected conditions on Kyushu warned Ugaki that they would be plagued by epidemics in the coming rainy season and warm summer months. On April 25, Ugaki finished his journal entry with a word about Nazi Germany: "The Red Army finally entered Berlin. Hitler remained in the city to encourage defenders, but their fate is now sealed. He who attempted to wipe out the Bolsheviks is now going to be destroyed by them."

The following day, things seemed even worse. The Allies were meeting in San Francisco, planning the new world order. Ugaki found it mortifying that they were discussing how to govern Germany and Japan after the war. Ugaki thought of Yamamoto and the 41,000 other souls enshrined at Yasukuni* and was ashamed. That night the moon was full.

April 26 marked the five-year anniversary of Ugaki's wife's death. He picked a dew-sprinkled rose to dedicate to her and attended a private memorial service. The B-29s continued their daily assaults. The next day was the emperor's birthday.

Hirohito ate only the food available to the *tokkotai* pilots that day. Kanoya was struck by fifty B-29s while others hit all over Kyushu, as usual. The Japanese crews were becoming despondent. Ugaki recorded that they had barely any planes left and "the crews are so exhausted they just didn't care about anything anymore." Ugaki did not even bother having them drag the aircraft out of the shelters. He knew the Zeros would all be destroyed in a daytime attack. And it was too difficult to fly at night in the rain. Ugaki alternated between harsh practicality—not ordering aircraft readied—and wildly irrational enthusiasm. He determined, when his search aircraft could not find the American fleet, that the task force must be withdrawing. In his diary, he notes that he decided to hit the Americans with a harsh blow and "recover materials from the enemy after destroying him." Then, just a few sentences later, he writes, "I don't regret the passing of the spring. Spring will come again, but what I fear is that a chance to recover the war situation won't come again."

Kiyoshi and the others spent their last days wandering around on the footpath that wended its way among the rice fields. He listened to the spring insects buzzing and frogs croaking. Allied planes had knocked out all electricity so the men lit an oil fire inside the schoolhouse in a small tin pineapple can. Their shadows swayed in the darkness. They shared care of a small puppy at the school. Ownership passed from the dead to the condemned. The dog had a greater chance of life than they.

Kiyoshi washed his face in the cold creek in the mornings, waiting

---

* Yasukuni shrine is the Shinto memorial to Japan's war dead—those who died in service of the emperor. The shrine book contains the names of nearly 2.5 million Japanese, including Kiyoshi Ogawa. Included in the book are the names of Japanese officials who were convicted of war crimes by the postwar tribunals.

for Admiral Ugaki to collect enough planes and for the American fleet to come within range of their meager fuel supplies. The pilots drank sake and played sentimental Japanese songs on an old organ at the abandoned school, like the 1940 hit "Who Would Not Think of His Hometown" by Noboru Kirishima. The feeling at the base had incongruously picked up the peaceful southern atmosphere Kyushu was known for. The equanimity, though, was shattered throughout the day and night by Allied bombs and strafing attacks but, remarkably, returned just as quickly as it was broken.

The next day, the American 330th Bomber Group returned, supplemented with aircraft from the 19th Bomber Group. They dropped nearly 200 500-pound HE bombs. Ninety-seven of these had long delayed action fuses, which severely demoralized the Japanese. The 330th returned yet again the next day and dropped more delayed action fuse bombs—with up to six-hour delays.

The Japanese antiaircraft guns and fighter planes were slowly vanishing from Okinawa. Turnbull flew the early hop on Saturday, April 28, with good weather over the island. The antiaircraft fire was "heavy but meager" (the Japanese were firing large rounds, but not many shells). They probably would not get hit. Turnbull dropped the usual load of four 500-pound GP bombs, now with a seven-to-fifteen-second time delay, hoping to penetrate the deepest caves before detonation.

The Japanese seemed to be using all of their fighters as kamikazes. Their Zeros no longer challenged the American bombing runs on Okinawa and the biggest threat became colliding with another American bomber.

On April 30, a group of Marines was pinned down by Japanese guns on a ridge outside of Shuri town on Okinawa. The Avengers were called in. McCain, the gunner in W. H. "Lips" Foucart's plane, was hit by shrapnel. They called him Lips because he never stopped talking. Foucart made an emergency landing on Okinawa at the former Japanese airbase at Yontan where the Americans had constructed a new hospital. Regulations forbade combat aircraft to fly solo, so Turnbull escorted Foucart in. It gave him and his crew a chance to see the war from the ground. They were some of the few naval airmen who got to see close up and level what the land they were attacking looked like, and the results of their aerial attacks. "We just bombed the crap out of that place," Gelderman said.

Stone, brick, and concrete structures landscaped to resemble formal gardens crowded the perimeter of the landing strip—the cemetery crypts of Okinawan families. The tombs formed excellent hiding places for Japanese snipers. Some had been reinforced with concrete and the U.S. soldiers were shot at from these locations sporadically until the American armed forces captured the entire perimeter.

A ground crew pulled Turnbull's Avenger into the bush, where they camouflaged it. Turnbull introduced himself to the pilot of the Army Grasshopper scout plane that landed just after him, and the pilot gave him, Gelderman, and Weincek a brief tour of the American side of Okinawa.

That afternoon the three men had a great time firing off their .38-caliber revolvers at bottles and everything else inanimate they could find. They were wined and dined at the Bachelor Officer's Club before heading out in a jeep looking for places they had bombed and for souvenirs. Because Turnbull wanted to be a teacher, they toured a native school. Later, they snuck into some of the old crypts and made off with as many funerary vases as his TBF could fly.

That afternoon, they came across a captured Japanese ammunition depot. The pilots loved bombing ammo dumps. The explosions were spectacular. Turnbull though had never seen one up close. He walked almost like a child at a country fair, looking through the crates and boxes of ordnance and ammunition. An Ohka flying bomb lay on its belly among the detritus. It looked to Turnbull like the kind of toy airplane that children fly around in circles attached to a chain at an amusement park. The sight of the Ohka had a powerful impact on Turnbull. He knew more than ever after that that the Japanese would use suicide during the rest of the war: they had built an entire class of aircraft that required suicide.

IJA leaders realized that the Zero was a poor suicide weapon; overburdened by a large bomb, it could barely maneuver. They ordered a study made on planes designed specifically for suicide missions.

Navy Sub-Lieutenant Mitsuo Ohta designed the rocket-propelled manned missile called Ohka, after the bright, but ephemeral cherry blossom—a symbol of fleeting youth and death. Americans called the manned warheads Baka—Japanese for fool.

The Ohka was called a manned bomb, but it was more akin to a human-guided cruise missile, with a small cockpit. They were sortied mainly from the Kanoya. The Japanese began production of Ohkas in September 1944. The Ohka was about twenty feet long with a seventeen-foot wingspan, and less than four feet high. The Japanese packed 2,646 pounds of their most powerful explosive into the Ohka. Powered by three solid-propellant rockets, it could reach 576 miles per hour, much too fast to be intercepted or shot down by any American fighter or antiaircraft weapon. The Ohka program is indicative of Japan's absolute collapse. The project was plagued with problems throughout its brief but dogged existence. Twenty-four Betty mother planes were on a training mission at Konoike in February 1945 when Al Turnbull, Caleb Kendall, and the *Bunker Hill* fliers attacked Japan for the first time. The Bettys were left unprotected and uncamouflaged on the field. Task Force 58 bombers bombed the base all day long, destroying every one of the precious Betty bombers. Admiral Ugaki knew that Mitscher was coming and was disgusted by the waste of so many good aircraft.

The technological challenges of building a manned missile, powered by rockets and launched by a mother ship, are daunting. Yet the Japanese designed the manned bomb in about a week. The craft had to be carried in a mother plane to within fifty-five miles of its target to have a chance of hitting. The already slow and vulnerable twin-engine Betty bombers assigned to carry the weapon were slowed further by the increased drag of the missile, to less than 160 knots—easy prey for the American fighters that could fly at twice their speed. The Bettys had to carry less fuel in order to get off the ground with the heavy Ohkas, and they burned more gas, which significantly reduced range. The Betty had no armor and did not carry self-sealing fuel tanks. American fighter pilots nicknamed them "flying lighters." Each of the Betty bombers was manned by six or seven Japanese. Nearly all of the slow Betty bombers were shot down. And the real problem was the psychological challenge faced by the men who flew the missiles and their flight crews. The squadron that manned the Ohka was called *Jinrai*—God's Thunder. The individual pilots are often called Thunder Gods in English translation. The Thunder God pilots began transferring to Kanoya on January 20, 1945, the day the *Bunker Hill* left the West Coast for Hawaii. They waited a full two months for their only mission, all the while knowing they were condemned.

The Ohkas had enormous destructive potential, but they came too late in the war. Some did terrible damage to American ships, but the Ohkas sank only a single U.S. naval vessel. Four hundred thirty-eight Japanese died in Ohka attacks, including fifty-six Ohka pilots.*

Ugaki learned of Hitler's death in the morning on May 1, 1945. After the usual B-29 runs against Kanoya, a squadron of B-25s made a low approach over Shibushi Bay beside Kanoya. The medium bombers had apparently followed a Japanese squadron. They approached, as Ugaki noted, "at an awfully low altitude." As though to insult the wretched Japanese student-pilots, the Americans kept their navigation lights on. They bombed and strafed the Kanoya field back and forth destroying aircraft and killing twenty men. That evening, Ugaki wrote about Hitler's death: "His spirit will remain long with the German nation, while the United States and Britain will suffer from communism someday and regret that . . . Hitler was killed."

B-29s attacked at midnight, then again at dawn the following day. The bombing seemed almost endless. Kanoya was being hit by bombers from Tinian, Iwo Jima, Ie Shima, Saipan, and from the new runways on northern Okinawa. But mostly they were hit by bombers launched from the dozens of carriers massing south of Kyushu. The frequency of the attacks made it almost impossible for the Japanese to launch aircraft.

Torrential rains fell at Kanoya during the first four days of May as Kiyoshi waited to die. Admiral Ugaki managed to sortie the fifth

---

* One hundred eighteen Japanese planes were destroyed in Ohka attacks. The destroyer USS *Manner T. Abele* DD was sunk.

Kikusui. One hundred twenty-five young Japanese pilots died. The *tokko* sank and badly damaged many small vessels, including destroyers. But as the Japanese ran out of aircraft, the danger to the carriers receded. Amidst the rain, the *Bunker Hill* received a paint job in the middle of the combat zone.

The Germans in Italy surrendered on May 3. That evening Admiral Mitscher announced that Task Force 58 had shot down more than 1,000 enemy planes in Okinawa since Love-Day on April 1, 1945, barely a month earlier.

When Turnbull went to bed that night he wrote in his diary at the top of the page: "Thursday May 3, 1945, Italy is Ours."

The men aboard learned that the *Bunker Hill* had been ordered to remain at Okinawa until June 1, 1945. That meant they would be home by Independence Day.

19. VOLUNTEERS

The son's solicitude for his mother
Is surpassed by
Her solicitude for him.
When she hears what befell me today,
How will she take it?

—YOSHIDA TORAJIRO (SHOIN)

By late spring 1945, the empire of Japan had virtually no tanks and almost no fuel. A public health crisis loomed and the population faced famine. One third of the Japanese had lost their housing and clothing. They had no contact via ship with China. Even coastal trade had nearly halted. In desperation, Japan's military leadership forced more and more young men to join the kamikazes.

Kamikaze pilots were coerced incrementally, in a manner not dissimilar from tactics of coercion used for millennia by governments and armies, along a gradual but unmistakable path to suicide. They were taught from the time of birth that the finest way to live is to lead a life of service to one's family and the nation. When they were drafted, they received identical haircuts, wore identical clothing, and trained in identical methods, behaviors, conduct, and comportment with their comrades. The hardships and injustices they endured forced them to rely on each other. Any who voiced dissent were severely punished and shunned. Finally, they were brought together into a large room and asked communally whether they would be willing to die for their mothers, sisters, fathers, and country. They answered resoundingly, unselfishly, courageously, and tragically, "Yes."

This future sacrifice still seemed an abstract idea. They were train-

ing with a group of gifted peers at a military base far from the front
lines. The enemy was still distant. No one wanted to appear faint-
hearted. No one wanted to seem selfish, or unpatriotic. So of course
nearly every student signed "YES" when asked if they would give their
life for their country. Some months later, a few were taken aside and
ordered to fly to a forward base. This made things much more real.
Still, they were together and this was not yet suicide, merely a flight to
a forward base. No one wanted to lose face, so they climbed into their
aircraft and flew south.

At the new base, reality dawned in a terrible way. Each morning
a few were sent off to die. Death was everywhere. American bombs
fell each day. American planes strafed them. The food was awful. No
one was allowed to leave. It was cold. They huddled together each
night for warmth, and each afternoon a few more were dead. Some
remained in denial, while others sank into depression. One evening
they were given their orders. The next morning, they would fly. Still,
some hope remained. Not everyone flew every morning. But on the
following day, they would step into a truck that drove them to a sodden runway where their Zero fighter was waiting, warming up. They
had to get in the air quickly before patrolling Allied aircraft struck.
They could not turn back. How would they explain themselves? So
many of their friends already had died. They could not abandon the
men in their squadron. They probably would be killed carrying their
awkward loads long before they sighted a carrier. If they made it all
the way to the heart of the fleet, there would be no escape, no way to
return without being overtaken and shot down. So there was nothing left to do.

Even so, many kamikazes pulled out at the last minute. Perhaps they
lost control of their plane. But the human drive to survive is extraordinarily powerful and even in the face of vast organized bureaucratic
coercion this flame struggles on to the very end.

The kamikaze's task was daunting. The Japanese had so few bombs
left that the student pilots at Yatabe practiced flying with water heat-
ers and tree trunks strapped to the belly of their Zero to simulate
the weight of the warhead they would bear. Taking off from a short
field carefully watched by U.S. scout planes, with a bomb their plane

could barely carry, they had to navigate over the sea, passing the vigilant CAP and American radar picket destroyers, finally arriving at the heart of the U.S. fleet.

The kamikazes were perilously exposed at each critical mission juncture. American aircraft attacked the base at odd intervals night and day. Ground crews had to fuel, arm, and drag the aircraft into launch position in the fastest possible time. The moment their aircraft was ready the pilots took off. They could not afford to circle even once to form their squadrons. They joined up while moving forward.

Their navigation skills were rudimentary. American pilots drilled constantly on navigation techniques. The Japanese utilized only the most basic skills: looking for landmarks, timing runs on particular headings, matching these to their air charts. Many kamikazes were sent up without a chart or even a watch. They could navigate only by sight, and probably relied on following their fellows more than anything. Formation flying therefore was critical. Flying in formation, though, was challenging even for the most experienced American pilots. Kiyoshi for the most part probably just followed along with the others.

I asked the poet Iwama what he thought was the hardest thing about flying a kamikaze attack. He replied clearly: "Dying."

Iwama worried most about the last 500 yards.

The kamikaze completed his mission in a steep, barely controlled dive, adjusting for buffeting wind, his own speed, increasing lift, and the target's speed. He was blinded by AA explosions, and burdened with an unwieldy bomb. The kamikaze planes were often pierced by large and small shells fired from the target ship's hundreds of machine guns, as well as rockets and shells fired from the destroyers, frigates, battleships, and cruisers surrounding her and the CAP. All the while, thoughts of life, of friends, of country, and above all of mother, entered the pilot's head. How could he hold on to that stick? How could he not turn his eyes away at the last minute? More than one American sailor has said that he remembered meeting the gaze of the Japanese pilot just before impact.

Their time at Yatabe should have been one of exhilaration, as they learned to fly the most agile fighter plane in the world.

After the war, former Japanese ground crews reconstructed a Mitsubishi Zero from the parts of several wrecked Zeros found scattered around Kyushu for display at the Kanoya Peace Museum, a homage to the dead *tokko* pilots. The cockpit is surprisingly small. It is difficult for a six-foot man to fit inside; a big pilot's body is uncomfortably wedged in by the metallic sides of the narrow fuselage.

The aircraft was astonishingly light. Its aluminum skin was so thin one could easily dent the outside merely by pushing a hand against the cockpit walls from the inside. The fighter offered only a slight sense of any boundary between the aircraft and the world outside. The aircraft's sides would barely slow a .50-caliber bullet. This fragility leaves a feeling of extraordinary exposure. But it is what allowed the Zero to be such an agile and tenacious fighter in air-to-air combat. It could turn and dive and rise probably faster than any other fighter.

All the advantages of speed and agility were erased when 500-pound bombs were locked to the Zero's belly. The aircraft became ungainly and difficult to control. Even crashing into a ship became a challenging maneuver.

Training Zeros at Yatabe.

A dial on the left side of the cockpit, difficult to reach, adjusts the trim and must be set before the pilot initiates a dive. Kiyoshi would roll the dial forward, shrinking the flaps, decreasing the wing area, and forcing the nose downward as the plane loses lift. The Zero could not descend at more than 15 degrees until the very end of a crash dive or it would pass 400 knots in speed and become uncontrollable.

A persistent American myth holds that kamikaze pilots were given drugs or plied with alcohol before their mission. IJN student pilots were not given drugs to keep them awake, nor to make them more compliant. The farewell ceremony in which Japanese drink from a sake cup with their fellows is traditionally done with water. Water symbolizes purity. In some of these ceremonies, rice wine may have been used, but for Kiyoshi, at the formal ceremony at Yatabe, the students drank water. The kamikazes required all the clarity their minds could muster to stay focused enough to get past the American defenses.

The kamikazes were directed to attack aircraft carriers whenever possible. The ideal target on a carrier, according to the Japanese records, was the central deck edge elevator. The next best thing was the fore or aft elevators. The Japanese felt that destruction of any of these sections had the greatest likelihood of disabling, at least for a time, the huge carriers.

A kamikaze pilot's greatest technical flying challenge was judging *hikiokoshu*, the powerful lift generated from high speeds, during which the aircraft nose begins to raise up as the pilot dives at around 45 degrees. They were told over and over how difficult it would be to hold the nose down. Many kamikaze planes popped up and missed their targets as they gained speed and lift in the last moments. Pilots could also fail to bring the nose up in time.

When the kamikaze sighted his target, he would radio back to Kanoya to notify the base in one final broadcast. Then, when they began their dives, they would key their radio mike as they fell. Their eager compatriots at the base gathered around the radio receiver counting off the seconds. If the mike was keyed long enough, they knew at least that their friend had made it to sea level and probably made a hit. Whatever the approach, one great fear of the kamikaze was that at the last minute he would shut his eyes involuntarily and miss the target, crashing uselessly into the sea.

The crash dive is more difficult than one might think. The Japanese did not have g-suits, so it was easy for them to black out from heavy gravitational forces. Kiyoshi and the other young *tokko* students were given only a couple of days to learn the skill. They would climb aloft in formations of four Zeros. When they reached 12,000 feet, the little squadron would dive individually in quick succession on a small target of white T-shaped canvas stretched on the landing field. At 1,200 feet they would yank back on the stick as hard as they could, pulling massive g-forces, and lift out. They did it over and over again. They were gaining skills, but they were also learning a simple, yet nearly impossible task by rote, so that it would become so mundane that they might be able to do it one last time over the American fleet.

They dove the last bit at 60 degrees—a much steeper angle than the Zero was designed to handle. When the fall began, they pulled negative g-forces that would float the pilot out of his cockpit seat. It was difficult to control the stick, which required more and more pressure to hold the nose down as they fell. Then, as he reached the point of no return and began to pull back, the pilot would have to be careful not to yank so hard that the plane would stall, but enough to pull out of the practice death dive. As the nose pulled out of the dive, pilots would experience positive gravitational forces, many times those felt on the earth's surface. Blood flow decreased. Many kamikazes blacked out. Some did not recover until their aircraft was hopelessly falling. When this happened, they would be smashed to bits prematurely in full view of their friends—mercilessly reminding all of the purpose of their training.

When they sortied on their final mission, kamikazes waited to arm their bomb until they entered the final dive. They pushed the nose forward into a steep glide of 45 to 60 degrees and picked up speed beyond 300 knots. The wings would start to shake and the high speed would create powerful lift along the leading edge of the wing. The nose would start to lift up, as *hikiokoshu* affected the aircraft's dynamics. If he could not keep the nose down, the kamikaze would overshoot the target and die for nothing. And there was always the danger that the nose would dip too low. Then his Zero would suddenly dip and crash-dive, futilely cartwheeling into the Pacific. The target itself, the carrier, would be moving quickly while firing a storm of bullets at the attacker. As the falling Zero begins to surpass 300 knots, it becomes almost impossible to control. The Zero was so fragile that high winds and g-forces could pull it apart in a steep dive. The wings start to shake violently as the plane gains speed. If the pilot tried to adjust the flaps, the aircraft's sudden increased drag often tore these attitudinal controls from the wing. The ailerons, too, become almost useless. Any significant movement to right or left would cause them to sheer off the aircraft. The metallic wings wrinkle up like the washboard sand on a beach that has been warped by ocean currents. The aerodynamics are irretrievably altered as the metal warps and the plane becomes uncontrollable. Even if a pilot could pull out of such a fast dive and was not quickly shot down, he would not be able to return to base. The Kanoya museum maintains wreckage of Zeros that had dived too fast. The metal along the fuselage is permanently wrinkled.

On May 8, Admiral Toyoda flew down to Kanoya to personally organize an assault against the American fleet. Ugaki and Toyoda spent the next day in a strategy conference. Between the army and navy they were able to scrape together 150 Zeros. They decided that day to continue the *Kikusuis*. They would launch the next one on May 11, 1945.

20. DESPERATION: MAY 8–10, 1945

Having renounced all,
I feel myself utterly nonexistent,
And yet when it snows,
I know
How cold I am!

—FUKUZUMI MASAE,
NINOMIYA O YAWA IN
NINOMIYA SONTOKU O ZENSHU,
XXXVI, 820

Alfred Jodl surrendered Nazi Germany unconditionally on Tuesday, May 8, 1945. Japanese propagandists explained the loss of Nazi Germany as a cultural idiosyncrasy:

> This phenomenon may be explained only by some fundamental differences between the oriental and the occidental philosophy on death and honor. For in this war of Greater East Asia alone we have known many instances in which our officers and men have fought literally to the last man. . . . The European war situation even in its final stage would have been quite different if the enemy had to encounter one million who reenacted the heroic stand put up by our garrisons on Iwo, Saipan, Attu, and other Pacific Islands. . . . Japanese troops have no taste for a thing called capitulation or surrender, every member is only too ready to fight to the last.

On board the *Bunker Hill*, the men stopped to listen to the broadcast of the German surrender. World War II in the Pacific had become the only war for American soldiers and airmen. The full force of the most powerful war machine in the history of the world was now available to assault the failing Imperial Japanese Empire.

Every Allied ship within range of Okinawa fired every single gun precisely at noon that day to signal to the Japanese that millions of troops, thousands of ships, and billions of tons of matériel were now available to finish the war in the Pacific. The entire resources of the United States and her allies could be concentrated against the starving, depleted Japanese.

In May 1945, the *Bunker Hill* steamed with Task Group 58.3, alongside four other carriers. The *Essex* served as the task group flagship. The *Bunker Hill* led as the task force flagship. The *Enterprise*, the *Randolph*, and the *Bataan* cruised with her.* On May 9, Air Group 84 was ordered to use incendiary bombs on civilian areas of Kikaigashima, because intelligence believed the Japanese were hiding their aircraft inside civilian homes. Turnbull flew the second strike carrying 1,000 pounds of incendiary bombs. That night, the *Bunker Hill* withdrew from the immediate combat area to resupply. They would be back in combat, and fully loaded with volatile fuel and explosives, by the next morning, Monday, May 11.

About the time the American guns fired the massive volley celebrating the end of the war in Europe, Admiral Ugaki and Admiral Toyoda made their plans for the sixth *Kikusui*. The main destructive force of the sixth *Kikusui* was intended to be the Ohka corps.

---

* The formation of the task groups changed constantly. If a ship were damaged, or needed special supplies, it might leave the combat zone and be replaced by another ship. When it returned, it might rejoin as part of a different task group. The carriers of Task Group 58.3 were given heavy support by two battleships, the *Washington* and the *South Dakota*, and five cruisers: the *Pasadena*, the *Springfield*, the *Astoria*, the *Wilkes-Barre*, and the smaller USS *Oakland* (CLAA). She also had the support of three destroyer squadrons. There were many other support ships in the task group, including oilers, supply, and hospital ships.

The Japanese believed that the awesome destructive power of the Ohka represented their last, best chance to halt the American advance. The Ohkas, though, carried by the lumbering Betty bombers, had great difficulty penetrating the American fleet defenses and rarely succeeded even in making it to the outlying picket destroyers. Ugaki thought that if he could sink the destroyers before they warned the American fleet, then the Ohkas might get through.* He determined on a new two-tier assault tactic for manned missile attacks. First the Japanese would send their most expendable, least experienced *tokko* pilots against the American picket destroyers. Their sole purpose would be to open a hole in the American line that the Ohkas could use to penetrate to the carriers in the center. Kiyoshi was chosen for this task. He would break trail for the *Jinrai*. This was the *samurai* equivalent of striking the enemy in the eye. Many kamikazes grumbled when given orders to attack the smaller picket ships, as they felt degraded at trading their lives for a destroyer.

Pilots Mitsuo Yamazaki and Koji Katsamura were ordered to sortie before dawn and crash their Ohkas into the American runways on Okinawa to disable the airfield and prevent land-based planes from hitting the attack force later in the day. The Japanese determined that

---

* Admiral Ugaki seems unaware that the large *Kikusui* assaults were clearly visible to fleet radars (the large radar arrays on America's biggest ships) far ahead of time, and that the fleet could afford to send hundreds of skilled fighter pilots to meet these assaults long before the slow, overburdened Betty bombers could reach their target. The Japanese expended needless effort, aircraft, and men's lives over and over in attacking picket ships. Based on surveillance of Japanese bases (American pilots noted the buildup of diverse types of aircraft at Kanoya and other fields on Kyushu just before the *Kikusui* raids) and transcriptions of Japanese coded messages, the Navy had a fairly good idea when each mass attack was to begin. The destroyers were capable of giving valuable early warning, but the radar aboard the *Bunker Hill* and other carriers could see fairly well for at least seventy miles, which usually gave the carriers ample time to establish a defensive perimeter. The CIC rooms, which were supposed to manage information coming in from destroyers and other sources all around the combat zone and then quickly vector the CAP out to meet any threats before they arrived at the heart of the task group, were much less effective at dealing with information from other ships than the Japanese knew. Moreover, the large number of carriers in the fleet allowed them to keep a CAP protecting the task group at all times.

the sizable explosion of their manned missiles could knock the airfield out for at least several hours. The two *tokko* pilots complained bitterly over the ignominy of their sacrifice to their commander, Okamura (who had shepherded the Ohka project from its inception). Intentionally crashing on a runway was debasing. But the order held.

Though Admiral Ugaki had almost no aircraft left, he managed to gather six Rensen (Zero trainers) on Kyushu near Nagasaki the day before their mission.* One of these Zeros would be flown by Kiyoshi Ogawa.

---

* The kamikazes flew three types of Zeros for the sixth *Kikusui*, the Rensen, an old trainer model, the more modern 21, and the latest Zero, the 52. Kiyoshi was assigned to a Rensen Zero with tail number 33. He was scheduled to depart at 5:00 A.M., but his plane probably developed mechanical problems, because Kiyoshi departed more than an hour and a half late, and he did not fly in a Rensen.

Every history of the Second World War published until now has identified Kiyoshi's aircraft as a Judy. I was puzzled when I interviewed American gunners from the *Bunker Hill* who insisted that Kiyoshi flew a Zero. When I traveled to Japan the first time, all of Kiyoshi's kamikaze comrades maintained that Kiyoshi had to have flown a Zero—he had never been trained to fly the more complex Suisei (Judy). I learned that Kanoya did not service nor utilize Judys. Finally, I traveled to Kanoya, and the records at that base also indicated that Kiyoshi had flown a Zero—but they were only partial, and in no way dispositive. I located a photograph of isolated plane wreckage aboard the *Bunker Hill*. I showed this photograph to historians at the Japan Defense Research Institute: Mr. Shibata, an expert on World War II military aircraft at the JDRI, and Mr. Masuo Kimura, also an expert on World War II Japanese military aircraft technology, specializing in engine manufacture.

The two men were able to immediately identify the engine wreckage in the photo taken aboard the *Bunker Hill* as Japanese. Isolating the specific make and type of engine was a greater challenge. Mr. Kimura did not sleep for three days while examining old records, both U.S. and Japanese, with World War II aircraft engine diagrams, including the original instruction manuals for Judys and Zeros. He succeeded in identifying Kiyoshi's engine and plane type. Kiyoshi flew a Mitsubishi Zero model 52 HEI with a Sakae type 31 Model A engine.

The Suisei is powered by a Kinsei model 62 engine. The cylinder is connected to the engine by a pair of rods called push rods. In the Kinsei engine, these two rods come out of a single hole. In Kiyoshi's wreckage the push rods exit through paired holes. It is therefore impossible that his engine was a Kinsei—and therefore he could not have been flying a Suisei, a Judy.

The Rensen—a two-seater Zero used for training (one seat for the pilot, one for the student)—was also used in kamikaze missions and was utilized on May

The morning of May 10 broke clear at Kanoya. The days were getting longer. On his last full day, Kiyoshi had nearly fifteen hours of visible light. The Fifth Air Fleet sent two Myrt 11s and one Dinah on reconnaissance missions at 5:00 A.M. and 6:30 A.M. They sighted numerous American carriers south and east of Okinawa and determined that the American fleet was returning to within range of their kamikaze and *Jinrai* bomb forces stationed at Kanoya and the other hidden bases in southern Kyushu. Ugaki sent out two more pairs of Myrts on reconnaissance missions. But he decided not to attack that day. The American fleet was too far south, and in any case would likely be within closer striking distance by the next day. The delay gave Ugaki one more day to fully prepare the sixth *Kikusui*. Five Japanese night fighters reconnoitered Cape Sata, Kurd Island, and Iwo Jima. Upon

---

11, 1945. It has an elongated canopy, which looks in profile remarkably like a Suisei, and carries an 800-kilogram bomb—three times the size of the bombs carried normally by the *tokko* Zeros. This would explain why so many historians have said that Kiyoshi flew a Judy. The Rensen used a Sakae 12 engine. The push rods in the Sakae 12 engine exit through paired holes, nearly identical to those in Kiyoshi's wreckage. But in between the holes for the push rod there is only one bolt hole in Kiyoshi's wreckage. There are two bolt holes in between the holes for the push rods for the Rensen's Sakae 12 engine. The gear housing for Kiyoshi's engine lies at the edge of the wreckage; it clearly has sixteen gears. The Sakae 12 has only six gears, so clearly Kiyoshi's engine was not a Sakae 12 and therefore he was not flying a Rensen Zero trainer.

The regular Zero fighter, 52 HEI model, in use at Kanoya in May 1945, utilized a Sakae 21 or Sakae 31 engine. There is virtually no difference between the two. Both have two bolts between the push rods, both have double push rods in a single hole, and both have sixteen gears. The only significant difference between the Sakae 21 and the Sakae 31 is the shape of the bottom of the gear case. The dislodged gear housing in the corner of the picture lies on its side. The bottom of the gear case is clearly visible. A close examination of the dislodged gear housing case reveals that Kiyoshi's engine was a Sakae 31.

Japanese records detailing Kiyoshi's flight indicate that Kiyoshi Ogawa was assigned to a Rensen Zero. The newly discovered records from Yatabe Air Corps show Kiyoshi was ordered to, and flew, a Zero type 52. The only Zero that used the Type 31 A engine (and that not coincidentally was often flown from Kanoya) was a type 52 HEI C. That is what Kiyoshi flew.

the scouts' return, operational instructions for the next day's *Kikusui* assault were issued.

The kamikaze orders were optimistically specific. The squadrons were broken down into independent teams of four to six aircraft, each with its own leader. The individual pilots were assigned a specific take-off time, a specific route to fly, and a specific goal. Each pilot within the team was assigned a wingman. Teams with similar missions flew together. The team's objective fit precisely into the overall tactical and strategic goals for the day's battle, and the broader struggle for Okinawa and the war. Kiyoshi's group was part of the force called the *Daishokaiteigun.** The *Daishokaiteigun* was split into five squadrons of two to four planes each. Kiyoshi was in the Third Squadron. His wingman was the team leader, Yasunori Seizo.

Yasunori Seizo was born on March 28, 1924, on a farm in Kamikgoori town, outside of Ako-ken in Chushingura, Hyogo prefecture. Kiyoshi was in the *jyuyonkikai* (fourteenth intake). Yasunori joined earlier, in the thirteenth intake. Their training was similar, though Yasunori had much more flight time. Yasunori did his preliminary flight training at Tsuchiura, Tsukuba, and then Yatabe and Konoike. He was finally transferred to Kanoya at about the same time as Kiyoshi.

Yasunori's parents and ancestors on both sides were farmers. Ako is a particularly patriotic region. The 47 *ronin*, perhaps the most fanatically loyal and filial heroes in a country renowned for its patriotism, hailed from Ako. The Seizo children all had to rise early and work in the fields before school. When they returned home, they immediately went out to work again. They had no heavy equipment. Everything was done by hand. But every child in the village worked just as hard, so the Seizo brothers did not think of their lives as particularly difficult.

Ako town provided no organized sports. The children worked nearly every day so had no time for that kind of exercise. But whenever the children managed to get some free time, they practiced Kendo together. Yasunori ended up a 3 *dan*.† The Seizos were a patriotic family in a

---

* *Dai-shokaitei-gun* means literally "the big group of the destroyers with radar picket," *dai* meaning "big," *shokaitei* "destroyer with radar picket," and *gun* "group."

† Roughly a third degree black belt.

region known for its devotion, in a country renowned for its nationalism. All five of his brothers, like their father, joined the armed services.

They grew rice in paddies that they flooded with water from a nearby river using a set of small canals and sluiceways. The brothers worked in the fields side by side each day. Sometimes they sang songs together to pass the time. But on New Year's they celebrated. Then they were allowed to play together and sing, and it was a great relief. They played *karuta*, a Japanese card game, and *koma* (tops). They whittled their own tops and threw them together to see who could bounce someone else outside a circle or keep his spinning longest.

The Seizo family was bankrupted by the international Great Depression. They had no way to pay for Yasunori to be educated. Instead, they arranged for Yasunori to go to a *shihan gakko*, a normal school for teacher training—one of the many that were being established by the Japanese government to extend Imperial Japanese hegemony over Manchukuo. Yasunori was fifteen years old. His father never saw him again.

Yasunori was more shy than his siblings and much less vocal. He was most likely to accept their father's beliefs without question, or at least without objecting. This trait concerned his brother Sansaku; he wished that Yasunori would speak his mind more often.

Yasunori was sent to the new Japanese territory they called Ryojun. It was the city his father, Masanosuke Seizo, had fought to secure, which Western nations called Port Arthur. Finally now again part of China, the city is called Lushun. The school was free, and the government paid for all of his living expenses. But he had to promise to become a teacher in Manchuria in return for his education and support. Yasunori hated Lushun. He would do almost anything to get home. One reason that Japanese imperialism failed so severely is probably that the Japanese, perhaps more than any other nationality, intensely dislike living outside their home country. Port Arthur has a pleasant climate and was one of the most vibrant ports in Asia. But Yasunori was miserable there. He longed to return to Japan. The war offered an opportunity. Yasunori volunteered for the 13th Naval Reserve student enlistment (*jyusankikai*). He was released from his

Yasunori practicing Kendo in a hangar.

teaching obligation, returned to Japan, tested well, and entered the flight program.

Yasunori and Kiyoshi spent the last three weeks of their life together. Yasunori would be the leader of the third squad, and Kiyoshi was his wingman. They were intimately connected during the three-hour flight to the *Bunker Hill*. They signed their death scroll together, but would never have met if not for the war.

Two other aircraft flew in their little squadron, piloted by Ishijima Kenzo and Tadanori Sasahara.* The latter two were schoolmates from Rikkyo University. The four men, all former students, flew together as brothers for this last flight.

Yasunori's group's primary objective was to destroy the *shokaitei*— radar picket ships. If they could not locate the pickets, they were to attempt to sink the capital ships of the American naval force. If they were unable to locate the Navy, they were to head back toward Oki-

---

* Tadanori Sasahara is sometimes referred to in the Japanese records as Tada-nori Shinohara. Shinohara is a way of pronouncing the symbols for Sasahara used often in the Kyushu dialect.

*Yasunori around the time of his
induction into the navy.*

nawa and attack the transport and supply ships at Chujo Bay* (which
had recently been renamed Buckner Bay for Lieutenant General
Simon Bolivar Buckner).

The group of five squadrons of the *Daishokaiteigun* were to head
south 293 miles to Okinoerabu Island, just north of Okinawa. A chain
of islands, part of the Ryukyus, called the Nansei Shoto stretches
from the southern tip of Kyushu down to Okinawa. Each island lies
within sight of the next. So all the kamikazes had to do was wait for
a sunny day, and then fly south following the islands to Okinoerabu.
From Okinoerabu they would fan out into their individual squadrons
searching for radar picket targets. The Japanese had not had any contact with the American fleet since 2:00 A.M. Ugaki did not know where
the task force was located, but hoped that by fanning out, his pilots
would eventually run into the American task force. Kiyoshi's squadron would be heading south at 165 degrees from Okinoerabu.

The pilots tried to stay with their wingmen at all costs, and the

---

* The first suicide troop of the war, the men who piloted the midget submarines
at Pearl Harbor, had trained in Chujo Bay.

Yasunori standing in front of a Zero, probably on May 10, 1945.

wingmen were to remain with the group until they found their target—the picket destroyers. Finally, they would dive together. Yasunori Seizo flew plane number one, with tail number 101. Kiyoshi Ogawa was assigned plane number three, with tail number 33.

Four aircraft from the 801st unit departed Kanoya at 11:00 P.M. on Thursday, May 10, searching for Task Force 58. At 2:11 A.M., on May 11, they located what they believed to be the American fleet about 100 miles off the southern tip of Okinawa. But they were immediately pursued by American night fighters and so could not confirm their sighting. But the *Bunker Hill* confirmed the Japanese. They showed up on the ship's radar at 2:04 A.M. and she went to Torpedo Defense—sending the gunners to their battle stations.

Ten minutes later, as the Japanese recon planes continued to approach, the entire crew of the *Bunker Hill* went to full General Quarters. The radar-equipped night fighters of the American CAP were vectored out and chased the bogies away before the Japanese recon could make a positive identification of the fleet, but the Japanese scouts reported to Ugaki it was a large group of American ships.

Friday, May 11, 1945, dawned cloudy at Kanoya. It rained later. The day began disastrously for the Japanese, plagued by the incompetence of poorly trained men flying poorly maintained aircraft. Ugaki assem-

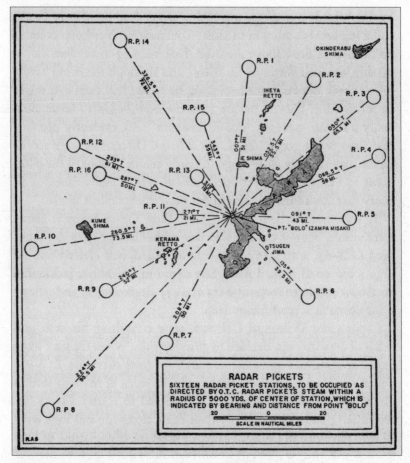

The American Navy encircled Okinawa with floating radar stations—destroyers specially equipped with the finest radar—to warn of any attack on the nearby vulnerable fleet. Japanese leaders reasoned that these radar stations had to be destroyed before any assault on the American Navy could succeed. Kiyoshi's assignment was to sink a radar picket destroyer.

bled eighteen Judy and Val dive-bombers at the nearby 2nd Kokubu Airfield. They were just about to take off when another group of aircraft attempting to land crashed in their midst. The collision set off a chain reaction of exploding bombs and gasoline tanks, which damaged two Zero fighters, eight of the Judys, and seven Val dive-bombers. The scheduled attack of the Judys on Task Force 58 was canceled.

Instead, ground crews hauled the Zeros out of caverns dug into clay hillsides, then up steep ravines, to the battered airstrip. They loaded the fuel and munitions that were destined for the *Bunker Hill*. Finally, crews started the engines of the planes meant to carry their comrades to death.

That morning, Flying Officer Fujisaki, an enormously talented pilot, wrote to a kamikaze friend:

These days suicide attack groups go out almost daily against the enemy carriers off the shores of Okinawa. In a few days it will be my turn. Frankly, I think this situation is the outcome of incompetence and stupidity on the part of the high command: it seems they are relying solely on the eager devotion of the young now. Suicide pilots also have a symbolic value. It was not the young however, who started the war. It is as if our leaders had broken off the writing of a novel they had started and which, for lack of inspiration, they are incapable of finishing. They are leaving it to the young men to bring it to a conclusion, but the young are not fully conversant with the plot! In a sense, we are scapegoats. What is the use of complaining? We are obliged to carry out the orders imposed on us. You and I are atheists. We shall never again have the pleasure of seeing each other, not even in the Great Beyond of believers. I hope that you will carry out your suicide mission successfully. Good luck, and goodbye forever.

Fujisaki flew his last mission on the same day as Kiyoshi. The officer listening to Fujisaki's last radio transmission wrote to Ryuji Nagatsuka that as Fujisaki dove, instead of steadily keying his mike, Fujisaki tapped out his wife's name in Morse code.

In the early hours of May 11, Kiyoshi and his group leader, Yasunori, watched their last sunrise, then rode in a truck out to the airstrip. The apprehension on their final morning was debilitating. Men in the truck with Kiyoshi were miserable. Lieutenant Junior Grade Takehiko Shibata, who was to lead a squadron of kamikazes, alternately boasted of how he would skim the ocean and strike his target dead-center, with cries of "Mother, the navy is trying to kill me!"

There was a measure of relief in finally sortieing. But Kiyoshi and

Opposite: Japanese map of flight plan, May 11, 1945: The map is copied from a secret Japanese record documenting the kamikaze attack plan of the Yatabe Naval Air Corps on May 11, 1945. Okinawa lies at the bottom of the picture. Okinoerabu is the small island immediately above Okinawa, where the attacking squadrons were meant to rendezvous, then branch out. Kagoshima Bay at the southern tip of Kyushu is on the top right. The attackers sortied from Kanoya Naval Airbase, which is midway down the Osumi peninsula, forming the eastern edge (right side) of Kagoshima Bay. The northernmost named island, small, isolated, and out of line, is Kikaigashima. Kikai is traditionally an island of isolation and exile, a mythic place in the Japanese mind, beyond the political and cultural control of the emperor. It serves as a desolate place of banishment in the literature of Japan. During the Second World War, Kikai became a place wholly beyond the healthful aid of the emperor. Admiral Mitscher knew it to be a haven for kamikazes. Mitscher's airmen were sent to Kikai so often that they began calling all routine patrols "Kikai." The island fell under near-constant American patrol, bombardment, and strafing. American fighter pilots attacked it for practice.

his fellows were delayed because of the crash at Kokubu. The kamikazes stood idle beside the runway for nearly two hours, waiting to die. Finally, at 6:40 A.M., they were issued their last order: "Pilots, to your planes!" The two hours wasted on the tarmac wrecked the mission logic. Kiyoshi was supposed to sortie an hour and a half before the *Jinrai* so he could clear a path for them. Instead, he left twenty minutes *after* the scheduled departure time of the *Jinrai* squadrons.* Before he departed, Kiyoshi had tucked into his breast pocket the poem that Iwama had written for him at Yatabe, neatly folded, and a photograph of four friends who had already flown their missions. He slipped an airman's timepiece over his head, which rested just over his rib cage.†

---

* Kiyoshi's entire *San Kutai*—Group Three—was off the ground by 6:42 A.M. Jim Swett and his CAP squadron of Marine fighter pilots caught up with some of the Bettys carrying Ohka missiles and their escorts half an hour before Kiyoshi saw any American ships.

† He had a photograph of four friends—young student pilots who had flown on an earlier *Kikusui* mission from Kanoya: Shigejiro Kashiwakura (Waseda University), Yasuo Ichishima (Waseda University), Yusaku Hirabayashi (Hose University), and Yonezo Matsumura (Nippon University). Yasuo kept a diary of his wartime experiences, which is helpful in piecing together Kiyoshi's life.

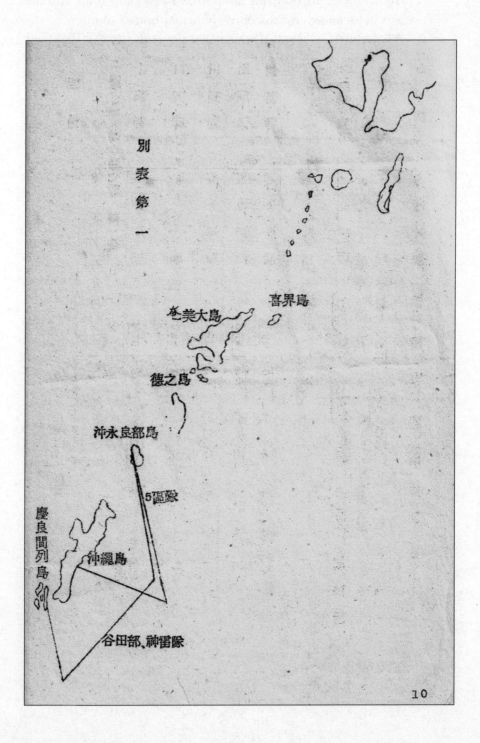

別
表
第
一

喜界島

奄美大島

徳之島

沖永良部島

5班隊

慶良間列島

沖縄島

谷田部、神雷隊

10

By 6:45 A.M., Kiyoshi and Yasunori Seizo had joined up with the others in his *buntai*. In loose formation, they headed south.

Kiyoshi arrived above Okinoerabu about two hours later, and passed over the jungle at Sotesto and by the staggeringly beautiful white sand beach at Wanjo, then out beyond the coral reef tightly circling the small island.

The four Japanese student *tokko* pilots in Group 3 joined up and headed south at about 6:45 A.M., toward their rendezvous with the other kamikaze squadron members. Okinawa loomed into view twenty miles or so ahead of Turnbull's Avenger as Kiyoshi and his comrades left Kanoya behind at about 7:00 A.M.

Kiyoshi and his fellows zigzagged from one visible landmass to the next as they wended their way southward along the Ryukyu island chain. They split up, probably around 8:00 A.M., at the last major island: Okinoerabu. Okinoerabu is a tall coral island, with striking hills, caves, and a rainforest, and white sand beaches ringed by reefs beneath beautiful blue near-tropical ocean. It is only thirty-five miles north of Okinawa. Some of the pilots continued to the American bases on Okinawa. Others, like Kiyoshi, turned more or less south, searching for the destroyer escorts of Task Force 58. He never found them.

Instead, he turned west of his southern track, and headed directly toward the *Bunker Hill*.

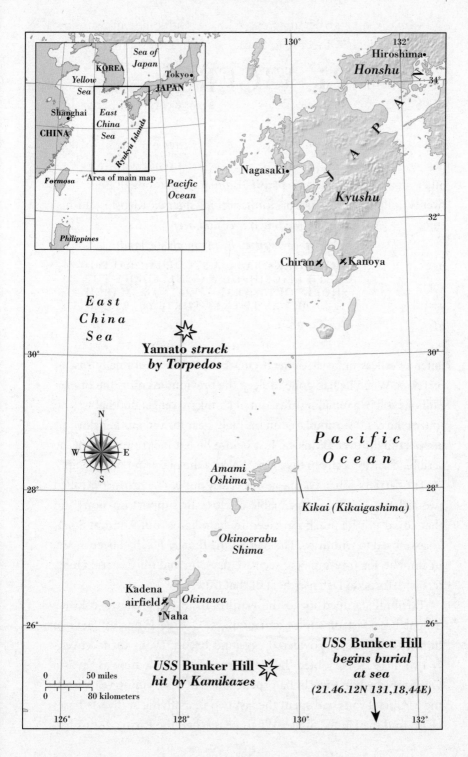

Sea of Japan

KOREA

Yellow Sea

Tokyo•

JAPAN

Shanghai•

CHINA

East China Sea

Ryukyu Islands

Formosa

Area of main map

Pacific Ocean

Philippines

130°

132°

Hiroshima•

Honshu

34°

Nagasaki•

Kyushu

32°

Chiran

Kanoya

East China Sea

Yamato *struck by Torpedos*

30°

30°

N

W   E

S

Pacific Ocean

28°

28°

Amami Oshima

Kikai (Kikaigashima)

Okinoerabu Shima

Kadena airfield

Okinawa

•Naha

26°

26°

USS Bunker Hill *hit by Kamikazes*

USS Bunker Hill *begins burial at sea* (21.46.12N 131,18,44E)

0   50 miles

0   80 kilometers

126°

128°

130°

132°

21. VICEROY

At Takeyama Naval Training Corps—
Just a single postcard, nothing special,
But I kept reading it over and over,
Because it was written by my mother's hand.

—MITSUTAKA BABA, A STUDENT DRAFTED
WITH KIYOSHI; HE WAS KILLED OFF THE
SHORES OF NA TRANG, VIETNAM, MARCH
1945; HE WAS TWENTY-THREE YEARS OLD

After a restless night at General Quarters, Al Turnbull finally rose at 3:30 A.M. When he had gone to sleep the previous evening, the *Bunker Hill* was still in a refueling area, out of kamikaze range. But that was no longer the case. Turnbull put on his flight gear for yet another close air support flight over Okinawa. Just before he left his compartment, he scribbled sardonically in his diary "Back to the ole' grind once again."

The carriers' job in Okinawa was nearly done. The Army controlled two airbases on Okinawa capable of close air support missions and that could not be much damaged by kamikazes. But Admiral Spruance refused to withdraw. The men of the *Bunker Hill* had been at sea, in combat, for fifty-nine consecutive days, on and off General Quarters and Torpedo Defense most of that time.

Turnbull stamped up to the wardroom in the predawn cold for a light breakfast of apples and oranges. George Lyons sat next to him with a plate of powdered eggs and bacon. Lyons turned twenty-two in 1945. He joined the Navy around the same time as Kiyoshi Ogawa. But while Kiyoshi had spent much of his training years waiting for fuel, Lyons had spent the last two years flying at diverse bases all around the United States. When he reached the Pacific, Lyons had more than 2,000 hours of flight time. After breakfast, the two pilots joined the rest of their squadron in the ready room. Turnbull wrote out the communication and navigation elements of the mission plan on the board and the ship's code name for the day. On May 11, 1945, *Bunker Hill* was called "Viceroy."

The darkened flight deck buzzed with men and machinery readying and launching flights. Strike aircraft were brought up on the ship's elevators, four planes every minute. Aircraft had been repositioned on the deck so that the fighters and bombers would be able to take off as expeditiously as possible. All the planes were loaded full of ordnance, including napalm. Each had been fully refueled with high-octane aircraft engine fuel.

The aircrews and plane captains were standing by each aircraft, checking systems and gauges. They wiped down any excess oil that might have overflowed a valve and checked off every necessary item for the flight. Conscientious plane captains stuck a clean strip of tape over the engine cowlings on the Corsairs. The tape prevented excess oil from staining the pilot's windshield.

And then "Pilots, man your planes" was ordered from the bridge to every single ready room at the same time. Fighter, dive-bomber, and torpedo pilots and their crews exited the side doors of their ready rooms, some of them slipping their life vests over their heads as they ran onto the gangway and up the companionway from the gallery deck, then out the hatchways on the flight deck from the port side of the island structure.

A moment later, as the pilots climbed up the wings of their assigned aircraft, a second command came from the bridge: "Stand by to start engines." Only the launching crews and the plane captains were left with the pilots in the predawn light as they started each plane for takeoff.

Turnbull's plane captain climbed onto the left wing and handed Turnbull a metallic clipboard. Turnbull scribbled his signature across the bottom, indicating his receipt of one government-issued TBF Avenger number 308 in working order. Then the plane captain stepped down off the wing and disappeared behind a protective barrier.

The only men left now were the launching crew and the pilots.

The Landing Signal Officer (LSO) gave Turnbull the sign to turn up his engine and check his magnetos and oil pressure. The huge aircraft shook and the engine pulled against the brakes. Finally, the LSO gave Turnbull the signal to taxi into line for takeoff. Simultaneously, crewmen ran beneath the wings on either side of his plane, dropped to their knees, and removed the chocks. Turnbull began to roll forward.

The flight crews crawled quickly away from the Avenger as it rolled toward the ship's bow. Turnbull taxied up to the LSO, who stood amidships by the island structure. He stepped on his brakes, then pulled a lever to spread his wings hydraulically and lock them in place. The Avenger was a powerful plane, with an enormously powerful engine. Even so, with a full load it needed every inch of the ship's flight deck to get airborne. Turnbull had seen every kind of aircraft drop off the end of the flight deck after making an unsuccessful takeoff run. When that happened, the carrier would plow over the fallen plane. If a pilot sensed a failed takeoff, he would try to steer his plane sideways out of the ship's way. The aircraft had no ejector seats; even if the plane made it to the ship's sides and was not bowled over, the wake behind the carrier would hit the stricken aircraft and take it under in seconds. The pilot almost never had a chance to get out.

Still at the center line beside the LSO, Turnbull dropped his flaps and opened up the engine cowling around the engine's power plant to get more cooling air inside during the crucial takeoff. The LSO stood at the tip of Turnbull's starboard wing. He signaled Turnbull to crank his engine all the way up, which he did while standing hard on his brakes. Turnbull then checked all his instruments one last time—fuel, oil pressure, engine heat—and adjusted his altimeter to the correct barometric pressure. Everything checked out okay. He showed the thumbs-up and the LSO gave him the wave with both red hand-signal lights. Turnbull let the brakes go and the seven-and-a-half-ton plane lurched into the darkness just as the first rays of the morning sun began to shine, lighting his way to the enemy in the east.

The whole way across to Okinawa, Turnbull worked the throttle with his left hand against the port side wall of the Avenger while he held his right hand on the joystick, keeping the plane straight and level for most of the trip. He saw a lot of Japanese aircraft on the way over and knew something was up. The sixth *Kikusui* was starting.

Turnbull's launch was quickly followed by others. Caleb Kendall launched next with a group of fighters. Major Archie Donahue followed with a group of Corsairs. Jim Swett flew CAP with his Marines. All were in the air by 6:30 A.M.

Along with bomber units from the *Essex*, Turnbull's twelve-plane Avenger squadron was to serve as a special attack group to support ground forces assaulting Shuri.

Turnbull flew the trip to Okinawa, as he did all of his missions, with a small notepad clipped to an elastic strap around his knee. It was his job as communications officer to take notes on the mission to be used in preparing a briefing for Slabo Bacon, the intelligence officer, upon their return. As soon as he launched from the carrier and pulled up his wheels, Turnbull would take his hand off the joystick, grab a pencil, and record conditions flying to the target, weather, resistance, their heading, wind direction, altitude, flight time to waypoints, anything unusual, and their effects on their final target destination. The Avengers flew in tight combat formation all the way over and back, so to avoid collision he also had to remain constantly aware of what the planes in front and on either side of him were doing.

Each pilot wore a steel Hamilton wristwatch with a gray canvas band issued by the Navy. Turnbull would note the time when he first saw enemy territory, and again when he first sighted the target. Then he would make a note just as he arrived over the target and began his dive. On the return he would note the weather over the target and make a note on all communications between the aircraft and Viceroy base during the mission.

The weather at sea was clear in the early morning, but the sky filled with moderate cumulus clouds at about 2,000 feet covering 80 percent of the sky as the sun rose. Sailors called this weather a "kamikaze day." The puffy clouds formed perfect hiding places for the kamikazes to scuttle along as they approached the fleet. A light wind drifted from the southeast at 3 to 7 knots.

When he checked in with Viceroy Base, Turnbull was informed that a series of gun emplacements was threatening American troops. The commander on the ground diverted them to destroy the guns, burn out the caves, and bombard Japanese supply stores on a ridge south of Yonabaru town. Turnbull's squadron dropped on the new target, but the assault was largely uneventful. As they flew the eighty miles or so back from Okinawa, the weather held fair: bright skies and temperatures in the upper 50s.

George Lyons, flying alongside Turnbull, was glad they would not be landing at night. Lyons had only been on the *Bunker Hill* three months. His first flight had been in the dark, and it had been scary. Lyons, like Turnbull, was both pilot and navigator. He studied the small air chart at his waist, trying to figure out where he was and where he was going. He marked the time traveled, speed, approximate wind speed and direction, and then made his best guess about his location. If he calculated accurately *and* the ship had maintained course, the flight group would come back upon her. But if the *Bunker Hill* had been forced to deviate, there could be serious trouble. For the most part, his work was all dead reckoning. The wind was a big factor. The Avenger had no anemometer to judge wind speed. Lyons had to fly down low and study the shape of the waves. He also had to maintain radio silence, but in 1945 the carriers often would give the pilots a short burst of instructions. "In the early part of the war there were problems with people getting lost," he said. "There were many unfortunate accidents."

The Avengers formed up over the carrier. When his turn came, Lyons descended, dropped to the deck, and caught the arrestor cable on his tail hook. His plane, emptied of perhaps 5,000 pounds of fuel and munitions, came to a complete stop in less than 450 feet. It took the combined efforts of more than 3,000 men aboard that vessel, and many others protecting her in the carrier battle group, to allow that remarkable feat: the launching and landing of a war plane from a ship. Once safely down, the pilots would sometimes drain alcohol from the fuel canisters for the torpedoes and mix it with fruit juice. They called it "good stuff." But now, Lyons just wanted his coffee.

It was 9:30 A.M.

The Avengers always returned from their strikes in four three-plane groups. On this morning, Marty Woll flew in on the outside wing, so he would be the last to land. But Lieutenant James T. Hagen came in before him, nosed up, and crashed the barrier. Woll and Turnbull had to fly around a couple of times waiting for the aircrews to clear the wreckage so they could land.

A bogie was reported ten miles out (about two minutes) from the *Bunker Hill*. GQ sounded again and landing operations for the early morning flights were discontinued. But flight crews continued to raise aircraft to the flight deck for the noon mission, overcrowding the landing space.

Burning through his fuel, Woll flew in for the second time only to see the *Bunker Hill* turning out of the wind. He radioed down to the bridge asking Viceroy politely what the hell they were doing. He needed to land. The *Bunker Hill* radioed back that radar had contacted bogies and he should try to join up with nearby American fighters who would protect him. He found a fighter circling the task group and fell in beside him. Turnbull and the others circled the fleet along with returning aircraft from more than a dozen other carriers. Controllers could not land the American planes while kamikazes were nearby, but by sending the Americans circling all around the fleet, they inadvertently made it easier for the kamikazes to sneak in amid the confusion. Aircraft seemed to be circling everywhere above the fleet, sliding in and out of the low clouds. Neither the lookouts nor the controllers could keep track. The bogies that had halted the landings had either disappeared or blended in with the American planes. The *Bunker Hill* turned again into the wind and resumed landing the returning strike.

Turnbull's plane caught the number two wire. He turned number 308 over to his plane captain and headed down to the ready room in his flight gear for a cup of coffee and to file his report for Slabo Bacon.

When sailors are called to highest alert for the first time, they are extremely vigilant. But when they are called for the thirtieth time in just a few days, the same men are often much less alert.

The gunners formed the *Bunker Hill*'s final line of defense. If the enemy got past them, the *Bunker Hill* could be destroyed. When they cruised close to Okinawa, Japanese spotter planes lit up the ship's radar so often that it just did not make sense to leave their stations at all. Gunners left only to relieve themselves or to grab a little food to share with their mates. Most stopped returning to their quarters even to sleep. They lay down fitfully at their battery, or on the deck beside it. Jim Spence, Stanley Nicas, Robert Earl Harris, and Jim Walker all served as gunners aboard the *Bunker Hill*.

A ship's level of readiness for battle is determined separately for its various divisions. Gunnery for instance is often kept at a higher level of readiness than, say, the cooks. General Quarters is an "all hands" command. Every single person aboard ship is required to be at their battle stations when GQ is sounded. Torpedo Defense requires only the gunners to go to their battle stations.

During previous battles, when ships were so close to enemy activity, they would be on constant GQ. But Okinawa dragged on too long. It was impossible for the ship to operate—for the men to eat or sleep or wash—when the ship was nearly always at GQ. So the Navy created new subconditions of readiness to allow the ship to function while remaining wary of enemy assault, reserving the highest degrees of readiness for times when bogies were nearby—the times when a ship faced greatest danger.

One-Easy is a modification of Torpedo Defense. It requires that all gunners go to their battle stations, but a single man from each gun, or one out of every three men on a gun system, was allowed to leave the battle station for a few minutes. The men had a brief chance to relax—use the head, grab a shower, or pick up coffee and toast for the rest of the crew.

One-Easy allowed some of the hatches opened to ease the passage of men around the ship and bring much needed fresh air belowdecks. One-Easy still required that the large watertight hatches be closed but allowed crewmen to open the scuttles (the small, circular hatch lids centered on the larger, watertight hatches) between the second and third decks and the living and working spaces on the fourth deck to remain open for access to the strong box—the ship's protected center.

When Admiral Ugaki's scout planes stumbled across the *Bunker*

Hill around 2:00 A.M. on the morning of May 11, they caused the entire ship to go to GQ. She was called to various degrees of readiness throughout the morning, as Japanese search planes and feinting attacks pressed at the edge of the fleet. Jim Spence, Stanley Nicas, Robert Earl Harris, Jim Walker, and the rest of the Gunnery Department remained at Condition One-Easy after GQ. The other departments, however, went back to Condition Able, so as to give the men some much needed rest.

By 9:45 A.M., the efficient flight deck crew had filled the aft deck with fresh planes stacked wing to wing, fully fueled and armed with .30- and .50-caliber shells, bombs, the new air-to-air rockets, and napalm. Crews brought aircraft up so quickly for the noon launch that the deck became too crowded for returning flights to land.

The *Bunker Hill* had been completely resupplied the day before and carried approximately 90 percent of her fuel capacity. The ship held about 1,873,000 gallons of ship's fuel and about 250,000 gallons of avgas.

Pilot Marty Woll had awakened that morning with a raw, prickling rash on his forearm; it irritated him, itching throughout that morning's mission. Combat missions required intense concentration. Woll had to read the map coordinates, mark his position, and watch out where all the other planes in his squadron were. He had to stay in formation, keep an eye out for hostile aircraft, drop his bombs on target, and remain wary of his fuel use and all his instruments. As soon as he landed, Woll marched straight to the ready room and tore off his flight suit and gear. He felt like a wimp for bothering Paul "Doc" Schroeder about a rash, but there was no way he could keep at peak intensity while continuously scratching at a nasty inflammation.

As Woll headed for the infirmary, Beads Popp lounged in the ready room with a group of other fighter pilots waiting for his sortie, scheduled for noon. Pilots milled in and out. Some, like Caleb Kendall, had just returned. Popp's friend John Sargent, with the Texas drawl, sat in the back.

Popp's sortie was to be a search and destroy mission (they had no bombers to escort). They did not have to remain in disciplined formation heading over AA-protected installations. Instead the fighters would hunt targets of opportunity. The men loved these kinds of missions. They could just head over to Okinawa, drop ordnance if they carried it, fire missiles at anything moving, and strafe the hell out of picket boats off the Kyushu shoreline. These open missions were often less dangerous than staying aboard ship on *Kikusui* days.

Skipper Chandler Swanson briefed them on the latest information about their flight: weather, navigation, defenses. Afterward, they all sat in the ready room, doing what war pilots do—talking, smoking, praying, reading, sleeping, reviewing, and joking—all the while waiting for the familiar words to come over the intercom telephone system: "Pilots, man your planes."

Pre-launch was the hardest time for most of the men. They talked quietly. They studied their maps. If there were any particular issues on that mission, they hashed them out. They made sure they knew well how they were going to match up and how they would go in. But they had flown together often, some of them since the very beginning of the war. They already knew what to do. It became mostly a matter of waiting.

Popp walked below to get a little chow before his flight. He sat down in a big chair in the wardroom and closed his eyes. It was quiet there, almost serene.

Colonel James Swett flew CAP that morning with Walter Goegle and Ralph Glenndenning. Swett had shot down at least fourteen enemy aircraft and only one ally by May 11, 1945. He was sent up early that day to lead the Marine detachment of VMF-221 over Task Force 58. Fred Briggs flew as Swett's number four man, "Tail End Charlie." They spent their morning "chasing kamikazes all over the sky." The Combat Information Center aboard the *Bunker Hill* vectored them first northeast toward Kanoya to intercept a Betty. The big twin-engine dive-bomber was one of the *Jinrai* attack planes that Kiyoshi was clearing the way for. The Betty, still carrying its Ohka bomb, slogged along but did not go down easy. The Marines lit her starboard engine afire quickly, then formed up above her.

Swett's squadron rolled down, one at a time, from their high-altitude advantage and raced in singly, raking her broadside. Then they pulled out tight beneath her belly, giving her waist, tail, and turret gunners the least return fire profile. Just as one Marine became vulnerable to return fire, the next would begin his attack dive, diverting the Betty's gunners.

Fred Briggs finished his run on the Betty just as Ralph Glenndenning began his dive atop her. The Japanese crew managed to release their Ohka. The suicide missile fell from the bay and dropped several hundred feet. The Ohka produced no exhaust; the doomed *Jinrai* pilot had not yet ignited the rocket engines. Briggs swung his plane hard over and gave a short burst from his wing guns. The fragile manned bomb exploded with extraordinary violence. Briggs is the only man known to have shot down an Ohka in air-to-air combat.

Debris from the Ohka struck Briggs's plane but he rolled out to safety. Almost immediately the CAP was vectored straight back out to help shoot down a Frances. They all knew then, because of the assortment of Japanese aircraft types, widely dispersed and all headed south and west, that the enemy had launched another *Kikusui*.

A few moments later, Swett dove on a Judy. He told me sixty years later: "That poor kid . . . I got a good look at his face and he looked up at me, knowing full well that he was a dead man. And he was right." The Judy was too low for the pilot to bail out. He hit the water hard and exploded. It was Swett's sixteenth confirmed kill. And his last.

Swett shot down the Judy near Okinawa, ninety miles from Viceroy Base. The squadron was running low on fuel, and nearly out of ammunition. Swett ordered his CAP back to the *Bunker Hill*. Thirty minutes later, about 9:45 A.M., Swett and his fliers arrived above the *Bunker Hill*. Thirty aircraft sat parked on the carrier's flight deck. Those on the flight deck carried (over and above their armament of .50-caliber and 40mm machine gun shells, rockets, bombs, and napalm) approximately 23,000 gallons of aircraft fuel.* By way of comparison, the 767s that hurtled into the World Trade Center carried approximately 21,000 gallons of fuel when they struck. Another forty-eight planes lay tied below on the hangar deck.

Swett and his patrol circled, waiting for the pilots to push the waiting aircraft forward. More and more aircraft returning from patrol began joining up with Swett's little CAP. He had been on station above the *Bunker Hill* for about fifteen minutes. The clocks aboard the *Bunker Hill* reached 10:00 A.M. with Swett still circling. Nearly twenty planes, returning from mission, all low on fuel and almost out of ammunition, joined up with Swett. His squadron circled low, at about 1,500 feet. Swett knew that one or more of those seeking to join up with him might be enemy. He checked constantly as he flew above the task group.

As soon as Turnbull returned to the ready room, he read through the jottings from his kneepad notebook and began writing a document that would become the intelligence report for his mission. This report would be given to the air group commander, Chandler Swanson. Admiral Mitscher, Byron White, and Swanson, meeting together, would use it to determine what to hit on the next strike and what specific munitions and aircraft to use on that strike. Usually the second strike would be heading out almost immediately, so Turnbull had to complete his report quickly. The ordnancemen were often already loading armament when the first strike returned.

Turnbull slipped off his flight suit and quickly put on a khaki shirt and pants and his Navy-issue heavy leather flight shoes with thick rubber soles. William A. "Stump" Edwards was duty officer that morning, in charge of assigning aircraft for the next strike. Stump was the youngest and smallest pilot in the squadron. He was reputed

* The Report of Battle Damage Received states that they did contain machine gun ammunition, but there were no bombs nor rockets on the planes. This is contradicted by the men who fought on the scene, many of whom provided numerous illustrations of burning napalm and other explosions.

to be the shortest pilot in the Navy. The rumor on the *Bunker Hill* was that he wore blocks of wood under his flight shoes just to reach the pedals. The wall telephone began buzzing as Stump stood writing on the chalkboard the pilots' names and plane numbers for the upcoming strike. On the phone was the flight deck officer, who was calling to say that several defective planes sat blocking the flight deck and needed to be taken forward to the deck edge elevator to be brought below and repaired.

The only pilots available to move the planes, like Turnbull, had been up since 2:30 in the morning and had just flown a four-hour combat mission. None of them wanted to get back into their sweaty flight suits merely to taxi aircraft.

But Stump, the duty officer, began writing pilots' names next to the numbers of the aircraft that had to be taxied below. The chosen pilots became furious when they saw their names being posted. Turnbull says he had never heard so much swearing in four years in the Navy. They cursed at Stump, shouting at him to yank someone out of the sack to move the planes. Stump put up with it for a while because he knew how tired they all were and knew it was not fair.* But the planes had to be moved before the CAP could land and before the next mission could be launched.

Turnbull, as communications officer, was not on the list, but he decided to go topside and move one of the planes himself. He put down his pencil and told Stump he would take a plane. Then he walked over to George Lyons, who had just flown back beside him from Okinawa.

Lyons sat in his pilot chair, just beginning to decompress. Turnbull asked him to come topside and help.

"I just got this coffee," he protested.

Turnbull picked up the cup, climbed on top of a leather chair, and announced sarcastically to the pilots, "No one touch *this* coffee."

Then he grabbed his helmet off the wall hook and headed topside.

---

* The Navy found that pilot efficiency (the time pilots could reliably remain in combat) had dropped from nine months in 1944 to four months during the kamikaze battles at Okinawa.

Reluctantly, Lyons followed. It was one of the luckiest moments of his life.

Lyons climbed into the cockpit of an Avenger on the stern flight deck and was just about to start the engine for warm-up when he saw three green planes, the red rising sun painted on their tails, break through the clouds. They were coming in at three o'clock, just a couple of hundred feet behind one another. Lyons froze. Why, he wondered, was no one shooting at them?

PART II

RENDEZVOUS
WITH DEATH

I have a rendezvous with Death
At some disputed barricade,
When Spring comes back with rustling shade
And apple-blossoms fill the air—
I have a rendezvous with Death
When Spring brings back blue days and fair.

It may be he shall take my hand
And lead me into his dark land
And close my eyes and quench my breath—
It may be I shall pass him still.
I have a rendezvous with Death
On some scarred slope of battered hill,
When Spring comes round again this year
And the first meadow-flowers appear.

God knows 'twere better to be deep
Pillowed in silk and scented down,
Where love throbs out in blissful sleep,
Pulse nigh to pulse, and breath to breath,
Where hushed awakenings are dear . . .
But I've a rendezvous with Death
At midnight in some flaming town,
When Spring trips north again this year,
And I to my pledged word am true,
I shall not fail that rendezvous.

—ALAN SEEGER

Alan Seeger, an American, graduated from Harvard University. He volunteered for World War I and was killed charging into German machine guns near Belloy-en-Santerre during the battle of the Somme. Three hundred thousand German, French, and English died in that battle.

22. YASUNORI SEIZO

Born all alone,
To die, also all alone.

Yesterday, I loved,
Today I anguish,
Tomorrow I die.

—FROM A POEM BY SØREN KIERKEGAARD
SCRIBBLED IN THE DIARY OF SHIN HASEGAWA,
A UNIVERSITY STUDENT WHO DIED IN A
KAMIKAZE ATTACK OFF OKINAWA IN APRIL 1945

At 10:02 A.M., Jim Swett was leading his CAP in a slow circle under the morning sun. The *Bunker Hill* cruised off his left wing when he looked up and saw two kamikazes diving steeply, out of the clouds 6,000 or 7,000 feet up, about a mile on his left, and right on the *Bunker Hill.*

"It was not the kind of a dive a plane pulls out of," Swett told me.

He picked up his mike and shouted, "Viceroy Base, there's two kamikazes diving on you." Within ten or fifteen seconds of Swett's warning, Yasunori Seizo released his bomb.

Swett and his men were flying in tight formation. They could only look over to the *Bunker Hill* for a second or two at a time or risk running into a wingman. Fred Briggs saw Yasunori break through the clouds above the *Bunker Hill.* It looked like a shadow more than anything. He thought it must be a Mustang and wondered what an Army land-based plane was doing way out there. And then the kamikaze broke free of the overcast and Briggs saw the red meatball.

He grabbed his microphone to alert Colonel Swett, but Swett was already taking a violent turn toward the Japanese plane. The gunners

283

on board the *Bunker Hill* saw it about then and began firing a heavy barrage. But it was all too late. Yasunori had begun his final dive.

The basic physical facts of Yasunori Seizo's kamikaze attack on the *Bunker Hill* on May 11, 1945, are clear: he dove in a controlled, shallow dive over the starboard side of the ship, astern and angled forward. It seemed almost as though he was coming in for a landing, but too steep, too fast, and firing all his guns at once in a steady barrage. Yasunori's line of strafing bullets moved forward diagonally, across the deck through the parked aircraft. He released his bomb, which, more aerodynamic, tumbled ahead and blew through the flight deck just aft of the number three elevator.

Edward Leahy, a plane captain, was going through the final check on his Corsair, positioned way aft on the flight deck. He leaned in, buckling the airman's seat belt, when his pilot looked up and shouted: "Jesus Christ! Duck!"

Leahy stood transfixed by the undercarriage of Yasunori's Zero. His pilot scrambled out of the cockpit, leapt onto the opposite wing, slid down it, and ran for the side of the ship as Leahy finally shouted, "Jap! Jesus!" He watched, horrified, as the enormous yellow 550-pound bomb fell. It occurred to him that the weapon was much too big to be a bomb. He had watched smaller American bombs being loaded for months now. Yasunori's bomb appeared enormous, five or six feet long, and it was tumbling directly toward him. Leahy leapt off the wing and dove belly-first to the deck.

The armor-piercing bomb* hit first, only a moment ahead of Yasunori's plane. It crashed through the flight deck, ripped apart a passageway in the gallery deck, then broke through the ceiling of the hangar deck, and shattered a hole in the ship's port side before it finally

---

* Armor-piercing bombs have delayed fuses that activate the moment the warhead strikes the target. Japanese armers tried to time the delay in the fuse so that the bomb would pierce the flight deck, then explode inside the hangar deck of American carriers. The delay on Yasunori's bomb was a split second too long—the bomb's momentum took it through the flight deck, then outside of the ship before it exploded.

detonated, about twenty feet outside the *Bunker Hill*, just above the water. Shrapnel tore through crewmen and gunners along the ship's port side, stabbing hundreds of holes along the armored walls of the *Bunker Hill*, many below the waterline. Sailors, especially in the gun tubs and on the port side of the hangar deck, were torn apart.

The bomb's concussion threw Leahy across the deck. He smashed his head against the tire of another Corsair and was knocked unconscious, his eardrum shattered. He came to as fires spread around him. His head reeled and blood trickled from one ear. Men seemed to run past him shouting nothing. Aircraft and machinery were bursting into flames all around him, some exploding, but nothing made any sound. All he could hear was a terrible ringing. Wary of the flames, he sprinted unsteadily toward the starboard side and jumped onto the relative safety of the catwalk. He lay for a moment, with a small group of sailors, and looked aft searching for a way out. One sailor was cut off behind them, surrounded by flame. The lone sailor stood up high on the catwalk and dove off the side of the ship.

Shrapnel penetrated the hangar deck where it ignited fuel tanks in parked aircraft and set off a series of secondary explosions inside the ship. One after another, the aircraft inside the hangar deck caught fire and exploded in an unstoppable chain reaction. The fires grew so hot that the reinforced steel framing the number three elevator twisted. Burning fuel poured down an open hatch and spread fires into the protected box.

After releasing its payload, Yasunori's plane continued its shallow dive and crashed the aircraft just in front of George Lyons's plane, skidding across the crowded deck. The Zero sliced through the aircraft on deck, whose propellers were already spinning, throwing deadly shrapnel in all directions, ripping open their fuel tanks, and setting gasoline fires blazing. Within thirty seconds, most of the aft portion of the flight deck was ablaze.* In a violent skid, Yasunori's

* Yasunori struck at frame 143 just aft of the ship's number three (aft) elevator (572 aft of the ship's bow). He slid diagonally about twenty-eight feet forward. The *Bunker Hill*'s framing members were placed every four feet. Thus frame 143 is 572 feet aft of the ship's bow.

plane dragged at least one Corsair and a long section of the catwalk, crowded with sailors, over the ship's side and into the sea.

From their vantage point, 1,500 feet above the *Bunker Hill*, Jim Swett and his squadron watched, horrified.

Swett told me later, "He just cleaned house. God, it was a terrible mess."

Flip Gerner sat astern in his Corsair cockpit idling on the flight deck as Yasunori began his dive. Gerner's wings were folded and pointing upward, his engine warming up, spinning the propeller hard. His plane captain was hooking up his harness when Gerner looked up at a small plane diving at them. The Zero clipped the upraised left wing of Gerner's Corsair before crashing hard into the next plane and ramming Bud Millholland's Corsair. Gerner watched Millholland's plane rip violently over the side, locked with the kamikaze. As other aircraft quickly ignited, the pilots were surrounded by an inferno.

Yasunori's strafing had mauled the Marines on the gun battery

Number three (aft) elevator twisted from heat of fires set by Yasunori's crash, as seen from the burned-out hangar deck.

immediately below the Air Aft lookouts, halfway up the aft portion of the island structure. A Marine officer, commanding 20mm double Bofors machine cannons, was severely injured. Shrapnel from Yasunori's bomb blast severed most of his lower body. Despite the flames that were rapidly approaching, the Marine ordered his men to remain at their post. His comrades could not carry him to the forward aid station. But they stayed with him. They gathered towels and shirts and stuffed them into the lower part of his torso, stanching the flow of blood. The injured Marine asked for an American flag. Someone ran through the debris to retrieve the colors. The Marine clutched the symbol to his chest as he lay dying and held the flag tight until he bled out. His men remained at their guns until their weapons no longer functioned.

Bud Millholland was widely regarded as the most attractive man aboard the *Bunker Hill*, perhaps the best-looking man in the Pacific Theater. Even in an air group of brave and handsome men he stood out. Millholland's Corsair hit the water right side up, just moments after the explosion of Yasunori's bomb. Unfortunately, Millholland's plane was loaded with napalm.

Millholland survived the drop, but his napalm ignited the surface of the ocean all around the plane, which was sinking fast. He had no choice but to jump over the side and into the flaming Pacific. Millholland tried to dive through the jellied surface and swim beneath the flames, but the napalm stuck to him. It burned so hot that the fingers of his left hand fused together into a swollen, oozing mitten. He tried to swim below the flames but was forced to rise several times, pulling for air that was not there—the fire consumed all the oxygen near the surface.

Turnbull stepped out on the deck and had climbed into his assigned Avenger to move forward when Yasunori appeared. Suddenly the planes arrayed on his port side began to vibrate with tiny explosions. Turnbull knew instantly they were being strafed. He could hear guns blazing—his first thought was that this was an odd sound to hear from the deck of a ship. Then he looked up to starboard and saw Yasunori flying down hard at the deck, all his guns firing. The bullets streamed down, tearing up the deck and the aircraft on Turnbull's port. The line of strafing bullets streamed forward down the deck away from Turnbull as Yasunori's dive continued. Turnbull sat in his Avenger, transfixed as the flames grew around him. And then he saw Kiyoshi falling.

Flight crewmen had just hooked a rubber-wheeled mule tractor to George Lyons's Avenger when he looked up and to his right and saw three green planes with big red balls painted on their tails diving at the ship. One had dropped his nose and seemed to be headed directly toward Lyons. A moment later, Yasunori released his bomb. The streamlined warhead fell ahead of the Zero, over Lyons's head, and blew through the flight deck. Yasunori's Zero crashed through the nose of the plane in front of Lyons. He tore that Corsair's engine out of its fuselage, setting its wildly spinning propeller tearing across the deck. The Corsair's cockpit split in half and a fireball engulfed the pilot. Fuel spewing from torn lines flooded all across the crowded flight deck, and then flamed. Yasunori was on fire, too, as he scraped through a line of other aircraft causing explosion after explosion along the burning deck.

Lyons leapt out of his plane and ran toward the stricken pilot, still belted into the burning cockpit of the decapitated Corsair in front of him. Then he halted as he spotted Kiyoshi Ogawa coming in hard.

23. I FOUND THE ENEMY VESSELS

The weather is perfect. There are no clouds ahead. This looks like the day.

—LAURENCE GOULD'S RADIOED MESSAGE
TO COMMANDER RICHARD BYRD BEFORE
HIS FLIGHT OVER THE SOUTH POLE

At 9:58 A.M., Kiyoshi Ogawa radioed Kanoya using Morse code: "*Teki kubo miru*"—"I found the enemy vessels."

And then, a moment later, "I see an enemy plane."

Only a moment after that, Kiyoshi radioed: "I see the enemy aircraft carrier."

Kiyoshi came in along the same bearing as Yasunori, but banked hard around the starboard aft quarter just after Yasunori's plane hit. He was able to mask his plane from the ship's aft guns that were buried beneath the wall of smoke that Yasunori's sacrifice had kicked up along the flight deck. But he came in above the top of the mushrooming smoke cloud and was highly visible to the forward gunners.

Kiyoshi turned hard around the stern of the *Bunker Hill*. Then, despite the terrible AA fire, he barrel-rolled his plane and dove nearly straight down—70 degrees—toward the base of the island structure at the center of the *Bunker Hill*. A bull's-eye for a kamikaze pilot.

In his final message, at 10:02.30, Kiyoshi spoke his last words: "Now, I am nose-diving into the ship."

Kiyoshi must have seen his comrade's near-perfect crash and the mayhem it had caused on the *Bunker Hill*. But he would have had almost no time to reflect on what he saw.

The gunners aboard the *Bunker Hill* had virtually no warning of Yasunori's dive. But they had twenty to thirty seconds to find Kiyoshi and begin shooting at him.

Every American gun was trained on him. The twelve 5-inch guns were firing proximity fuse shells like machine guns; seventy-two 40mm rapid-fire machine antiaircraft cannons were tearing at his plane; and another fifty-two 20mm rapid-fire machine antiaircraft guns were striking his fuselage—and that was just from *Bunker Hill*. Dozens of other U.S. ships, among them at least one cruiser and four Navy destroyers, were also firing at Kiyoshi.

Kiyoshi was well beyond an attitude and speed that could be reasonably controlled. Yet, somehow, Kiyoshi did steer the plane while being struck by innumerable AA guns and fired on by hundreds of others.

The leading edge of his port wing exploded almost dead-center, as it was hit by a 40mm cannon. The shell ripped out a big chunk, but the wing did not break off. Kiyoshi steered directly into the smoke and fire, knowing that the result of success would be his death and the deaths of many others, men not unlike himself.

Kiyoshi released his giant explosive at precisely the right moment. The near instantaneously fused SAP (semi-armor-piercing) 250-kilogram (550-pound) bomb fell just ahead of his Zero. The warhead penetrated the deck of the *Bunker Hill* at the ship's most vulnerable point—adjacent the deck edge elevator and only twenty-five feet port of amidships.*

George Lyons knew then that the bomb had struck his ready room. He continued running toward the injured pilot as the deck around them began to ignite. Lyons reached the shorn aircraft and climbed up to the cockpit where he found the stricken pilot alive and literally smoking. The pilot's skin had blackened as though he was dirty, but otherwise he did not seem too bad. He spoke with Lyons normally, but had trouble moving. In fact, the stricken flier was mortally wounded, although he probably did not know he was dying. In those days, the primitive nylon pressure suits were not fire-retardant. The

---

* Kiyoshi's plane crashed to starboard of the centerline, at the intersection of the island and the flight deck between frames 90–91 (360 feet aft of the bow).

pressure suit's steel zipper hung down from the burned pilot's throat. The rest of the suit had melted away, blackened and indistinguishable from the pilot's own skin. Severe burns shock the body. Adrenaline flooded all the doomed man's tissues and blocked pain signals to his brain. The burned pilot, although dying, felt no pain and was nearly able to walk.

Just above the ship, Kiyoshi's plane burst into flame, but he pressed home his attack. His right wing smashed into the catwalk of Primary Fly (Flight Control), where Commander Fraunheim normally stood, guiding flight operations, and just aft of the ship's bridge, where Captain Seitz stood fifty feet away. The wing then tore down the side of the island, ripping out about ten feet of the catwalk in front of the hatchway on the navigation deck and the signal bridge walkway, beside the flag signal boards where Wally Girts was stationed. Kiyoshi kept his fingers keying the Morse code mike as he fell. The mike went silent thirty seconds later, 10:03 A.M. The Zero missed killing Admiral Mitscher and Arleigh Burke by less than twenty feet.

Jim Swett banked sharply around the stern as Kiyoshi, opposite him on the port side of the *Bunker Hill*, also turned hard. Swett saw the cloud of flame and smoke rising from the gallery deck ready rooms and his heart ached. Swett and his men tried to raise the *Bunker Hill* repeatedly, but no one answered. He knew his friends were dead.

A remarkable pair of pictures of the *Bunker Hill* under attack, taken by photographers aboard the USS *Randolph* (CV-15), and only recently declassified by the National Archives, reveals the precise timing of the four explosions caused by the two kamikaze aircraft and their two bombs. The first photo is taken after Yasunori Seizo's aircraft has hit the aft deck. The lighter graying smoke of the initial crash and bomb detonations atop the smoke spire is being supplanted at lower altitudes by a growing thick black petroleum-based plume. Fire from the chain of explosions begun by Yasunori's crash lights the deck amidst the dark cloud. Smoke from a secondary explosion is moving ahead of the major fire in the stern as aircraft on the deck begin to explode one after the other. But only the aft portion of the *Bunker Hill* is aflame. The smoke plume trails the ship, angling sharply off the *Bunker Hill*'s aft quarter because the carrier is still steaming quickly.

Kiyoshi lived for approximately half a minute from the time he commenced his dive until he hit the deck of the *Bunker Hill*. He died on impact, his airman's navigation watch buried deep into the bones of his chest. It was pried out later by Robert Schock, a seaman aboard the *Bunker Hill*.

The primary blast zone from Kiyoshi's bomb formed a jagged sphere approximately fifty feet in diameter and three decks deep.

The gallery deck was forced upward where it shattered against the bottom of the flight deck, then continued upward, blowing a gigantic hole through the flight deck. Debris from both decks fell all around the ship. Herbert Ferguson stood mesmerized in a control room beside Admiral Mitscher as he watched four-inch teak deck beams splintering and falling through the air like burning matches. Ferguson was a cryptographer, decoding top secret messages from the Pacific Command for Admiral Mitscher. Ferguson normally worked in CIC from nine to five. But on May 11, 1945, he was serving on special bridge duty, standing behind Admiral Mitscher. The admiral sat at his usual place, flag plot, the most forward compartment on the navigation bridge, one level above the flight deck and open to the elements. Ferguson's friend from Harvard, with whom he normally worked, was locked in CIC in a small compartment they shared, suspended above the hangar deck, just forward of where Kiyoshi's bomb exploded.

Kiyoshi Ogawa's plane is caught in this photo, a blur falling at about 70 degrees and headed straight for the ship's center. The picture stops time perhaps one second before Kiyoshi is obliterated.

The light from the detonation of Kiyoshi's bomb explodes out from the deck edge elevator and through the hangar deck, just as many of the pilots in the ready room are killed. Inside this major blast one can see the lighter, secondary explosion from Kiyoshi's collision with the ship's island. The picture likely records the precise moment of his death. A third kamikaze is visible near the top of the smoke plume in high-resolution copies of this photograph.

Kiyoshi's Zero smashed into the flight deck where it meets the hangar deck, driving the engine through a mule tractor and three feet into the island structure. The crash ignited gasoline fires around Kiyoshi's wreckage. The blast also immediately ignited fires on three decks (gallery, hangar, and flight) in which trapped men were cooked alive. These fires eventually spread into the protected box through open hatches. Parts of Kiyoshi's plane broke through decking and entered a passageway. The metal fragments killed a sailor making his way to the engine rooms. Kiyoshi's fuselage did little other injury. His aircraft engine had received so little damage that photos of the engine even reveal which Nakajima factory built it. Kiyoshi's body was thrown to the deck from the Zero's shattered cockpit, still very much recognizable.

Alarmed by the concussion of Yasunori's crash, Al Nadeau peered out his hatchway in the island and saw fire and smoke where the number three elevator had been. The narrow doorway blocked his view of Kiyoshi's plane, now diving steeply almost straight down at him. Nadeau could not believe this was happening.

An air traffic controller talker, Nadeau worked Fly 2 at the base of the island. Fly 3 was one deck above him on the catwalk, just outside the flag boards ten feet above Nadeau's head. Kiyoshi's bomb exploded almost precisely as his plane hit at the base of the island, one door aft from Nadeau. A tremendous flash of fire shot right through the island structure.

"By Jesus," Nadeau said. "Them Japs really got us this time."

He jumped through the hatchway, past the bomb-blasted hole, and ran toward the bow, up along the starboard ship's edge, past the 5-inch guns arrayed along the side of the flight deck. Throughout the attacks of the first two planes, the gunners had stayed in their positions, still shooting. Now most of the gun mounts swung around and were shooting aft at yet another kamikaze.

George Lyons held the arm of the badly burned pilot who had barely escaped Yasunori's crash. The man's whole body was smoldering. Lyons rushed, half carrying, half dragging the injured Corsair pilot across the burning deck. They fell into the catwalk and dove behind a 20mm cannon, where a gunner blasted away at another kamikaze.*

---

* A still unidentified kamikaze flew close by and behind Kiyoshi—the one that Woll and Lyons saw shot down from the port side of the flight deck. This aircraft can be seen in enhanced photos of Kiyoshi's last dive. Another kamikaze flew in low, just over the ocean at the starboard side. Leahy and Volkema saw it destroyed. Herbert Ferguson, too, saw this kamikaze just before the flag bridge was shuttered. Many other kamikaze aircraft attempted to hit the *Bunker Hill* that morning. Gunners on both sides of the *Bunker Hill*, bow and stern, claim to have seen or had a hand in shooting down Japanese aircraft at that time. Probably half a dozen additional kamikazes came close to finishing off the *Bunker Hill*. But the ship's gunners put up a shield of lead, and the battle group around her

Lyons, crouching by the 20mm gun, which had just shot down a kamikaze on the stern, looked forward along the hull of the *Bunker Hill* searching for safety. The island superstructure was obscured by thick smoke. He looked down for a long while, thinking of jumping, considering the distance to the water and his probability of survival. But sailors choking on the fantail reached up to help him. He handed the injured pilot down and climbed over a discharge pipe and joined them in the relative safety of the fantail.

Art Volkema had served most of the war as a lookout in Air Aft, perched high up just behind the stack on the back side of the island. But he was transferred to the ship's bow on May 10. When the sounds of Yasunori's crash cracked in his ears, Volkema turned aft to watch Kiyoshi fall. He saw Kiyoshi's bomb destroy the flight deck in a gigantic explosion that caused hunks of pipe and other debris to rain down on him and the other men in his gun tub at the ship's bow. He thought that would be it. But the horrendous explosion seemed endless, growing bigger and louder as more ordnance and fuel ignited.

In despair, Volkema watched as the men he had worked with in Air Aft leapt from the burning lookout position. Some landed in the sea. Others were crushed on the deck. Every man at his old position was killed in the attack.

When Yasunori hit, Herbert Ferguson ran from the bridge out onto the little catwalk to look down at the fires on the aft deck. Then he looked up and saw Kiyoshi flying straight down at him. As Kiyoshi fell, Ferguson thought to himself that the kamikaze was in perfect control of his plane. He seemed to spin the fuselage a tiny bit at the end in order to fit past the bridge and slam directly into the base of the island. Kiyoshi's wing tore down a section of the catwalk ten feet

---

closed ranks. Just after Kiyoshi crashed, three more kamikazes were shot down by screening destroyers surrounding the *Bunker Hill*. The log of the *Enterprise* (CV-6) states that at least five more kamikazes were shot down in the vicinity of the *Bunker Hill* that morning. The *Bunker Hill*'s radar was out so all available men were ordered to watch the skies, looking out for more kamikazes. Gunners aboard the *Bunker Hill* watched gunners on nearby radar-equipped ships. When the surrounding ships moved their guns, these lookouts ordered the *Bunker Hill*'s gun bays to swing at the same part of the sky.

Before and after Kiyoshi's crash: Photograph of the Bunker Hill's island before Kiyoshi crashed. Note the public address speaker beneath the flag boards and the officers observing behind the boards at Primary Fly.

The same area after Kiyoshi's crash. The public address speaker remains, but not much else. Note obliterated mule tractor at ground zero. Admiral Mitscher's habitual station was on the lower catwalk, just above the strike record drawing board, about twenty feet from where Kiyoshi's wing struck.

Commander Fraunheim supervises recovery of Kiyoshi's wreckage. Pieces are piled into a crate of Boy Blue Washington apples—carried fresh from Bremerton on the ship's final deployment.

The hole in the flight deck torn by Kiyoshi's bomb. Note the wheel used to dog down a hatch on the doorway torn apart at right.

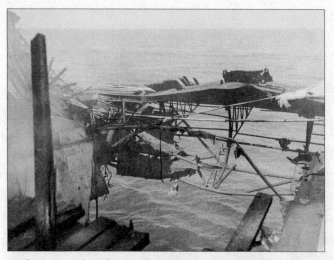

In this image, the calm Pacific Ocean may be seen rolling through what was recently the deck edge elevator. It has been obliterated.

Kiyoshi's crash. The front section of the mule tractor that Kiyoshi smashed lies in the foreground. Two sailors had been seated inside when he struck.

from Ferguson. He stared, frozen, as Kiyoshi obliterated two men operating the small mule tractor below his catwalk. The explosion blew Ferguson against a bulkhead wall in the bridge, unconscious and deafened.

Wallace Girts was a skivvy waver—a signalman attached to Admiral Mitscher. Girts raised and lowered the flags on the flag boards just outside flag plot. He was standing at his station when Yasunori struck the *Bunker Hill*, but he ducked inside the meager protection of a narrow passageway in the island when he saw Kiyoshi diving. Kiyoshi's wing tore out the catwalk where Girts had been standing, and shredded the flag boards. Then the whole ship shook. Pieces of Kiyoshi's plane ripped through a flag office just behind Girts, killing three officers and seven men on Mitscher's staff. Girts watched Mitscher look out past the starboard side observation deck catwalk to make sure destroyers were picking up the sailors who had been forced off the decks.

Arleigh Burke ran below with Frank Dingfelder to the battered radio room at the bottom of the island. A dozen or so men stood inside, confused and choking. Flames quickly spread toward them. Burke and Dingfelder dragged and led the barely conscious radiomen to safety. They made it out just ahead of the flames. Burke remained until the last man exited, then climbed back up the ladder to Mitscher's side. Burke had breathed in more of the foul air than any of the other men and could not speak for several minutes. Hot, acrid smoke followed them up the ladder, pouring into flag plot. Admiral Mitscher and his staff were cut off from the rest of the ship and the fleet. Most of the radars were out and many of the radio frequencies failed. Even the VHF radios stopped working. For a time, the *Bunker Hill* could listen to radio chatter but not be heard, but this last channel burned out quickly. The *Bunker Hill* was reduced to communicating by flags, though Kiyoshi's crash had torn out half the flag boards. No one on the other ships knew whether Admiral Mitscher was alive.

Swett, still banking hard when Kiyoshi's bomb exploded, could not afford to reflect on the loss of his friends in their ready room. He was now in charge of a group of planes that were nearly out of fuel and ammunition, with no place to land. Their refuge had become an inferno. They were largely unable to defend themselves, much less the fleet. His first task was to land his crews safely. As he banked by the *Bunker Hill*, though, Swett flew close enough to see his shipmates jumping over the side, many without life jackets or safety gear.

He should have guided his squadron immediately to safety on another carrier. But he could not leave the sailors alone in the sea. Instead, Swett led his men around again, then dropped his nose down toward the sailors in the water.

Swett's squadron dove on their comrades, as they would have an enemy ground installation. He and his men flew in with their sticks hard forward, skimming the sea. Instead of dropping bombs, they threw out their dye markers. Then they removed their life preservers and made another run, throwing their life jackets out to the struggling sailors. Finally, Swett and his men, perilously low on fuel, dexterously worked their life rafts out from under their seats and cut loose the tie-downs with their Bowie knives. The life raft was affixed via their seat to their parachute harness. Cutting free the life raft rendered their chutes useless. But every Marine pilot cast theirs off. They finished the final run, pitching the ungainly life rafts out to the men struggling below them. The water was full of black oil and mud from the ship. Then Swett saw the sharks. They appeared enormous to him, circling around the men splashing in the windless sea.

When they had nothing left to give, Swett hauled his men from carrier to carrier, looking for a place to land. The *Enterprise* welcomed them. It was the first time a Corsair ever landed on the Big E. But by May 1945, the Fifth Fleet was so well supplied that the *Enterprise* had no room for the sixteen Corsairs. As soon as Swett climbed out of his plane, the deck crew pushed the brand-new fighter over the side.

The *Enterprise* steamed ahead, leaving the stricken *Bunker Hill* behind followed by several destroyers and a cruiser. The big carriers would become too easy targets if they slowed to help the wounded. The *Bunker Hill*'s hull fell quickly out of Swett's sight, but everyone could see the pyre of smoke rising high above the far horizon. The smoke was a reminder to him of his friends . . . and a beacon leading remaining kamikazes to the stricken ship.

Marty Woll left the Avenger ready room to get some cortisone for his rash. He got lost below, but found another pilot looking for sickbay. When Yasunori's bomb exploded astern, the two were climbing down a ladder into the armored area of the ship below the hangar near the deck edge elevator. A sailor leaned down the hatch above them and shouted that they had been hit. He slammed the big hatch cover down over their heads.

They heard the dogs (steel latches used on ships) locking the big cover in place. Moments later, Kiyoshi's huge explosion rocked the ship. Woll was protected by the steel deck of the hangar. He felt the explosion more than he heard it—the reverberations of Kiyoshi's bomb shook through the hull and all around him.

Woll stood alone with the fighter pilot. They paused in the dark, uncertain in the maze of passages below the hangar deck. The two lost pilots knew that every hatch would be dogged within minutes and they would be trapped under the fires.

Woll rushed up the ladder to the hatch that had just been slammed closed above them. He lifted this small hatch and popped his head up into the hangar deck to a scene of absolute horror. The ship had collapsed all around the opening. The sailor who closed the hatch was obliterated.

Fire burned all around. The gallery deck had disappeared. Steel beams were bent by the heat. Machinery that raised and lowered the 16,000-pound deck edge elevator lay melted, twisted, and broken. The elevator had been halfway down. It looked as if someone had dropped it on its side.

Ammo had been piled just aft of the small hatch in preparation for loading into the next group of attack craft. The heated munitions began to explode all over the hangar. Bullets tore past Woll on all sides and he knew he had to get his head out of there immediately. But the fighter pilot below him wanted to get out of the smoke-filled room just as badly and was pushing Woll up into the inferno around the elevator. Woll shouted, but could not make himself heard above the din of fire and explosions. Woll kicked hard and they fell together on the floor, lost and disheartened. Their darkened compartment filled with smoke.

The two men built a step-ladder out of some cots spread out in the room and climbed up so they could suck the clean air coming in through the ventilation system. They could survive on that air, they believed, indefinitely. Suddenly, however, the ventilation air turned thick, black, and poisonous and began furiously pouring out of the vent that had been giving life to their lungs. They crawled forward and entered another pitch-dark room. It took a few moments, squinting and feeling around in the dark, before they realized they were crowded in with six dead men. The two pilots retreated quickly back to their first position and locked the hatch behind them. Then they split up.

Woll crawled on his hands and knees heading aft, feeling his way as he dragged along for hundreds of feet, until he reached two petty officers who had come to search and rescue. They threw him bodily up a ladder into what he thought was a dark, crowded room. He sat for many minutes before he realized he was standing on the open fantail in broad daylight but shrouded in smoke. He had crawled from midships to the stern. George Lyons eventually appeared. Together, they shared an oxygen mask.

Blaine Imel flew a Marine Corsair in VMF-221 under Colonel Swett aboard the *Bunker Hill*. He had flown sixty combat missions and shot down three Japanese planes in six months. Imel stood in the VMF ready room a few doors down from Caleb Kendall. Two hatches led to his ready room: the usual narrow hatch leading to the twisting hallways on the gallery deck above the hangar, and a second, small escape hatch that led to a narrow catwalk on the port side. The ship was slammed hard and shuddered. It felt as though they had struck a rock; Imel nearly fell to the floor. Half a minute later they were hit again, even harder.

The overhead light brightened for a moment, then turned amber, faded to blue, and went out. The ready room filled with smoke and fell into total darkness. Imel's eyes burned. The Marines, working together, quickly lay face-down on the floor and locked arms. Flames covered the little catwalk outside, so they scuttled together toward the steel passage that linked the ready rooms. But when they opened the hatch, an eerie light flooded in. The steel passage glowed orange-hot, impassable. They were trapped. The airmen decided to make a run for the burning catwalk. Imel prayed silently for forgiveness as they shuffled toward the flaming hatch to the outer hull.

The flames had moved off a narrow section of the catwalk immediately outside of their ready room. The pilots stepped out onto a tiny island of survival twenty-five feet long. The only section of the catwalk not covered in flame miraculously lay in front of their ready room. A locker of .50-caliber belts had heated up and the rounds were exploding, not all at once, but like an angry child beating a drum. They made their way over and dogged down a hatchway in front of the locker, blocking the bullets.

A giant set of cubbyholes, tacked onto the side of the ship like a series of post office boxes, held the new five-foot-long 140-pound HVAR rockets that had so devastated the Japanese ground troops. The rockets were growing dangerously, visibly hot. The Marines grabbed a fire hose and began to sprinkle the hot steel, but the hose had rotted full of holes. In a moment, it lost all pressure. Instead, they started a rocket brigade, passing the hot rockets hand over hand and pitching them into the sea.

The catwalk kept getting hotter. Fires blocked both ends. Rolling gently forty feet below them, the Pacific offered solace. The men pitched overboard all the unexploded ordnance they could reach, then the officers ordered the men to abandon ship. After splitting the life belts and jackets between them, they uncoiled a Jacob's ladder.* But the ladder lines had rotted and it tumbled into the sea. They all watched it fall, realizing they, too, would soon make that drop. Imel gazed downward, thinking about the four giant propellers churning the water

---

* A Jacob's ladder is an emergency ladder on the outside of a ship. (In the book of Genesis, Jacob dreamed of a ladder that went straight to heaven.) These are usually made of chain or wood, with wood or metal rungs, and can be unrolled to abandon ship.

behind them. The ship was still making 20 knots. He had watched the sea many times from this catwalk and wondered whether he would have the courage to jump. And then he stepped off the platform.

Imel hit the water hard and everything turned white. He struggled to the surface, gasped in clean air, and looked up at the listing *Bunker Hill*. He could see the fires all along the flight and hangar decks passing above him. Smoke filled the air. The *Bunker Hill* receded into the horizon. For the first time in months, everything was quiet. Experiencing a brief moment of absolute solitude and calm, Imel breathed in deeply. But this moment of serenity was quickly interrupted as he became aware of more and more terrified sailors struggling in the waters around him. Someone had found part of the torn rope ladder and they clung to it together. An hour or so later, a destroyer plucked them from the sea.

Slabo Bacon, communications officer for the Avenger squadron, worked most of the day at his desk in the small office just off the Avenger ready room. Bacon survived the initial blast from Kiyoshi's bomb, then dashed down a burning passageway suspended above the flight deck. Most of the passageway collapsed a moment after the explosion. Bacon tumbled down amid pieces of the collapsing hallway into the burning hangar deck. He struck his head and lay for a moment, unconscious, on his back in a pile of debris atop the hatch that Marty Woll had shut a moment before. Pieces of different decks, aircraft equipment, and parts of the deck edge elevator lay around him. They all began to burn, and the flames surrounded him as he came to.

Fuel and oil from the flight deck poured into the hole torn by Kiyoshi's bomb. The fuel accelerated the debris fires beside the ruined deck edge elevator. These flames spread and climbed over and around parked aircraft on the flight deck, which quickly became part of the growing conflagration.

Stanley Nicas commanded one of the double 5-inch guns behind the island on the starboard side. The four armored gun mounts stood like gigantic double-barreled army tanks stuck to the side of the flight deck. More than a dozen men worked inside each. Radar aimed the gun. Powerful electric motors swiveled the gun mount so quickly that the men inside could barely hold on.

Nicas never saw either of the kamikazes. But he heard Yasunori's explosion and immediately locked down his gun, bolting his men inside. Nicas heard more and more explosions around his armored mount, but the radar continued to aim his gun, so he kept his men loading and firing. After a few minutes the power line to his gun burned out. The firing stopped, but the explosions outside continued. He opened a narrow viewing hatch to look out at the deck. The *Bunker Hill* appeared to be completely engulfed in flame. Nevertheless, Nicas knew he could not allow his men to abandon their weapon. He buttoned the gun back up. A filtering system mounted on the turrets of the 5-inch guns scrubbed the air coming in. The air inside became brutally stultifying, but remained just clean enough to keep the gunners alive.

Jim Walker sat inside his 20mm gun tub at the stern end of the flight deck, learning to play pinochle with four other gunners, Rex Road, Eddie Radcliff, Eddie Harris, and Fillingame. The 20mm guns remained inaccurate until enemy planes flew within a mile of the *Bunker Hill*—seconds from impact. Their gun mount hung far aft, so close to the stern that Walker could climb down to the fantail to sleep. Much better than the noisy flight deck crowded with men and aircraft, it had a rail that kept him from rolling over the side in the night. Walker had worried about falling overboard since the day he boarded the *Bunker Hill*. He feared the ship's huge propellers chopping him up.

They heard a strange whine coming from the engine of a plane they thought was landing (Japanese radial engines sounded different from the American planes). Fillingame craned his head cautiously up over the edge of the flight deck to check out the strange sound, just as Yasunori's bomb exploded. The deck became an inferno almost instantly. Gasoline gushed from broken hoses and split fuel tanks. Burning fuel sloshed down the deck and poured into their gun tub. The fuel quickly ignited and Walker caught fire. He leapt over the side, aflame.

Walker sank deep when he hit the sea and could feel the screws he had feared for so long, churning as he tumbled under water . . . voomp . . . voomp . . . voomp . . . voomp. Burning fuel burned his chest, head, arms, and legs. It blackened his face and seared his clothes. But he kept swimming, until he met up with another gunner from his mount. They had both burned and swelled so black that neither recognized the other. Millions of nerves in his skin were dead and could sense nothing. But the unburnt, or less badly burned, portions of Walker's skin remained sensitive to the enormous pain he was suffering. Nevertheless, it did not yet hurt. His body had gone into shock, blocking blood flow to and pain messages from the injured parts of his body. His brain released so much adrenaline that he was able to swim, unaware of the terrible injuries he had sustained. He has no idea how long he treaded water. Eventually, a destroyer picked him up and he was deposited on the hospital ship *Bountiful*. When the damaged skin began to grow back a few weeks later, the pain became nearly unbearable.

Walker met one of his gun-mates years later at a reunion. Both had jumped off the ship when their guns melted. His gun-mate swore, though, that when he returned to the *Bunker Hill*, somehow at the bottom of the gun tub, the pinochle cards remained where they had dropped them, unharmed.

Thomas Martin, the ordnance man who used to box the stewardsmates to alleviate stress, was in the gallery deck armory, retrieving ordnance, when Yasunori's bomb detonated. The lights went out immediately. The ship's gallery armories, filled with volatile weapons, were the most dangerous compartments on the *Bunker Hill*. Tons of high explosives filled each armory compartment. Full armor, including airtight armored hatches, protected the gallery deck armory. When the lights went out, the armory sank instantly into complete blackness. Martin could not see his hands. Perhaps twenty seconds later the lights came back on. Relief among the men in the room was palpable, but short-lived. Kiyoshi's bomb exploded a moment later and plunged them again into blackness. This time the lights did not come back on. Smoke somehow penetrated the airtight armory. Poisoned air quickly filled the room. Martin could not breathe. The men all around him began screaming, confused.

The protected arsenal had become an agony. Martin lay on the deck, terrified, knowing he had to get out. He struggled to visualize the twisted passageways in the suspended armory compartment. He pressed himself against the deck, sucking barely breathable air along the floor. As he crawled blindly, aircraft on the flight deck above him began first to burn then explode. The fires below him on the hangar deck grew and spread. Then the floor he crawled on began to warm. Petroleum fires burn much hotter than domestic conflagrations. The heat rose upward, surrounding Martin's bombproof armory. The floor grew so hot that his hands began to blister. But whenever he picked up his head, he coughed violently, tearing at his lungs. Martin then lay down and crawled again, lost in the dark as his hands cooked. Small fires began breaking out in various parts of the room at once—anywhere papers or wooden crates had been left on the superheated floor. The smoke became so thick that the fire light was no help. He had to lay his whole body on the searing floor, sliding along burning his chest and thighs, to suck the cleaner air.

The steel arsenal, heated above by the burning flight deck, and below from the fiery hangar deck, had become an oven, cooking the men and munitions inside. Martin heard his friend Bakely's Kentucky drawl in the dark. Bakely had found a hatch, but could not loosen the searing dogs. Martin crawled toward him, coughing violently, then passed out.

Al Skaret was on damage control watch, just below the hangar deck in a little cubicle, at ten in the morning on May 11, 1945. The room had a small desk and all sorts of firefighting and damage control tools and equipment: ropes of all different sizes and Chem-Ox masks. Skaret wore headphones with which he could connect to virtually any area of the ship instantaneously. He was listening quietly when the first bomb exploded. "We felt a big jar of the ship and right away I said, 'I think we have been hit by a torpedo!'"

Men isolated all around the ship began calling for help. Skaret heard it all through his communication headphones. Men called up from the laundry. They could not see. They could not breathe. They were trapped.

One of the shipfitters in Skaret's unit slipped on a Chem-Ox mask, then made his way through the smoke and fire to the laundry room. He led six men who lay dying inside to clean air.

Skaret remained at damage control watch for an agonizing half hour. He controlled the ship's list by managing the void tanks from this central location. A series of handled levers hung above his desk. When ordered by Commander Shane Hastings King or Carmichael, Skaret pulled one of the handles to remotely release a valve on a tank, allowing seawater to pour in. Alternatively, the same tank could be pumped clean by pulling a different handle. Skaret transferred millions of pounds of fuel oil and seawater around the ship at Carmichael's orders to keep the *Bunker Hill* on a relatively even keel.

Minutes after Yasunori's crash, Commander King ordered Skaret to open up void tank number 120. He cranked hard on the lever to begin to balance out the ship. When things quieted down, Skaret stepped outside his cramped office. Then he heard a sound that changed his life.

"I saw, I heard, this *pounding* on a hatch." It was one of the huge hatches leading down to the mess hall. Four men could walk abreast through that hatch. Just then, though, a lieutenant rushed by Skaret. "'Say Lieutenant,' I says, 'there's somebody on the other side. Let's open up this hatch.'"

The defensive plan for the *Bunker Hill* required that all watertight bulkheads be maintained shut throughout General Quarters. Crewmen had dogged everything closed per GQ regulations—six dogs held the heavy doorway locked. No one had the authority to countermand that most basic element of the damage control plan. Naval regulations required that Skaret ask an officer before opening the door. The same regulations required the officer to say no.

The sailors handbook, called the *Blue Jacket Manual*, stressed loyalty to the chain of command above all. Whenever a sailor was uncertain about a course of action, he was required to seek out advice and then follow orders from a more senior officer. No one could violate the chain of command.

The young lieutenant ordered Skaret not to unlock the hatch. Then he left. Skaret stood alone on one side of the doorway, listening to the men crying out, scratching, banging, and pleading for him to open the door.

Skaret listened to the dying men struggle for two or three minutes, until the last stopped knocking.

Skaret has second-guessed his obedience to those particular orders for the rest of his life. His work as a damage controller took him ranging throughout the ship just a few minutes later, and it was not until long after the fires were under control that he opened the hatch.

Herbert Ferguson, lying by flag plot, came to and made his way to a porthole where he gazed aft at half the ship engulfed in flame and explosion. At least thirty fully armed and fueled planes were burning out of control on the flight deck by 10:30 A.M. Fire and smoke poured forth from two gaping holes blasted through the ship: one on the side where the deck edge elevator had been, and a second, Kiyoshi's crater, forty feet across the flight deck. Everything in the hangar deck seemed to be on fire. The gallery deck was destroyed. A third cavity, this one in the ship's side where Yasunori's 250-pound bomb had exited, boiled with fire from more burning planes and exploding fuel. Half the flag officers had been killed or taken out of the battle.

A few moments after Ferguson came to, about thirty minutes after Kiyoshi's bomb exploded, the last unidentified kamikaze appeared, flying in low and fast to starboard behind three F6Fs. The friendly planes broke away, waggling their wings violently to signal to visual observers and radar operators (who saw the change in their profile) that they were friendly. The guns on all ships were brought to bear as this Zero penetrated in close and headed directly toward the *Bunker Hill* below flight deck level. The action report concluded, "The enemy had apparently given a great deal of thought to the most effective approach for suicide attackers." The *Bunker Hill* had an open bridge. Like the captain of a clipper ship, the Essex skippers steered in the open, exposed to all weather. When it rained, the captain and bridge crew got wet. The bridge still had no transparent windshield, but the newly added steel hatches could be sealed temporarily to offer some protection from shrapnel. As the last kamikaze closed in, officers and crewmen in the bridge quickly locked down the new steel covering hatches. The flag bridge darkened. Ferguson could hear the fires and explosions outside. He knew that another kamikaze was headed straight at them. He could hear, too, the ship's AA guns blasting away above the crackle of flames and secondary explosions. No one spoke. A spotter in the bridge peered through a small gap and marked out the distance to the onrushing kamikaze. They all knew their lives were being measured in seconds. Ferguson looked through the shadows at Admiral Mitscher. Nothing more could be done. Mitscher's expression indicated no fear. From the deck chair, Mitscher calmly surveyed the ship's various instruments, the only indications of the ship's condition in the darkness of the shuttered bridge.

The *Bunker Hill*'s 5-inch guns blasted away. Then the 40s came on line. Crewmen all over the ship stood, transfixed, watching the gunners in the tubs on the outside of the *Bunker Hill* fire and load, then fire and load again as this final kamikaze plane came relentlessly forward just fifty feet above the sea. Guns from all over the ship fired steadily at the kamikaze. More AA weapons from the *Wilkes-Barre* and a dozen or so other ships near them rapidly fired at the Japanese pilot. Enthralled crewmen watched the tracers firing off and arcing in, flashing small explosions on the attacker's wings and motor.

Finally, the 20s opened up and the kamikaze exploded. The concussion passed across the *Bunker Hill*, shaking the bridge, but the

Yet another kamikaze is taken under heavy AA as the Bunker Hill *burns.*

pieces splashed harmlessly into the sea. The bridge lookout shouted that the kamikaze had been destroyed. It was 10:30 A.M., twenty-seven minutes after Kiyoshi's crash. The guns went silent.

Crewmen alongside Ferguson immediately lifted open the bridge hatches and portholes. Bright Pacific sunshine poured in, immediately followed by thick black smoke. The fight was far from over.

The island and the center of the ship, enveloped in smoke and flame, remained beyond reach of the medics. None could move forward or aft on any deck between the two bomb blasts in the devastated central area of the ship. Instead, medics and crewmen laid the wounded on desks and mess tables. Corpsmen hung IV bottles from asbestos-sheathed vents. They set up several temporary emergency care facilities as close as they could get to the main disaster area, beneath the hangar deck, on the bows of the flight deck, and in the bunking areas of the forecastle. Blast survivors, stumbling, carried, or dragged by others, arrived with wounds the doctors expected: legs twisted sideways, blood seeping thickly out of chests and stomachs

Temporary dressing station on forward flight deck: corpsmen with oxygen tanks attempt to revive an injured seaman. Beside him, another lies dead.

Sailors carry a stricken comrade across the smoldering flight deck.

Amid a heavy barrage of AA, another kamikaze is flamed by 5-inch AA fire (top right) to starboard of the Bunker Hill.

A kamikaze (in center of photo) is splashed near the side of the Bunker Hill *by escorting destroyers, just after Kiyoshi's plane exploded.*

torn by shrapnel, shattered and cracked bones protruding through torn skin. The wounded appeared disoriented, staring, shocked by their own mangled bodies.

The flight deck aid station was located well forward and remained relatively peaceful. But Doc Schroeder had limited access to most supplies.

Small groups of men stumbled through the smoke and darkness to sickbay, but for the most part these men were unable to find their way out. They cared for each other through the smoke and wet darkness as best they could. None of the shipboard doctors was able to work his way to the sickbay until long after the fires were brought under control.

Edmund Skacan knelt by the wing of a fighter plane on the hangar deck, tying it down along with Frank Slawick and John Johnston. Johnston was crouched by the tail, Slawick standing on the left side of the plane and Skacan down by the starboard wing, when Yasunori's bomb tore through the ceiling and exploded aft of them.

A ball of fire filled the hangar deck toward the rear of the ship. The three men saw it, heard it, and felt it, but they had no idea what it was. At first Skacan figured a wing or belly tank must have come off and exploded. He sensed, but could not see, small particles, shrapnel whizzing through the air around them. Skacan and Slawick turned toward each other screaming:

Men on other carriers in the task force watched the Bunker Hill *burn, as they had so many other ships during the Okinawa campaign. They were powerless to help. Most who saw the smoke and flames figured the* Bunker Hill *would sink.*

"What the hell was that?"

"Let's get out of here!"

But Johnston did not reply. He had toppled over, dead. Skacan and Slawick ran across the deck, through hangar deck control and into a tiny alcove with a small porthole. Trapped with a dozen other frightened men, they crouched in total darkness, listening to the fire and explosions just outside their door.

A moment later, Kiyoshi Ogawa's plane struck and exploded just across the hangar. Their room filled with smoke. The trapped sailors began to panic. One began to shout that they would all suffocate. Another quieted them, then calmly slid open the dogs, and pushed the small hatch cover out. A welded steel ladder with sharp, narrow rungs of darkened steel ran up the side of the ship, just beyond the hatch, rising to the flight deck. One at a time, the men swung out above the calm Pacific rolling past forty feet or so below them. They climbed in slow, single-file toward the burning flight deck.

Forward of the island the *Bunker Hill* remained unharmed. If they could make it to the bows, they would survive. Skacan had just been issued a new pair of leather shoes. The sailors resoled all of their footwear by hand with a synthetic rubber that was much more waterproof and better gripped the slippery decks. It also made the shoes last a lot longer, perhaps even until that rare occasion when the Navy paid for new ones. But Skacan had not yet had time to resole these shoes. Now he climbed up the narrow ladder, the leather soles bent over each sharp rung. He wondered about slipping and thought to himself, "Of all the times to get a new pair of shoes."

Skacan continued up the ladder and alighted beside the standing 5-inch guns. He stood before ground zero of the kamikaze attack. Wreckage of machinery and aircraft lay cast randomly about. Fires burned in clusters at all sides. Some flamed small, others burned super-hot. Everyone was dead.

Small munitions continued to explode all around them. The bullets and casings, unencumbered by gun barrels, fired in random, cartwheeling trajectories marked by little trails of spent powder. Skacan ambled almost in a daze, wondering, "What the heck is all this destruction?" Fear gripped him. He thought of the *Franklin*, which he had seen burning less than two months earlier, and of all the men who had died aboard her. He felt an overwhelming desire to be safe and began to cry.

But he had to keep moving forward, to get beyond the bomb crater and the wreckage of Kiyoshi's plane to the clean air and safety of the ship's bow. He made his way through some of the wreckage and realized, only slowly, that arms and legs and other pieces of men lay scattered all around him. Remnants of skin and chunks that were not recognizable, except that he knew they had recently been part of someone, lay indiscriminately about the wreckage on the deck. Skacan became confused as he stumbled through the mess. He wanted someone to tell him what to do, but no one seemed to be taking charge.

Soon enough, though, many of the men on the *Bunker Hill* would take on leadership roles on their own. The officers and men began to fight the fires and care for the wounded, but at the very beginning, no one that close to the fire seemed to know what to do.

Skacan picked his way forward through the debris. Wrecked equipment littered the deck; interspersed with it at completely random intervals lay pieces of the dead. Skacan looked down at a piece of meat. The bone was sticking out, part of someone's upper thigh. "Christ, it looked like the shank of a ham, you know?" Skacan said later. He decided then that he would never eat ham again.

Skacan felt the .50-caliber ammunition whizzing around his feet and legs. He had watched the guns fired and a few times even seen strafing toward the ship, always well overhead. But he had never heard or felt rounds coming close, let alone so low.

Skacan's little group worked their way forward toward the jagged hole in the center of the *Bunker Hill* that Kiyoshi's bomb had torn open. Fire and smoke belched up through the cavity. Dozens of men on the other side struggled with fire hoses directed into the hangar deck. Thick waves of white steam billowed up mixed with the murky fog rising from the petroleum fires. Skacan and the others ducked around a set of 5-inch guns, then, hugging the island structure, they found themselves face-to-face with Kiyoshi Ogawa, who lay dead on the soaking deck, a few feet from the island and just beyond the crater ripped by his bomb.

Kiyoshi wore a flight jacket or the top of his flight suit. His white scarf, still clean, clung to his neck. His lower body had apparently been shorn off, or sickeningly folded up behind him. He had been tossed clear from the crashing Zero. No one yet had touched him. "He looked fine from the top up," Skacan said.

Skacan stood on the wrecked and still burning flight deck staring, transfixed, at young Kiyoshi's remains. He brought himself nearer, leaning in close, almost as though the dead man's body or clothes would offer him an explanation or understanding. But Kiyoshi's round, unblemished face held no message for Skacan. He seemed perhaps, more than anything, absolutely ordinary. The dead kamikaze was wearing a ring. Skacan thought about taking it, but decided he had better get out of there before things got worse. He left the body lying on the deck.

All of the ship's guns aft of the island were either destroyed or left useless. Shrapnel from Yasunori's bomb raked the gunners on the ship's port side aft. Then his plane dragged Millholland's Corsair across their mounts. Burning fuel surrounded the gunners and leaked into their sponsons. Flames and poisonous smoke forced them over the side. Finally, ammunition from various aircraft detonated and tore through the survivors and the aircraft themselves caught fire. Kiyoshi's bomb severed the sprinkler lines designed to water down the gunners' ready-service ammunition and their own ordnance exploded all around them, igniting additional fires. Few survived. Each of the other guns aft of the island faced the same destructive forces.

All of these gun crews faced flame and smoke. Fire burned power and communications lines to the tubs, so the guns had to be moved by hand and aimed by sight. But most of the gunners could not see through the smoke, and the guns were ineffective when hand-operated. Their ammo had either detonated from the heat or had been pitched over the side. Many of the surviving gun crews aft of the island were eventually forced over the side by smoke and flames.

Death, for the most part, appeared to come randomly aboard the *Bunker Hill*. Some men burned, while others, nearby, survived unscathed. But a few found ways to survive when men nearby suffocated. Seaman Donald O'Brien, lost in the bowels of the ship after the first explosion, made his way in the dark smoke to the galley and eventually stumbled into the bakery. The poisoned smoke quickly filled the bread storage room. Men tore into the loaves and held the bread to their mouths, breathing through it as a primitive filter. When the bread became blackened thick, they tore into a new loaf. It burned their lungs, but O'Brien and those with him survived.

Despite the swift spread of fire and explosion, the ship's crew rallied almost immediately and began extensive damage control work. The collective response of the American sailors and airmen aboard the *Bunker Hill* saved the ship, and allowed them to save each other.

Within minutes of Kiyoshi's crash, fire hoses were laid out along the flight deck, but the explosion had cracked a water main. As a result, few of the hoses carried water. All damage control within the hangar deck was supposed to be overseen from within Hangar Deck Control (HDC). But the fires destroyed HDC. Crewmen had never drilled to control an emergency without HDC. Most of the sprinklers and fire curtains were run directly from HDC, so many sprinklers were never turned on and fire curtains remained open. When crewmen finally opened sprinklers manually, their pipes had already cracked or the sprinkler heads had melted from the heat. Aluminum wheels controlled the water mains, but many melted in the heat (stainless steel wheels would have withstood fires more than 1,000 degrees Fahrenheit hotter). The Navy had purchased the ship's fire hose nozzles from both the Fog Nozzle Company and the Rockwood Sprinkler Company. The different nozzles were not interchangeable. No one realized this until they faced the terrible need to link disparate hoses and nozzles to fight the fires. The Navy only recently had begun to outfit ships with firefighting foam. Crewmen discovered that the anti-fire foam could not travel long distances through the hoses. It just got stuck. When it did come out, there was not enough to make a difference. The foam just slickened the deck and made it harder to main-

The engine of Kiyoshi's plane lying on the flight deck of the Bunker Hill. *Close examination confirms Kiyoshi definitely flew a Zero fighter.*

tain footing while fighting the fires. Some hoses had to be stretched so far that they burned while being rolled out to the fires. Most of the emergency bilge pumps failed.

All lights went out for a time, except for the small cubic, plastic battery-operated yellow battle lanterns. Losing the lights may seem inconsequential compared to the damage from blast and fire, but loss of lighting had contributed meaningfully to the loss of at least one earlier carrier. Humans, even men trained for war, tend to panic in unlit, enclosed spaces. When one adds being surrounded by fire at sea in a ship that may be sinking, while explosions continuously shake the compartments overhead and below and poisonous smoke is being pumped in all around the men, it becomes clear how loss of lighting compounds all the problems the ship faced. It is much easier to face these dangers when one can see. But when one is lost in a maze of interlocking passages in the dark, perhaps alone, perhaps, too, hearing the panicked voices of others, then order and discipline, and therefore damage control ability, can be irretrievably lost. In a short time, even the battle lanterns lost much of their effectiveness because their four-inch-diameter lenses became coated with the poisonous particles suspended in the dense smoke.

24. FIRE

—CAPTAIN PHILLIP RUCK-KEENE OF THE
BRITISH SHIP *FORMIDABLE*, SENT FROM
FLAG BOARDS THROUGH SMOKE POURING
FROM DECKS AFTER BEING STRUCK BY
A KAMIKAZE, MAY 4, 1945

Roma Dussault was standing in his quarters deep inside the ship with a group of other plane captains when Yasunori's bomb penetrated the flight deck and exploded. No one knew what to do, but most of them decided to try to hurry forward through the lower decks and then up to the flight deck. Alone, Dussault headed aft. He planned to try to make his way to a large double hatch that would give him access to the hangar deck. He figured from there he could climb up to the flight deck.

After running hurriedly down darkened passageways, Dussault bumped into a friend, Douglas Balfour from California. Together, they found their way up to the hangar deck. But when Dussault lifted the hatch to enter, the hangar deck already was filling with thick black smoke. He could see live wires, torn and snapping back and forth, arcing bright electrical bands against the steel cabin top.

The burning hangar deck terrified them. But the two men realized they would die below. Together, they continued to climb up into the fire- and smoke-filled hangar swathed in eerie shadows from smolder and arc light, hounded by impossibly loud blasts from exploding fuel and ammunition. They scurried, crouching, across the ship to an alcove that had two red steel wheels holding flat, four-inch fire hoses wrapped around them. A large valve opened the hoses to seawater pumped up from Engineering far below them.

Balfour held the hose while Dussault spun open the valve. He turned it up to full blast immediately (they had not had training on how to use the hoses). The twisted, high-pressure hose kicked straight and threw Balfour across the deck. He slammed into a steel oil cart, which toppled over and pinned him. Balfour screamed for help, but Dussault had to shut the valve before he could move across the deck and pull Balfour out.

Despite his fear, he freed Balfour and together they managed to close down the corrugated steel hurricane roller curtains along the starboard side of the ship in order to cut off more oxygen from the interior fires. They climbed outside one of the roller curtains onto a narrow weather deck above the sea and just beyond the flames.

A wide, steel chain Jacob's ladder ran down the side of the ship from the weather deck nearly all the way to the Pacific. Dussault moved away from the heat to the edge of the weather deck. Men pinned on the flight deck above him jumped or fell, forced by heat and flames. The first bodies missed him by mere inches. The heat radiating out from the hangar deck across Dussault's little balcony

The Corsair above Roma Dussault that dripped aluminum onto him as he clung to the ladder.

A hastily shut steel roller curtain appears twisted outside the hangar deck, probably a little forward of where Roma Dussault clung to the steel Jacob's ladder. Men on the weather deck outside struggle to pass an injured seaman on a stretcher forward. Firefighting water streams down upon them, along with debris from the burning flight deck above.

Men just forward of Dussault crawl along the narrow side edge of a stowed gangway trying to get forward of the flames inside the hangar deck.

Melted engine and propeller on the flight deck of the Bunker Hill. *Pooled aluminum dripped from the ship's scuppers and burned men on weather decks below.*

became unbearable. Dussault decided to climb down the ladder to escape the high temperature. But the bodies of men higher up on the ladder trying to escape the flight deck continued falling, barely missing him.

Dussault climbed around to the inside of the ladder and held on to the metal rungs. Fires raged above and below him, but he had found a tiny place of safety clinging to the steel rungs of the chain ladder. There he met a new problem. The aircraft on the hangar deck were melting and their molten aluminum poured off the deck, falling from the ship's sides in gobs. It hit his shoulders and burned through his uniform, then his skin, searing him painfully. He gripped the ladder hard as, one by one, his mates fell past him into the sea.

Dussault remained perched on the ladder, his arms and shoulders burning as dozens of men fell past him into the ocean. Behind the ship Dussault could see destroyers slowly crisscrossing, looking for men to pluck from the sea. But the rescue ships could not pick up the men quickly enough. Many of the swimmers thrashed, wounded and bloodied. Others, exhausted, lay almost still. Dussault, alone on the ladder, watched, horrified, as the sharks approached through the clear Pacific waters. He could see a feeding frenzy begin a few hundred yards behind the ship. Dussault's skin was being burned. His arms were tiring. Yet he was determined not to jump into the shark-filled seas, and began to climb back up toward the flames.

25. SMOKE

You were just babies in the war.

—KURT VONNEGUT,
SLAUGHTERHOUSE-FIVE

Commander Carmichael was in his office "filling out paperwork for the government" when he heard the first explosion. He immediately headed for the Engineering Department twenty-eight feet below the deck. For most men it would be counterintuitive to go to a place so cut off from any help. For Carmichael, there was never a thought of going anywhere else. He sprinted along the passageway, then jumped down a ladder to a hatch one level below the flight deck, just as Kiyoshi Ogawa's plane made its final plunge.

As he was running, a big chunk of metal—part of Kiyoshi's engine—crashed through the flight deck at the island and into the stairway just above his head. It struck a sailor in the ladderwell as Carmichael passed by next to him. The fellow collapsed like a sack, instantly dead. Carmichael didn't even pause. His only thought now was to secure the engine rooms. "I had to get to my duty station," he said. "I would not have stopped going to the engine room if that engine had fallen on ten people."

Within minutes of Kiyoshi's crash, the disaster that the ship's architects warned of in the late 1930s began to occur aboard the *Bunker Hill*: horribly toxic smoke was being sucked by the ship's huge blowers down the central duct and sent throughout the ship where it began to kill the men inside.

The smoke was many times worse than smoke in any domestic fire. It was composed of particles of combusted petroleum, lead, and bronze from ammunition, copper from the ship's wires, aluminum, steel, battery acid, hydraulic fluid, lubricants, fuel, and—everywhere—lead-based paints. The *Bunker Hill*, from a modern perspective, may be seen as a mobile Superfund site. Anything that could burn did, and many things that they thought could never burn melted and partially dissipated into the poisoned cloud. Even the "fireproof" asbestos curtains in the hangar deck dissolved.

The smoke and suspended particles, especially in the boiler rooms, seared the men's lungs. It tore at the lining of the pulmonary tree. The toxic smoke, filled with poisoned microscopic irritants, traveled far beyond the lung's water barriers all the way to the end of the smallest bronchial tubes.

Carmichael ran down a second flight of stairs and came out at an entrance to the galley. Two mess cooks carrying a tub of raw pork chops stepped into the passage. Panicking as they saw the ship's officer running toward them, they dropped the meat all over the passage floor. Carmichael hit the greasy slop and almost went down. Regaining his balance, he continued on and finally reached the engine room. Within a couple of minutes of Kiyoshi's crash, Carmichael had established himself in command at Engineering. Officer Walter Sottung from New York was running the number one engine room. Carmichael, by his mere presence, relieved him. Carmichael would take charge of the Engineering Department and run it from inside engine room number one.

He would spend the next twenty hours or so keeping the whole Engineering Department in operation while the ship burned above him and the crew struggled to douse the flames and to survive.

Carmichael knew the *Bunker Hill* would withstand whatever happened on the decks, so long as his men remained at their posts. And he was determined to keep them there. But only a few moments into the struggle, he realized that many of the men around him would soon die.

Carmichael had long been aware that the *Bunker Hill*'s ventilation was the ship's fatal flaw. He knew, too, that nothing could be done about it. He and his crew were expendable. The ship remained essential. It took only a minute after Kiyoshi's bomb exploded before

Carmichael knew for sure that the air intakes along the flight deck by the island were blanketed in smoke. The men behind and just to his right began coughing uncontrollably. He looked up at the vented duct, the only source of clean air to his compartment. A horrifying, soot-ridden, poisoned gas poured forth thickly from it. Everything in line with the airflow blackened immediately. It was as if every gauge, every piece of equipment, every inch of every man's face and hands, all of their clothing, the walls, the floors, even the air itself had been instantly painted the darkest black.

Carmichael clasped a mask over his face, but tiny particles of sulfurous soot clogged it almost immediately. He peered forward at the indecipherable gauges, then wiped the glass face of one. For a moment he saw the needle. But only seconds later, it vanished under heavy soot. He moved his hands again over the glass face of the gauge, but even his fingers disappeared. Carmichael squinted through the blackened room and began rubbing vigorously along with the other sailors. He kept a fair idea of the temperature of his engines and the pressure he was generating by wiping constantly and keeping his nose only inches from the gauges.

The smoke permeated every inch of their room. It wracked their lungs, burned their throats, seared their nostrils, and scratched their eyes. They could not spit it out, they could not cough it out. At first, the smoke filled them with fear. The men felt trapped, starved for air, and in pain. But soon after, their carbon monoxide–soaked minds seemed to tell them that everything was okay, that there was no need to worry so much about the machinery. It would be all right to lie down next to a friend for a while and get a little rest. And with each passing hour, more and more men settled down in the muck. Those that did rarely rose again. They fell asleep and slipped into unconsciousness. Yet others, right beside them, remained at their posts.

To understand the disaster that befell Carmichael's men, it is important to keep in mind the difference between an engine room and a boiler room. Boiler rooms were rooms where the men tended fires that heated water to make steam. The steam was then transferred in pipes to the engine rooms. The superheated steam then powered the turbines in the engine rooms. The engine rooms were hot, but the boiler rooms were blistering. Smoke was deadly every-where inside the ship, but there was more of it in the boiler rooms than anywhere else.

Powerful fans sucked fresh air through intake vents along the flight deck, through central ducts throughout the ship. But the intakes on the flight deck were pulling in one of the most toxic brews of gasified chemicals ever assembled. Carmichael knew that things in the boiler rooms must be much worse.

The boiler fires required enormous volumes of air to feed the flaming diesel fuel. The *Bunker Hill* burned more than 7,000 gallons of fuel in an hour. A gallon of fuel oil requires a minimum of about 1,300 cubic feet of air to burn. Nearly ten million square feet of foul air were drawn into just the boiler rooms of the *Bunker Hill* in the first hour after Kiyoshi's bomb exploded. The central fresh air duct's connection to the boiler rooms was enormous, and it emptied right above the heads of the men working in those rooms.

As the *Bunker Hill* burned above them, the boilermakers were trapped in a horrifying Catch-22. If they continued to fire the burn-ers, they would have to bring in so much foul air through the ventila-tion tubes that they would likely all asphyxiate. But if they decreased the amount of air coming in, the temperatures inside would rise to nearly 145 degrees. The boilers would have to be shut down, or the men would die of heat prostration. Or the boilers would burn through all remaining oxygen and the men would have nothing left to breathe. If, on the other hand, they shut down the boilers, then the ship would lose power. The lights would fade out. All of their comrades within the ship would be left lost in a strange, disquieting, near-total dark-ness. Intership communications would fail. Communication within the ship would become barely feasible. The *Bunker Hill*, still burn-ing on five decks and filled with smoke, would lie dead in the water, well within range of Admiral Ugaki's sixth *Kikusui*, a sitting duck for further kamikaze attacks. All power to her pumps would be lost. She would then no longer be able to fight fires, nor clear the bilge of the already alarming amount of water she had taken on. Engineers would not be able to manipulate the void tanks and the ship would begin to list out of control. The *Bunker Hill* would almost certainly have to be abandoned. The men in Engineering, working twenty-five feet below the surface and nearly eighty feet below the top deck, would stand very little chance of again seeing daylight.

Carmichael knew the crew's situation all over the ship was desperate. He listened to the calls coming in on the various telephones around him and envisioned conditions on the decks and in isolated compartments throughout the carrier. If they could not keep the boilers running, the ship would be lost and the lives of every man aboard the vessel would be imperiled. The loss of an Essex could jeopardize Army timetables on Okinawa.

Carmichael understood, too, that few of his men in the boiler rooms would survive. Three men in his room had already collapsed on the gratings. They could not be revived so long as carbon monoxide saturated the room. Things, he knew, would be much worse for the boilermakers.

He could have allowed the men to abandon the boiler rooms immediately. No one would criticize him. Engineers had abandoned their stations on other ships. Carmichael knew that if he ordered his men to stay, many would die, but he also knew the ship might be saved. To him the choice was clear. The ship must not be lost. The men in Engineering would remain at their stations.

The chief engineer stands by the ship's throttles in the forward engine room. From there, he can see each significant gauge and almost everyone in the engine room. Although Carmichael could not see more than a few feet in any direction, he had perhaps the best vantage in the ship to understand the grave nature of the battle ahead.

The *Bunker Hill* had been built during a transitional period for the U.S. Navy. Antiquated, sound-powered telephones lined the hull, hallways, and bulkheads throughout the ship. They formed a sort of intercom system always geared up, but actuated only by the sound of a human voice directed into the microphone. The phones had no dial and used no electricity until a human voice passed into the system. A set of hotlines hardwired between essential divisions provided instant communication.

A phone bank mounted to a bulkhead on his right connected Carmichael to hardlined phones throughout the ship. Two talkers, assigned permanently to Carmichael, stood by his side wearing headphones, ready to connect him to anyone, anywhere on the ship, at any time. If Carmichael wanted to speak with Commander King, or with any area of the ship, he would say, "Get me CIC," or "Get me the bridge," and the talkers put him through. Using principally this system, Carmichael was able to direct the operations of the physical plant to control the power production and send necessarily limited power wherever needed. But the ultimate method of intraship communication was the public address system, which had speakers throughout the vessel.

Ten minutes after Yasunori's crash, Carmichael heard a dangerous rumor spreading through the ship's phone system that the *Bunker Hill* was sinking. As an engineer, he knew that fires alone could not sink the *Bunker Hill*. The topsides, even the interior, decks, and island could burn, but as long as the hull was not pierced, the *Bunker Hill* would not sink.*

Hundreds of men stood, though, in imminent danger of burning alive and suffocating. Panic was the greatest danger. If the men left their posts, if they stopped fighting the fires, if the panic spread, those trapped in the interior would never make it out. So long as the men remained at their posts, though, the officers could salvage the vessel. It was vital, given those conditions, that the men not feel that the ship was going down.

Carmichael waited, concerned, as the tension built and minutes passed. Scuttlebutt passed more and more desperately that the *Bunker Hill* was sinking. Men had begun jumping overboard.

Carmichael listened intently for Commander Seitz to come on the phones and correct the serious misapprehension. He could not understand why the captain was not speaking to the crew at this crit-

---

* It is, of course, possible that secondary explosions could have set off the internal magazines and then the *Bunker Hill* would have been in terrible and immediate danger. But the heaviest reinforced steel protected the magazines from heat and explosion.

ical juncture. He waited for a full thirty minutes for word from the bridge. Finally, he could stand it no longer. The men needed to know that the chain of command still functioned.

He opened the public address system and announced:

> This is the chief engineer speaking. This ship is not sinking. It is not in any danger of sinking. And it will not sink. So put your minds at rest on that.

Many sailors point to the time they heard those words as the defining moment in the struggle to save the *Bunker Hill*.

Carmichael had taken charge. Everything they had learned and studied and drilled for reasserted itself. The Navy was there as it had promised to be. Carmichael would lead them out of the mess.

After taking control first of his own engine room and then the surrounding compartments, Carmichael, working closely with Commander Shane King, managed most of the damage control from deep within the hull of the *Bunker Hill*.

He began by checking with each of the engine rooms via the ship's wired phone system to make sure that they were sufficiently manned and undamaged. He made a quick count of available personnel in the engineering compartments to ensure he would have enough men to continue to run the machinery. Then he checked to see that the fires were lit in each boiler and that the steam pressure was up in each of the turbines. He had just finished satisfying himself that the basic conditions for operating the physical plant aboard the *Bunker Hill* were met when the calls began to come in.

Patrick King served as an engineering talker. He stood only five foot, three inches tall and weighed 108 pounds. The men called him "Baby" or "Pee Wee." But he did not mind so much. King relayed orders directly from the bridge to the engineers via a set of headphones that connected him directly to another crewman in the bridge. It often felt as though he was in charge of the entire ship himself. When he relayed an order—"Get those engines up"—every man in the engine room jumped at his word. King occupied a privileged place in the darkened, isolated compartments. All the topside news came to King first. The talker on the bridge would whisper to King the hot scuttlebutt on the bridge and describe happenings on the outside of the ship.

King never heard Kiyoshi's explosion, but he felt it. The talker in the bridge shouted, "They just hit the island." King thought the ship had run into an island they were attacking.

"What island?"

King's friend on the bridge told him about the kamikaze, and that the admirals had decided to slow the task force down and protect the *Bunker Hill*. But that if she took another hit, they would have to abandon her because they could not afford to lose two Essex carriers. King worried, but did not consider leaving his post.

George Thorne worked for Carmichael as a fireman in the boiler rooms. His job was to keep track of six gauges, making small valve adjustments when necessary so that the pressure never got too high or too low on any of the pumps.

The boiler rooms maintained a constant ambient temperature of 110 degrees. But when the smoke poured in, the temperature spiked. The last time Thorne could see the room temperature gauge it had risen to 139 degrees. He spread rags on the hot steel floor grates so he could walk. Soot filled the air and covered everything. It smelled like gasoline and burning tar. Within minutes, Thorne could not see his fingers when he rubbed his nose. Coughing violently, he held his battle lantern right up next to the indicators and wiped the soot away.

He could read the dials only for a moment after swabbing the glass, before the gauges quickly disappeared again into the thick, fouled air. With his hands, Thorne would feel his way to a new gauge, hold his battle lantern close, and wipe again.

Soon, though, the soot-blackened air became so thick that even with his head held close and constant wiping, Thorne could not make out the dials. So he placed his hands on parts of the engine, or the pumps, and sensed by the *feel* of the system—a combination of sound, vibration, and temperature—whether the pumps were overheating. Thorne had been aboard the *Bunker Hill* for years, and knew the boiler rooms intimately. A housing near the drive shaft gave him the most accurate sense. He set and reset his valves by the timbre of the machinery and kept the pumps flowing.

Fred Deans supervised a crew that tended the number four boiler. He had finished his eight-hour shift when Yasunori struck, but ran straight back to his boiler room.

Deans knew that the watertight doors above him were being locked down and the hull was filling with firefighting water. He could not leave now no matter how much he wanted to. He simply had to keep the boiler pumping steam.

The big boiler room became so dark and filled with smoke that Deans could not see the other men. He shouted to them above the noise. Sometimes they answered through their masks. Sometimes they didn't.

The Navy-issue Chem-Ox gas masks held chemical canisters meant to purify the fatal gases, but the purifying canisters lasted only an hour or so. They filled up long before the fires were out, long before Deans could be relieved.

The Chem-Ox masks were a surprisingly complex system that required more than a dozen steps to fit properly.* Many men wear-

---

* The Chem-Ox system included a gas mask that fit over the entire face of the sailor, with a diaphragm that allowed for some minimally comprehensible voice communications. The mask connected to a charcoal canister by two rubber hoses. These hoses attached two pair of sacks that hung across a sailor's chest and that acted as artificial lungs, powered by the intake of air into the sailor's own lungs. But before it could work, the sailor had to remove the protective top of the charcoal canister and then screw up on a small handle on the bottom of the canister, until it punctured the softer interior copper top. This allowed the moisture contained in each sailor's exhaled breath to activate the charcoal. When Al Skaret first exhaled into the Chem-Ox mask, the artificial lung sacks filled via the rubber tubes. They forced moist air into the internally opened canister. Each exhale afterward forced air from the artificial lungs, which pulled more moist air through the purifying charcoal canister and removed most of the impurities, leaving a more highly oxygenated air for Skaret to breathe. Sailors had to be careful to pull the mask extremely snug about their whole face; the slightest crack would release the suction in the artificial lungs and allow the poisoned air to come directly into the mask.

ing the masks died on the *Bunker Hill* on May 11 because they had neglected one of the key twelve steps. Most simply forgot to pull off the piece of tape that activates the chemical canister. With the tape on, the mask remained ineffective.

The men in Deans's boiler room were beginning to die. One after another, they lay down or collapsed and never got back up. Carbon monoxide poisoning is insidious. It clouds the mind like a sleeping pill. Many drifted off and never woke up. After an hour or so, Deans's Chem-Ox canister filled, and stopped purifying his air. He became light-headed, then started to pass out. He knew that he had to find filtered air. Stumbling through the dark, he reached into the muck for one of his dead friends. He found a body floating in the filthy bilge with a Chem-Ox mask still on. Deans felt around the chemical canister for the tape. The sticky seal remained intact. The dead seaman had never activated his canister. Deans took the mask the sailor would never use. Elastic held it tightly to the blackened man's sodden face. Deans had to hold the dead man by the head and hair, then pull the mask across the bloated lips and nose. He wanted so much to just lie down and rest. But he knew that if he did not get up, his entire boiler room crew could perish. For the next ten hours, he and a handful of survivors kept the boilers fired. "It never was dead in the water; we kept it going," he said.

Sitting in an Avenger on the flight deck, Al Turnbull, horrified, thought Kiyoshi had crashed right into the flag plot and killed Admiral Mitscher and Arleigh Burke. He sat in his cockpit, staring, as explosions built in front of him. Fire burned where Yasunori's bomb exploded. A second, enormous fire grew where Kiyoshi's bomb detonated. Another fire, where Kiyoshi's plane had hit, flared quickly. A line of fires where Yasunori's plane struck and dragged across the decks began to spread in all directions. All the flames were coming together into one great conflagration. The first planes hit by Yasunori were burning out of control. Each time one of their belly tanks exploded, its gasoline spread fire to the aircraft on either side of it or in front or behind it.

Each plane followed an almost predictable course through its own destruction. First the aircraft wheels melted, hissing as they burst, releasing an acrid, smoldering fog that rose quickly. The planes clanked as they dropped to their struts when the wheels melted, and sank closer to the deck fire. The intense heat melted the brackets and struts, too, and the planes dropped again, to their bellies. Their props bent under the heat and weight, then melted. Rockets, bombs, and strafing rounds stored in the fuselage and wings began to explode. Some of the aircraft carried napalm and the sticky fire spread across the wooden deck. Their gas tanks cracked, leaking fuel across the deck that burned almost instantaneously, or the fuel tanks exploded violently. Eventually, everything burned. The part of the fuselage surrounding the engine disintegrated and the motors fell to the decks. Aluminum mechanical parts warped, then melted. Finally, the strongest steel of the engines melded together.

The deck fires raged from where Turnbull sat transfixed aboard his Avenger, all the way forward to the island, a nearly unbroken fire about 450 feet long. Heat from the burning aircraft, gas, munitions, and deck structure scorched against Turnbull's skin through the sides of his aircraft. The smoke quickly made it almost impossible to see forward more than a few feet. Turnbull knew the ship was now at General Quarters and that all of the escape hatches leading belowdecks were closed tight. The men stationed inside would not be allowed out until the fires were under control. Turnbull knew, too, that many of those men would never make it out alive. He did not really think about what to do next. At that moment, Turnbull's training kicked in. His primary mission changed; he knew he had to do anything he could to save the ship and give aid to as many crew as possible. He literally leapt into action.

Turnbull jumped out of his plane—which was still in good shape— and ran down the deck toward where the fires had started. Flight crews brought a hose forward. Turnbull jumped into line on the heavy hose and helped them to guide it onto the fires. At first, the men had trouble holding the powerful stream of water to the fire, but the water quickly fell to a trickle, then failed completely. Water mains controlling firefighting water to the aft portion of the ship had cracked from the heat in the hangar deck.

The entire aft portion of the Bunker Hill *was bathed in a poison-ous black smoke. Hundreds of men crowded the fantail to escape flames and asphyxiation inside, but the open deck astern was inun-dated with deadly smoke. In the photo the* Bunker Hill *is beginning a list to port.*

The *Bunker Hill's* forward movement created its own wind on the calm day, which cleared the bow of smoke, but drove the flames and poisoned air sternward, spreading aft toward Al Turnbull, who was isolated with a small group of surviving crewmen on the rear of the flight deck. The fires astern now linked him inextricably with the enlisted men who had brought out the hose. Turnbull had become their de facto commander. The bridge gave no instructions. The crew-men on the hose with Turnbull decided to get out of the way of the onrushing flames as quickly as they could. But the six men were stuck. They could not move forward because of the fire. They tried going below through a series of various hatches, but the hangar deck blazed

Two worlds aboard the Bunker Hill. *Forward of the island the ship remained almost wholly undamaged, and cruised as though nothing were wrong. Below and astern, though, hundreds of men lay dying. Dozens of men crowded together on the ship's fantail. The smoke was so thick that many did not realize that they were on an open deck—outside.*

up at them and fire blocked all escape hatches downward. They eventually ran for a catwalk and ended up crouched along the starboard side of the *Bunker Hill*, on the stern section aft of the furthermost gun platform, just behind the last set of 20mm quads.

As the fires spread closer and closer to the men, the aircraft parked near them began to burn, then explode. With each successive explosion the conflagration grew in size and intensity. Turnbull and the other men decided that their only choice was to abandon ship. If they remained, they would burn alive. They would not stand a chance in the Pacific, though, without flotation. Each of the TBFs on the deck contained a life raft for their crew. Marty Manger and Turnbull decided to cross the blistering flight deck to the nearest two planes to try to secure life rafts. They crawled across the deck, trying to keep their heads and bodies below the level of the flying debris, while hurrying to avoid the flames and live ammunition whooshing around in every direction. Both remained entirely focused on getting to the closest planes, retrieving the rafts, and returning to the catwalk before those planes exploded.

Luckily, the closest planes were Avengers and both pilots knew well the location of their life rafts: a small hatch accessible on the starboard side, adjacent to the compartment where the radioman flew. Turnbull had no idea where the life raft was in any other aircraft aboard the ship.

Turnbull could feel the *Bunker Hill* slow as the engineers diverted remaining energy to water pumps and electrical generators. Half of the ship, from the island aft, disappeared in a cloud of dense black smoke. Men on the fantail could not see more than a few feet in any direction. But the airflow around the ship created an anomaly in the thick smoke: the area right around Turnbull's little group remained strangely clear. A darkening ceiling of heavy smoke curled chaotically just above their heads. The smoke fell in swirling curtains on all sides of them. Smoke churned up in front of them, then cascaded down behind them and spun in eddies on all sides. But at that moment, the air around them remained clear.

Above them, sharp explosions sparked brightly. The two pilots had no way of predicting a safe course across the deck, nor a safe time to make their run for it. As each successive plane exploded, it became more and more difficult to see the two Avengers that were their targets, only twenty feet or so away from where they crouched in the catwalk.

Turnbull and Manger together leapt up from the catwalk and sprinted to the Avengers. After retrieving both raft containers, they raced back across the flight deck and jumped into the protection of the sunken catwalk.

They worked out a procedure to abandon the ship: a strong swimmer would go first and a strong swimmer would go last. They would send the enlisted men, whose lives were now in their care, in the middle. Turnbull would jump first, then Manger, who had life-guarded at the Jersey shore, would throw out the first life raft. In quick succession, the four enlisted men would jump. Turnbull would quickly swim to the life raft and row it along, picking up the enlisted men. Finally, just after the last enlisted man jumped, Marty Manger would throw out the second raft and jump himself. He could then climb into that raft and row in the opposite direction. They would all meet in the middle: two rafts and all six men.

During their cadet instruction, Turnbull and Manger learned how to abandon ship from an aircraft carrier. They knew to cross their arms, point their toes, and try to go straight down. As soon as they hit the water, they were supposed to let their legs and arms out in a prone position to stop their downward movement, then go kicking away from the ship and up for air. They went over these instructions with each of the men. Everyone was worried about going over the side, but there seemed to be no other alternative to burning to death on the catwalk.

Turnbull had spent so much time swimming in the ocean and racing the very long distances between the piers at the Santa Monica, Venice, and Redondo beaches, that he probably had less trepidation than the others. The carrier was cruising around 10 knots, so it was similar to jumping off a fifty-foot bridge into a river from a car going 15 mph.

Turnbull stood along the edge and leapt out. He made a perfect jump, arms wrapped tightly across his chest, but he was buffeted on the way down and hit the ocean hard on his left side. He let go his arms, pushed out his legs, and stopped himself, then kicked hard up into the churning water of the carrier's wake. It had been only a few moments, but as he looked up, Turnbull could see the blazing *Bunker Hill* steaming straight as a die blade away from him. He was alone.

26. WATER

Art Volkema, still in the forward gun tub, looked down the starboard side of the *Bunker Hill* as the cruiser *Wilkes-Barre* sprayed saving water across the carrier's decks. He was transfixed by the sight of men in misery around him. Sailors, some already afire, streamed off the side of the *Bunker Hill*. Several struck the deck of the *Wilkes-Barre*, cruising thirty feet below them. A few splashed in the water and passed miraculously safe between the two warships, then floated forlornly into the open Pacific.

Volkema looked to the very top of the island where the bugler stood to make his call. The men called it the Zenith. The lone man, consumed by asphyxiating smoke, stood out and leapt over the edge. He fell 137 feet down to the Pacific.

Captain Robert Porter of the *Wilkes-Barre* had been protecting the *Bunker Hill* from kamikazes for most of the Okinawa campaign. He knew when he saw the smoke that the stricken carrier would not be able to fight the fires on her own, and that the crewmen pinned at the sides of the ship would die without help. He headed the *Wilkes-Barre* at flank speed toward the *Bunker Hill*. Porter knew that he would have to bring the two ships dangerously close together in order to be of any help, and that he would risk his ship—and his career—by attempting the maneuver. It takes a particular kind of courage for a captain to put his ship into harm's way. But that is what he did. Porter smashed his own ship, and one of the greatest capital ships in the American Navy, to save a few dozen men. The collision pushed the burning *Bunker Hill* hard to port. Everyone aboard recalls the jolt of collision, and then the metal grinding as the *Bunker Hill* rolled and slid into a turn. Men trapped inside thought the ship had been hit by another kamikaze, or was making final groans before she sank.

340

The Navy had recognized that Essex carriers were vulnerable to low-flying kamikaze planes, especially on the starboard side. Just before the ship sortied in 1945, shipyard workers in Bremerton installed three quad gun tubs, each holding two double-barrel 40mm cannons, low on the *Bunker Hill*'s starboard side. The new gun placements worked. The men in these tubs shot down one of the last kamikazes headed toward the ship. But the ship was not designed to have gun mounts tacked on the sides, and there was no emergency provision for the gunners if the hangar deck caught fire. When the fires spread inside the hangar deck, these gunners became isolated, cut off from the rest of the ship, and surrounded by flame.

The *Wilkes-Barre* collided with two of the *Bunker Hill*'s new quad gun tubs (numbered 15 and 17) on the after starboard side of the hangar deck just as the flames began to threaten the 40mm gunners. Their gun tubs were crushed, but the men were able to jump to the cruiser's decks and safety. Porter's firefighting water from the *Wilkes-Barre* probably saved many others on the hangar and lower decks. He rescued men through portholes and played water out on isolated groups of men in various parts of the ship. A striking photograph, shot from the *Wilkes-Barre*, shows a group of men boxed in by flames in the hangar deck. Small groups of these trapped sailors attempted to make their way around the flames by crawling outside the ship on the narrow edge of a ladder held sideways against her hull. The *Wilkes-Barre* sprayed water on these men and held the flames in the hangar deck away from them as they made their perilous way forward around the fires. Porter's crewmen threw small ropes across to the *Bunker Hill*, then used those ropes to pull heavy lines between the two ships. They tied their own fire hoses to these stronger ropes, and *Bunker Hill* crewmen pulled the fire hoses to the *Bunker Hill*, aiming water from the *Wilkes-Barre* to where it would do the most good. At the same time, men began to devise a way to evacuate the wounded from the burning ship. Crewmen rigged pulleys to the heavy ropes, but had no stretchers. Instead, the crews tied huge mail sacks, about five feet around, to the guy wire and pulled the wounded back and forth to the *Wilkes-Barre* suspended like parcel post. They stuffed the men in two at a time. With each wounded man the cloth sacks became heavier with blood. The injured men were dipped up to their waists in their comrades' blood as they swung across the Pacific to the *Wilkes-Barre.*

The high-octane avgas inside the fifty or so aircraft stored in the hangar deck had either exploded or caught fire after leaking from cracked tanks. Dussault paused, trying to figure out a way to make it through the hangar deck. But impenetrable flames blocked the hangar. So he resumed his climb to the flight deck.

Every man aboard knew that the Japanese had never sunk an Essex carrier, but that the *Bunker Hill* was hobbled and severely wounded. Her radars and most of her guns no longer functioned. Her planes were burning or could not fly. She could not communicate with other

A wounded sailor rides in a mail sack across to the Wilkes-Barre *from the Bunker Hill's fantail. Injured men were evacuated from the flight deck and isolated weather decks of the* Bunker Hill *to the safety of the* Wilkes-Barre. *Men were carried over in mailbags hastily converted to breeches buoys. The mail sacks filled with bodily fluids. The last of the wounded were scrunched waist-deep in a sinuous liquid—mostly their comrades' blood. The cruiser had insufficient sickbay space for the wounded and most were eventually transferred to hospital ships.*

Seawater is directed from the Wilkes-Barre *in a stream to the deck fires of the* Bunker Hill. *A 40mm gun sponson, which was wrecked by the* Wilkes-Barre, *can be seen in the center of the frame.*

ships. Even her flag boards were out. If Admiral Ugaki had learned what terrible shape they were in—how limited their defenses were, and how little maneuverability they had—he would have sent every kamikaze left at Kanoya to the *Bunker Hill* immediately. For the crew aboard the wounded ship, anticipating the next wave of Japanese aircraft to finish them off was like waiting to die.

But the cruiser *Wilkes-Barre* covered them on the starboard side with all her guns. A destroyer patrolled just in front. Three more lined her port side. Other destroyers crisscrossed behind her. Their crews pulled sailors from the ocean and stood ready to defend from the rear. For the moment, the *Bunker Hill* was safe.

Slabo Bacon came to lying in a pile of debris on the hangar deck, surrounded by flames. He could see the ocean racing by just outside the hole where Kiyoshi's bomb ripped out the deck edge ele-

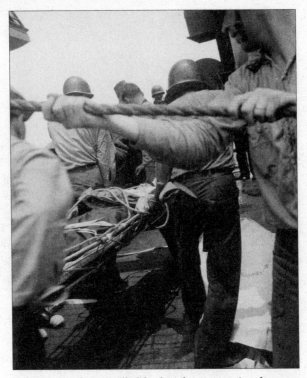

Injured men were pulled by hand on guy wires between ships, suspended from whatever could be found at hand—stretchers, Jacob's ladders, or even mail sacks.

vator. Bacon climbed around the flames and up to a stanchion that held the remains of the twisted deck edge elevator. Heat and fires prevented him from getting far enough out to jump. But neither could he retreat. He clung to the torn stanchion, waiting. Heat surrounded him, and the fires moved relentlessly closer. Bacon held fast with little hope of rescue for nearly an hour, when suddenly the sea outside the deck edge hole grew dark. The destroyer *English* had arrived along the port side of the *Bunker Hill*. Crewmen from the *English* played water from their fire hoses into the gaping hole in the side of the *Bunker Hill*, all around Bacon. They could not rescue him, but they kept him cool and held the fires off. Eventually, firefighters aboard the *Bunker Hill* trained their own hoses on him and someone climbed down and

A shoeless wounded sailor is passed in a stretcher to the Wilkes-Barre.

lifted him out. They carried the blackened and burned communications officer to a temporary aid station.

The destroyers *Stembel*, *English*, and *Sperry* came alongside the *Bunker Hill*'s port side at 11:03 A.M.—one hour after Kiyoshi had struck. Crewmen aboard the *Sperry*, busy loading 5-inch shells below, were called to the top deck. The men were stunned to see the huge carrier heeled, towering over the *English* just ahead of them. Kiyoshi's explosion had torn open the carrier's deck like a jagged tin can. Smoke poured out of gaping holes in her sides. Crewmen from the *Bunker Hill* were jumping overboard. Some made it onto the decks of the *English*. Many fell into the ocean. Destroyer crewmen gaped, horrified, at the line of men floating past them in the ocean. The crew threw all of their life jackets into the sea, but the floating men disappeared quickly in their wake.

The cruiser Wilkes-Barre *(CL 103) offers aid alongside the* Bunker Hill. *Some men jumped to the cruiser's decks when the ships came together. Lines were passed between the crews and fire hoses from the cruiser were pulled across to fight fires directly aboard the* Bunker Hill.

Men aboard the destroyers sprayed their water straight through the holes in the ship's side, directly onto those crewmen who were trapped, surrounded by flame. They discharged streams of water onto the ready-service ammunition spaces, cooling them down and preventing explosions so that the crews aboard could continue to fight the fires. The destroyer USS *The Sullivans* picked up men who had jumped or were blown overboard and transferred wounded off the sides of the *Bunker Hill* along transfer whips. A green Irish clover had been painted on her forward stack, in remembrance of the five Sullivan brothers who had been killed on November 15, 1942, when their ship, the American cruiser *Juneau*, was sunk by the Japanese off Guadalcanal. The five brothers had enlisted together after Pearl Harbor in Waterloo, Iowa.

In order to launch their air groups, aircraft carriers were loaded with massive amounts of extraordinarily combustible materials. A partial listing of highly flammable substances aboard the *Bunker Hill* on May 11, 1945, is daunting: approximately two million gallons of diesel fuel, 200,000 gallons of high-octane avgas, hundreds of thousands of .50-caliber, 20mm, 40mm, and 5-inch projectiles, napalm HVAR rockets, torpedoes, and 50-pound, 100-pound, 500-pound, and 1,000-pound bombs of assorted types: SAP, AP, GP, and incendiary.

The destroyer English (DD-696) *sprays water on a 20mm gun battery on the* Bunker Hill's *port side in the afternoon of May 11, 1945. The destroyer* Sperry *(DD-697) moves in on her stern, followed by the destroyer* Stembel *(DD-644). Water from firefighting is pouring from holes along the ship's sides, most likely blown open by Yasunori's bomb. Probably no one in this battery survived the fight. The* English *evacuated Admiral Marc Mitscher and Arleigh Burke a few hours later. Before they carried away the admiral, the* English *sent coffee to the* Bunker Hill *crews using the lines set up to carry Mitscher.*

The Sullivans *(DD-537) cruises to pick up survivors from the kamikaze attack, May 11, 1945.*

The structure of the ship itself created a range of miscellaneous dangers. The *Bunker Hill*'s electrical machinery and many of her electrical outlets utilized electricity four times more powerful (and deadly) than standard AC outlets. Thousands of miles of electrical wiring ran throughout the hull. The ship may be likened to a gigantic homemade pipe bomb with every type of industrial explosive in the United States packed tightly inside. And now the Japanese had lit fires all over it.

Commander George Seitz had skippered the *Bunker Hill* for four months. After Yasunori struck, Seitz altered course back and forth trying to get the Pacific breeze to clear the fresh air intake vents and the decks of smoke. But the light breeze had fallen to zero. By 10:30 A.M., a single continuous, gigantic cloud of poisoned black smoke hung about the ship from the deck edge elevator to the fantail. Finally Seitz directed the ship to 140 degrees true—southeast—taking her most directly away from the kamikazes.

Fighting fires aboard the *Bunker Hill* was a nearly impossible task. The ship was moving forward, up and down in the swells, and rolling slowly side to side. Firefighting water trapped inboard slicked the floors and hid obstacles in the already darkened rooms. Men trying to fight the fires slipped and fell in the muck. They worked amid poisoned air, often without oxygen, in darkened corridors flooded with their own firefighting water and seawater that flowed in through holes smashed by Yasunori's bomb. Chemical foam sprayed to douse electrical fires spread everywhere, slicking the decks and making it almost impossible to maintain footing. Temporary bilge pumps failed. Electric lights burned out, but electrical lines stayed hot. Electrocution remained a hazard throughout the struggle. It is difficult to comprehend the heat produced by petroleum and explosives burning out of control on a military ship. No construction material has been invented that can withstand those temperatures. The fires burned so hot they cracked water mains, melted sprinkler heads, burned fire hoses, jammed hose valves, and melted hatches shut.

Before World War II, U.S. citizens expected to take much more responsibility and initiative for each other's health and safety. Axes hung on the walls of every movie theater and most public places in the United States a generation ago, and men knew how to use them. They are still required aboard ferries and other commercial vessels. Without hesitation, individual sailors and damage control teams on the *Bunker Hill* chopped holes with these axes through the wooden decks to drain firefighting water down into the lower reaches where it would make the ship less top-heavy and unwieldy. It piled up, finally, above the locked hatches over the engine compartments, trapping Carmichael and the other engineers under three feet of oily seawater.

The inside of the *Bunker Hill* was almost completely waterproof. Compartmentalized, watertight decks and sealed compartments protected the ship from flooding if the hull were breached. No seawater penetrating the hull from the sides or below can enter these rooms. But designers did not plan for water being poured in from the top. After the SS *Normandie* (USS *Lafayette*) disaster, designers feared that if the fire hoses poured too much water into the *Bunker Hill* from above, the aircraft carrier might topple over.*

---

* BuShips figured that, because of all her extra weight, a single torpedo hit in 1945 would do as much damage as two torpedoes to the *Bunker Hill* as designed. The problem was so serious that BuShips recommended a reduction in ready-service ammunition to 500 rounds per 40mm barrel and 1,440 rounds per 20mm gun. But no gunner near Okinawa thought he would be safer with *less* ammunition at the ready.

Water from the ship's firefighting efforts quickly began to flood the interior of the ship. Hundreds of thousands of gallons of firefighting saltwater (weighing more than eight pounds per gallon) poured in from the *Bunker Hill*'s pumps, those of the three destroyers on her port side, and those of the giant cruiser *Wilkes-Barre*. Water also entered through holes in the hull hacked by the shrapnel from Yasunori's bomb, flooding compartments in the stern. The carrier began to list to starboard.

Much of the water from the flight deck and open hangar deck at first flowed out through scuppers (holes cut into coamings since the days of sail to allow seawater to wash out of decks). Soon, though, debris blocked the scuppers, and water gathered along the coamings, poured down open hatches, filled waterproof compartments open at the top, flooded over locked hatches, and made its way inexorably to the bottom of the ship where it filled the bilges and then rose higher and higher into the engineering compartments.

The *Bunker Hill* grew heavier and more sluggish every minute the hoses ran. Fire hoses typically pump 500 to 1,000 gallons per minute. If the Navy's hoses pumped in the middle of that range, then each of the dozens of hoses added 6,225 pounds to the *Bunker Hill* every minute.

The seawater shattered hatchway doors and filled the *Bunker Hill*'s lower decks. The weight of the firefighting water pushed the *Bunker Hill*'s bows five feet deeper into the sea. The ship listed further and further to starboard.

When rescue and firefighting parties opened watertight doors in the interior, all of the water held inside (or outside) those watertight compartments sloshed freely inside the ship, exacerbating the flooding. Over the course of the day-long rescue effort, the *Bunker Hill* took on well over one million pounds of water. Many of the crewmen thought that the top-heavy ship would turn all the way over. Chief Engineer Carmichael knew she would not. He transferred fuel oil to port to counter the list, and jettisoned 60,000 gallons of fuel—nearly half a million pounds—from the starboard tanks.

The ship had been taking on water for three hours. Commander Seitz had to clear the decks. As sailing captains had done for thousands of years, Seitz ordered his crew at 1:30 P.M. to execute a 70 degree turn in order to heel the *Bunker Hill* and spill the seawater and burning detritus off the hangar and flight decks. Seitz would use what was then called centrifugal force to tip the ship, and push everything out.

Talkers heard Executive Officer Dyson over their headphones relaying the order: a long turn with all hangar deck doors open. No one knew if it would work, but most of the crew figured it could not get much worse.

The helmsman slowly spun the wheel to 2.5 degrees rudder. The ship turned, slowly at first, and then harder. Then she began to heel. The list increased to at least 6 degrees. The *Bunker Hill* began to vibrate as she leaned over. Many sailors point to this moment as the time they were most afraid. They thought that the ship would just continue to roll until she was upside down.

Seawater and fuel sloshed out of the hangar deck doors. Sailors pushed thousands of tons of munitions, rockets, bullets, 5-inch shells, 20mm and 40mm shells, fuel drums, the last of the aircraft—anything that might burn—into the sea.

It was an inspired maneuver. Sailors I interviewed fifty years later recall the seawater and blazing equipment pouring over the ship's side, finally clearing their way to fight fires and rescue comrades.

The Navy account said that, in turning, the *Bunker Hill* shifted the load of water across the ship and "dumped the heart of the roaring inferno on her hangar deck out into the sea." The Navy announced that after the maneuver men with "lips too burned to cheer rushed forward with fire hoses." Others, pinned beneath burning decks, knew they would be saved.

Carmichael controlled the ship's list as captains had throughout maritime history. In the days of sail, crews and ships at sea for long periods of time were almost daily shifting cargo from port to starboard or forward and aft to keep the vessel at the most advantageous trim. Millions of pounds of fuel stored in gigantic tanks built into the ship's sides formed the ship's ballast. Carmichael moved this fuel between various tanks to keep the ship on an even keel. When the ship leaned too far to one side, Carmichael radio-telephoned up to damage control officers such as Al Skaret to open empty tanks and spill or pump fuel oil from one side of the ship to the other. Carmichael could have created the same list achieved in the hard turn by ordering certain valves opened up to move fuel oil within the hull. In fact, Carmichael managed the ship's list carefully during the period after the attack and ensured that the ship maintained sufficient list so that firefighting water would continue to slop off the decks.

Throughout the fight, Carmichael moved fuel back and forth, flooding and counterflooding void tanks, to improve the footing for the crew, especially on the high flight and hangar decks where the list was most strongly felt. He eventually decreased the *Bunker Hill*'s angle of heel to a single degree to starboard, which allowed the water to continue to run off the ship's sides. The ship's engines and boilers could not function safely when the ship was severely heeled. The boiler's fluid uptakes ran best when the ship was horizontal; each increment of list decreased their productivity. Cooling water and fuel could not flow properly through engine pipes when the ship heeled markedly.

The idea that the *Bunker Hill* was saved by Seitz's hard turn to starboard continues to irk Carmichael sixty years later. He says that no one mentioned the turn until they were docked safely at Bremerton. A reporter asked a ship's officer to say something exciting or heroic about the attack—the officer came up with the turn. The hard turn certainly forced tons of burning fuel, water, and debris to slide overboard, and many of the men fighting the fires say that it made an enormous difference to them at the time. They credit the turn with saving their lives. But they are not engineers, and the chief engineer makes it clear that this maneuver, whatever was intended from it, was not necessary to heel the hull.

Despite the list and the turn, there was still too much heavy saltwater on every deck. They had to get it overboard. Virtually all of the many emergency pumping systems designed to remove massive amounts of water from isolated decks on the Essex carrier failed. The crew tried first using the standard submersible electric pumps, but power was out to most of the vessel, especially in fire-damaged areas (where pumps were most needed). When crews were lucky enough to find power, the filters on the electric pumps quickly jammed. The men carried in handibillys, but the fiercely pumping sailors wore out these hand-operated bilge pumps within hours. They rushed in heavy-duty gasoline-powered bilge pumps, but these failed, too—their ignition systems had been flooded by the saltwater and the crew could not start them. Finally, the crew carried in portable eductors, which they rigged in the interior second, third, and fourth decks and in the number three elevator pit. The eductors were designed to carry liquids containing suspended particles in other ship's applications. But they performed miracles of bilge pumping.

Fire and flood, two usually opposite threats, are particularly relevant to men at war upon the sea. Uncontrolled, they invoke universal fear. Men aboard the *Bunker Hill* drilled constantly to deal with the threat of the ship burning or sinking. It was not until the *Normandie* turned turtle in New York Harbor in 1942 that most Navy men began to think hard about the dangers posed by water spread throughout a ship to fight fires. But Commander Seitz and everyone aboard remained well aware of the dangers of adding so much weight to the already weight-critical ship. The men dealt splendidly with the threat posed by water. Fire, though, and the smoke it spawned, remained their worst enemy.

27. HELPING OUT

Turnbull's two crewmen, George Gelderman and Jack Weincek, had walked together to the aircrew ready room immediately after they landed around 9:30 A.M. Gelderman's head had ached throughout the combat mission that morning. Instead of hanging out with the other crewmen in the ready room, he walked down to his quarters. Weincek stayed behind with more than a dozen other men to drink coffee and talk with his squadron mates. Kiyoshi's bomb killed them all.

Gelderman, who survived the blast, made his way through darkened passageways until he found himself in the burning hangar deck. He undogged a small hatchway, and peered, disbelieving, into the burning hangar. Blue and orange flames engulfed the deck from the floor to the gallery and to the flight deck above. Everything seemed to be on fire, so he pulled the small hatch shut and spun the wheel hard to retighten each of the dogs. He rushed back down the steep ladderway in total darkness as smoke filled the passageway, then stumbled along the familiar hall back to his quarters, coughing violently, only to find his bunkmates crowded in the darkness. They quickly held a brief conference. It appeared that the ship might not survive. They figured that in the current emergency they were expendable. No one would come looking to rescue them, so they had better find their own way out. The radiomen assumed the dispensary would be a hub of activity from which they could find a route to safety. Gelderman and the others wrapped wet towels around their heads and trudged single-file down the smoke-filled hallways toward the Medical Department.

Dewey Ray and Hoot Hutt survived both blasts. Along with their bunkmates, they made their way down the passageway toward their wardroom battle station.

In the wardroom, however, nothing could be done, so Ray and Hutt headed out and made their way to the junior officers' bunk room, located on the same level as the hangar deck but about as far forward on the *Bunker Hill* as one could go. Corpsmen had converted it into a temporary infirmary. They immediately began to lend a hand, injecting morphine into the wounded.

They struggled with the men as best they could. Triage is one of the great advancements in emergency medical care. It was probably first utilized during the Napoleonic Wars, but became a mainstay of treatment procedure during the Second World War. Doctors utilizing triage separate patients into three categories: those who can survive without immediate attention, those who can survive only with immediate attention, and, finally, those who are least likely to survive, even if immediate care is given. This sifting of the wounded in situations with high casualties saved hundreds of thousands of people throughout the last century by efficiently distributing limited medical resources. In practice aboard the *Bunker Hill*, though, it meant that men lay dying in makeshift medical care facilities, confused, and wondering why no one was paying any attention to them. Other men, caregivers, worked around the dying, trying not to let the terror and pain of the suffering men, and their own guilt at ignoring them, delay their treatment of those who might survive. None of the officers had experienced such massive casualties, and triage of wounded was foreign and discomfiting to them.

Sailors carried Slabo Bacon in on a stretcher, but he was so swollen and covered with black soot that Ray did not recognize him. He looked at Bacon blankly, and then moved on to another injured man. Bacon lay in shock on the stretcher, overcome with guilt. Ashamed to have survived, Bacon figured Dewey Ray had snubbed him for leaving the pilots.

Neely, the black stewardsmate who had slept beside the ready rooms, lay across the aisle from Bacon, also badly burned. Neely's wounds were beyond medical help, placing him at the bottom of the triage system. The only thing the medics could do was to shoot him up with more morphine.

These were horrible shots. The men had to squeeze the morphine through a fat needle that extended out of a small metal roll, like a miniature tube of toothpaste. Dozens of men with no medical training waded through the wounded, injecting them with the powerful opiate. Hutt penned a large "M" on Neely's forehead after shooting him up, as a sort of battlefield medical record of his dosing, mostly to keep the next volunteer from giving him too much of the drug. Dewey Ray leaned around and spoke gently with him for a few minutes. Then he twisted back and talked quietly to Bacon, whom he finally had recognized. When Ray turned again to Neely, the young man was dead.

Eventually, they ran out of patients. Doc Schroeder knew that the most severely injured men could not be carried to his temporary aid station. He decided to go inside the ship to give aid. Schroeder walked through the heavy, darkened haze toward the hangar deck, which was still burning. Lethal smoke poured forth. He made it all the way aft to where the fires began. The next morning crewmen found his body on the gallery deck just below the island.

Meanwhile, Hoot Hutt made his way along the hangar deck, helping men to lay out hoses, and moving debris. Later, he wandered back through the wreckage of his squadron's aircraft on the flight deck. He found Miller, one of the fighter pilots who never made it out of his cockpit after Yasunori's crash. Miller's skin and muscle had burned off his leg. His femur stuck out of his charred thigh. Fires by then had moved well aft of Miller's body, but the deck remained hot enough to set off 20mm and 50mm ammunition around Miller's burned plane as Hutt removed his body. Hutt felt strange, as though the loose ammo firing around him was not particularly dangerous. Larger and scarier 40mm rounds exploded almost constantly farther aft, along the ship's starboard side. Hutt carried Miller's body up to the bow and laid him out alongside other dead men.

Hour after hour, men throughout the *Bunker Hill*, men like Gelderman, Ray, and Hutt moved through the ship, looking for survivors, trying to help. They did not know what the fate of the ship would be. Still, they pressed on.

Most men live their entire lives without really knowing whether or not they are cowards. We live denying death. Even in war men struggle to keep death out of their thoughts. But inevitable death confronts those at war most immediately, and consideration of the most fundamental ideas and emotions—death, courage, murder, fear, and voluntary death—were inevitable aboard the *Bunker Hill.*

Beads Popp left the safe wardroom to man fire hoses on the flight deck. Popp had abhorred Beno Dyson, the ship's executive officer. No one on the *Bunker Hill* worked more by the book than Dyson. He made the 84th the only air group in the Pacific Theater that had to wear neckties at every evening meal. Popp always felt a measure of contempt for Dyson's officious dedication to naval form. "Naval Academy all the way," Popp said later. That changed when he saw Dyson commanding men on the broken deck.

Wrapped in bandages and unable to stand on his own, Dyson remained at his post, calmly directing the ship's personnel in fighting the fires—just as calmly as he had when canceling their leave or calling muster. Popp thought to himself, "This is what the Navy is all about."

Born and raised in Jersey City, Ordnanceman Pete Probo was a big man. He could carry 250-pound bombs by himself and stack them twelve high in the ship's magazines. Ordnancemen worked around the clock, either taking care of a flight that had just returned from battle, preparing a new group to head out, or changing munitions on a ready flight because someone altered the target. They bunked as close to the flight deck as possible and grabbed sleep whenever they could. Probo roomed with thirty other men in a cramped gallery deck compartment. Every time a plane landed, it felt like it would slam through the wooden deck above him into their quarters. Sometimes, on hard landings, the planes did break through the planks.

Probo had worked through the early hours of May 11 to get Turnbull's mission in the air and was sleeping soundly when Kiyoshi's bomb exploded about 100 feet aft of his bunk. He awakened to the sound of his bunkmates shouting, "What the hell was that?" Fires quickly spread to the aircraft stored below Probo's quarters. His room heated up.

Probo searched for his shoes for a few moments, finally got them on, and headed for the hatch. But when he opened the door he was thrown backward by an onrushing wall of smoke and heat. Eleven other men stood on the hot floor of the compartment, trapped with him. The catwalk, he knew, was only twenty-five feet down the hallway beyond his bunk room. From there they could abandon ship. But flames filled the glowing hallway. Their room was an oven, getting hotter and hotter. Officers estimated afterward that the temperature inside the compartment had risen to 220 degrees. The men were cooking.

"Little Joey" Olivera bunked near Probo. Olivera had received a letter from home the week before. His brother had been killed in Europe. Now, Olivera panicked and began shouting. Probo gave him a short right jab across his lower jaw and laid him out. They carried Little Joey to his bunk and set him down, unconscious. The walls began to smoke.

When the floor became too hot to stand upon, the men climbed onto the bunks together, scrambling bed to bed like children playing "don't touch the ground." They began to pray, silently. Then, as the smoke thickened, they prepared to die.

"This is it, boys," Probo said, grimly, as he took out a soft pack of unfiltered Philip Morris cigarettes. He handed each of them a cigarette and they sat together in the bunks of their burning room, smoking. All of them, even those who never smoked, smoked that morning.

Probo, still puffing, recited the Hail Mary and Our Father. He looked at the huge bronze ashtray* and then, almost for lack of anything else to do, made a desperate proposal. Probo suggested that they try banging on the ceiling. Safety, in the form of the flight deck, remained only eight inches or so from their heads. But thick insulation hung overhead, beneath four-inch teak planks that were seated on one eighth inch of steel plating. Everyone on deck was busy fighting fires amid the frequent explosions. No one would hear them. But the men had nothing to lose and nothing else to do. Everyone grabbed

---

* Throughout history, men on long military assignments and POWs have fought boredom by fashioning items from their ship's detritus. These works were often utilitarian—and sometimes whimsical—trench art. Probo and his bunkmates cut solid bronze ashtrays out of the 5-inch shell casings.

something: wrenches, hammers, ashtrays. They clambered up to the top bunks and began desperately, fiercely banging on the ceiling.

Miraculously, someone heard them. That crewman ran to find a sailor he knew had been a lumberjack in Oregon. The lumberjack arrived with a fireman's axe. He chopped through the deck in just a few minutes.

The eleven men with Probo all made it out without a scratch.

The burly Probo had trouble fitting through the opening. His friend Tony Faccone helped pull him through. Probo cut his hand coming out of the hole, but declined the Purple Heart. The Navy later retrofitted the Essex carriers with escape hatches for the men in those compartments.

Tony Faccone took one of the most famous photographs of the Pacific war. *Life* magazine published the picture and it became the cover of the *Victory at Sea* record albums and the best-selling official U.S. Navy collection of Pacific war photographs, compiled by Edward Steichen.

A sailor who had been a lumberjack axed through the deck. He saved Pete Probo and ten other ordnancemen who were cut off from aid in a room consumed by flames. The axe is in foreground, right.

Faccone had been trained to develop photos, not to take them. But he learned the workings of the Navy's huge Kodak cameras. When Yasunori struck, Faccone was in the photo lab drying the prints and listening to Tommy Dorsey's "Not So Quiet, Please."

Had it not been for a brand-new modification made to his lab, Faccone would have perished. After Pearl Harbor, the Navy's BuShips hurried the Essex carriers through production. Construction always exposes design problems, and it soon became clear that lack of emergency exits, jammed passages, and deficient ventilation could directly result in loss of life. Each time the big ships returned to the United States, the Navy made modifications to improve safety for the crewmen. BuShips ordered new emergency escape portholes cut into the side of the *Bunker Hill* when it returned from the first damaging kamikaze battles in the Philippines in 1944. The Bremerton shipyard cut a small hole out the side of the photo lab. Faccone and the other men loved having their own window to the sea. In the end, this window saved him. When his compartment filled with smoke, Faccone climbed through the window up to the flight deck, and ran forward to safety near the bows. There he ran into a Navy photographer who gave him a Kodak K-4 still camera.

Faccone lay down, his stomach flat on the deck, and placed the one-foot-square camera directly in front of his head as a shield from exploding ordnance. Reverberations rocked him. Bullets and other shrapnel whistled past. The fire raged in front of him. Debris, some of it afire, fell around him. But he stayed, lying behind the camera, and snapped photo after photo until he had used every inch of film.

Because his camera was resting on the flight deck, Faccone's photos gave a striking perspective in which the deck stretches impossibly long. Shot from that low angle, the ship looms, a compelling war machine, yet it is dwarfed by the immensity of the conflagration arising out of, and towering over it. In his famous shot, the bulging fire hoses draw the viewer back along the deck, past three sailors. The men aboard, though tiny in comparison to the ship and the danger, are occupied with the immediacy of their tasks. They look hurried but not afraid. Men in a gun tub at the edge of the frame are moving quickly, almost a blur. Behind them all, the deck is torn open like a tin can. Dozens of men stand at the edge of the inferno, each at their station, fighting the flames. The *Bunker Hill* in that moment represented everything it meant to be fighting the kamikazes at the end of the war.

After Kiyoshi's crash, Al Nadeau, the talker from Fly 2, had run across the flight deck and jumped into the sponson that wrapped along the

The photograph of the Bunker Hill *taken on May 11, 1945, by Tony Faccone that became emblematic of the U.S. Navy's struggle against kamikazes during the battle for Okinawa in the last months of the war.* Life *magazine published the photo in July 1945, and it became the cover of the hugely popular series of* Victory at Sea *record albums, as well as the best-selling book of naval war photographs* U.S. Navy War Photographs: Pearl Harbor to Tokyo Bay, *edited by Edward Steichen. The talker holding his huge helmet down over his ears is Art Volkema.*

port side of the flight deck. He found himself lying with four or five other guys in a six-foot-by-six-foot cargo net sponson box holding life jackets. They were all just trying to keep their heads down. Nadeau lay pressed tight against the netting, suspended fifty feet above the open ocean. Smoke rose behind him in a thick black plume two miles into the cool Pacific sky.

Nadeau looked down at the sea rushing past beneath them, his cheeks and mouth forced through the holes of the rough manila rope netting. Belowdecks and inside the hangar an inferno was building. The planes were melting. Rockets ignited and .50-caliber ammunition was firing and ricocheting throughout the ship's crowded interior. The main munitions stores were still a few decks below the flames, but the safety hatches had been breached. Nadeau figured it was only a matter of time before the fire ignited the arms stores and the ship exploded.

In 1942, the Navy had begun firefighting training for all sailors and developed new equipment under the guidance of two former professional firefighters from New York and Boston who became Navy lieutenants. The carriers had new gasoline-operated water pumps, portable steel-cutting outfits, rescue and breathing gear, and foam-generating fire mains. It turned out, though, that much of this equipment was of little value.* More than anything, the Navy relied on its men.

Hearing the GQ whistle call, Nadeau climbed out of the sponson net onto the flight deck. He ran across to a group of men struggling to stretch out the high-pressure hoses toward the burning hole torn by Kiyoshi's bomb. Nadeau knew that when the water was released, those hoses would be difficult to control. He took a position four men

---

* The Japanese had very little firefighting and damage control training. The American training proved invaluable, but much of the new equipment failed. The steel-cutting rigs required compressed gas, which was too combustible for use near flames. The foam generators were useless because firefighting water spread everywhere and broke up the foam, making it impossible to stand on the slippery, foamed decks. It was impossible to start most of the gas-operated water pumps, and those that did start quickly clogged with debris. The RBAs, Rescue Breathing Apparatus, were a great help, but the *Bunker Hill* needed many hundreds more than they had shipped.

back from the nozzle and held on as hard as he could just as the water jetted through. The four sailors sprayed saltwater into the gaping, twisted deck hole. Fire and thick black toxic smoke poured out. He had been on the hose less than five minutes when W. T. Hatch came up behind him.

Hatch was a first class petty officer, roughly the equivalent of a sergeant in the Army. Today Nadeau explains, "When he says do something, I say 'How fast?' He came over, grabbed me and says, 'There's some guys trapped over by the island structure, come with me.'" Hatch led Nadeau back to the same island hatchway Nadeau had escaped from just after Kiyoshi's crash. A steep ladder staircase, so narrow that only one sailor at a time could use it, led below. Fires on the lower deck appeared to be breathing. Thick black smoke poured forth and spouts of flame shot up the stairway, then were sucked back inside, back and forth. Hatch told Nadeau that men were trapped in a compartment below. Hatch asked him to climb down the burning ladder with a fire hose and try to make his way to the compartment and free the trapped men.

Nadeau doesn't know why he was picked. He is not particularly small (to fit down the hole) nor so brawny as to rely on his strength in an emergency. Perhaps he was just last on the hose.

Other sailors tied a rope around Nadeau and handed him a fire hose gushing saltwater. Belowdecks, Nadeau could hear the terrified screams of men cut off from rescue, pinned down in rooms, beginning to burn, running out of air, or being poisoned by the smoke and fumes as the deadly gas swamped the ship.

The steep metal staircase leading to the lower deck glowed too hot to step on, so crewmen put Nadeau in a jury-rigged boatswain's chair. As his shipmates lowered him down the companionway, Nadeau sprayed the hose everywhere, trying to carve a path toward a radar room where he could see the walls on fire and hear men screaming. The rescue rope they used to lower him quickly burned to ash and he fell to the deck. Nadeau stood up, surrounded by flame. He turned aft and fired the hose down the corridor, cutting a path down the terrible hallway. Streams of fire burst forth from all directions. But the strongest flames darted in front of him. Nearly all the oxygen had been burned or sucked out of the hall. Thick, black, oozing smoke was poisoning his lungs. Nadeau coughed violently, unable to breathe. He knew he was not going to make it, so he turned around and rushed back through the flames to the companionway. The men atop reached out to him, but he would not abandon the trapped crewmen. Nadeau shouted up to his mates to throw down a Rescue Breathing Apparatus. He stood then at the bottom of the ladder, spraying his fire hose in fast circles round and round.

Nadeau can't explain it, but he was becoming oddly accustomed to this place, a world where men were not supposed to be, where thick hemp lines combusted and military aircraft melted into the decks. Someone dropped down an RBA. Nadeau slipped it on. He was surprised at how well it worked and pulled in deep breaths of clear air. Fortified, he made his way once again down the passageway on the broken gallery deck to the radar room hatch. Six dogs held the hatch cover watertight. Heat had caused the steel dogs to expand, jamming them all in the locked position. Nadeau kicked with all of the force he could muster and released them one at a time. But the last dog would not budge. He kicked as hard and violently as he had ever kicked, but he could not loosen the last, scorching dog. It seemed to be melted shut. He could not do it alone and he knew he would not get help. Perhaps he could get more tools. The men inside would perish unless that door could be opened.

Nadeau stepped back again to the hatchway. His mates dropped down a fireman's axe. Nadeau forced himself down the long hallway a third time carrying the heavy axe, the RBA, and the gushing fire hose.

With everything he had, Nadeau whacked the final dog. At last the hatch tore open. Five men, all alive, lay inside. One was on his knees praying. Smoke inundated the room, and the walls around were sprouting flame. Nadeau directed the stunned crewmen down the hallway past the shorn pieces of Kiyoshi's plane, forward in the island to the second ladder up to the flight deck. The last man out ahead of Nadeau was Mike Bauriedle, another plankowner. To this day, Bauriedle speaks of Nadeau with tears in his eyes.

28. DAMAGE CONTROL

Crewmen aboard the *Bunker Hill* faced two monumental tasks. They had to contain the fires and they had to escape the war zone. During the first hours after the attack, crewmen fought hard but were losing on both aspects of that fight.

Under normal circumstances, the *Bunker Hill* would rely on her defensive systems to make good her retreat. But every single defensive system aboard the ship had been severely damaged by the two kamikazes. The flight deck, hangar deck, and two elevators were wrecked. All her aircraft burned. Most of the pilots and their crews had been killed within the first ten minutes of the assault. The Combat Information Center, which controlled ship's operations, and hangar deck control, which managed damage control, were knocked out. Thirty minutes after the first bomb exploded, electrical power, communications, and radar failed. Essential personnel lay dead and dying. By 10:30 A.M., the *Bunker Hill* could no longer effectively defend herself against further attack. The Gunnery Department had been rendered ineffectual.

All of the guns aft of the island stood destroyed or abandoned. The forward guns had little ammunition, almost no power, and could not be fired accurately, as the cables connecting the guns to their radars and power had melted. Surviving electricians laid new cable to portable generators but firefighting water rendered them useless. The AA guns had to be loaded and aimed manually and targets could only be sighted visually. Sailors pitched much of their ready ammunition overboard and fresh munitions stores remained mostly out of reach. STS bomb elevator shafts had cracked or passed directly through continuously raging fires. Gunners volunteered for long bucket brigades passing ammunition to the mounts on the flight deck, but the ammo had to be jettisoned again when the stubborn deck fires reignited.

The ship, slowed to single knots, lost maneuvering speed. Smaller warships surrounding her on all sides streamed water across her flaming innards. The water slowed the flames, but the shielding vessels kept the *Bunker Hill* boxed in, unable to maneuver even when the boilers returned to full capacity.

The hangar deck fire raged out of control and spread even as the crew cleared the ship to contain it. The forward elevator, though, functioned and the men relocated aircraft and other accelerants from the hangar deck to the flight deck as quickly as they could, then pushed the war planes and other potential fuels over the side throughout the morning. Nevertheless, the hangar deck fire continued to spread inside the ship's protected box, following fuel as it leaked down a large open hatch. Once inside the protected area of the ship, the flames could move more freely through and around the inner decks.

The *Bunker Hill* had been built with a series of internal watertight compartments to defend against the typical threat to warships—torpedoes. Thick bulkhead walls traveled from the ship's bottom all the way to the hangar deck. These bulkheads were watertight, but only to a level of five feet on each deck. These five-foot bulkheads compartmentalized damage, preventing flooding from spreading. If a single compartment were breached, it would have to fill up with five feet of water before it could spill over the bulkhead and begin to flood the next compartment. Steel screens covered the remaining distance from the top of the bulkhead to the ceiling on each deck to allow fresh air pulled through the ventilation system to circulate between the waterproof compartments. After the hit, though, smoke—not fresh air—poured through the screens and saturated every compartment in the hull.

Insidious smoke, the by-product of fire, could not sink the *Bunker Hill*, but had the capacity to suffocate every crewmen inboard. Men in the messing halls and galley and small rooms throughout the ship piled tables and chairs, desks, mattresses, wet towels, sheets, and pillows—everything they could find—against the porous screens to hold back the foul smoke. The makeshift barriers delayed entry of the smoke. But many of the men manning the barricades were eventually overcome. These crewmen were found in small groups throughout the ship, tangled together, lying on top of and around their furniture redoubts, all dead of asphyxiation.

The armored third deck, just below the hangar deck, would have stopped most of the fire, but sailors left an extra-large hatch open and the fire spread easily to the second deck, inside the armored box. At each deck within the box, the flood of flaming fuel atop seawater spread horizontally as the fuel pooled up at the coamings, then overflowed and spilled down to the next deck. Water was never supposed to penetrate the box. The doors in this middle section of the ship were not watertight—they did little to slow the spread of smoke, fire, and flood.

The smoke hung so thick, and the fires burned so hot, that firefighting crews could not even enter the box to begin firefighting. They played hoses down the top of the hole in the flight deck.

The men were powerless to douse the flames on the flight and hangar decks. In the ship's official report, the flight deck fires are described as "controlled" by 10:30 A.M., but this is misleading. "Controlled" is a term of art, which to a firefighter describes a fire that though it cannot be extinguished, can be "controlled" from spreading beyond a defined area. Crewmen never really controlled the flight deck fires. Wind off the bow prevented the flames from moving forward. Flight deck fires burned fiercely after 10:30, but at that point they had consumed all of the aft part of the flight deck, and therefore could not spread further.

The "controlled" flight deck fires, though, had already launched conflagrations on the hangar and gallery decks, which had spread into the protected box. These fires raged, uncontrolled, for hours, until they had burned up every ounce of fuel, ammunition, and combustible material.

The *Bunker Hill* represented the culmination in design and construction techniques a generation in the making. The Essex Class, with their aircraft and trained pilots, were the most expensive and difficult ships to replace in the Navy arsenal. Survivability of the ship, therefore, not necessarily the crew, became one of the key design factors.

Damage control, which for the Japanese navy was seen as defensive in nature, and therefore almost a misconcern, became a guiding principle, not merely in the training of the men, but in the ship's design.

BuShips learned to build redundant systems throughout the ship, thus the boilers and engines could all be run independently and interchangeably. The ship could run fast backward and move fairly easily with three of four propellers out. Water pressure could be maintained even with the loss of multiple mains in various portions of the ship. Nearly every machine had a backup aboard, with ample spare parts. There were only two ways to sink an Essex: open up her hull under the water, or pour so much water in from above that she toppled over. Commander Carmichael remained with his men throughout the struggle to save the ship. He initiated this effort by taking total control over the imperiled Engineering Department. The six rooms, composed of the two engine rooms and four boiler rooms, were the heart of Carmichael's operations, and that is where he concentrated nearly all his energies in the first fifteen minutes after Kiyoshi's bomb exploded and fires consumed the ship above his men.

Carmichael knew that the bottom was not seriously holed and he would never allow her to capsize. He exuded the confidence of an engineer who knew the ship would last—he had drilled and planned for this type of disaster since taking command of the Engineering Department—and his men felt his assurance.

In many ways much of his life had been a preparation for this time. He had worked for years in Western mines under dangerous conditions, with explosives and toxic gasses close at hand. Carmichael's engineering degree and naval training gave him the specific knowledge he needed to keep the systems running. And the Civilian Conservation Corps had taught him how to lead.

In succession, Carmichael called each engine room and fire room to receive detailed reports of the deteriorating conditions. Once he had assured himself that the largest systems (the boilers, engines, turbines, and generators) remained functioning, he began methodically using the talkers and the various phone systems to contact each area under his command throughout the ship to determine its status. Carmichael made a complete survey of every engineering watch around the ship. He knew the names of all 528 men under his command and he called around to make sure that their leaders had made it to their watch or had someone covering. He ensured that sufficient men, capable physically and mentally to carry out their assigned tasks, stood at hand, and then he turned his attention to the worsening conditions in his own area.

Carmichael appeared to be the only significant ship's officer on the intercom. When crewmen throughout the ship heard Carmichael's calm voice speaking to his men in scattered compartments, his quiet resolve assured them. Many came desperately to believe that Carmichael, so graceful under pressure, would save them. Men began calling in to Carmichael on the various phone systems from all over the ship, scared, coughing, shouting, often frantically, that they were burning to death. He told me stoically, "There wasn't anything I could do about it."

Men struggled to escape. The ship burned below, above, and all around them. Smoke poured into their redoubts. Somehow, though, their phones still worked. They called to let the rescue parties know their whereabouts.

Even at the very end, many expected to be rescued. It did not seem possible that they could be perfectly healthy, standing on the same ship with their comrades, able to speak back and forth, and yet be facing imminent, inevitable death. They simply could not accept that they were about to die. And they held to the idea that so long as they struggled, so long as they remained conscious, so long as they could talk to their friends on the intercom, something would be done. They would be saved. The cavalry always arrived.

But Carmichael understood from his vantage point in the engine room that for many of these young men rescue would not come, only a slow and agonizing death.

Fifteen electricians had raced to their battle station in a central compartment when Yasunori crashed. Flames quickly surrounded their waiting room. The compartment heated up, then began to fill with smoke. They could not escape. But they could hear Carmichael speaking calmly on the telephone and they called out to him for help. They spoke calmly to him at first, careful about interrupting him, to ask when firefighters would arrive to lead them out. Carmichael knew none would be sent. He tried to keep them calm, although he knew what was coming.

As the minutes wore on, the electricians called Carmichael with increasing frequency telling him that the room was getting hotter. Again and again they called, asking for their rescuers. But Carmichael knew that their compartment stood beyond the help of any man. Hardened steel around them had turned liquid.

As their room filled with smoke, the heat for them became unbearable. Some began to pass out. Then they began to die.

Carmichael shouldered this burden and continued to run the ship. The *Bunker Hill*, with her 3,400 sailors, remained his priority. And so he ordered his talkers to cut the lines.

"It sounds kind of cold," he would later say, "but there was no choice there, and it was better to spend my time directing and checking out how our equipment was functioning where something could be done."

Despite the danger to himself and his engineers, trapped well below the waterline and with deck after deck aflame above them, Carmichael maintained the good order and discipline he had trained so long to keep. His men acted routinely. They had been at war for years and drilled for this kind of eventuality every day. They all were scared, but they stood surrounded by familiar equipment, making familiar noises, in a familiar room, and doing work they were all well used to completing together. The routine, familiarity, and Carmichael's stolid example filled them with a confidence that allowed some engineers to keep to their tasks even as their friends lay down in the muck around them.

As the minutes wore on, engineers in other compartments began to call in, too, asking for help, for rescue or relief, and finally asking for permission to leave their posts. The men were coughing and in pain. Some lay dying from smoke. But Carmichael knew that already. He was aware of the ship's fatal flaw. He had worried over it. There was nothing that could be done.

Much of the fuel from aircraft spotted on the flight deck poured through the elevators and bomb holes in the flight deck, and onto the hangar deck where it blew up the aircraft stored there, spilling, in turn, more fuel, which poured through the tragically open armored hatch. From that hatch it fell down each companionway, until it came to rest on top of the hatches above the men who had been sealed inside the main engineering compartments. Perhaps two to three feet of sea-water had been pumped into the *Bunker Hill* as part of the firefighting effort. Much of this water was now on top of the escape hatches of the engine and fire room compartments. Atop the seawater burned six inches of lighter-than-water fuel.

Even if Carmichael had wanted to release all his men, he knew after the first half hour that there was no way they could open those hatches and survive. He thought of perhaps opening up a small reservoir, hoping that the burning fuel would fall past his men's heads and into the bilge and then somehow get pumped out of the ship without igniting the fuel that fired the boilers or any of the other sensitive equipment in the engineering rooms. But that seemed laden with tremendous risk, especially when compounded with the fact that the men still could not leave their posts without essentially dooming the ship.

Carmichael could stand the loss of men. Even his own men. But he could not get replacements for the men in the now isolated rooms. The machines could not operate long without human intervention. Carmichael had to figure out a way to keep enough men alive to save the ship.

All the men still standing were coughing violently. Sooty, black, bloody pieces of something that looked like lung were coming up from each of them. Five or six of his men had lain down early on and died almost peacefully. Carmichael described them "fading away," which is typical of carbon monoxide poisoning.

He tried to keep the others on their feet and focused on the work at hand. Describing the scene, he said, "We had a young talker in the engine room, who I had placed there deliberately alongside me because I thought he was a little bit of a weak sister, and I thought if he was with somebody like me, we could kind of keep him on his feet as long as he needed. But, well, he was determined not to stay on his feet."

The young sailor slumped down and ended up on the floor where he slipped in and out of consciousness. Carmichael kicked him to his feet again and again. The engineering chief, Sottung, slugged the sailor whenever he walked past the young man and brought him back each time. But then the young sailor would fade away again. With repeated kicks and jabs, Carmichael and his second kept the awkward sailor alive. He survived physically, but Carmichael explained afterward, "he was never any good, a mental-head, probably as much from our care as from anything else."

Carmichael is unforgiving of those officers who abandoned the ship. The enlisted men working in the number one fire room were beginning to die. But those who remained standing continued their vital work.

As the day wore on and smoke continued to pour into the boiler rooms, men began to die also in the number two fire room. Both rooms then began asking Carmichael permission to shut down operations and evacuate the poisoned compartments. Unruffled, Carmichael answered unequivocally, as though their situation remained no more serious than a drill. He said, "No."

By late that evening, only one man was alive in the number one fire room. He called in to Carmichael and they spoke together quietly for more than an hour. His name was Berenstuhl. They had worked together for many years. They were only a few yards apart, but it was a distance neither could traverse. And they both knew it. They spoke calmly to each other on the phones. Berenstuhl began to fade in and out. But Carmichael talked him through setting every gauge and every dial so that the engines could run themselves for as long as possible after Berenstuhl passed out. And then the line went dead.

Despite the certainty of a slow attrition. Despite the horror of the dark. Despite the dread that every sailor has felt for millennia—what Melville called "fear of the abyss"—these men stayed.

They seemed to make a collective decision to try to manage the boilers for as long as they possibly could to give their mates on the ship a fighting chance of surviving. They knew that they would die. They understood that Carmichael knew they would die. And yet they stayed.

They stayed to fight the Japanese, they stayed for each other, and they stayed for their friends in other parts of their ship. They stayed to save the *Bunker Hill*. But mostly they stayed for Joseph Carmichael.

Kiyoshi's assault killed more men from Engineering than from any other department. To this day, Carmichael carries the scars from the soot, visible on X-rays, deep in his lungs. The other scars, those that come from leading men to their deaths, are harder to see. Carmichael understands deeply that in war men must die. On May 11, it fell to him to order his own good men to remain at their posts and die.

29. RESCUE

Crewmen aboard the *Bunker Hill* had trained for years to deal with fires, water damage, and medical emergencies. But no one ever taught them specifically what to do if they were hit by a kamikaze. For a moment, most of the crew, like Al Turnbull, had watched in wonder as the *Bunker Hill* and all her planes caught fire. But within minutes, without direction from the bridge, hundreds of men, in every part of the ship, began to take initiative on their own. They fought fires, kept the engines running, and tried to save their mates. They performed a thousand acts of courage that will never be recorded. Above all, they did their duty.

Jerry Hanson worked on emergency crews around the clock. First he fought the fires. Then he struggled through the interior rescuing trapped men and carrying out the dead. Finally, he worked in the hangar deck morgue where he tied his comrades in makeshift body bags with two fifty-five-pound 5-inch shells knotted around their torso.

Everyone knew the ready room exits had been blocked by flames. But most of the sailors figured that the vast majority of the men stuck on the gallery deck remained alive, hunkered down, simply awaiting rescue. Flames died down sufficiently in the late afternoon to cut holes in the deck to let the waiting pilots come up and breathe free air.

Everyone wanted to get the pilots out as quickly as possible. Rescue crews chopped a hole through the flight deck above the nearest ready room. They needed someone lanky enough to fit down the narrow hole, but strong enough to deal with any problem on the gallery deck. A chief ordered Jerry Hanson to go first into the dark hole, and lead the pilots out.

The pilots were the raison d'être of the *Bunker Hill*. The efforts of the men who built the *Bunker Hill*, the men who sailed her, manned her guns, kept her boilers fired, and her aircraft working, all were directed at the final task, which depended entirely on the bravery of these pilots. The airmen flew into combat every single day during Okinawa, and the crew looked up to them and were anxious to see them freed.

Two men held Hanson's legs and began lowering him into the pitch black hole. The stench was overpowering. Fuel oil, gasoline, burned rubber. And, above all, the horrifying reek of burned flesh. Survivors from the *Bunker Hill* all remember the pungent odor of burned flesh. Perhaps the worst thing about that smell for so many of the crew was its haunting familiarity. Their friends' burned bodies smelled horrifyingly recognizable to all of them. The burned dead smelled sweet like the backyard barbecues they had loved so much at home. It left them with longing and a guilt that the years have not erased. Not one of them has forgotten that smell.

Rescue crews cut the hole just large enough for Hanson to squirm inside. As they lowered him further, his body plugged up nearly all the light. He was hanging upside down into a crowded hallway. Hanson had no idea where he was, but sensed something terribly wrong. As he twisted his way inside the stinking passage, he became aware of a massed presence just below his arms. Slowly his eyes adjusted to the dim light.

Hanson was staring down at the blurred jumble below him, peering hard, when he suddenly realized that the heap was an enormous tangle of dead and burned men.

The pilots had had no way out. All of them were dead. Most lay charred beyond recognition. Heavy soot and poisoned air blackened even those who died of asphyxiation. The burning hangar deck beneath them had cooked the dead from below. The flight deck afire overhead broiled them from above. The men died in blackness, in a world lit fleetingly only by fire and bewildering explosion. In the confusion, they had become tangled together in a terrible knot worse than any nightmarish image by Hieronymus Bosch.

Hanson began screaming. He shouted loudly at the walls and the men above him holding his legs. "Get me out of here. All these people are dead!"

Many of the pilots in that pile had flown Avengers. They were the man left behind by Al Turnbull and George Lyons. Their bodies remained in that hallway for hours, until rigor mortis had set in. Recovery crews could not disentangle the bodies, nor remove them down the hallways. Eventually, crewmen cut the hole much larger. They lowered down a block and tackle and tied lines to the dead men, then pulled them up and out of the uneven opening. Sometimes the bones would break as the men were ripped from the passage. Sometimes their limbs came off and dark, cooked liquids seeped out.

Hanson said later: "It was like how you would imagine, ah, hell would be, I guess."

Pilots trying to escape flames surrounding their ready room raced through the pitch black passageways. As the flames consumed all oxygen, the pilots would have become increasingly befuddled, taking in more and more carbon monoxide. They died tangled, confused, tortured, and frightened beyond description, probably in intense pain. Their bodies were discovered first by Jerry Hanson when he was lowered head-first into a hole cut in the deck. This is what he saw when his eyes became used to the light. The wall-mounted telephone at right indicates how high these men were piled upon each other.

Immediately after the strike, Al Skaret began moving oil around various void tanks to keep the ship from listing too much. On direct orders not to open a hatch, he had listened as men struggled on the opposite side. Thirty minutes after the first bomb exploded Lieutenant Petrofsky, a damage control officer, grabbed Skaret out of the office to survey damage to the *Bunker Hill* for Commander King. Skaret liked Petrofsky. The tough young lieutenant would stand nose-to-nose with the roughest sailors on the ship and, according to Skaret, "tell them what he thought."

Throughout the afternoon, as the fires raged, the two men walked through some of the most heavily damaged and dangerous portions of the *Bunker Hill*. They made their way into the protected box on the lower decks. They traveled far aft to view damage from Yasunori's bomb along the ship's port side. They entered compartments where the shrapnel from Yasunori's explosive punctured the heavily armored ship's side along the waterline. When the ship heeled to port, more of the holes from Yasunori's bomb dipped below the waterline, and sea-water streamed inboard. The largest holes were the size of a bowling ball. Water gushed in as though fired from a high-pressure main.

Skaret saw sailors in those comparments wading through in waist-deep water. These men grabbed anything they could to stop the inflow, including the time-honored method—probably going back to the ancient Greeks and Phoenicians—of stuffing pillows, mattresses, and sheets into the leaky holes. It stanched the flow to a significant degree. Carmichael's induced list to starboard fortuitously kept some of the shrapnel holes in the port side storerooms raised just above the waterline. By sunset, the *Bunker Hill*'s bilge pumps were removing more water than the firefighting efforts were adding.

Skaret was one of the few sailors who saw a great deal of the *Bunker Hill* that day. He and Petrofsky often had to feel their way through darkened corridors. Commander King, concerned that the spark from a battery could ignite gasoline fumes permeating the ship's interior, forbade them from using battle lanterns. Feeling their way through the dark, they walked and stumbled along blind passages filled with foul, inky water, touching different types of equipment to determine its temperature, trying to figure out which areas were still burning or in danger of flaring up again. They wended their way past the dead to find holes in the ship's side, abandoned machinery, and clogged passageways. Most important, they needed to ascertain—if they could—the condition of the engine rooms.

They put on Chem-Ox masks and grabbed battle lanterns from the walls.* Hull crews had placed these flashlights, set in orange or yellow plastic cubes holding lead batteries, strategically throughout the *Bunker Hill*, but they were not much use against the smoke. Al Skaret and Petrofsky climbed down the vertical escape ladder, in pitch blackness, as the smoke billowed up from below. They made their way twenty-five feet below the waterline of a vessel that many thought was sinking into one of the engineering rooms.

The mask's face piece was made of shatterproof glass about the size of aviator's goggles, with extremely limited peripheral vision. Skaret's voice vibrated through the rubber diaphragm, making it almost impossible to understand him.

Skaret had never been in an engine room in his life. The spaces are gargantuan, some of the largest rooms on the ship. Their ceilings are twenty-five feet high, almost as tall as the hangar deck. But nearly all of the space, vertical and horizontal, is taken up by a complex maze of interlocking pipes, tanks, hoses, valves, and dials. The only way around inside is on narrow catwalks of interlocking steel mesh plates, most of which have no railings. These walkways are bisected constantly and at odd angles by various tangled pipe, valve, and dial arrangements. It is perhaps the most alien environment on the ship, even under normal conditions. When Skaret and Petrofsky arrived, the compartment was so full of sooty smoke that even the off-white beam of the square battle lantern did not penetrate more than a foot. The two men lost sight of each other almost immediately.

Al Skaret was scared. There seemed to be no one in the room. He

---

* The engineering compartments were filled with machinery that produced sparks and live flames, so there was little danger of explosive gasses in those rooms.

figured the crew for that room must all have died. No one was moving. Anyone there was either dead or passed out, invisible in the smoky shadows. He wanted to rush back toward the ladder where they had entered and climb out. But Skaret knew he had to wait for Petrofsky. He had been taught the buddy system in damage control. Either you dragged your buddy out or he dragged you out, but no one left without their buddy. Skaret remembered from his training—and from his training others—that the Chem-Ox mask he was wearing would last only about an hour—less if he began breathing quickly, perhaps a little longer if he could control his breathing. But it is particularly hard to breathe calmly when you think your oxygen is running out.

Determined to find Petrofsky, Skaret moved carefully in the heat among the pipes and valves. Because he could not see the ground, he moved slowly, stepping lightly lest his foot settle onto the body of a fallen sailor. He began to think Petrofsky must have died. But he could not bring himself to leave the room without his buddy. He started back, trying to work his way to where he had entered, but Skaret was lost.

His oxygen was running out. He hadn't found anyone he could help. He had not found anyone at all. Now he could not find his way out. He tried to calm his breathing, and said a simple prayer, one repeated by servicemen since the dawn of war: "Dear Lord, help me get out of here."

He felt around until he finally found a railing, then followed it up a narrow passage back to an emergency ladder in an escape tube. His Chem-Ox mask was depleted. He would certainly die if he remained any longer, and so, though troubled about abandoning his lieutenant, Skaret climbed the ladder. It was pitch black in the narrow tube. He looked up confused to see the moon high above. He climbed toward it, hand over hand. As the light slowly came into focus, Skaret realized it was one of those little square battle lanterns. A sailor stood over the escape tube, pointing it down as Skaret made his way up. The sailor said, "Boy, I've been here a long time. Your officer left a long time ago, and he told me to stay here until you came out!"

Once out of the engine room, Skaret continued his damage survey, pausing when he could to rescue men or to aid firefighters. That evening, he joined a group of men trying to put out one of the most stubborn fires, which burned in a large berthing compartment on the gallery deck in between the two bomb blasts. It had been left to burn itself out, but continually flared up. Now, in the evening dark, it would become a bright beacon for enemy search aircraft and kamikazes.

The firefighters tried to force their way through a burning hatchway, but the gooey black smoke was too thick. They retreated, and donned Chem-Ox masks. But the smoke inside was so thick and black that they almost immediately lost their way and retreated again. They returned a third time, wearing lead-in lines like Theseus entering the Labyrinth. But the fire hoses were not long enough. They retreated a third time. They brought in more hose, but the couplers did not match the original hose, so they left again. Finally, they returned to the flaring room, only to find that it was so cavernous that their lead lines were now not long enough. By this time, Skaret had had enough. He took over leadership of the firefighters from an officer, grabbed a dozen coils of Manila rope, and led the men in.

The fire had grown steadily worse while the men fiddled with equipment. Now it burned all around them. Still, they waded in through the saltwater that had accumulated to the top of the gunwales at the hatchway doors.

Flare-ups of staggering brightness punctuated the darkness, yet illuminated nothing but shadows in the thick and deadly smoke. The flashes destroyed whatever night vision the men had developed. They could barely see each other. No one could hear anything. The fires burned beyond their control. Their tiny inch-and-a-half hose had no effect on the flames. Skaret knew they would make no difference. Over the din, and making signs with his hands, he ordered them out of the room.

As he moved toward the exit, the first in and the last to leave, Skaret was pulled up short. His lead line had tangled on a bunk. Instinctively, he jerked it hard. In doing so, he wedged the rope tightly into a steel crevice behind the metal bunk. He was locked in.

Al Skaret looked up, horrified. His comrades were disappearing into the smoke. He tried to twist free, but instead entangled his head in the mass of lines. He was trapped. "I could just see this sailor in front of me . . . just leaving me there . . . and I yelled as much as I could through the muffled diaphragm speaker. But it just sounded like mush, and there was so much noise in the room." Straining forward, Skaret managed to brush the sailor in front of him with his fingertips. The sailor glanced around and saw Skaret tied up. They worked at the line simultaneously, then marched out together.

The officer in charge determined not to send the men in again. Instead, they would cut through the teak and Douglas fir that covered the deck and fight the fire from above.*

When rescuers finally broke through the wood, the firefighters burned through the steel layer of the flight deck with acetylene torches. Once inside, they realized that this sporadic but tenacious fire in a gallery deck berthing compartment was caused by the 440-volt electrical system. If Skaret and his men had been able to spray water on it, especially while standing knee-deep in saltwater, they probably all would have been killed.

The firefighting and struggle to save the ship, and the horror of seeing comrades die, was relieved at times by peaceful moments of almost transcendent grace. At some point, Skaret climbed up out of the dark and muck to a clear deck, bathed with golden light. There, he watched, mesmerized, as the shining white hospital ship *Bountiful* pulled alongside the *Bunker Hill* as the evening sun set. The red cross shone out brightly against the former troopship's gleaming sides. The *Bountiful* had originally carried twenty-four mules and 1,500 men of the American Expeditionary Force to Nazaire, France, in 1917. She was the first ship Skaret had seen since the war began that was not trying to hide itself, and it filled him with a new hope for the *Bunker Hill*.

---

* The *Bunker Hill* as built had a teak deck of three-by-six boards. When sections of the flight deck were repaired at Bremerton, the teak was replaced sporadically with tough Douglas fir.

30. BURN

Humans can be injured from pressure, sharpness, cold, and heat. But
heat has always been the most terrifying. Anyone who has ever been
burned for a moment by a simple match knows how shockingly painful even a slight burn can be. In nearly every human culture and religion, the worst punishments—such as eternal damnation—call for
fire. Dante reserved the hottest places in hell for the worst offenders.
Fire has been almost universally considered the most terrifying and
effective agent to produce extreme pain.

Fire is insidious. It can kill by many varied means. The fires on May
11 killed crewmen in three principal ways: burning, oxygen deprivation, and inhalation injuries. Most men suffered injury from a mixture of the three.

Burn pain is enormously complex and difficult to control. It has a
duration far beyond that of most injuries. A broken leg hurts, but the
pain departs long before the bone is healed. Burn pain can be acute
for years and years, and last a lifetime. Burns also produce scarring,
and the disfigurement adds to the fright that burns induce.

Skin is an organ that prevents the body from evaporating or leaking fluids, holds in heat, and protects from bacteria. When skin is
exposed to severe heat, all three functions are lost. The body immediately loses a tremendous amount of fluid and heat, and becomes vulnerable to a range of bacteriological infections.

Most organs lack sensory perception to a significant degree. It

would not hurt much to have a hole cut straight through your brain—
the beginning of the hole through the skin of your scalp, however,
would cause enormous discomfort. Skin contains millions upon million of nerve endings.

The exquisitely sensitive nerve endings are buried at the deepest layer of the skin. When the outer, protective portions of skin are
burned, the buried nerve endings are powerfully stimulated, sending
out millions upon millions of messages to the brain. The mind inter-
prets all of these stimulations as intense pain. The greater the temperature and larger the size of the burn, the more the body feels pain.

Most of the burn injuries aboard the *Bunker Hill* were caused
by explosions and combustion of highly flammable materials. Fuel,
explosives, and napalm generated intense heat that burned the full
thickness of human skin. When heat burns the skin all the way to its
last layers, the nerve endings themselves are destroyed. The pain stops.
Burns, though, are rarely uniform. Around the periphery, and along
horribly painful islands amid burned areas, some nerve endings are
invariably left undamaged. These transmit signals of intense pain.

The mind reacts to this pain by shutting down blood flow to and sensory perception from peripheral and painful areas. The badly burned
person may not realize the ferocity of his injuries. Blood flow is directed
solely to essential organs: the heart, lungs, and brain. The severely
injured areas, lacking blood flow, quickly became anaesthetized.

Most burn victims, like the pilot that George Lyons tried to save,
would quickly succumb to fluid loss, or infection. Ironically, those
with severe burns normally retain consciousness for some period of
time, and are often so deeply in shock that they might not describe
themselves as being in pain at all. But the body cannot long maintain
those levels of system shutdown. Cells and organ systems deprived
of blood and oxygen very quickly begin to die. When men like Tom
Martin,* who had been transferred, finally received care aboard the
Bountiful, they were injected with massive doses of adrenaline to keep

---

* Martin was the airman who passed out beside his friend Bakely in a burning
armory. He regained consciousness aboard a hospital ship but has no idea how
he got there, except that Bakely saved his life.

their blood flowing. This was a serious medical error, which accelerated blood flow to—and fluid loss from—burned areas. After Martin survived through the 12th of May 1945, his greatest threat became infection and dehydration. Such secondary injuries, which today would be routinely salvageable, were often lethal during the Second World War. It took several days for many of the burn victims to die.

The amount of suffering they sustained in their final hours and days is simply indescribable. Doctors wrapped Martin in painful bandages to try to control infection. His main treatment was merely unsophisticated pain management through injections of morphine.

Recovery for Tom Martin and the others who survived their burn injuries and exposure to carbon monoxide was a painful, often crippling process. Modern dressings would have significantly reduced his scarring. But these men faced and have experienced a lifetime of pain, mutilation, disfigurement, and scarring. Martin spent the first years after the war moving from hospital to hospital as he made his way back to Cambridge, Massachusetts. During this time, his burned nerve endings were constantly regenerating, and with every new growth, he felt the intense pain again. He experiences the pain of the *Bunker Hill* fires still today, and will continue to relive the pain of that morning for his entire lifetime.

All of the pilots in their ready rooms were killed by Kiyoshi Ogawa, but they died in various ways depending on their proximity to the explosion. Those found burned, but still sitting in their chairs, had been killed by the shockwave of Kiyoshi's bomb. When his bomb exploded, it sent out a wall of superheated air, which essentially crushed everything within a narrow radius of the explosion. Concussion killed these men, including John Sargent, the Texas pilot who used to tease Beads Popp. John Sargent was the pilot who smuggled his puppy "Blackout" aboard the training cruise before they all left for combat.

Sargent was Hoot Hutt's wingman. He had just made ace. When he was hit by the shockwave from Kiyoshi's bomb, every single cell in his body was rapidly compressed, and then decompressed, in the space of a microsecond. Each blood vessel burst: Sargent suffered a

massive capillary leak, similar to getting a bloody nose, only throughout the entire inside of his body. Though Sargent's skin was burned,
the strongest evidence of trauma was the trickle of blood that leaked
from his ears.

Sargent was identified by Hutt and Popp. The two men were horrified when they entered the ready room. Their friends' bodies lay
tossed about, scattered and dismembered, "just blasted all over." Rob-
bie Robinson had lost the top of his head. "It was just gone," Popp
told me.

Many of the pilots were still seated in their high-backed chairs.
Some were doubled over. A number were more badly burned on particular parts of their body, a shoulder, or ribs or their scalp, so that
their singed bones stuck out through the cooked flesh. One pilot sat,
still in his ready room chair, with all the skin burned off his head.
His body was badly burned, but all the flesh on his face had burned
entirely off. His blackened skull stared out blankly propped up on his
body by the remains of his neck.

The thing that bothered Hutt most was lifting his friends' bodies to
take them from the ready room. They had burst inside and he could
hear the blood and other fluids running back and forth within their
bodies as they tipped.

Out of the eight men in his group, Popp was the only one to survive, just because he had left the wrong place at the right time to grab
a snack.

Often after fires we read that people died peacefully in their sleep.
Most domestic fires produce relatively little smoke. There are not sufficient particulates in the smoke of a domestic fire to stimulate the
tracheal-bronchial tree and awaken victims. Unfortunately for the
men aboard the *Bunker Hill*, even those who were not burned, death
would have been exceedingly painful. Carbon monoxide poisoning
was delivered amid poisoned air saturated with painful particulates.
Many experienced a terrifying, sharp, searing pain to the depth of
their lungs with every last breath.

Airborne soot would have added the horror of blocked lung passages to the last minutes of many men who died aboard the *Bunker Hill*. The nerve endings of the tracheal-bronchial tree are exquisitely sensitive. Even microscopic irritants are powerfully noticed and experienced both immediately as fear when the lungs momentarily cease to function, and as pain when the body coughs to expel the threat. A tiny piece of the shell of a peanut caught in one's throat for a moment causes a massive bodily response. This horror, magnified a thousand-fold, was how many men aboard the *Bunker Hill* experienced their last moments. They died amid a combination of air hunger and, perhaps, the complete inhalation of particulate matter.

When air becomes absolutely impenetrable, as it did inboard of the *Bunker Hill*, doctors examining the dead sometimes find the tracheal-bronchial tree has completely filled with soot, almost like a clay mold. It is a terrible way to die. Had the men in those compartments been autopsied, it is likely that their entire bronchial tree would have been a cast of soot.

Men who died in the boiler rooms succumbed to carbon monoxide (CO) poisoning. It is a slow and insidious killer. The CO first causes a headache, then makes it difficult to reason, followed by an intense desire for rest. Men with apparently nothing else wrong with them, no longer coughing, simply sat down and went to sleep. Internally deprived of oxygen, they lay down and died.

During normal breathing, the lungs take in air, which contains about 20 percent oxygen. The oxygen travels into the lungs where it is absorbed by blood. Blood carries the oxygen to cells throughout the body. Without this constant influx of new oxygen, all cells will die. Blood alone cannot absorb much oxygen, but blood is filled with hemoglobin, which can carry about five times its own volume of oxygen. When the cells use the oxygen, they convert it into carbon dioxide (CO_2) which is poisonous to the cells. Hemoglobin also binds well to carbon dioxide, and carries the CO_2 back to the lungs where it is released in an exhale just before the blood picks up a new supply of fresh air including oxygen. So the hemoglobin pulls the oxygen out of the air in the lungs, carries it through the bloodstream to cells, and then carries the waste products back out for disposal via the lungs.

Unfortunately, hemoglobin bonds even more efficiently to carbon monoxide than it does to oxygen—210 times more easily. If hemoglobin is given a breath of air that contains the usual 20 percent oxygen and, say, 3 percent carbon monoxide, the hemoglobin will carry very little or no oxygen at all to the lungs. The body will be poisoned and quickly succumb.*

Fire exacerbates carbon monoxide poisoning. It burns the oxygen and creates CO. The oxygen portion of air during a fire can become 80 percent or 90 percent carbon monoxide. Remaining oxygen is insufficient for survival, and what little exists is pushed out of the bloodstream by the carbon monoxide.

Men dying of carbon monoxide poisoning do not struggle through death. They tend to lie down and go to sleep, peacefully, if permanently. Death by oxygen deprivation is very different from carbon monoxide poisoning.

Air hunger—oxygen depravation—is the most powerful stimulant of the flight/fight response. It attacks humans at our most basic level. It is one of the most frightening states humans experience, and has long been used as a method of torture.† As any fire burns in an enclosed space, it quickly consumes all available air. The Nazis used Zyklon B, a cyanide poison, which simulates oxygen deprivation, in their death chambers. Nazi guards left accounts describing those being murdered as scrambling on top of each other trying to get to the top where they thought there might be good air.

The men on the *Bunker Hill* who died fighting, like those whom Al Skaret heard bloodying their fingers while struggling to open steel hatches, died of oxygen deprivation.

The casualties in the ready rooms were extraordinary. Caleb Kendall and sixteen other fighter pilots were dead. Many other pilots,

---

* The only treatment is to give patients an immediate supply of 100 percent oxygen. Otherwise, the hemoglobin just won't let go of the carbon monoxide. Ironically, the color of hemoglobin carrying carbon monoxide is cherry red. So persons dying of carbon monoxide poisoning look great—full of color. But they are dying.

† This is why waterboarding is such an efficient method of instilling terror.

mostly from the Avenger ready room, including Phil Wainright, were discovered in the hallway outside the ready room. They died of a horrifying combination of heat, oxygen deprivation, inhalation of particulate matter, and carbon monoxide poisoning.

Those pilots knew they were in danger, they felt terrible anguish, and they understood they had to get out. Oxygen deprivation initiated the most primitive areas of their brain geared only for survival, to take control.

Doctors often comfort those nearest and dearest to the dead in burn cases. They tell loved ones that the victims never knew what happened. This is comforting, but in some cases profoundly misleading. If Phil Wainright, who died in the hallway, had lived, his mind would not have allowed him that terrible memory.* But at the time, he would have been fully cognizant of his pain and anguish as he and his friends clamored, burning. Lost in darkness and smoke, without oxygen, suffering the confusion of carbon monoxide poisoning while heat from fires raged all around, the pilots, so selfless for so much of their service, would have spent their last moments thrashing and scrambling in a total panic in the dark. The human survival instinct at its most basic level would take over almost completely. So, they ended, tangled in shadows.

---

* The mind produces three types of memory. Long-term memories are fully consolidated, those that the mind maintains both an inclination and ability to remember. Intermediate memory can be held and recalled for a time, but will eventually be forgotten. Most people recall what they had for breakfast this morning, but few can tell you what they ate for breakfast three weeks ago. Breakfast is usually an intermediate memory. Immediate memory, similar to RAM on a computer, is fleeting. If you were to hear a series of numbers read aloud, you might be able to recall the first ten or fifteen, but at some point, immediate memory would be overwhelmed. You could recall none but the last handful heard.

Memories produced by a mind under the effects of carbon monoxide are perhaps the most fleeting immediate memories of all. The brain has no ability to consolidate those memories, and when Phil Wainright passed out, it destroyed any chance of the memories of those last minutes in the ready room and hallway being consolidated. Had he survived, it would be highly unlikely that he would have recalled the incident. But at the time, he was fully aware of anguish and pain.

31. ADRIFT

Al Turnbull treaded water and watched the *Bunker Hill* cruising away. He knew a raft and men floated ahead of him, and so he began to swim in the direction he had watched the smoking carrier steam. From his vantage point, now only a few inches above the sea, he could not see any other ships. It seemed the entire task force had disappeared. But the *Bunker Hill*, with her trail of smoke, gave him a clear beacon to follow. Turnbull swam in the water watching the smoke rise a few thousand feet into the air above the stricken ship. Winds hit the smoke spire at the higher altitudes, causing it to dissipate and spread horizontally over the sea, a great dark cloud. Sometimes, though, the whole sky calmed, allowing the smoke to rise higher and higher, blending gradually into the upper horizon, trailing off behind the carrier. He didn't panic. There was barely a breeze and the ocean lay quiet and peaceful. Slow Pacific swells gently lifted him up, then lay him down in their troughs. No whitecaps, nor waves broke the silence. Turnbull never doubted that all he had to do was to follow the carrier and he would find a life raft.

But though Turnbull continued swimming, he found nothing. He began to think about the size of the ocean around him and wondered whether he was on the correct path. He thought, too, about the size of the life raft canister that he had carried across the burning deck. It was not much bigger than an ordinary bedside lamp—maybe four feet long, with a little painter attached. The ocean looked very large.

Turnbull swam and swam. He was glad the Navy had painted the canister yellow. But the more he swam, the more he realized how impossible the odds were against his ever coming across the little round yellow life raft thrown from an aircraft carrier steaming away at 20 knots.

389

The Bunker Hill, *burning at sea below heavy cloud cover, is surrounded by escorting destroyers.*

And then he found it. The canister floated, bobbing up and down quietly on the surface, almost directly in his path. Turnbull swam straight over to it and yanked the cord on the CO_2 bottle. As the raft inflated, it automatically deployed a yellow dye marker so that anyone flying over him could easily spot his raft.

Turnbull's first thought, though, was of the enlisted men who had jumped overboard right after dropping the raft. Turnbull popped out the diminutive wooden paddles and quickly snapped them together. He placed the oars into the stiff rubber oarlocks and began rowing straight in the direction of the smoke from the *Bunker Hill*. The ship had long since disappeared, but the smoke from her burning decks remained visible, still thick. He found no one. The ocean around him gently rose and fell, eerily peaceful. On the catwalk, his life had felt like a crowded hell of inescapable fire and noise. Now he sat, quietly, comfortably paddling, completely alone.

Turnbull always flew with a crew. He had not experienced pure privacy since he signed up after Pearl Harbor, and he knew that after even a short time alone in the water, thoughts and perceptions become unreliable. He began to doubt himself almost immediately. He could not at first decide whether he had rowed the boat too far, or not far enough, to find Marty Manger and the men who jumped off the flight deck after him. Finally, he turned the raft around and began to row in the opposite direction. He again used the smoke from the *Bunker Hill*, now directly in his vision as he rowed backward, like a man retiring in front of royalty. He headed back to the dye marker in hopes that the task group would locate him.

The small life raft contained an emergency bag with K rations and equipment. When Turnbull reached the dye marker, he spilled out the contents of the bag into the center of the raft and tied the empty bag to the painter on the bow of the life raft, then tossed it overboard to fill and act as a sea anchor, keeping him buoyed more or less in that spot.

Turnbull lay in the raft. He had a little food, a Bakelite sextant, and several fishing lures, with a fishing instruction booklet. The sun, glinting through broken clouds, warmed him and the sea anchor held him amid the dye mark. He felt safe inside the raft. But he could not stop wondering about the other men and what had happened to them. The sea made gentle sounds as the raft settled back and forth in the soft swell. The familiar buzz of an aircraft engine broke the quiet. Turnbull looked up to see an F6F Hellcat diving on him. The pilot wiggled his wings and Turnbull waved back, knowing the pilot had plotted the raft's position on the metallic navigation board strapped across his right knee. Soon Turnbull's location, expressed in longitude and latitude, would be radioed to a destroyer that would pick him up, and allow him to rejoin the men of his squadron.

After waiting another twenty-five minutes in his little raft, Turnbull heard a deafening engine boom and looked up to see the 600-foot Cleveland Class cruiser *Wilkes-Barre*, the third-largest class of American warship, headed at flank speed straight toward him.

Cruisers and destroyers acted both as antiaircraft picket ships and plane guards for the carriers. They picked up downed pilots and returned them to the carrier. Each plane guard ship carried a rescuer who specialized in pulling pilots from the sea. These human plane guards wore a rubber belt mounted with a steel swivel eye on the back. The plane guard looped a long manila throw line to the swivel. When the destroyer got as close as it could to the downed pilot, he would dive in and swim to the man in the water with the throw line trailing out behind him. The rescue swimmer grabbed hold of the pilot, and crewmen on the ship pulled them both back to safety with the throw rope. It was almost like Japanese cormorant fishing.

The plane guard, wearing his rescue belt, stood on the bow of the onrushing cruiser, ready to dive in and pull Turnbull to safety. But an officer with a megaphone stood up behind the rescuer and shouted out: "We'll be back for you!" The cruiser would not stop for a single man in the water while the *Bunker Hill* burned out of control. It passed about forty feet to the side of his little raft.

Turnbull rose up on his knees and waved, trying to indicate he was physically okay. Then he slumped back in the raft and settled down to await rescue as the *Wilkes-Barre* motored out of sight. Within minutes, he had drifted off to sleep. Around 2:00 P.M. he awakened sharply, vomiting blood, probably from stomach injuries sustained in his leap off the flight deck. He continued to vomit, until he dry-heaved for a long while, and then began to feel better.

Three o'clock passed, then four. Turnbull began thinking that he might have to wait out in the sea for a nighttime rescue. Again, he took stock of his situation. He located his Very pistol and slipped one of the three cartridges into it. The Very was a single-shot, breach-loading handgun that fired a 10-gauge flare a couple of hundred feet into the sky. The red flare burned for about five seconds. A Bakelite grip held the rustproof aluminum barrel. A thin lanyard tied to a key ring on the bottom prevented unsteady hands from dropping the gun into the sea. American pilots throughout the Pacific relied on the Very pistol for nighttime rescues. It looked very much like the plastic signal pistols required by the U.S. Coast Guard today on many vessels.

Having spent so much time swimming between piers in Southern California, Turnbull felt comfortable even alone in the raft. He knew what to expect, from the ocean and from his own mind. He allowed the thoughts that led to panic to pass through and concentrated on what he could do to help rescuers find him. While the ocean appeared glass calm, Turnbull realized that he was still riding on the energy of big Pacific rolling waves. And just as in Los Angeles, they were rolling in sets. There would be a small wave and then something a little bigger. Finally, several large waves would pass in succession. At the top of each of these big waves, Turnbull could see far in every direction. But when his raft sank in the troughs between them, he could not see more than a few feet. Turnbull waited for the top of the waves to scan the horizon, straining on his knees, then rested in the troughs. Dusk began to fall, and with it Turnbull's hopes of a rescue. He knew that his chances of a nighttime rescue were slim and that few are rescued beyond the first twenty-four hours of going missing. And then he saw a mast. He was at the top of a crest in a large set. And he could barely make it out in the falling light.

Turnbull waited eagerly for the next set to come by, then searched from the wave tops along every stretch of the horizon where he had seen the boat. But he saw only the graying ocean. He began to wonder whether he might be hallucinating. He had been alone in the sea for half a day, asleep, exhausted, and heaving blood. He knew he wished for a boat. But now he could not see one, and he could not be sure he ever had. It was hard to recall precisely his memory of the mast. yet he could not shake it.

He waited anxiously, second-guessing until the next set of waves. He saw nothing until he reached the peak of the highest wave and then, for a moment, he thought he saw the mast again. The sky was darkening, though, amid a lowering haze. He could not be sure. Perhaps he was dreaming it. He measured time and the onrushing darkness by wave sets. The light fell, and it become increasingly difficult to see any distance with each succeeding set of waves. If a rescue boat cruised nearby, he wanted to fire his flare. But if he were only dreaming, it would be terrible to waste a flare on a hallucination. He had to be sure. But if he waited, the ship might turn away from him and not reappear.

On the next set, Turnbull saw the mast again. But it disappeared, and he could not be sure. The mast was almost impossible to make out in the lowering light. He decided to wait. The next set would tell him. But he saw no mast on that next set. And again nothing after that. All the pilots had great vision, at least 20/10. Turnbull scanned as hard as he could. As the last light of the day slipped beyond the horizon, Turnbull's raft crested another swell and he saw the mast clearly. He fired the Very pistol. Never before had he seen such a beautiful firework display as that single red flare blazing a red trail into the evening sky, straight at the mast of his hoped-for rescuers.

The mast turned to head toward him. Soon he could make out the cross bar at its peak and then the USS *Cushing* came fully into view. The destroyer had been dispatched to zigzag across the *Bunker Hill*'s path to try to find survivors. Whenever the *Cushing* zagged, she had disappeared from Turnbull's vision. Then when she zigged back, he could see her from the crest of the waves.

As the *Cushing* pulled close to Turnbull, he could hear the commands from her captain to "Stop engines" and then "Reverse engines." They turned the ship around and got to within about thirty feet of Turnbull's raft. Crewmembers came to the side of the destroyer with machine guns and fired into the water all around his dinghy, beating a path between him and the ship. Turnbull didn't understand until he looked directly into the water, and not at the horizon. Sharks surrounded his little raft. They had trailed the task force for weeks, feeding on the food and garbage discarded by the ships and the occasional enemy dead from the Japanese naval craft that challenged Task Force 58. When the firing stopped, Turnbull heard the captain's voice order "Stand by to come aboard."

The crew threw out a line to Turnbull. He wrapped it around the CO_2 inflation bottle. The plane guard pulled Turnbull's raft around to the starboard side and climbed down the Jacob's ladder to the last rung. The rescuer leaned out with one hand on a rung and slung his other arm under Turnbull's shoulder. Then the huge plane guard lifted Turnbull up out of the raft with that one arm.

Turnbull screamed in pain. He shouted so loudly the men told him later they could hear him in the engine room. When he had jumped from the *Bunker Hill*, he splashed though the ocean surface a little sideways. He kept his arms crossed over his chest, but they slapped the water so hard that his elbow snapped half the ribs on his left side. The broken ribs tore into his insides and caused the internal bleeding that made him vomit in the raft. During the hours he had been in the water, Turnbull had been acting on pure adrenaline. He never felt the pain until the plane guard lifted him up. He still cannot believe he had rowed the life raft with cracked ribs. The huge plane guard, undeterred by Turnbull's screaming, carried Turnbull up the ladder like a child, under one arm.

Crewmen helped Turnbull down to sickbay. Medics taped his sides and gave him a glass of hot tea. Turnbull, still wearing the wet khaki pants he had changed into just after his flight, appeared to be an enlisted man, perhaps a Marine. No one had yet asked him his rank or duties. They kept him on a gurney through a bad night of wild dreams. His head, side, and back ached terribly, but Turnbull was safe and alive.

The war continued, essentially uninterrupted. The *Bunker Hill* and all her crew had become expendable.

32. RECOVERY

We will not regret the past, nor wish to shut the door on it.
—WILLIAM WILSON, 1939

Night fell. The hellish day aboard the *Bunker Hill* was coming to an end. Most of the crewmen still alive would survive, and everyone now knew the ship would not sink. By and large, the flight deck fire and most of the hangar and gallery deck fires were extinguished, though some of the isolated fires in more combustible areas burned stubbornly though the night. These fires were controlled in the sense that everyone was pretty sure they would not spread (everything around them already was burned). But they could not be extinguished. The *Bunker Hill* was saved. The hard work of recovery—of the ship and her dead—was just beginning.

It became clear immediately after Kiyoshi's strike that the *Bunker Hill* could no longer function as flagship. Admiral Mitscher had to be transferred at the earliest possible time. But early on, the fires burned so out of control that crews could not get to him. Instead, Mitscher ceded authority over the task group to Admiral Ted Sherman, then waited out the fires. Around 4:00 P.M. Arleigh Burke ordered Commander Gus Reade to gather the admiral's staff. Nearly six hours had passed since Kiyoshi's bomb exploded, but the stairways in the island structure were still glowing hot and impassable. Reade had to climb outside the island and work his way below down the gun directing system. Reade had been a pilot during World War I. He became a successful banker, but volunteered for World War II to serve with Mitscher. He was the first flag officer to see the forward section of the hangar deck, which had become the ship's temporary morgue and hospital. Bodies lay side by side, mostly in neat rows. Dead men charred beyond recognition lay beside sailors who breathed, lying almost equally charred but still alive, crying in pain. Chaplains knelt, leaning into the dying men, whispering last rites and granting absolution. Reade climbed back to flag plot and told Burke that half of the flag officers had been killed. Many others were badly wounded.

The destroyer *English* came along the starboard side of the *Bunker Hill* at about 4:30 P.M. Still, Mitscher could not get to the flight deck. Officers and crewmen rigged a Jacob's ladder to the side of the island, and Mitscher climbed over the edge, and into a breaches buoy, which swung him from the still burning carrier to the destroyer, which transferred him to the *Enterprise*. A photograph taken of Mitscher in the flimsy transfer swing shows him smiling, though gaunt and forced. Kiyoshi's bomb destroyed Mitscher's office and sea cabin, along with all his personal papers and clothing. Mitscher had given his sea cabin over to his doctor, who was killed in the explosion. The aging USS *Enterprise*, built in 1936, became the new flagship. After Mitscher transferred, the task group turned back to the war. Commander Seitz remained aboard, in command of the *Bunker Hill*, and would guide her home for repairs. The *Bunker Hill* was left with a small contingent of destroyers to protect her retreat.

Periodically, during the struggles to douse or escape the flames, crewmen crossed the flight deck past the island structure. Most were shocked to see Kiyoshi's body just lying there beside the wreckage he had caused. Many of the sailors had been fighting since Pearl Harbor, but this was the first time they had seen the enemy, dead. Many times they had watched the Japanese pilots flying toward the ship trying to kill them. They often spoke, casually, of killing the "Japs." But on May 11, they were confronted with the terrible reality of losing so many of their friends, and of nearly being killed themselves by someone they had tried very hard to kill. People from Gunma prefecture in Japan are known for having almost Western faces, with a nose that appears Caucasian. American propaganda pictured the Japanese as being fundamentally different from Americans. Every sailor who crossed in front of the island recalls the moment they saw Kiyoshi's young face, so pale and unblemished. The sight of his body forced them to confront the war emotionally, in an entirely new light.

When Gelderman first saw Kiyoshi's broken body lying by the cockpit, half a dozen of the ship's company stood around it. One walked through the wreckage intently scrutinizing everything. Then, fixing on Kiyoshi's body, the sailor lifted up Kiyoshi's hand, shaking it and pulling at a ring on Kiyoshi's fingers. The flesh on the hand loosened, then sloughed off, and the ring finally slid free. Gelderman could not believe it. The thief shook the ring, casting off bits of Kiyoshi's flesh that still clung to it, then wiped it on his pants, and slid it over his own finger. Kiyoshi's hand, cast aside, lay amid the wreckage. It had been torn from his bones, yet somehow maintained its shape, like a delicate glove, crushed. Gelderman was still dazed from all the smoke, and the idea of going after souvenirs was far from his mind. He was sickened by the crassness of that moment.

Art Volkema had wandered down the flight deck late in the afternoon, around the time that Mitscher evacuated the ship. He, too, saw Kiyoshi lying on the deck, a white scarf still wrapped around his neck, as men picked up pieces of his plane as souvenirs. Volkema watched crewmen rifle though Kiyoshi's body, taking out what appeared to be his wallet and other personal items. He returned later in the day and saw that Kiyoshi's scarf had been taken.

Roma Dussault says that a group of sailors put a grappling hook into Kiyoshi Ogawa's body and tore him out of the wreckage of his plane, then dragged him around the flight deck like Achilles with Hector. But other accounts do not mention this.

The ship's deck log and battle diary contain no record of Kiyoshi receiving military honors as is required by international treaty. It is unclear what was done with his body.

Edmund Skacan was dazed both by the hellishness of the interior, where he had been working to find bodies, and by his struggle to survive the initial explosions. Now, as he made it to the ship's top deck, he was filled with confusion. He had no idea what to do. And then he heard the poised authority of an officer on the public address system order with assured clarity: "Sweepers, man your brooms. Clean sweep down fore and aft."

Amid all the fear and confusion that had been Skacan's world for the last several hours, he experienced at that moment a sensation of profound trust. Skacan thought back to the afternoon of his father's funeral. He was a little boy, confused and lonely, small and scared, watching his mother as she scrubbed the floors. There had been a flurry of activity that afternoon and an air in the house that somehow everything had changed. But when everyone had gone, his mother removed the special outfit she had worn to honor her husband, and put on a house dress and began to clean. She knew what to do.

Now standing on the charred deck of the *Bunker Hill,* Skacan decided that he might as well sweep. For the first time in almost twenty years, he finally understood why his mother had changed clothes and spent the evening of his father's burial cleaning the house. It was time to move on with the work of living.

Around 9:00 or 10:00 P.M., the boilermen belowdecks finally received word via intercom that the fires were under sufficient control for them to be relieved. They had been in the boiler rooms for ten hours straight—much of it spent locked in, under rising water, knowing that failure meant death.

Eighteen men had gone in to the number two boiler room when General Quarters had summoned them to their battle stations. Only seven survived to climb their way toward the upper decks. Getting out was terrifying. As they opened a dogged hatch, water came churning in, carrying a body that knocked the men to the floor. The engineers resealed that hatch and clambered to an alternative exit. But three feet of water flooded the deck above, and they had to wait three more hours while temporary pumps dumped the extra water overboard. The filthy water sloshed around the lip of the coaming. Repairmen who would have pumped it out had been trapped by flames at their battle assembly station on the third deck. All of the men in Repair 3 died. Their bloated bodies bobbed in the filthy water gathered around the hatch. Rigor mortis had begun to set in.

Some of the men looked like they were waving and smiling as their bodies floated by.

Carmichael went immediately to the number one boiler room to check on Berenstuhl. The hallway outside his engine room was jammed with bodies. Soot lay everywhere. Emergency lights glowed eerily through the smoke but helped Carmichael find his way. Bodies lined the lengths of passageway after passageway. These were, many of them, men Carmichael had worked with for years, but he did not at first recognize their burned and charred bodies. He had to identify them, though, and he knew this was best done before their trip topside for burial. He leaned down among the dead and picked up a young body by the shoulders. He stood the bloated, blackened sailor against a bulkhead, just below a glowing red emergency light. Holding the body up by its limp shoulders, trying to recognize the lifeless face in the weak reddish light, Carmichael still could not make out which of the young men who worked for him he was holding. Then Carmichael dug his left forearm in hard against the dead man's chest, bracing the sagging body firm against the bulkhead, just below the diffuse glow of the emergency bulb. This freed up Carmichael's right hand. He used his right fingers and thumb, like a parent cleaning a wayward child before dinner, and he rubbed and brushed the oily soot from the sailor's dead cheeks, below his eyes and across his nose, staring intently, trying to remember, to recognize.

Most of the engine men had never left home before the war. Many of those who survived never left again. Some of the dead sailors had already given three years of their life to the *Bunker Hill*. Carmichael wanted to know who each of them was. He shook the dead man a bit to move his head so the light reflected off the young sailor's cleaned cheeks. He finally recognized him. He laid him down gently and picked up the next sailor beneath the light and began again. He spoke to them as they became known to him. "Yeah, I know you," he would say, and then reach for another.

Carmichael moved on, determined to get inside the first fire room. When he finally got through the hatch he knew, even in the subdued light, that everyone was dead. It was hard to distinguish the bodies from the machinery. Thick black soot and filthy bilge water had sprayed everywhere. A heavy, deadly grime covered the room. Carmichael made his way over to the main control panel, where the gauges hung, impossibly dirtied. Berenstuhl lay below them, dead. No one in the room survived.

But the boiler was still running. Berenstuhl had set the gauges perfectly before he died. The boiler had functioned without human intervention for more than an hour. The last engineer had died at his post, making steam to keep the engines running, taking the *Bunker Hill* out of range of the Japanese bases on Kyushu, and giving power to light the interior of the ship so that the injured could be treated or rescued and the huge pumps could drive saltwater into the flames.

Surviving crewmen worked intently under gruesome conditions to recover and identify their friends' bodies. They understood that their dead comrades would be cast into the sea the following day. The *Bunker Hill* was still in the war zone. They could not stop to bury the dead. Rather, the sailors would be pitched over the side as the ship hobbled away from Japan. Few in the crew grew up in anything like a seafaring tradition, and it bothered them to their core that their friends would be dumped overboard with no marker, no grave for their families to visit. Every crewmen fought to see that their friends were identified before their bodies were pitched into the sea.

It was, too, a cleansing act for the survivors, an act of contrition for having survived.

Hundreds of dead men lay scattered alone and in small groups throughout the ship. Volunteers combed the hull searching for their dead comrades in the darkened passages. By the next evening, about fifty would remain missing. Forty-three were never found. Some would not be located until the ship had made her way back to Ulithi. Beginning late the first afternoon, and continuing until burial began the following day, as the *Bunker Hill* trudged away from battle, crewmen trudged their way into the waterlogged muck of locked and darkened compartments to find the soggy, burned bodies of their friends. Recovery of the dead began on the flight deck; the survivors worked their way through the ship, carrying out their comrades.

They could have avoided the awful task. Crewmen aboard the *Franklin* (which had been struck on March 19 by conventional bombs) had locked down the inside of their ship and left their comrades to rot until they reached Pearl Harbor. Medics and crews from other ships were left the recovery work. Not so on the *Bunker Hill*. Her crews carried their comrades out as a sort of grim honor guard for the fallen. They never considered leaving their friends to others. And like the poet in "Sam McGee," they came to loathe not merely their work but their loads as well. Duty-bound, though, they stayed with their friends till the very end.

Gunner Robert Earl Harris had waited out the fires on the crowded fantail, amid the sailors and pilots who also had sought safety there. By evening many of these men still on the fantail lay dead.* The 40mm guns on the port side received the brunt of Yasunori's bomb blast. Most of the men on these guns appeared to have been killed instantly. When Harris arrived to empty out their ammunition, he found their bodies still strapped into their guns. Harris and some of the other gunners unhooked those men and tied their charred bodies onto stretchers, then carried them to the forward end of the flight deck after the fires had burned out.

George Lyons and Marty Woll had survived on the fantail until the fires were brought under control. Then they made their way forward. The after part of the ship appeared to have been completely destroyed. The planes they had been taxiing had all burned. Melded engine hulks and hardened puddles of aluminum marked where the two Avenger pilots had run from their aircraft. An aluminum shoe print showed where a sailor must have accidentally stepped in the molten metal. Crossing the island was like boarding an entirely different ship. There, compartmentalization had worked. The flight deck forward of the island remained entirely undamaged.

Everything aft of the forward fire curtain in the hangar deck, about midway to the ship's bows, had first burned, then the heat intensified. Edmund Skacan peered into a compartment where spare propellers

---

* Most of these men, though they were able to find some safety on the fantail, probably died from CO poisoning and inhalation of particulates.

had been stored. "Everything just melted like a candle," he said. Aircraft had turned to ash.

Deeper inside the ship, recovery became problematic.

Beads Popp led a group of forty-five seamen into the hull to locate bodies and drag them up to the hangar deck for burial preparations.

Compartments in the center of the ship had gone to a condition of full watertight security the moment Yasunori's bomb exploded. The

A burned torso and leg hang over the coamings into a hatchway flooded with firefighting water. The ladder in the background was twisted from heat or blast. A discarded helmet floats among the detritus in the corner of the photo. The hatchways to the ready rooms opened around a coaming, or toe rail, which allowed water from the fire hoses to build up to about six inches deep in each of the compartments, more in some, a little less in others. The pilots' dye packets activated amid the putrid fire-pumping water, then mixed with their cooked flesh, clothing, furniture, equipment, and grime—all of it dyed a sickening, thick, slimy, greenish color that left search parties stained and with a spooky feeling in the wreckage of those rooms.

steel doors and hatchways had been closed ever since, so Popp and his men were the first inside. Popp saw men there who had died in agony, trying to crawl through steel. They died of terrifying asphyxiation, their hands and fingers a bloody mess. They had struggled to the very end to save themselves and their comrades. Popp and his crew put them into bags and tied them up, then dragged them into a bomb elevator that was still working and sent them up to the hangar deck.

As recovery crews moved deeper into the ship, light disappeared entirely. Everyone still within that dark middle of the ship, it seemed, had died. Firefighting water, carrying the grime of three years at war, filled each compartment to the hatch opening. Crewmen slogged through absolute blackness, in sticky water up to their knees at times, their palms held out open in front feeling their way along, dreading what they would touch. They could not see the bodies. Sometimes they would bump them, but could not be sure, until they had touched, running their bare hands and fingers in the darkness along the wet cadavers. No one gave them the nicety of rubber gloves.

The bearers held the dead face-up by their arms and legs, pulling and pushing them along, working the sticky blackened bodies through sooty muck. The corpses had stiffened, and recovery teams had trouble bending the dead over the coamings, below doorways, and through the smaller hatches. Seamen hauling the cadavers slipped repeatedly into the muck while struggling the dampened dead up the steep stairways. Sometimes crewmen wrapped the dead in soggy blankets to avoid looking into their faces as they bent the bodies along.

The dead men made terrible sounds when the men contorted them to slip through hatches and hauled them up steep ladders. The corpses dripped on them as they hefted the dead up ladders. Sometimes the cadavers came apart as survivors forced the stiffening loads through narrow passages. They pushed and pulled the bodies up, deck after deck, until finally reaching the broken light of the hangar deck. There they lay the men in a long line of other dead. The officers were kept separate, in their own lines.

When Popp finished the job that day, only five men of the original forty-five were still with him. He has never had a nightmare about it, nor even lost sleep, but to this day, when his mind meanders back to that time in the darkened interior, carrying out the mutilated bodies of his comrades, he wonders whether it really happened. They laid the bodies out in grim processions hundreds of men long, each with a tag on their toe waiting for a friend to confirm whom they had been. Some never were identified. A rabbi, a Protestant minister, and a Catholic priest stood by performing Last Rites, one at a time, over each dead man.

Late Friday night, Marty Woll and some of the other pilots gathered in Chandler Swanson's room and shared a bottle of booze. Fortified, they climbed into the darkened hangar deck morgue to identify their friends' bodies. They did not have to do it; the morgue had been darkened for the night. But the dead pilots would be slid overboard the next day and Woll and the other survivors felt they owed it to their mates to give them that one last look. They walked in the dark along the line of pilots who had been laid out side by side along the hangar deck. Most had asphyxiated. Their faces were black with soot but, for the most part, not badly burned. Woll could not get out of

Wounded and dead were quartered side by side in the hangar deck. Four wounded men huddle in a corner smoking cigarettes, surrounded by dead men on stretchers. Just outside, men in the light begin to clean the ship.

his head the question of why they had died and he had survived. He knows that everyone who goes through a survival experience comes out with those same guilt feelings. But they are powerful nonetheless, and difficult to live with. The pilots faced death every day in combat, but rarely were confronted with the gripping reality of dead men's remains. Final identification of the dead was probably the hardest task of Woll's life.

Crewmen and medics identified most of the dead through their dog tags. But many, particularly the younger sailors, did not always wear their tags. Some could be identified by the nametags on their clothes, especially their leather belts, which resisted the fires that burned human skin.

A few men were identified idiosyncratically. Jerry Hanson had a friend who wore a special belt buckle with three bullets welded to it. It was the only buckle like that he had ever seen. When Jerry found a

J. Waite "Slabo" Bacon, torpedo squadron intelligence officer, briefs pilots and crew in their ready room before a strike: note the asbestos-covered ventilation shaft and steel stanchion with cutouts in top center.

The ready room post-fires: note the same steel stanchion and ventilation shaft. This room was filled with pilots when Kiyoshi's bomb exploded nearby.

The pilots' ready room after Kiyoshi Ogawa's attack.

body, charred beyond recognition wearing that familiar belt, he knew he had found his friend Purdon.

Carmichael was not satisfied with identifying men through their clothing. He knew the young men were always trading clothes. It seems that no one else aboard was satisfied either, unless it was the last available option. Crewmen lined up unidentified bodies on the port side forward on the flight deck. The ship's company walked the line of dead. They wrote the names of their friends on a small paper tag tied to the dead men's barefoot toe.

Robert Earl Harris spent much of the next day or so at his gun on the fantail. Medical corpsmen worked to identify the most badly burned and mangled bodies on the fantail beside Harris's gun. The faces of the naked bodies had burned beyond all recognition. Many had lost limbs. Sometimes they carried in a head attached to a torso and nothing else. Fresh, clearing air blew along the open fantail and the medics could work there without too many men scrutinizing their

Injured crewmen, one without shoes, look down at fallen comrades lining the foredeck.

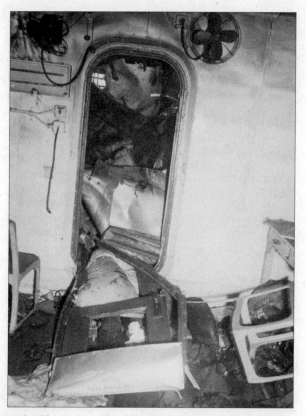

Sailor blown through a metal doorway on the gallery deck.

gruesome task. Harris remained at his gun, isolated with his crew, watching. The corpsmen wrenched off the lower jaws of each dead man with a sort of bloodied steel tong. The jaws held stubbornly to each cadaver and had to be twisted and pulled before they tore free. Medics then used rags to clear the blood and burned flesh and filth from the dead men's teeth. Only then, the medics began the slow, grim process of visually comparing the fillings to records from the ship's dentist. Afterward, they squashed the jaws back on as best they could. And then these dead were returned to the long grim line.

Carmichael returned to the engineering rooms. Their regular lights were down, but there were some emergency lights burning. A thick layer of soot blanketed each compartment. The survivors lay about amongst the dead, equally blackened. Most had been below for

Wreckage inside the ship.

eleven hours. Soot had blown continuously in their faces and hair and on all the exposed parts of their bodies. Their comrades had died beside them. Survivors no longer looked like real people to Carmichael. They appeared as unearthly entities.

Carmichael set about to restore engineering. The rooms all needed to be cleaned. But first survivors had to remove the dead. Carmichael began carrying them out like the big drill machine he used to huff. Everyone pitched in.

"I have often thought about those bodies I had to step on to make my way up to the bridge. . . . It reminds me of when I watch the news and they show a tenement fire, and the reporter walks up to a woman and they have just told her that five of her children were up there and they have all burned to death, and the reporter says, 'How

The deck edge elevator warped, not from the force of Yasunori's bomb, but from the heat of the gasoline fires from aircraft above and below it. Men have hung clothing out to dry as the Bunker Hill *makes her way home. The temporary patch on the hole made by Seizo's armor-piercing bomb can be seen at top right corner.*

Destruction in the hangar deck. Light shines through the elevator (center left). Melted aluminum has spread about the floor. The warped number three (aft) elevator is bent at right.

Sailors pull a melted wing from the detritus of the fires in the hangar deck to pitch it overboard.

do you feel, madam?' Well, it is about the same thing, there isn't any way you can say. . . .

"These trials that our generation went through, sometimes I think they make too much of it, we were just living and doing the things that you had to do in those times, that's all."

Carmichael helped take out a couple of bodies from the Marine compartment where the regular Leathernecks slept, not the pilots. The fire had been bad inside their compartment and the marines were particularly crowded in; the ship was not designed to carry a large Marine contingent. Carmichael found one man who had crawled behind and underneath a bunk and then curled up into a fetal position. The guy just died. "He decided to die. Sometimes guys just do that." The chief engineer figured that the unfortunate marine got panicky, stopped struggling, and gave up. Carmichael likened these deaths to drowning men. He said that some men trying to swim will go down and give up and they die. He continued, "Now the guy that survives is the guy who struggles constantly, and the umpteenth time he comes up somebody grabs his hand and he is saved. The instinct that he has to survive is stronger than in other people."

All of Carmichael's men in the number one boiler room were killed and half of the men in the number two boiler room died.

No ship in the world was more powerful than the *Bunker Hill.* Yet the carrier and her crew of 3,400 were nearly destroyed by two fragile Japanese aircraft—dated fighters armed with bombs they could barely lift. Three days after the surrender of Nazi Germany, Yasunori Seizo and Kiyoshi Ogawa made the most devastating kamikaze attack of the war. They killed 393 men aboard the *Bunker Hill* and injured more than 250 others.

The *Bunker Hill* did not sink, but she was knocked permanently out of the war.

PART III

AFTERWARD

The Navy Hymn

Eternal Father, strong to save,
Whose arm hath bound the restless wave,
Who bidd'st the mighty ocean deep
Its own appointed limits keep:
O hear us when we cry to thee,
For those in peril on the sea.

O Christ, whose voice the waters heard
And hushed their raging at thy word,
Who walkedst on the foaming deep,
And calm amid its rage didst sleep:
O hear us when we cry to thee
For those in peril on the sea.

Most Holy Spirit, who didst brood
Upon the chaos dark and rude,
And bid its angry tumult cease,
And give, for wild confusion, peace:
O hear us when we cry to thee
For those in peril on the sea.

O Trinity of love and power,
Thy children shield in danger's hour;
From rock and tempest, fire and foe,
Protect them wheresoe'er go;
Thus evermore shall rise to thee,
Glad hymns of praise from land and sea.
—WILLIAM WHITING

33. DAMAGE

Americans often look for extraordinary explanations when faced with tragedy. Naval officials recoiled from accepting that a couple of poorly trained kamikazes could sink the most powerful ship in the world. Many refused to believe that Kiyoshi had simply slipped through the elaborate defenses of two large task groups and randomly wrecked the flagship.

Since Midway, America had dominated Japan in the Pacific. The United States won every battle after the Essex carriers arrived on station. They had sunk the Imperial Japanese Navy almost with impunity and established an elaborate defensive system to protect the Navy. American scout planes kept Japanese bases under frequent surveillance. Radar picket ships and ground-based radars on Okinawa allowed for early warnings of Japanese missions. The carriers were surrounded by concentric defensive circles—oncoming kamikazes that made it past the combat air patrol and ground-based aircraft on Okinawa, then had to contend with the guns from hundreds of destroyers, cruisers, and battleships before arriving at the carriers protected in the center of the fleet. America cracked the Japanese code, and had advance warning of the *Kikusui* large-scale attacks. It did not seem possible that all of these elaborate, technologically advanced, quantitatively superior, and expensive defensive systems could be overcome by suicide tactics. Intelligence officers manufactured wild theories to explain the tragedy. But the fact is that Japan's will to sacrifice its nearest and dearest became Japan's greatest weapon.

Crewmen clearing wreckage from the *Bunker Hill* on May 12 found an IFF—Identification Friend or Foe—antenna near Kiyoshi's crash site. The antenna probably tore off the fuselage of an exploding Corsair and came to rest amidships near Kiyoshi's wreckage.

Desperate to explain the tragedy and their newfound vulnerability, American personnel theorized that the Japanese had cracked the ever-changing American IFF signals and been able to either fabricate or recover and repair an American IFF radio antenna, and then use that antenna and code to sneak to the heart of the task group. This is a staggeringly unlikely scenario. The Japanese could barely feed their pilots at Kanoya. They had almost no fuel for their aircraft. On many days, the Japanese did not even *have* aircraft. Japanese air forces were in no position to conduct the massive effort needed to crack the American IFF codes, nor to manufacture a new, parallel IFF broadcast system. If the Japanese had made such an elaborate intelligence breakthrough, they would not have entrusted it to a lone kamikaze with as little experience as Kiyoshi Ogawa. The reality of Kiyoshi's attack is much more banal. Yasunori and Kiyoshi probably did what all the other kamikazes did. They merely lucked into finding a target and getting past the massive American defensive force. They succeeded not so much because they were better, but because the sheer number of kamikazes made it inevitable that some would make it through. Japan's embrace of suicide, and the young pilots' complicity in that determination, was the great leveler of World War II. Kiyoshi probably followed home a returning American flight, and then hid in the clouds or slid in toward the *Bunker Hill* along a radar void.

The United States suffered a significant tactical defeat in the battle for the USS *Bunker Hill*. Two inexpensive Japanese planes carrying a single bomb each were able to kill or injure more than 700 American naval men, including most of an air group that took many years and millions of dollars to train. Yasunori and Kiyoshi destroyed nearly 100 aircraft and caused the loss of thousands of gallons of fuel and tons of armaments. They crippled and permanently took out of combat one of the most sophisticated, expensive, well-protected, and difficult-to-replace ships ever built.

Primary responsibility for the success of the *Bunker Hill* attack lies with the Japanese. Yasunori and Kiyoshi drove their attacks home with reckless but well-directed abandon. Yet military losses rarely can be tied to any single cause. The fires aboard the *Bunker Hill* would probably not have penetrated below the hangar deck had the large starboard hatch been properly closed, and the ship should not have remained so long in the combat zone on a kamikaze day with fueled aircraft on deck. In that sense, the *Bunker Hill* was caught unprepared.

One could argue that it was the fault of the lookouts and gunners aboard the destroyers riding picket on the perimeter of the battle group for missing Yasunori and Kiyoshi entirely. Or the fault of the CAP for not seeing the two kamikazes earlier. Or, perhaps, the radarmen and IFF operators on all ships for not identifying Yasunori and Kiyoshi, and for failing to vector the CAP out to engage them long before they penerated critical airspace. Whichever squadron allowed the kamikazes to sneak in behind them to the heart of the fleet could have prevented the disaster. So, too, responsible are the spotters and crewmen who did not clear the decks and get a fresh CAP in the air in time to intercept. The task group commander may be at fault for putting the ship on Condition One-Easy, instead of General Quarters.

Regardless of how the kamikazes were able to penetrate the fleet that morning, the ship's officers and men performed magnificently after the first explosions. Doctors and medics took over the galleys as temporary aid stations and morgues. They strung emergency lighting and performed surgical work on food preparation counters and lay the dead out on messing tables. The gunners recovered immediately and shot down the remaining kamikazes. Sailors moved the ship's hospital to an emergency station on the flight deck, manned the hoses, and rescued trapped and injured men. They fought fires and made their ship safe from further explosions. They formed replacement gun crews to defend themselves from further attacks. They began repairs even as fires raged. They kept the boilers steaming and the ship running, and moved the *Bunker Hill* out of harm's way.

Carmichael's engineers made up one quarter of the *Bunker Hill*'s dead. Ninety-nine men out of the just over 500 in Carmichael's department were killed. Thirty-seven additional engineers were wounded.

Despite their extraordinary losses, the engineers trusted Carmichael. He kept them engrossed in doing their work, too busy trying to read gauges and keep the pressures correct, even in those almost impossible conditions, to think about the reality of their situation.

Seamen aboard the *Bunker Hill* and on vessels surrounding the ship thought she would not survive. She had sustained astounding damage, was useless as a carrier, and at first served merely as a target and later as a simple, wounded transport vessel bringing the men home. Yet, ship's officers kept the men focused on their work—each at their task and station. Together, they kept the ship afloat.

The *Bunker Hill* would limp back to Ulithi under her own steam. She would go on to Pearl Harbor and finally to Puget Sound, where she would be the most damaged ship to return from battle to the Bremerton Navy Yard. The last shots she fired were those that brought down the final kamikaze.

Her big naval guns and rockets had helped keep the Japanese at bay, but the carrier's job was largely done. There were no Japanese ships left to sink. America owned two airbases on Okinawa from which land-based bombers carrying heavier loads could strike Japanese targets and provide close air support much more effectively than carrier-based aircraft. Less than ninety days after the attack on the *Bunker Hill*, the United States dropped the atomic bomb on Hiroshima.

Arleigh Burke later wrote that the most important lesson he learned from Admiral Mitcher was precisely the opposite of what he had studied his whole life in the Navy. In peacetime, the war college had always taught officers to determine the minimum-sized force required to complete any mission. Mitscher did the opposite. He determined the maximum-sized force that could possibly be spared to do a job. That way, the enemy would likely be defeated even if their resistance had been underestimated. "If you are going to hit an enemy," the fighting admiral said, "hit him with everything you have got."

The Navy learned significant lessons from carrier combat in World War II, lessons that guided military policy for fifty years following the conflict. The most specific significant lesson learned from the attack on the *Bunker Hill*, sadly, was one that already was known: the Essex-class ventilation system could be lethal.* Tragically, Japan's new suicide weapon was uniquely capable of exploiting this fatal flaw.

Nearly 3,500 men served aboard the *Bunker Hill* in May 1945. The ship's crew faced about the same level of crime as any small town in America about that size. During any disaster that destroys public order, there has always been to some extent a societal devolution into looting, even for those who have never before committed a crime. While so many of the greatest generation struggled and fought to save the lives of their fellows, a surprising number (though no one will ever know how many) became, for a time, thieves. Carmichael did not see any looting firsthand. But he saw disturbing evidence.

Carmichael roamed through most of the *Bunker Hill* after the fires making a rough damage assessment. The *Bunker Hill*'s post office was located below the hangar deck, aft of the island structure, in the heart of the most havily damaged portion of the ship. The post office functioned, too, as a sort of bank, where crewmen kept safe deposit

---

* The damage report recommended supplying air to the ship's interior from multiple sources and dramatically increasing the number of RBAs—Rescue Breathing Apparatus. It recommended, too, the elimination of the main vent trunk that supplied air to the engineering spaces: "This trunk almost forced the abandonment of all engineering spaces and has done so on other carriers." It suggested instead that individual supply ducts be led to each space. There were other technical recommendations—improving pumps and gas masks, giving more firefighting training, and redesigning the ship so that there were exits from the engineering compartment directly to different decks; all engineering compartment exits—main and emergency—emptied to the second deck, which was flooded with three feet of water and burning fuel. It provided no safety. The hangar deck coming had no scuppers. The Navy did not want light escaping from the scuppers and giving away the blacked-out carrier's position. But without scuppers, firefighting water and burning fuel piled up on the hangar deck. Flapper valves on scuppers would let the water flow out while keeping the light in. Water on the hangar deck endangered the *Bunker Hill*'s stability and maneuverability and made it much more difficult to fight fires. There were not enough extra sections of fire hoses on various decks. When men stretched multiple sections over a long distance, the middle of the hose often caught fire, making the whole operation useless.

boxes. Carmichael discovered a hole the size of a basketball, nearly perfectly circular, burned through the steel covers to the safe boxes. It appeared to him as though a 16-inch shell had been fired through the post office and had passed directly into the safety deposit boxes. He walked around the post office trying to find an entry or exit point for the shell. But he found no other hole.

Carmichael examined the hole more closely. The edges had been neatly burned and crumpled. It took him a moment to realize that he was looking at a break-in. A crewman aboard the *Bunker Hill* was reputed to have won more than $30,000 at poker since the ship left California. While the ship burned, an intrepid thief made his way to the post office deep inside the ship, through fires and smoke, past men in need of help. He carried an acetylene torch through the flames, and while others struggled to douse the fires, the crook burned through a single set of safety deposit boxes. He knew what he was looking for.

When Carmichael peered inside, the only box cut full-through sat empty. The chief engineer told me he would not have ordered anyone into that portion of the ship during the fires; it was too dangerous. He remains astounded at the bravery, audacity, and patience of the thief.

For twenty-four hours after the attack, sailors of any rank could walk around unescorted and unexplained anywhere on the ship. For many men it was the first time in three years that they were not held strictly accountable for their time or location. Much had been destroyed. Much else was pitched overboard. No official counts were made of items damaged or cast off. Naval order and discipline broke down, at least in terms of minor offenses. Theft after the disaster aboard the *Bunker Hill* was particularly disturbing precisely because it became, for a time, widespread. Wrongdoing went far beyond one or two miscreants taking the ring or wallet of the attacking enemy or stealing the watch from John Sargent's burned wrist. Men stole items from all around the ship. Even the small safes in the dead pilots' private quarters were pilfered for their personal possessions—cigarettes, cash, and stashes of whiskey.

Looting, even of souvenirs, was punishable by death, and the general disorder aboard the *Bunker Hill* in the hours after the ship was saved provoked a harsh response from the officers. Joe Brocia was issued a Colt .45. He stood guard over the line of dead men in the hangar deck, in charge of two Marine survivors. Crewmen had torn the rings and watches off their dead comrades. Every single enlisted man was ordered to the hangar deck. The pilots, officers, and surviving Marine crew armed themselves with handguns, then stood guard at every hatch. No sailors were allowed to pass until a complete search had been made of the enlisted men's private gear for stolen goods. Dewey Ray supervised a search of crew's quarters. They opened up every crewman's locker, searching for items pilfered from the bodies and lockers of the men killed in battle.

Those found with contraband were locked in the brig, stripped of their clothing, and sprayed hard with saltwater from a fire hose day after day. They subsisted on only bread and water until the ship arrived at Ulithi. Then they were taken off. No one knows what became of them. There is no record in the ship's log of these disciplinary actions.*

---

* Disciplinary actions aboard the ship are regularly recorded before May 11, 1945.

34. BURIAL AT SEA

On May 12, 1945, for burial at sea, crews wrapped the dead respectfully. Each knot was meticulously tied. Everyone understood that the bodies would be dropped twenty-five feet into the ocean, and that the wrapped cadavers would not slip gracefully into the sea. Most slapped violently as they hit, and men in the hangar deck winced as the crack reverberated into the air. Sometimes when crewmen threw trash overboard, eddies formed by the ship's wake carried the garbage along behind them. Bobbing in and out of the froth, disappearing and then popping up again, jetsam might dog the ship for hours. The dead, buried at sea, needed to stay down. So the burial crews stretched eighteen-foot strips of dark navy blue canvas across the dining tables like super-long tablecloths, six feet across the table and six feet hanging down from either end. They laid the bodies of their comrades on top and then placed two fifty-five-pound, 5-inch projectiles on top of each body, one cradled along the dead men's chests, the second between their legs. They then folded the extra six feet of canvas over their feet up to their heads. The remaining six feet or so from their heads folded down to their feet. Forty-foot lengths of rough cordage were then wrapped around the body, a half hitch tied every eighteen inches or so, securing each body within their weighted shroud.

Edward Christian was a ship's carpenter who was nearly killed in the carpentry shop when Kiyoshi's bomb exploded. He had begun the war carving wooden chocks for the airplanes as they headed into the Pacific. He went on to carve planks to repair the decks where planes had crashed and made dovetailed wooden boxes to send home the personal effects of men who had died in combat. When Yasunori's bomb blew holes below the waterline, they were stopped with wooden plugs that Christian had carved. His last job was to build the seesaw chutes that slid the dead overboard. The Navy had never buried so many men at once, and no one knew how long it would take. Ship's carpenters had constructed only three burial chutes originally. But it would have taken all that day and night to bury the dead three at a time. So crewmen hastily added three olive drab stretchers to spill the dead faster into the sea.

At three minutes after noon on Saturday, May 12, about 380 miles south-southwest of Naha Town, Captain Seitz ordered the flag brought to half-staff for the burial at sea of 352 officers, crew, airmen, and members of the admiral's staff from the USS *Bunker Hill*. The service lasted until sunset. To this day, it is the largest burial at sea of American personnel in the history of the U.S. Navy.

Honor guards draped an American flag over the bodies. A priest, a Protestant minister, and a rabbi performed a joint funeral service. When a sailor had been identified, his religious leader prayed over him. When they buried unidentified remains, all three spoke. Crewmen then slid the remains out from under the American flag, down into the sea, six at a time.

By mid-afternoon, the chaplains were all crying. By the end of the day, exhausted mentally, spiritually, and physically, they could barely

Six dead crewmen from the Bunker Hill *are buried from makeshift chutes on a small weather deck outside the ship's hangar deck. The first three wooden chutes were constructed by the ship's carpenters. But crewmen added three more ramps using canvas stretchers to try to get the job done more quickly. The bodies have been wrapped in cloth and weighted down. Finally, a hemp line has been tied to hold the bundle together as the men are plunged into the sea.*

mumble the requisite prayers before the assembly line was tipped, and the dead men slid into the sea.

Little by little, the Honor Guards worked their way through the stacked bodies of their shipmates. The burial became too much at times and sailors would drift away. Some wandered to the ship's stern and looked back, horrified at the wake. Despite their efforts, many of the tightly sewn canvas shrouds had filled with air. The bodies rose, bobbing to the surface, then swayed sickly back and forth in the whitewash behind the *Bunker Hill*, marking her path away from Kyushu. Some were caught in the ship's eddies and followed after her, washing in and out of the stern wave. Sharks followed the *Bunker Hill* for days.

The *Bunker Hill* limped out of the battle zone. The wounded ship headed first to Ulithi where she would unload munitions and ensure that she could safely return on her own to Hawaii. She had departed Ulithi two months earlier, the most powerful ship in the most powerful fleet ever assembled. She returned to the giant naval base, crippled, never again to participate in offensive operations.

35. GOOD-BYE TO ALL THAT

—TITLE OF ROBERT GRAVES'S
FIRST WORLD WAR MEMOIR

World War II went on without the *Bunker Hill*. The fighting on Okinawa became even more desperate, and the kamikaze attacks viciously continued. On May 14, twenty-six kamikazes sent by Admiral Ugaki penetrated close to the fleet. Nineteen were shot down by the CAP. Six more were downed by AA fire. One, piloted by Tomi Zai, made it through.

Zai's Zero remained under attack from the CAP and under the full antiaircraft barrage of the entire task group for thirty to sixty seconds— an eternity under that kind of fire. His plane was hit many times, but somehow he pressed his attack home. He struck the *Enterprise* at the forward elevator, blowing huge pieces 400 feet in the air and warping the deck. Fires raged in the hangar deck and destroyed every single plane aboard the carrier. The *Enterprise* never returned to war.

Arleigh Burke wrote that the attack on the *Enterprise* was a nerve-wracking experience. The Japanese kamikaze pilots had circled wide around the task group, avoiding the early warning destroyer picket group, then came in on the carriers from behind. They were only twenty-five miles out when they finally were picked up on radar. The big carrier was so close to enemy land bases that Mitscher could not take the time to evacuate the ship to transfer the flag. The *Enterprise* first had to withdraw from enemy waters. The fleet retreated with her. Japanese kamikazes, using some of the last aircraft on Kyushu, forced the withdrawal of the Americans. The retreat, of course, was temporary. Japan had nearly run out of aircraft, and had lost almost all ability to resist.

But Mitscher was shaken. He had been given command of the fast carriers because the Navy wanted an aggressive admiral who would take the fight to the Japanese. Yet, it was the Japanese kamikazes who had brought the fight to them. Japanese suiciders achieved what the Japanese navy never could.

When Mitscher transferred from the *Enterprise*, the fast carrier task force had no undamaged carriers left that were not already carrying an admiral. So Mitscher and his skeleton staff doubled up with Admiral Gerald Bogan on the *Randolph*. Only two months earlier, Burke and Mitscher had seen their first kamikaze attack when a Japanese Frances bomber crashed the *Randolph* in Admiral Ugaki's long-range Tan operation. During the sixty-two days after Tan, Admiral Ugaki launched ten *Kikusui* attacks of 860 IJN aircraft (supplemented with 605 army kamikazes). Approximately 500 additional kamikazes dove in spontaneous suicide attacks during that period. The suiciders sank seventeen ships and damaged 198. Many damaged ships, like the *Enterprise*, the *Intrepid*, and the *Bunker Hill*, were never to return to the war. Other Essex ships, like the *Hancock*, the *Ticonderoga*, and the *Randolph*, missed significant parts of the war due to damage sustained from the kamikazes.*

The *Bunker Hill* arrived in the safety of Ulithi on the evening of the 14th of May. Her dead had been buried, her wounded tended to. Not everyone, however, had been accounted for. Al Turnbull was still missing. Everyone figured he was dead.

---

* The U.S. Strategic Bombing Survey states that in the seventy-eight days between April 6 and June 22, 1945, twenty-six ships were sunk and 164 damaged in suicide attacks.

Three thousand nine hundred thirteen Japanese Kamikaze Special Attack Unit pilots died during Special Attack missions against U.S. and Allied forces. Two thousand five hundred twenty-five were navy fliers. Most were between eighteen and twenty years old. Some were seventeen. The others (1,388) were army pilots. Most of these were between eighteen and twenty-four. There are no accurate records of the number of Japanese pilots that died in spontaneous suicide attacks. It is estimated that approximately 500 Japanese pilots initiated spontaneous suicide attacks during Okinawa. The kamikazes damaged 288 ships, including thirty-six carriers (sixteen major carriers). They sank thirty-four.

36. DESTROYER RESCUE

Al Turnbull, however, was still alive, rescued at sea by the USS *Cushing* after being in the water for nearly eight hours. Turnbull's left side looked as though it had been painted the colors of a rotten, split grapefruit. A corpsman taped Turnbull up, and crewmen began talking to him for the first time the following day. The men with whom he was now sharing bunk space were trying to determine whether he was a Marine who had been guarding Admiral Mitscher or worked in the AA battery, or perhaps on the staff of Commander Seitz. These crewmen nearly fell out of their berths when Turnbull told them he was a pilot. Most had never interacted man-to-man with any officer. Perhaps none of the *Cushing*'s crewmen had ever before spoken with a pilot. At the time, few Americans had seen the inside of an airplane.

Turnbull became an instant celebrity among the enlisted men. He had, by then, lost almost all interest in keeping up the rule against fraternization. They asked him a hundred questions at once, wanting to know every detail of all his attacks on the Japanese. What had he seen? What had he bombed? Above all, what was it like to fly an Avenger?

When the ship's officers learned he was a pilot, they called a meeting of all the officers. There, Captain Volk introduced Turnbull and had him tell his life story, including the details of his two combat tours in the Pacific.

Later that day, under Doc Pool's orders, Turnbull took a nap. That evening, the *Cushing* joined TF 58.4 heading toward Ulithi. The *Bunker Hill* followed faithfully behind them, still smoking.

By Monday, the *Cushing* had begun escorting the big ships into Ulithi's protected harbor: the *Yorktown*, the *Shangri-La*, the *New Jersey*, the *Wisconsin*, the *Alaska*, the *Guam*, the *Independence*, and the

Langley. Turnbull, now stronger, sunbathed on the top deck until the *Cushing* herself dropped anchor in the area reserved for destroyers. Then he joined the flag staff for a nip before going ashore for a recreation party. There, he and the other officers were served bourbon and cake (unlike the enlisted men, who received warm beer preserved with formaldehyde). The same afternoon, the *Bunker Hill* motored into the anchorage proudly under her own steam.

Turnbull must have known the reality of what was waiting for him on the ship, for he opted to spend the night on the *Cushing*. The men toasted the country, the Navy, and their company into the night. Turnbull was named "Flight Officer" of the *Cushing* before he hit the sack. Not until the next day, May 15, 1945, did he leave the *Cushing* to return to the *Bunker Hill*. Just before disembarking, Turnbull painted a pair of golden Naval Air Corps wings on the ship's scoreboard—indicating the *Cushing* had bagged one Navy pilot from the sea in addition to the enemy aircraft they had shot down.

Ulithi Atoll, the site of the Pacific Fleet anchorage, is eighteen miles long and nine miles wide. The atoll's harbor on any given day in mid-1945 could contain more ships than the entire U.S. Navy presently maintains. The ships were berthed in various sections, depending on their size and use. Getting from one section to the other could be a complicated business, like crossing a stream on stepping-stones or transferring trains to traverse New York City. It took Turnbull nearly a full day but eventually a harbor launch carried him to the *Bunker Hill*.

As the launch approached the port side of the *Bunker Hill*, Turnbull began to see for the first time the extent of the damage. The launch circled around the stern where George Lyons and so many others had huddled, flames in front of them, churning propellers below. The dinghy then idled up the *Bunker Hill*'s starboard side where Turnbull had leapt into the sea four days earlier. He climbed up the gangway almost in a daze. Commander Fraunheim greeted him on the flight deck. Despite the horror and misery of the sight before him, it felt good to be back.

On May 15, Turnbull learned why Marty Manger and the four enlisted men with whom he had tried to escape did not abandon ship.

When they threw the first raft over the side to Turnbull, its painter had tangled and the raft had jammed on its way down. The men struggled for several minutes before finally untangling it. But by the time they were able to throw the raft overboard, Turnbull had fallen well out of view. That is why his swim to the raft took so long. Manger and the sailors had lost their leader and one raft. They decided against jumping, even as the fires continued to advance. Their situation was desperate. The deck was aflame and the steel catwalk had become so hot that their hands blistered instantly when they touched the rails. But then the cruiser *Wilkes-Barre* came alongside, and the men aboard her played water from their hoses onto Manger and his little group. The hoses cooled and kept them alive until a cable and boatswain's chair could be rigged to transfer the five across the wire onto the deck of the *Wilkes-Barre*.

While at Ulithi, Turnbull and Mouse Webster caught a boat to the *Shangri-La* to visit with some of their old squadron mates for lunch. Their tours of duty were just about ended. The war for them would be over soon. They were going home.

That night, they walked through the hull of the *Bunker Hill*, then Turnbull returned to his room where the usual bull session had started again. Beads Popp dropped in, so did Joe Neary and Mouse Webster. But it was different. Too many pilots were gone. The more they avoided talking about the loss, the more their awareness grew that their friends' deaths were the only thing on each man's mind. Still, no one spoke about it.

37. THE LONG VOYAGE HOME

—TITLE OF A SHORT SEA PLAY BY EUGENE O'NEILL

On May 17, the *Bunker Hill* departed Ulithi for Pearl Harbor. The next day, the surviving crew held a memorial service in the hangar deck to celebrate the lives of the men lost during the kamikaze attack. After the service, the men paraded on the broken flight deck under the hot South Pacific sun. The Marines fired three volleys in salute. Turnbull officially received his promotion that afternoon. He was now a "two-striper," a full lieutenant.

That night they had a party in Mouse Webster's room, but the joy in carmaraderie that had held them together through battle had disappeared. Kiyoshi Ogawa had killed half the squadron. Al Turnbull and torpedo squadron skipper Chandler Swanson left early for their bunks.

For most of their time in the Pacific, the airmen of the *Bunker Hill* had fought a war that had been very clean. They rarely had the opportunity to see the destruction they had visited upon the enemy, and those who were not assigned to fighters rarely engaged enemy aircraft. Turnbull tried to explain how the naval pilots experienced so much of the war without seeing death up close:

> If there is a way to fight a war, as World War II was, I can't think of a better place to be than on a carrier, flying. When we did damage, we didn't see it. We didn't see suffering, we didn't see maim. We didn't see death. We knew we did a heck of a lot

432

of killing. In some sense you might say we did a lot of murdering because we dropped bombs where there was civilians, but we never saw it. We came back, hot showers, clean clothes! Hot food, you just name it and it was a nice way to fight the war. . . . We saw no killing until we were kamikazied and then was the big mess. And I don't think anybody on the carrier was prepared for all that death and destruction.

Death followed the men all the way to Pearl Harbor. An electrician was killed during the memorial service. Crewmen recovered bodies throughout the long trip home. Al Skaret was in the chow line a couple of days after the attack. Someone opened up a storage room. Two dead sailors had barricaded themselves inside and tried to suck clean air through bedrolls. Their bloated bodies rolled into the chow line. Much later, someone found a body in one of the safety nets below a catwalk— a sailor blown over and killed by the concussion of Kiyoshi's bomb.

Most of the squadron reports had burned or disintegrated in firefighting water. Turnbull spent much of the rest of the sail to Pearl filling out forms, trying to piece together disparate reports from his missions, and writing letters home. He also helped the chaplain write condolence letters. The ship had no flight operations—no aircraft. There was no need. The enemy was far behind them. Turnbull's biggest problem was that some days he got too much sun, or had too much paperwork. He could not bring himself to exercise any longer. But he read magazines and learned to fall asleep in the sun. Life was becoming normal on the long, slow trip home.

Turnbull spent hours with his friends aboard the ship. They would start talking about combat and move to marriage, then crisscross the world in their enthusiasm for the life they were about to return to. It seemed clear that few of them would really come back to anything that they had left behind. They had changed too much, and they sensed that the United States and the world had changed, too.

On Wednesday, May 23, as he lay down in his bunk to sleep, Turnbull picked up a *Time* magazine and learned for the first time about the mass murders in Nazi concentration camps. He did not sleep that night.

The *Bunker Hill* arrived at Ford Island in Pearl Harbor on May 25 and began unloading her bombs almost immediately. WAVES sang to the men as the broken ship dropped anchor. The pilots swam at Waikiki and had their first real milkshakes since January. The men had their pictures taken for new identification cards to replace those burned in the fire.

The war they were leaving behind seemed to become even more cruelly brutal. While Turnbull was eating lunch on a beach, five Japanese bombers carrying suicide crews in lieu of explosives attempted to land at the American airbase on Okinawa. Four were shot down, one skidded in on its belly. A young suicide team ran out, hurling grenades and incendiaries at parked U.S. planes. U.S. soldiers watching could not believe it. The Japanese wrecked seven planes, damaged twenty-five, and blew up 70,000 gallons of fuel before they all were killed. One hundred seventy-six other kamikazes attacked the fleet that day.

Turnbull and some other pilots borrowed a plane from Hickham Field and flew the next day for the pure pleasure of flying—perhaps for the first time ever. They were no longer preparing for battle. They all knew the war would be over soon. Instead, they went sight seeing like normal tourists and watched *National Velvet*, starring Mickey Rooney and Elizabeth Taylor. Turnbull loved it.

Admiral Mitscher was relieved of command by Admiral Halsey on May 27. He and Commander Burke returned to the United States. Mitscher became chief of the Atlantic Fleet, a position he would hold until he died of a heart attack in 1947—he is buried at Arlington National Cemetery. Burke built the nuclear navy and served an unprecedented three terms as chief of naval operations.

The next day, Sunday May 28, 1945, the *Bunker Hill* departed Pearl Harbor for her return to Bremerton, Washington. The band played "Aloha Oe" as she pulled away and then "California, Here I Come." The ship was buzzed by all of the Navy's latest planes as she steamed away.

Consciously or not, the men aboard the *Bunker Hill* were slowly becoming prepared to live as civilians again. Their geographical journey from the front lines of combat to the shipyard at Bremerton, Washington, mirrored their psychological journey from deepest trauma to becoming able to function again in their own communities.

It began even as they were moving out of the direct combat area and people stopped shooting at them. At Ulithi, they were able to have decent food, change their clothes, and relax on dry land. A week later they were in Hawaii, where they got their first taste of what America was becoming: shopping, swimming, eating at restaurants. But each crewman remained a sailor, still showing up for their appointed tasks aboard the *Bunker Hill*. When the ship left Pearl Harbor and rounded Oahu on their starboard side, the men were all allowed to write freely, for the first time in years, that soon they would be home.

The tension of the combat zone faded as the crew became less and less susceptible to enemy attacks of various kinds. The ship stopped having General Quarters. Eventually, they lifted the sides of the hangar decks in the evenings, and the whole ship's company gathered to watch movies as the sun set below the port side. The sea calmed and tropical air wafted about them. For a brief time it was almost as if they were on a pleasure cruise in the South Seas. But no one could forget their comrades who had been laid out on that same deck only days before.

The ship moved through time zone after time zone as they pressed northeastward. The seas grew rougher in the northern latitudes. The crewmen began to secure the shipboard fans and wore jackets as they moved about the open decks.

On May 30, Turnbull sighted the shoreline of the United States for the first time in 131 days. On their approach to Washington, they passed through the Strait of Juan de Fuca and ate Boston baked beans with their dinner. The ship pulled into Port Angeles below the Olympic Mountains later that evening.

Even today, the men can vividly recall the look of shock and disbelief on the faces of the dockworkers who climbed aboard the *Bunker Hill*. They stood amazed at the destruction, at the massive steel stanchions that heat had warped into impossible shapes, and marveled that her crew had led her back.

Three weeks after the *Bunker Hill* docked at Bremerton, the American 10th Army pushed through to the southernmost point on Okinawa. General Ushijima and his chief of staff committed *hara-kiri*. The next day, the United States pronounced the island secured and held a formal flag-raising ceremony.

38. CHERRY BLOSSOMS

While waiting for an order to sortie, a kamikaze pilot is play-ing with ants.

—WRITTEN BY THE BUDDHIST MONK KENICHI
WATANABE AT KANOYA IN 1945, WHILE WAITING
FOR HIS ORDER TO SORTIE AS A *JINRAI* PILOT ON
A SUICIDE MISSION

The drawing of the *Yosegaki* is a common custom in Japan done to commemorate any significant event. It is a formal calligraphy, writ-ten on a square cloth with Chinese letter symbols radiating out of the center like the rays of the Japanese rising sun. The group name, or motto, is usually written in the center. During the war, squads often drew *Yosegaki* directly on Japanese flags. Each member would write a message or short poem and his name, from the center outward. Each writing served as a final notice—an explanation, a wish, or a state-ment of how the young men wished to be remembered. *Yosegaki* is both a poem and visual art. The circle symbolizes the unity of the group and their connection to the Japanese nation through the flag of the rising sun.

Kiyoshi flew in the seventh *Showa* Special Attack Corps, formu-lated on May 1 when the ten member pilots were chosen to fly the sixth *Kikusui*. The young men banded together that day and wrote a *Yosegaki*—it would become a death scroll.* It was shown to me by

---

* Many of the individual poems on the scroll, including Kiyoshi's, refer to the number 7 which has been auspicious in Japan for centuries. Since the eighth cen-tury, Japanese have celebrated July 7, the seventh month, with a ritual based on seven: they eat seven meals, take seven baths, make seven offerings, and assem-

the brother of Yasumori, who had received it from Hiroshi Sadakata, a kamikaze who was scheduled to fly with Kiyoshi, but who survived the war because his aircraft engine would not start that morning. Each individual message is specific to its writer.

Some writings, like the pilot Saburo Takahashi's, are starkly straightforward. He wrote: "I am going to break a deck and sink it."

Takahashi sortied just after Kiyoshi at 6:53 A.M. He died that morning. He was twenty-two years old.

Others, like First Sergeant Akira Saraumi's are more lyrical and poetic. Saruami wrote out the names of each member of the seventh Showa Special Attack Corps in the lower left corner of the scroll.* Later, he added his own poem:

> *For the sake of the country, I am going as if*
> *blossoms are falling. The scent of cherry blossoms*
> *in Naha, Okinawa, please reach to Japan.*

Saraumi writes that he is going to live and die like a cherry blossom that falls as soon as it blooms. He acknowledges that he will never return to his family physically—he will die near Naha Town on Okinawa—but he will be sensed at home through the scent and spirit of the cherry blossom. Saraumi sortied from Kanoya at 6:45 A.M. and died that morning. He was seventeen years old.

---

ble plant arrangements with seven golden and silver pins. Since the thirteen century, Japanese have made seven poems written on seven leaves and played seven games. In the Edo era they began placing seven ink basins on a desk, lighting seven lanterns to write seven poems. There are seven gods of good fortune, the Buddha took seven steps the moment he was born, and it is said in Japan that people are reborn seven times. It was a special honor to give each of these seven lives to the nation.

* Saruami wrote: "The members of the Showa Troop: Ensign Kenzo Ishijima; Ensign Saburo Takahashi; Ensign Kiyoshi Ogawa; Ensign Tadashi Mogi; Ensign Hiroshi Nemoto; Ensign Ryuzo Ishizuka; Ensign Tadanori Sasahara; First Sergeant, Naval Air Service Yoshikazu Kurono; First Sergeant, Naval Air Service Akira Saraumi; First Sergeant Kuruno Ichihisou."

Some pilots tried to comfort their loved ones, especially parents, by stating that they were happy about their situation. Ensign Tadashi Mogi wrote simply:

I am happy to get this opportunity to attack the enemy's carrier.

Mogi sortied at 6:53 A.M. He was killed that morning. Mogi was twenty-two years old.

The large Chinese characters written vertically down the center line were drawn by Morita Heitaro on May 1, 1945. Heitaro wrote:

Ah! Kamikaze *Showa* Special Attack Corps.

The Yosegaki of the seventh Showa Special Attack Corps. Yasunori Seizo signed at the bottom right corner.

Heitaro was one of the leaders at the base. He did not fly a mission that morning.

Moving clockwise from the bottom-left-hand corner, Tadanori Sasahara signed next, just above the squadron list. Sasahara had been on the tennis team at St. Paul's University (Rikkyo). His only combat mission lasted less than three hours. Sasahara signaled Kanoya at 9:21 A.M. that he had made contact with the enemy. American aircraft, vectored to intercept the sixth *Kikusui,* apparently caught up with him. The fight did not last long. Six minutes later Tadanori radioed that he was losing altitude. His last message was succinct: "Unable to continue." He crashed into the sea at 9:27 A.M. The final entry in the record of his flight, written by an officer at Kanoya, reads simply: *Mikikan*—"Never came back." Before flying, Sasahara wrote:

> Even though my body sinks down into the southern sea, my spirit will definitely guard the emperor's country for eternity.

He was twenty-four years old.

Ensign Ryuzo Ishizuka wrote next, in even lettering, horizontally, at what would be nine o'clock if the *Yosegaki* were a clock face. Ishizuka implored his audience to believe that his sacrificial death would at least prolong the war:

> I will fly south smiling since the continuing war will last long.

Ryuzo Ishizuka was killed that morning. He was twenty-two years old.

Kiyoshi Ogawa drew his poem in diagonal lines from the top left corner leading down to the center and pointed directly at Yasunori Seizo's poem in the bottom-right-hand corner. By this time, it had already been decided that Kiyoshi would die as Yasunori's wingman. Kiyoshi wrote:

> Young cherry blossoms will not die without flowering for the country. I am going to be a fire ball that shines seven times.

First Sergeant Kuruno Ichihisou from Hyogo prefecture signed in the center of the *Yosegaki*, just to the left of the large bold writing. Kuruno wrote:

I am going to dye the waves coming to the emperor's country red, and explode like a ball as a truly Japanese man.

Ichihisou sortied at 5:07 A.M. He died that morning. He was nineteen years old.

Ensign Hiroshi Nemoto from Ibaragi prefecture was originally in the sixth Showa squad. He survived two kamikaze sortie assignments before May 11, 1945. But on that morning he sortied at 5:19 A.M. as a member of the seventh Showa-tai. He wrote:

I made seven successful sorties.

Hiroshi died that morning. He was twenty-one years old.

Kenzo Ishijima, an Episcopalian, flew with Kiyoshi Ogawa as wingman to Tadanori Sasahara. He sortied at 6:42 A.M. His aircraft failed about an hour and a half into the flight—209 miles south of Kanoya. He radioed that he had run out of fuel. Ishijima likely had a leaking fuel line. He made an emergency landing on Kikaigashima. Kikai was not a safe place to hide. Ishijima died there within days of his landing.

Because he was not killed during his kamikaze attack, Ishijima was denied the two-level promotion that his comrades received. In many documents he is not listed as a member of their Showa troop. But he was one with them when they signed their death scroll. On the upper-right-hand corner of the *Yosegaki*, Ishijima wrote:

Since my body is a shell, I am going to take it off and put on glory that will never wear out.

Lieutenant Junior Grade Yasunori Seizo signed the death poem twice. This is probably a reflection of his senior status. His writing takes up most of the bottom right corner of the *Yosegaki*. Yasunori begins with the image of five brothers under the flag—a patriotic family protected by, and protecting, the country. They stand together as veterans. By placing himself one step ahead, Yasunori acknowledges, mystically, that he will die as a *tokko* before any of his brothers.

Yasunori's first poem read:

> Under the flag, five brothers who came out of
> one stomach are together. The fourth son goes
> one step ahead. Until the enemy surrenders,
> I will be born again and again to be a shield
> for the emperor.

And then Yasunori signed, simply:

Akou kenji, Yasunori Seizo

A healthy young man from Akou.

Yasunori was twenty-one years old.

Admiral Ugaki also wrote a short poem the day Kiyoshi was killed:

> Flowers of the Special Attack are falling,
> When the spring is leaving.
> Gone with the Spring
> Are young boys like cherry blossoms.
> Gone are the blossoms,
> Leaving cherry trees only with leaves.

News of the attack on the *Bunker Hill* was withheld by the American government until late July. On July 27, 1945, newspapers across the country printed dramatic photographs of the attack and struggle. The Navy circulated Tony Faccone's picture of the burning flight deck around the world. That same day, President Harry Truman announced from Potsdam that the Allies required Japan's unconditional surrender.

For more than 100 days, from April 1 until mid-June 1945, less than three divisions of Japanese held out in Okinawa, without support, against an American force twice as strong. Fourteen Japanese divisons and five independent brigades protected Kyushu. President Truman later claimed, and many Army sources agreed, that an invasion of Japan could have cost one million American casualties. This estimate is far from accurate. General Dwight Eisenhower said that he felt that the atomic bombing was unnecessary from the point of view of saving American lives. Admiral William Leahy, Secretary of War Henry Stimson, Secretary of the Navy James Forrestal, and Army Air General Henry "Hap" Arnold, all thought that dropping the bomb was unnecessary. Japan was broken and would have surrendered without an invasion.

The Japanese had no fuel, fewer than 10,000 trucks, almost no ability to manufacture weapons or ammunition, nor to transport supplies within Japan. They had almost no tanks left and remained wholly unable to defend themselves from air attack. Famine and disease threatened most of the population. Millions of Japanese civilians remained homeless. One by one, their cities were being razed. Japan's air forces had been ruined, her navy wrecked. The bulk of Japan's army was withering away in South Asia.

Nevertheless, on August 6, the first atomic bomb, dubbed "Little Boy," was dropped on Hiroshima. Two days after that, the USSR declared war on Japan and invaded Manchurian China. The next day, August 9, 1945, the second atomic bomb, "Fat Man," was detonated over Nagaski.

Five days after the destruction of Nagasaki, Admiral Ugaki received orders from the emperor to stop all hostilities. The following morning, he listened to Emperor Hirohito announce Japan's surrender, imploring the Japanese to "bear the unbearable."

Before each *Kikusui*, Admiral Ugaki had promised the young kamikaze pilots that he would "meet them at Minatogawa." Immediately after Japan's surrender was announced, Ugaki ordered dive-bombers to be readied for take off. His staff members drove him to the field, their eyes filled with tears. They had scrounged together eleven ready aircraft. All of the remaining pilots volunteered to accompany him. Ugaki departed at 5:00 P.M. and headed south toward the American fleet on the last kamikaze mission. He radioed back to base at 8:24 P.M: "We have succeeded in making a surprise attack." No more was heard from him.

There is no record of a Japanese aerial attack on August 15.

The morning after the Japanese surrender, Admiral Takijiro Onishi, the architect of the kamikaze program, committed ritual suicide. Onishi disemboweled himself at his home with a Japanese sword. The abdominal cut was cleanly done, but he botched the finishing slash of his throat. Onishi refused the coup de grâce that is normally given to those who have committed *hara-kiri.* Instead, he lay on his mat in penance, his blood flowing all that day. Before he died, Onishi left a letter:

I wish to express my deep appreciation to the souls of the brave special attackers. They fought and died valiantly with faith in our ultimate victory. In death I wish to atone for my part in the failure to achieve that victory and I apologize to the souls of these dead fliers and their bereaved families.

I wish the young people of Japan to find a moral in my death. To be reckless is only to aid the enemy. You must abide by the spirit of the Emperor's decision with utmost perseverance. Do not forget your rightful pride in being Japanese.

You are the treasure of the nation. With all the fervor of the spirit of the special attackers, strive for the welfare of Japan and for peace throughout the world.

Onishi also left a Haiku:

Refreshed,
I feel like a clear moon
After a storm.

His last word was *Sayonara*.

On August 22, the commander of the Fifth Air Fleet ordered that all documents relating to the suicide missions be destroyed. The surviving kamikaze pilots were sent home with a few thousand yen. Emperor Hirohito was never charged with any war crime, nor held responsible for the suicide units.

The Yokosuka naval base was peacefully surrendered to the U.S. Navy on August 30, 1945. The buildings where Kiyoshi and the other students trained were converted to schools and churches.

Japan signed the surrender terms in Tokyo Bay aboard the battleship *Missouri* on September 2, 1945. The dent in her side, where a young *tokko* pilot had crashed into her, killing only himself, was clearly visible to dignitaries of both sides.

EPILOGUE:
LOOKING BACK

For most of the men who sailed on the *Bunker Hill*, World War II and especially May 11, 1945, remain the seminal events in their lives. Nearly all the crewmen I interviewed had never left home before the war, and a good many never left home again. It is easy to forget, especially when we see them now in the twilight of their years, that so many of the crew were only nineteen or twenty years old when they served. Like teenagers everywhere, they felt indestructible. But they were not, and these men and their families still show the effects both physical and psychological of the war, and especially of Kiyoshi Ogawa's kamikaze attack.

Most of the men who survived the assault did not discuss Kiyoshi's attack, even with their own families, until decades later. During their time on the *Bunker Hill*, it was vital for them to deny daily the dangers they faced. Few could function while constantly aware that at any moment their life might end. So the Navy fostered and the men advanced a sort of collective denial of menace. Such denial can become debilitating after the fighting. Kiyoshi crushed the safe psychological world the men of the *Bunker Hill* had created. After his crash, their minds could no longer deny their danger. It was the final straw that utterly destroyed the men's ability to divorce their daily thought from the awareness that they could, at any moment, die. Every sailor seemed to recognize and understand that, but for the slightest chance, it could have been they themselves, burned beyond all recognition as an individual human being and cast overboard in a weighted gunny sack.

Everyone on the *Bunker Hill* had a battle station. When the ship was under attack, each crewman went immediately to his station. At least one sailor was assigned to virtually every single compartment in the hull. Some assigned sailor would therefore see, and could report, damage anywhere aboard ship during battle. This meant, though, that some men were sent to obscure areas during GQ. Al Skaret's friend who always carried the Mae West* was assigned to the crew's latrine. When Skaret entered the latrine late on the night of May 11, the smoke had mostly cleared. The fires had not spread there, but it was obvious that the smoke had been terrible. Skaret's friend (he has blocked out the sailor's name) had struggled to the very end, determined to stay alive for himself, for his wife and his young children. The lone sailor tore the benches off the troughs and lay down in the slop of the long toilets where the men used to float burning newspaper boats. When the smoke had displaced all the oxygen in the room, this man had ripped the outflow pipe out of the wall and wrapped his lips around the filth-covered flange, trying to suck air from the sewage pipe. Skaret found him, wearing his Mae West, asphyxiated there, his mouth still wrapped around the filth-stained tube.

No known survivor of the *Bunker Hill* again saw combat during World War II. Even Arleigh Burke and Admiral Mitscher were returned to the States as quickly as possible. Sailors who today live through the kind of harrowing combat faced by the men aboard the *Bunker Hill* are treated with a complex combination of physical and psychological therapies to deal with the stress that develops almost invariably in those who have lived through such trauma. Not so the men of the *Bunker Hill*.

Modern warfare has produced major advances in trauma treatment, especially battlefield treatment and emergency medicine. Reconstructive surgery barely existed before the Second World War. Now it is a specialized field with courses offered at every major American medical school. Unfortunately, major advancements in burn treatment did not come about until the Vietnam War. Fluid loss is now controlled intravenously. Hundreds of sophisticated antibiotics are available to control infection. Burns are treated surgically. During World War II, all the doctors could do was apply creams, change

---

* Nicknamed for the notoriously buxom film star, the Mae West was an enormous life jacket that fit down over the chest in two preposterously bulging chambers stuffed with white foamy floatation filler called kapok.

dressings, and administer morphine. Third degree burns over one third of the body were almost universally fatal.

Hundreds of men aboard the *Bunker Hill* were burned to various degrees. Roma Dussault's shoulders are permanently scarred. Liquefied aluminum pouring from the flight deck burned off the superficial protective layers of his skin. The nerve endings at the center of the burn were destroyed. But those at the periphery were exposed, irritated, inflamed, and stimulated—millions upon millions of nerves. Mere temperature differences in the air around a burn are enough to cause severe pain. The nerve endings begin to hurt more and more as they regenerate. The pain he experienced while clinging to that ladder is impossible to imagine.

Such burns can lead to devastating post-traumatic stress. The psychological effects of seeing one's skin falling off, or boiling, or melting, or smelling your own burnt flesh complicates individual treatment. Family dynamics are now understood to be essential to recovery, and family counseling has become an integral aspect of burn treatment. The terrible scarring contributes mightily to the challenges faced by families of burn victims. Even modern EMS technicians—paramedics and firemen—receive counseling when they have *seen* severe burn victims. Yet, there was almost no recognition of these effects on treatment during World War II. Most of the burn victims on the *Bunker Hill* have never discussed what happened even with their wives.

Many of the men who survived the kamikaze attack bear deep emotional scars. Others, like Joseph Carmichael, are more stoic in their remembrances. Perhaps because Carmichael had had a wealth of experience before the war, and also afterward, he is able to see events in the Pacific with more perspective, or at least philosophically:

Even the most horrendous thing you can think about is relatively common when you come right down to it. You ask me what does a man look like when he is dead? Well, to a person who has never seen it before, that may have one impact, while for someone else, who has seen this kind of thing more commonly, while it may not be something he likes to think about, well, it isn't necessarily going to upset his whole day, nor is he going to feel upset about it.

I might think afterward, why did he have to ask me about that? You know, I don't want to have to dwell on that . . . but I just can't fathom how people feel so emotional still. Now, I know that they do, and I know that some people talk about the *Bunker Hill,* and they get tears in their eyes in no time at all. Well, I feel I am very emotional about the *Bunker Hill* myself, but I have been through enough in my life that I know you cannot give way to those kinds of things. The thing to do, is not to pretend that this did not happen, but you just cannot let it rule your life.

Joseph Carmichael received the Navy Cross from Secretary of the Navy James Forrestal for his actions on May 11, 1945. He lived out a full life in New York City, raised a family, and became a successful banker.

Al Turnbull finished out his service and returned to Southern California where he and his brother opened up a retail paint and wallpaper store. He and his wife, Harriet volunteered to teach English as a second language to Japanese students at their local state college. They became good friends with many of the young Japanese scholars and have maintained relationships with them over the years.

J. Waite "Slabo" Bacon miraculously survived the kamikaze attack, and made a successful career at National Cash Register in Dayton, Ohio. He raised a family and served as best man at Al Turnbull's wedding.

George Gelderman left the naval base at Bremerton for Los Alamitos where he worked at a training camp until he was released. He used the GI Bill to attend the University of Washington. Four years after the first naval carrier raid on Tokyo, Gelderman got a call from Al

Turnbull. The remains of Ensign Brothers* had been located at an airmen's cemetery in Japan and were being returned to Los Angeles. Gelderman joined Turnbull, several other men from Torpedo Squadron 84, and Brothers's family members to bury him at Forest Lawn in Los Angeles.

The war remained a powerful and affecting part of Gelderman's life. He will never move entirely beyond the hours he spent lifting and carrying out the remains of his shipmates from their tombs within the *Bunker Hill*.

Edmund Skacan saw and heard and felt more than he shared with me. Probably more than he can share. He broke down often during our interviews and explained that he simply never talks about the war— not so much because he is afraid of how people will react to what he did in the Pacific, though that is clearly a factor, but of his own reaction. He does not know what he will do when forced to confront these stories. Each telling means reliving these moments of incredible pain, stress, doubt, and even triumph in his life.

Joe Brocia was trapped in a doorway after Kiyoshi's bomb exploded. He, along with a few men with him in the small compartment, survived. But men just a few feet away on either side were all killed. Eventually, he made his way forward to the bow and manned a fire house. For years after the attack, Brocia had a recurring dream that the Japanese were on the *Bunker Hill* and none of the American's ammo would fit their guns. He would lie in bed at night before he fell asleep, thinking over and over of strafing runs, worrying about whether he would be hit. But during the war, Brocia never really was aware of worrying about it. He maintained a fatalistic attitude—he figured that pilot skill made no difference. Getting hit was merely a matter of luck. Sometimes the antiaircraft shells would explode just to one side of him, or just to the other. There seemed to be no

---

* Brothers was the TBF pilot shot down beside Turnbull's plane on the first Tokyo raid.

reason that one plane would come home, while another pilot was killed.

Edward Leahy is now a retired Boston police officer. He lives on the top floor of a white double-decker in the same neighborhood of Dorchester where he was born eighty years ago, and where he has spent all of his life other than the three years he served as a plane captain aboard the *Bunker Hill.*

Leahy has not slept through the night since May 11, 1945. The morning of the attack, Leahy was crouched on the catwalk and a young sailor just beyond him was cut off by fire. This sailor stood up straight and tall at the edge of the flight deck and then leapt off, hands outstretched like Christ. To this day, Leahy is haunted by the memory. Tears well up in his eyes and his whole body shakes as he demonstrates how this sailor executed a flawless swan dive. The incident has become emblematic for Leahy of the horrors of that day. The unknown sailor sliced into the Pacific with perfect grace. His hands came together a moment before he hit the water. "He didn't even make a splash," Leahy said.

Leahy spent much of the next several days bringing bodies out of the ship's hold. He had never told a soul what he saw belowdecks. And he will not begin to now.

It is hard for *Roma Dussault* even now when he sees a truck that says "Mitsubishi" on the back. But when he is more reflective he thinks about the things that he knows were done on both sides and figures if he ever met a kamikaze, he would try to understand. After he got home, Dussault could not take his sons fishing because he could not bear to put bait on a hook. He did not want to hurt even a worm.

Jim Swett still dreams about the USS *Bunker Hill* burning. "It is an image I wish I could be rid of but I can't." He says that in the dreams, "I can just see those guys thrashing around in the water with a great big god-danged shark trying to get 'em ... We'd fly over and they were gone ... terrible, terrible, terrible."

When he returned to Seattle after the war, *Al Skaret* did not go back to being a journeyman machinist. He became a firefighter on Ladder One, where he served as a tillerman steering the back of a long aerial ladder truck. Skaret was stationed at headquarters on Second Avenue South and Main Street and put in twenty-six years fighting fires. Over the years, he got to know a lot about death, but he had seen most of it on the *Bunker Hill.* "Rigor mortis sets in pretty quick," he says.

Men aboard ships for extended periods, especially in time of war, tend to develop special bonds. There is an unspoken understanding among all men who served aboard ship in the Pacific, and especially among those who served together.

Skaret knew one sailor who was forced to jump off the ship just after Kiyoshi crashed. A destroyer picked him up, but he was covered with blood. Shrapnel had torn through him, pieces ripped through his lungs and a bit lay embedded in his tongue. The sailor spent a month in the naval hospital at Pearl Harbor, then finally shipped back to Bremerton. When he was finally reunited with his comrades, the injured sailor said, "I was so worried about you guys aboard ship . . . you know . . . all that smoke and fire and explosions. You guys must have had an awful time."

Bud Millholland was one of the pilots whose plane was blown off the deck of the *Bunker Hill*. He got out of the wreck and jumped through an inferno of napalm into the Pacific. Somehow he survived. He was picked up by a destroyer and flown out to the Navy hospital at Guam. Millholland was stabilized there before being flown to the burn center at Oak Knoll in Oakland, California.

Millholland went through a trying series of operations and was able to return to his alma mater, the University of Kansas, where he got a law degree and became a gifted, successful trial lawyer. But his life always seemed to have a dichotomy about it that he could not shake. One side of his head and face remained horribly disfigured from the burns. The other side somehow endured almost unscathed, his normal handsome self.

Archie Donahue was a seasoned Marine pilot. He had become "ace in a day" twice. In May 1943, he shot down five Zeros in a single mission. On April 12, 1945, flying from the *Bunker Hill*, he shot down five more over Okinawa. But on May 11, they had not found any Japanese on their mission. Irritated, Donahue refused to debrief his men, because "nothing happened." One of the younger officers threatened to report him for canceling the debrief, but Donahue walked out of the ready room anyway, followed by a dozen or so pilots. The few who stayed behind were killed a few minutes later.

Jim Walker was blown, burning, into the Pacific from the catwalk by his gun. The skin grafts on his arms have, for the most part, healed well. Fillingame, his bridge partner, survived, too. His hands were burned badly and his eardrum was broken, probably from the concussion of an explosion when he raised his head above the deck. Though almost everyone on battery six aft either abandoned ship or was killed, Eddie Radcliff is the only one from their gun bucket who didn't make it. Radcliff decided to make a run for it along the catwalk that connected all of the gun batteries on the starboard side of the ship. A large section of catwalk had burned and fallen overboard, but the break was obscured by the smoke. The men figured Radcliff must have been running as fast as he could and not seen the missing section until it was too late.

Eddie Harris, Jim Walker's loader, saw Walker for the first time since May 11, 1945, at the reunion where I interviewed them outside their old port in Bremerton, Washington, in the summer of 2002. When the two men saw each other, they were instantly transported, not to the horror of their last moments together, but back to the *Bunker Hill* and the bond they shared as teenagers manning a gun, far from home, against the Japanese.

On April 14, 1945, *Caleb Kendall*'s son, Tim, was born. On June 25, 1947, Caleb Kendall's widow, Brownie, received a letter from her husband, more than two years after he was killed. It would have been his twenty-seventh birthday. The date on the letter indicated it had been written the night before Kiyoshi's attack.

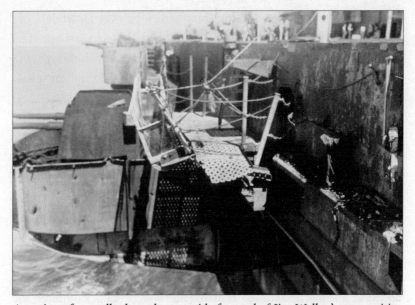

A section of catwalk along the port side forward of Jim Walker's gun position was torn away, probably by Yasunori Seizo's aircraft or an American aircraft dragged off the ship's side with the kamikaze. Eddie Radcliff probably did not see this missing section as he sprinted forward looking for safety at the bows. The larger 40mm double Bofors machine cannons are mounted in the gun tub behind the wrecked catwalk.

He wrote Brownie about how joyful it was to know that he had a son. And that he was so happy: "I am going to explode any second now," he wrote. Then:

> If only I could see you now and hold you in my arms and tell you how proud and happy you have made me. I am unable to express myself. . . . I'll be your humble servant now and forevermore.
>
> All I want now is to get home soon. . . . I'll be on the crest of the wave from here on in.

In 1941, the United States, fed up with the Japanese troop expansion into Indochina, had expanded the oil embargo to include all scrap metal. In 1973, the USS *Bunker Hill*, the last of the Essex Class carriers still utilized by the Navy, was towed out of Naval Air Station

San Diego where Turnbull trained, and pulled past the Hotel del Coronado where Caleb and Brownie Kendall began their marriage. The carrier was sold for scrap and taken to Japan. In a sense, though, the *Bunker Hill* still protects us. Heavy steel plate from the ship was transported to the Fermilab, where it absorbs accelerated particles.

Few Japanese pilots who made it all the way to the American fleet in 1945 returned to report on their observations, and the bodies of kamikazes that crashed American ships were rarely identified. Almost no information as to the specific results of any single kamikaze pilot's crash have been recorded. Happenstance enabled the identification of Kiyoshi Ogawa fifty years after his crash.

Kiyoshi flew with a small mechanical navigation watch hung around his neck. A sailor aboard the *Bunker Hill*, Robert Schock, pilfered the watch and several other items from Kiyoshi's dead body. Schock hid them away in cardboard boxes, left unopened for years. When he died, his grandson, Dax Berg, sorted through Schock's personal effects. Berg opened one box that contained war memorabilia. Among other items, Berg found several that appeared to be Japanese, including a canvas belt still attached to a flat steel belt lock. The manufacturer's label, in stark black Roman lettering, remains clearly legible and reads: *Seizousho Fujikura Koukuu Kougyu Kabushiki Gaisha*. Berg later learned that this was the name of a manufacturer of Japanese parachutes during the Second World War.* Berg had found Kiyoshi's parachute belt. He also found what appeared to be a letter, neatly folded, written in Japanese, and stained with blood. A torn photo of four young Japanese men in military flight suits lay beside the letter. The letter was Iwama's poem to Kiyoshi, and the photo is the picture of his four friends that Kiyoshi took with him when he sortied.

Amongst the other possessions, Berg found Kiyoshi's timepiece. The watch broke through Kiyoshi's rib cage as it buried itself into his

---

* The company is still producing parachutes and makes paragliders in partnership with an American manufacturer.

chest cavity. Kiyoshi's dried blood still clings to it, but it is impossible to read the time it stopped.

A small piece of fabric torn from Kiyoshi's life jacket held the key to the true story behind the destruction of the *Bunker Hill*. Robert Schock, perhaps unwittingly, had torn off a piece of Kiyoshi's life jacket. The cloth contained the first few letters from Kiyoshi's nametag.

The Japanese college students drafted in the war and forced to become kamikazes have stayed in touch. Like the American veterans of the *Bunker Hill*, the former kamikazes get together at reunions each year. They have gathered together extant records of their sorties, so it was easy for them to track down Kiyoshi's name. Kiyoshi is the only pilot with the letters OGA in his name who flew on May 11, 1945.

Berg gave the items to a translator, who tracked down Kiyoshi Ogawa's family through the group of Yatabe survivors. He returned the items to Sachiko and Yoko Ogawa, Kiyoshi's in-law and grandniece, who maintain a shrine for Kiyoshi in their home in Takasaki.

Perhaps the most astonishing fact about Kiyoshi for most Japanese, young and old, comrades and schoolmates, is not the fact that he died as a *tokko*, nor his enthusiasm, nor even his stunning success in destroying so much aboard the *Bunker Hill*. The Japanese remain amazed that some part of Kiyoshi survived. Many of the older Japanese especially feel a powerful connection to a person through his personal effects. This is true also in Western societies, where we value the signature of a president or the clothing of a saint. These iconic mementos help us to connect to an earlier time and make real the lives of distant people.

The parachute harness, the smashed timepiece, the bloody poetry, and a torn photo of dead kamikazes bring Kiyoshi instantly to the present. These mementos, for Kiyoshi's family, signify that he may rest, now at peace in his own country. His possessions, too, allow his story to be told and give the Japanese a particularly powerful insight into what their country was, what the student *tokkotai* were doing, and what that means for people of every age and in every sector of society there. But it is also important to us, perhaps obviously as the enemy of Kiyoshi Ogawa, but also now as the friend of Japan; as a nation that fought hard against men who used airplanes as weapons of mass destruction and suicide fifty years ago, and that has learned to make the children of those men and even many of those former kamikazes themselves, the greatest supporters the United States may ever have.

Kiyoshi Ogawa is remembered with special fondness by his classmates at Waseda and those who went through flight and kamikaze training with him. His friends get together each year and talk about him and others. They have done so since the war ended at private reunions. They invited me to join them and give a talk about this project. None of them realized until recently that Kiyoshi was one of the two kamikazes who had brought down the *Bunker Hill*.

Hisashi Tezuka attended Tokyo University. He was drafted with Kiyoshi, trained with him at all of the same bases, and became a kamikaze. The navy granted Tezuka a special four-day leave to see his parents just before he was sent to his *tokko* base. They all understood the implication of his unexplained leave. As in most *tokko* families, neither Tezuka nor his parents ever mentioned that he had been ordered to die.

Tezuka never wanted to kill himself. He felt, though, that there was no way he could disobey the order. He explained to me that all of the students were concerned with saving face, appearing brave, and not doing anything that would embarrass them in their last days.

Surviving kamikazes feel a duty to console and respect the souls of the dead pilots. Most now feel the war was wrong. Nevertheless, they also feel that the individual sacrifice that Kiyoshi and the others made was noble and good. Tezuka believes that the best way to honor the death of the kamikazes is by telling their stories to convince young people that war must be avoided. In this way, he says, "We may soothe the spirits of those who died." For Tezuka and many of the surviving kamikazes, the sacrifice applies not only to Kiyoshi Ogawa and the other kamikaze pilots, but also to those Americans who died in their attacks.

Osamu Numaga served in a front-line naval kamikaze base during the last months of the war. Each morning, he and nearly everyone

EPILOGUE: LOOKING BACK | 459

at the base would go out to the runway and watch the young *tokko* pilots take off. The pilots would circle once over the runway, their cockpit windshields pushed back, their white scarves billowing out behind them. The men on the ground would look up and point into the morning twilight, as they probably did for Kiyoshi on his last mission, gesturing to each plane, naming the pilot. "That is Kiyoshi" and "There is Yasunori," they would have said. All of the men in the ground crews would wave as the pilots fired off a few precious rounds, then flew out toward the sea to the south and west. Tears streamed down the faces of the crews left behind.

When Osamu Numaga finally made it back to Takasaki after the war ended, he walked to the Ogawas' home to find Kiyoshi. Mrs. Ogawa answered the door to Numaga and cried out, "My Kiyoshi's not coming home." They held each other and cried and cried. Mrs. Ogawa stood moaning, but sobbed out: "I am so glad you made it back, Osamu." Even now, sixty-five years later, Numaga wells up with tears when he thinks of the moment he learned of Kiyoshi's death.

Numaga still attends senior meetings in the village. Everyone sings karaoke military songs at the events. But he can never bring himself to sing with his age-mates. Numaga is overwhelmed with thoughts of all the young men he grew up with who died in the war. He begins to cry when he starts to tell me of these men, and their loss. Many of these friends of his were only nineteen or twenty. None of them has anyone left to carry on their name. Before they died, they were assured they would be remembered always and forever, but he told me, "These days no one remembers. People think the *tokkotai* did bad things—but they weren't bad. They gave their lives for their country."

Numaga explained, "It is not a straightforward kind of pain . . . each person's destiny is a fragile, arbitrary thing." Tears stream again down his face, and despite the nationalism that reigns in his less reflective moments, he looks at me and says, "I don't think we should ever fight in another war again. . . . We can't think like soldiers—it is too late to do anything about the olden days."

When *Tatsuo Ono* thinks of Kiyoshi now, and the sacrifice that he made and the tactics that the government approved, his emotions are powerfully mixed. Ono is overwhelmed by a feeling of loneliness but he is reluctant to say that *tokko* tactics were wrong lest he insult his friend's memory. Yet he knows how terribly wasteful the Japanese effort in the last years of the war had been. "The war was very stupid," Ono told me.

Ono spent most of his time after the war trying to forget all about his wartime experiences. Yet the difficulty and loss of that time period are inescapable. His best friend was killed in the atomic explosion at Hiroshima and he never got to know Kiyoshi Ogawa fully. They remain only *senyu*, wartime friends. Japanese naval *senyu* cherish that relationship their entire lives. However, every year when December 10 arrives, no matter how Ono tries to avoid his memories, he sinks into pain. It is the anniversary of the student draft, when he walked from the train station to the newly constructed barracks at Yokosuka.

Shinto Bushido teaches every Japanese soldier and sailor that "The way of the warrior is to die."

The Japanese developed a varied arsenal of suicide tactics by 1945. They utilized waves of suicidal infantry in ground assaults. Individual soldiers carried hand grenades into enemy lines as a sort of suicide mortar. Japan maintained various specialized suicide assault and antitank units. There were suicide snipers, suicide pilots of miniature subs, and human torpedoes, Scuba-equipped human mine swimmers (some merely carrying hand grenades and swimming along landing beaches in the night), suicide boats, suicide gliders, the Ohka, and conventional aircraft armed for suicide missions.

Tatsuo Ono and many of the other student draftees are particularly angered by the power of the military dictatorship to determine early in the final stages of the war that the reserves were 100 percent expendable, but the men trained in the military academies and all of the senior officers were *Honchou*, indispensable chiefs, who had to be saved because they were best able to preserve and rebuild the country. Only about 120 of the kamikazes were graduates of the Japanese Naval Academy. The ordinary students—gifted young men who studied math, science, philosophy, and economics, and who sometimes questioned the established order—made up the vast majority of those ordered on naval kamikaze missions.

Kenichi Watanabe, a student from Komazawa University in Tokyo who trained with Kiyoshi and was assigned to the *tokkotai*, became a Buddhist monk after the war. Watanabe was probably the tallest of the student draftees. His head is shaved now and he appears more serious (and taller) in his robes, though still a jolly version of the Dalai Lama. He told me: "In the state of emergency nothing makes any logical sense . . . we didn't have any sense of direction." There was something about the dislocation of war that united everyone who served in the military. Twenty of Watanabe's friends were killed as *tokko*, and he knew that they were dying one by one. They were sent to the war zone, which he called "merely a death zone." Watanabe holds a meditative image of himself heading to the war zone in a long line of students: The students cue in the order of their sorties. Each student in the procession carries the heads of those who departed before them. Those behind him in line carry Watanabe's head. Watanabe maintains, though, that they all departed with *shoyo*, a sublime sense of honor.

Fushakushinmyou is a uniquely Japanese Buddhist term signifying an extraordinary devotion, so complete that the practitioner will no longer worry even about losing his life or body in the search for truth. Watanabe's friends in the *tokko* corps spanned religious affiliations from those who still believed in the old systems of Japanese spirits to the Buddhists and Christians. Yet they all departed as *tokko* with what Watanabe called "the same conviction in their minds." The two most powerful forces in their lives were, first, their concern and dedication to their families, their parents, and siblings, and, second, their domination by the "hard" military. The students had to destroy all sense of self in order to survive the brutal indoctrination that came with their mobilization. This losing of their selves made it all the easier to sacrifice what was left to protect those they loved.

Kenichi Watanabe is one of the fourteen Yatabe student pilots who survived Kanoya. There are now only a handful left alive.

The kamikazes were kept segregated on their bases, not even permitted to practice flying. The sailors, too, were cut off together aboard the *Bunker Hill*. After January 1945, both groups faced death, each from the other. The men aboard the *Bunker Hill* waited daily for the kamikaze attack and the student pilots passed their time waiting for American bombs, or their own leaders, to kill them. These separation experiences contributed to each group identifying more thoroughly as members of their particular assemblage, to giving up their individuality. Two of the most basic human precepts are self-preservation and the prevention of homicide. The isolative experiences of the kamikazes and Navy men were designed to pierce this principle—to teach the young to take life and to die. The sailors and the kamikazes learned to function as parts of a weapons system. They killed and were killed not so much as individuals but rather as elements within that system.

In my research and interviews with the family and friends of Kiyoshi Ogawa and other kamikazes, in reading their diaries and last letters, and in conversations with their friends and parents and wives and siblings, I see bravery in spite of the fate assigned to them by the increasingly desperate leaders of Japan.

Admiral Onishi argued that in the end the purpose of these *tokko* attacks was to convince the United States that Japan would fight to the last man and thereby win a better peace. But the kamikazes' seeming contempt for death, and what appeared to U.S. forces as fanaticism for a lost cause, contributed in no small way to the American decision to use the atomic bomb rather than confront such a radical nation. The carnage aboard the Navy's flagship aircraft carrier *Bunker Hill* was likely in the minds of those who decided to use atomic force to end the war.

Halldór Laxness, the Icelandic Nobel Prize–laureate, wrote that terror is stronger than the sum of anyone's happiness. The kamikaze pilots sliced through the naval shield, bringing terror not merely to the men aboard the ship, but across America where it was terrifying to imagine a civilization in which individuals placed such apparently different values on their own lives.

The challenging lesson of the Pacific war may not so much be that aircraft carriers can extend American foreign policy across the world, but rather that a few determined men, willing to give their lives for a cause, may block that policy from ever being fulfilled.

AUTHOR'S NOTE

The bulk of this book is based on interviews with surviving airmen and crew of the *Bunker Hill* and interviews with surviving kamikaze pilots and their families and friends. But several printed sources were also invaluable. Of the primary sources I utilized, none were as helpful as the official reports generated by the officers and crewmen of the *Bunker Hill* and the action reports of various component squadrons and of Air Group 84. These proved most valuable in confirming individual recollections and the results of actions in which the *Bunker Hill* took part. These reports are all available now at the National Archives and Records Administration (NARA) in College Park, Maryland. Many were declassified at my request on May 15, 2003. In addition to these documents, I relied on similar records, ship's logs, and action reports from the vessels surrounding the *Bunker Hill* on May 11, 1945. The primary reports in which movements of the *Bunker Hill* and her actions are recorded are:

Bunker Hill action reports 1943–1945—including casualty reports
Bunker Hill Medical Department action report for May 11, 1945
Bunker Hill war diaries
Bunker Hill "Report of Battle Damage Received During Action of 11 May 1945"
Bunker Hill action summaries
Bunker Hill logbook

While researching this book, I made three trips to Japan. During these visits I met with more than 100 former kamikaze pilots and their families. Japanese students formed a memorial society for the students killed in the war, called *Watatsumi*. The president of the society, Dr. Hiroyuki Okada of Hosei University, sat with me for several interviews and gave me full access to all of the Watatsumi Society's files, including the official war records of nearly every kamikaze pilot.

The Naval Historical Center at the Washington Navy Yard and the Manuscript Division of the Library of Congress both maintain helpful archives, although most of the documents at the Naval Historical Center have been transferred to the NARA. The papers of Admiral Marc Mitscher (a severely abbreviated collection, as most of his papers were destroyed in the kamikaze attack) and the papers of previous commanders of the *Bunker Hill*, including Commanders John J. Ballentine and Thomas P. Jetter, are held here. Captain George Seitz's records are spread between the Naval War College, the U.S. Navy's archives, and the archives at Annapolis.

Sailors and airmen of the *Bunker Hill* shared with me their letters, diaries, photographs, personal papers, press clippings, casualty lists, Navy press releases, official Navy personnel service records, citations, mementos (including pieces of Kiyoshi's Zero fighter), diagrams, maps, service awards, ID cards, and insurance policies.

The *Bunker Hill*'s pilots also lent me many very helpful flight logs. Dewey Ray's flight log was especially clear and detailed. Al Turnbull's diary was recovered from his water-soaked quarters on the *Bunker Hill* and this, along with the diaries of other men, became an invaluable source.

NARA maintains all of the action reports, war diaries, logbooks, and action summaries of the *Bunker Hill* and other ships in the Pacific, but they also manage the Cartographic Division, which keeps records of World War II cartography, including aerial reconnaissance photographs of the Kanoya air base and the other air bases where Kiyoshi trained. These photographs, combined with the intelligence maps and intelligence estimates based on the photos and other intelligence data, were a great help in piecing together Kiyoshi's life at these facilities.

The U.S. Navy has always required that naval ships keep strict records of all actions. During World War II, the Navy began training sailors as photographers and assigned them to create a photographic record of their ship's time at sea. The *Bunker Hill* had its own darkroom and a dedicated group of photographers and photographer's assistants. The photography teams, trained by some of America's finest photographers, created a stunning record of life aboard the *Bunker Hill*. This remarkable still photography record was enhanced by the work of a small number of men who shot moving pictures, including images of nearly every takeoff and landing aboard the *Bunker Hill*. Most of this footage has disappeared, but a surprising number of photographs taken throughout the history of the *Bunker Hill*, from the laying of her keel through her commission and sorties in the Pacific, exist in the National Archives. I was able to find photographs of nearly every compartment aboard the *Bunker Hill* mentioned in my many interviews with officers and crew. The Archives also contain on microfilm the original blueprints for the *Bunker Hill*, which allowed me to follow along with the sailors as they told their stories about the ship.

The USS *Bunker Hill* Association, led by Al Nadeau and Al Perdeck, opened up their archives to me, including their remarkable collection of the ship's official newspaper, *The Monument*, published aboard the *Bunker Hill* throughout the war and afterward by the ship's alumni association.

During the course of World War II, the United States Navy grew from a military branch of a few hundred thousand men to a force of several million and the largest fleet ever produced. The Navy had to train millions of men for complex jobs and, as an integral part of its expansion, created a series of notably well-written books that explained in detail nearly every task necessary to keep the Navy fighting, from fixing broken electric motors to flying combat in a Corsair.

I read many of these manuals, ranging from weather prediction, to first aid, to raising chickens. Many included helpful diagrams of the ships, their guns, aircraft, and engines—just about everything aboard the *Bunker Hill*. All were enormously helpful to me in understanding what it was like to join a naval force rapidly becoming the largest and most powerful that had ever existed. Especially illuminating were the booklets explaining how to fire the *Bunker Hill*'s guns and giving pilots instructions on topics such as navigation and how to lead an enemy aircraft so that it could be shot down. The Navy also produced many smaller recognition booklets that illustrate enemy and Allied forces, including aircraft and ships. These booklets were excellent aids to me for understanding both critical differences in each side's forces and the challenges faced by pilots in discerning friend from foe. The basic manual for seamen is called *The Bluejacket's Manual*. The editions of this manual that were printed during World War II proved essential.

The best estimate of casualties from Yasunori and Kiyoshi's attack comes from the *Bunker Hill*'s action report. This report tallied 352 bodies buried at sea and one more, discovered later, buried at Ulithi. Twenty-four of those buried were never identified. Forty-two men were declared missing in action and never recovered, for a total of 393 men killed in action.[*] Two hundred sixty-four men were injured in the attack, for a total of 659 casualties.

There are few extant documents from the Japanese side dealing with kamikaze operations. A great many were burned during the war in incendiary and other raids. Most military records were destroyed intentionally by the Japanese during the long lag time between the Japanese surrender and American occupation. During that period many Japanese military leaders feared that the United States would hunt down those involved in kamikaze attacks. They made it a priority to destroy the kamikaze records. Disparate military records were also hidden away throughout the islands. Some of these turned up while Japan was still under American rule, although after completion of the Strategic Bombing Survey on July 1, 1946. These captured documents were sent to the United States, and eventually returned

---

[*] The action report was filed before crewmen found the body of the missing man who was buried at Ulithi.

to Japan. The Japanese Defense Research Institute has located only a handful of documents dealing directly with kamikazes. The library and records maintained by the Japanese Defense Research Institute are surprisingly limited. Unlike the Germans, who kept voluminous records and were loath to destroy even highly incriminating documents, the Japanese military was prepared to destroy everything.

General MacArthur, however, had directed that Army officials interrogate Japanese commanders and compile a series of monographs re-creating Japanese military records. Japanese Monograph Number 86 deals specifically with the Fifth Air Fleet, and operations from Kanoya and southern Kyushu, from February through August 1945. This monograph has been made available by Patrick Clancey at the Hyperwar Foundation. The records are fairly clear about the Japanese operations up to the launch of aircraft from the bases. After take-off, however, they begin to sound more and more like typical wartime propaganda of a power that is losing a desperate struggle, and determined to keep that fact hidden.

The official Japanese reporting indicates all sorts of successes for various kamikaze operations, but it is clear that few of those aircraft that had made it beyond the halfway point were able to return. And very few struck American ships. Forty out of sixty-four Zeros were believed to have been shot down before they arrived within range of the American fleet on May 11. After a long recital of the successes of the day (which made no mention of the damage to the *Bunker Hill*), the Fifth Air Fleet requested an entirely new set of aircraft. Essentially everything was lost in the day's *Kikusui*, including the escorting fighters.

Mr. Takehiko Shibata of the Japanese Defense Research Institute looked long and hard for any mention of the flight of Kiyoshi Ogawa. Finally, in desperation and in great thoroughness, he picked up a book the Americans had deemed too insignificant to haul back to the United States. It was entitled *Naichi Kokutai*, or "Domestic Corps." These records dealt with training and air transportation within mainland Japan. The book had apparently sat on various shelves, unopened yet never discarded, for nearly sixty years until Shibata-san flipped it open. He thought perhaps that because Yatabe was a "domestic airbase," the book might mention the specific names of people who had trained there, and that this would be better than nothing. Shibata searched through the extraordinarily dry book until he arrived near its center. Bound together with the long list of standard reports was a ten-page record, mostly handwritten, that documented the flying orders at Kanoya on May 11, 1945.

The newly discovered set of records dealt specifically with the student corps, the *Bakusentai* (literally "Zero Carrier Fighter Force"— another descriptor for *tokkotai*), who had been transferred to Kanoya from the Yatabe base. Kiyoshi Ogawa's records were transcribed into the book on July 10, 1945. The Yatable Air Corps at Kanoya printed the book, made a small number of copies, and sent it out to various naval departments. Only one copy of this book is known to have survived. The Kanoya records include attacks on April 16, April 29, and May 11, 1945. The document presents every known detail about Kiyoshi's flight orders, radio transmissions along the way, and the names of those who flew side by side with him toward the American fleet.

Several translators toiled through the Japanese sources in preparation for this book. Many of the older former kamikaze pilots speak a particularly dated form of an already complex language. Their poetry often utilizes even more archaic dialect. These translators' work became integral to the construction of the book. Ko and Kumi Tanaka translated many of my first interviews with the Ogawa family and with the poet Iwama. Snow Shimazu has tirelessly translated interviews, documents, diagrams, notes, official records, and letters from those who knew Kiyoshi Ogawa and Yasunori Seizo, including family, friends, those who trained together, and schoolmates. Philip Gayle accompanied me to Japan and assisted in simultaneous translation during interviews, and in transcribing and translating those interviews later. He was assisted by Jon Rodgers, Fukushima Sawako, Miki Nakamuri, Ben Dyck, and Kirsten Henning.

Two psychiatrist, Dr. Roger Gould and Dr. Robert Rodman, both of whom taught at UCLA, helped me understand the psychology of suicide. Dr. Timothy Haydock, Chief of Emergency Medicine at Northern Westchester Hospital in Mount Kisco, New York, and Dr. Bill Luterman of the University of South Alabama Burn Center (which deals frequently with victims of oil platform fires) helped me understand the physiology of burn injuries.

This book is primarily intended as a microhistory of World War II in the Pacific. I am particularly grateful to the work of Ronald Spector and John Toland. Much of my understanding of the war, and how I placed the *Bunker Hill* within that history, is based on their seminal books.

Many survivors of the *Bunker Hill* and their family members gave me newspaper clippings. Wherever possible, I have given a full citation for those articles. For a number of them, however, I found no way of tracing the original author or paper. In those cases I have listed all available information.

Al Skaret, the pipefitter from the *Bunker Hill* who survived to become a fireman, collected the stories of many of his shipmates. He asked each of them to describe their experiences on May 11, 1945. Skaret generously provided me a copy of this collection. The men who responded came from just about every department and seem to have, collectively, been in every area of the ship. Taken together, it is a remarkable record of heroism and war.

I met Caleb Kendall's son, Timothy, at a *Bunker Hill* reunion. He spent many hours talking with me about his family history over the course of four years and gave me all his father's letters from 1943 to 1945, his naval records, and many family photographs. Harvard University provided some of Caleb's college records. Tim also introduced me to Caleb's brother, Jim Kendall, and several others who knew Caleb and helped me piece together his life. The following men and women, and/or their families submitted to interviews, donated their diaries, private memoirs, letters, military records, or personal memorabilia:

Shinichi Akiyama, Takamasa Ariyoshi, Takeo Ayama, Nicolas Baki, Donald Balch, Michael Bauriedle, Carl Bergeson, Louis Boitano, Frederik Briggs, Joseph Brocia, Duncan Cameron, Joseph Carmichael, Dean Caswell, Warner O. Chapman, Robert Charleton, Mark Cintolo,

Ralph Condo, Roma Dussault, Abe Engber, Richard Ernst, Anthony Faccone, Herbet Ferguson, Robin Field, Eugene Fielding, Keizo Fujii, Carl Galub, George Gelderman, Joe G. Gilbuena, Wallace Girts, Ralph Glenndenning, Ebby Glockner, Walter Goeggle, Alexander Girts, Jerry Hanson, Russell Hanson, Robert Earl Harris, Yuko Hazenoki, Dixon C. Hightower, Don Hoit, Wilton "Hoot" Hutt, Blaine Imel, Edward Keller, Caleb Kendall, Masuo Kimura, Charles King, William Edward Patrick King, Dee Dee Knapp, Eichiro Koba, Hikota Koguchi, Fumihide Kohari, Edward Koschen, Masao Kunimine, Edmund Langevin, Everett Francis Lanman, Robert Lapointe, Edward Leahy, Norman Leonard, Marcel Levesque, R. C. Lillie, George Lyons, Sansaku Maeda, Thomas Patrick Martin, Frank Matone, Sachio Matsunaga, Iris McNelly, Daniel and Ann Mellow, Kenneth Morgan, Al Nadeau, Makoto Nakamoto, Charles Nettles, Stanley Nicas, Shouichi Nishikawa, William O'Brien, Sachiko Ogawa, Yoko Ogawa, Kaname Okawara, Tatsuo Ono, Joe Pallares, Harry Parker, Steven Piccolo, Wilbert P. Popp, Harold Lee Posey, Larry Prince, Nunzio Pete Probo, LeRoy Wayne Richards, Henry Roesler, Edmund Skacan, Ed Scollan, Takehiko Shibata, Yousuke Shiga, Junchiro Shoji, Billy Sides, Edmund Nicholas Skacan, Al Skaret, Kenneth Somers, Patricia Somers, Thomas G. Souders, Walter Susdorf, James Swett, George Thome, Al Turnbull, Frank Viscek, Jim Walker, Kinichi Watanabe, Clinton Webster, Jack Weienthaler, Arthur Wiese, Marty Woll, Fielding Zimmerman.

ACKNOWLEDGMENTS

Thank You, Vicki, for being the most thoughtful, resolute, inspiring, clear-eyed, and stirring supporter of my work on this book. I am grateful to you and for you. I want to thank especially my talented editor, Marysue Rucci, who stuck by me, always keeping at the heart of this story the men aboard the *Bunker Hill* and their struggle. Thank you also to Sloan Harris, without whose dogged work this book would never have been printed and whose unconditional support over the last five years consistently heartened me.

Henri Bloomstein and Jackie Green read through so many drafts and gave me countless detailed notes, and I can never thank them enough. Nevertheless, I value Henri's friendship even more than his countless contributions to the manuscript. Katie Hall's gifted eye and practical sensibility made me a better writer. I thank you, Katie, for wrestling me through the later drafts of this work, making possible this final version. Thank you, my children, Maxey, Summer, and Noah, for being the greatest blessing and most fun companions any father has ever had. I could never have written the book without the generosity and support of Ben and Iliana and Spencer Strauss. Special thanks also goes to Bonnie Strauss for her constant love and caring and to Roger Gould for his steady guidance. I would like to acknowledge my mother, Ethel Kate Kennedy, for always inspiring me, and a warm thank you to my hero, Senator Edward M.

A most important thank you, of course, goes out to the men of the *Bunker Hill*, her officers, crew, airmen, and flag staff, and the men in Quincy, MA, who built her. Without their sacrifice many more Americans would have died in World War II. This book is written for those who served aboard, and especially all of those who died in service aboard the *Bunker Hill* and among Allied forces across the Pacific. But it is also a memorial to the Japanese, in particular the kamikaze pilots, who died terribly, fighting another man's war: the student draftees, forced to commit suicide, many for a cause and a government they no longer believed in.

The men of the USS *Bunker Hill* Association were, by far, my greatest resource. I met first with George Lyons who introduced me to Al Nadeau, the head of the association. Al welcomed me into his home and introduced me to all four hundred living members. I joined him at four annual reunions. Without his help I could never have written this book. Al gave me access to all of the members, and their families, and eventually to many of their letters, diaries, and personal papers.

I first learned of the *Bunker Hill* story from my friend Timothy Dickinson. I appreciate his intellect and his unyielding friendship. My great friend and mentor David Michaelis taught me how to write and how to research. But the book never would have been given a hearing if Lisa Chase and Ted Widmer had not helped me put together the book proposal and taught me how to package it. My friend Dr. Wes Hill read my manuscripts, worked tirelessly and enthusiastically, anticipating and solving every problem, enabling me to make deadlines year after year.

I am particularly grateful to David Rosenthal for his support of the manuscript and the production of the well-illustrated story of the *Bunker Hill*. He saw from our first meeting how important it is to understand the war from both perspectives, and I am privileged that my book will be published under his gifted tutelage. Several people at Simon & Schuster worked diligently to complete the book. Ginny Smith and Meredith Chamberlain spent many hours learning new computer systems, taking my calls, and answering my queries. Gypsy da Silva, my production editor, carefully steered this book through production, aware of the emotion that the story of these men deserves. Paul Dippolito produced the wonderful maps and diagrams, and made more photographs work within text than I ever imagined. Rick Pracher and Jackie Seow designed the jacket and went through more iterations than an author could reasonably have asked. Fred Chase has made my impossibly bad punctuation at last comprehensible. The many contributions by Elizabeth Mason are appreciated as well.

My unreserved admiration and thanks go to Clay Tatum, David Lande, Evan Strauss, Rich Farley, Pedro Mezquita, Vio Barco, and Brando Quillici. Ashley Spillane carried out exceptional research. Troy Campbell's steady assistance and vision has been invaluable.

Roger Gould, Bob Rodman, John Jane, Henry Smith, Robert Gerner, Larry Ronan, and Ron Karlsberg helped me to understand the psychology of suicide and war-time service aboard ship. Donald Chisholm at the Naval War College shared unstintingly with me his personal recollections and collected documents about his uncle, Joseph Carmichael.

I want to express my appreciation to Tokuo Kasai, Mr. Shoji, General Sakamato, Kentaro Tokuhiro, Tadashi Takahashi, Corky White, and the many translators who helped me understand the Japanese side of this story, including especially Snow Shimazu. Yuko Hazeboki from Waseda University, and staff researchers and archivists at the National Archives and Records Administration, Presidential Libraries, the Library of Congress, the Naval Historical Center, and especially the Kanoya Peace Museum and the Japan Defense Research Institute.

I wish to thank, too, Melody Miller, Luz Brioso, Michael Kineavy, Scott Fay, Terry Alford, Charlie Shaw, Mike and Diane Binder, Clara Bingham, Michael Karnow, Lance Khazei, Marybeth Postman, David Bender, Kent George, Brian Tarr, Dylan Dyer, John and Buffy Stewart, Larry Spagnola, David and Susan Friedson, Brad Blank, Michael Stevens, Courtney Clark, Merle Miller, Jay Senter, Nina Houghton, Tommy and Katie McGloin, Louise Hamagami, Marc Shmuger, Victor Viramontes, Bob and Sarah Nixon, Warren and Karen Behr, Rahul Sonnad, John Wilbur, Dirk and Natasha Ziff, Liz Young, Steve Smith, Kevin Ward, Marsha Cohen, Sabrina Padwa, Paul and Priscilla Ryan, Jon Reiss, Jill Goldman, George Molsbarger, Wendy and Michael Riva, Susan and Chris Graves, Paul and Nicole Bushnell, Nick and Stephanie Meyer, Chris and Craig Gillespie, Bobbi Jean and Adam Barshay, Dan Tangerlini, Daryl and Robert Offer, all of whom helped.

I am thankful to Andy Karsch, Michael Mailer, Sasha Lazard, Mandy Lande, Annette Tatum, Kymberly Marciano, Shannon Shay, Drew Hayden, Richard Zuckerwar, Jimmy Shay, Ellie Cunningham Cary, Mike Caslin, Barry Clifford, Roger Freeman, Johnny Gates, Daniel Voll, Cecilia Peck, Kent Corel, Kip Koenig, Zaab Sethna, Douglas Cruickshank, Caroline and Natalie Behr, Harper Graves, Timothy and Anthony Shriver, and especially Ena Bernard, Patrick, Teddy Jr, Kara, Douglas, Molly, Chris, Sheila, Rory, Bobby, Mary, Courtney, Joe, and Beth Kennedy, and Mark Bailey, Vicki Gifford, Henry, Diana, Clara, and Jamie Michaelis. I am deeply grateful to Marty Walsh, Beth Haugland, Justin O'Brian, Darlene O'Kane, Barbara Souliotis, and Tracy Spicer for their loyal support.

Warmest thanks to Lynn Delaney, Bryan Idler, John Creamer, Henry Smith, Ginette Trask, Walter Thompson, Cheshta Buckley, Carolyn Alliende, Shane King, Andrew Glasso, Dolores Huerta, Buzz Hemphill, Ted Webber, Edmund and Kenneth Bureau, Mike McLaughlin, Professor John Stilgoe, and Michael Wilcox. A big thank you also to Elizabeth Blozan, who worked long nights transcribing hundreds of interviews and altering countless manuscripts.

My unqualified gratitude to John Seigenthaler, Dan Stern, Marybeth Postman, Charlie Lord, Michelle Cinque-Mars, Larry Cohen, Jim Meade, Virginia Desario, Linda Semans, Hank Gladstone, Joe Hakim, Bill Robinson, Douglas Spooner, Andrew Sullivan, John Barrette, Mike Schepps, Bill Macadam, Carolyn Wills, Krystin Keane, Margot Hathaway, Greg Egan, Milton Dicus, Joe Driscoll, Reverend Gerry Creedon, Mark Falanga, K. C. Soll, Bella Lantsman, Jerry and Lynn Hawes, Bob Hoffman, Liza Ingrazi, Paul Schrade, Steven Stamstead, Bill Rosendahl, Mike Bonin, and Dr. Jeff Sachs.

BIBLIOGRAPHY

GOVERNMENT DOCUMENTS

"General Arrangement Plans: USS *Bunker Hill*."

"Imperial Rescript for Soldiers and Sailors." *Imperial Precepts*, 1882.

"Report of Operations of Carrier Air Group Eight Based Aboard USS *Bunker Hill* (CV17)." March 15–October 26, 1944.

"The USS *Bunker Hill*: The Record of a Carrier's Combat Action Against the Axis Nations in the Pacific." U.S. Department of the Navy, 1944.

"The USS *Bunker Hill* Report of Changes," filed on 28 May, 1945 (a grim, specific summary of the deaths and injuries of crew-members).

Anonymous. "Pilot's Handbook of Flight Operating Instructions for Navy Models F6F-3, F6F-3N, F6F-5, F6F-5N Airplanes." Date unknown.

Anonymous. "World War II Histories and Historical Reports in the US Naval History Division." 1997.

Deane, J. R., and F. B. Royal. "Report on Operations in the Pacific and Far East in 1943–44." 1973.

Levy, E. S. (Carrier Air Group Air Intelligence Officer). "Report of Operations of Carrier Air Group Eight Based Aboard the USS *Bunker Hill* (CV17), 15 March 1944 to 26 October 1944." 1944.

National Defense Research Committee. "Weapon Data: Fire Impact Explosion." 1945.

Naval Analysis Division. *United States Strategic Bombing Survey (Pacific)*. Washington, D. C.: U.S. Government Printing Office, 1946.

Naval History Division. *Dictionary of American Naval Fighting Ships*. Washington, D.C.: Navy Department, 1959.

The Office of the Chief of Naval Operations. "U.S. Naval Aviation in the Pacific." United States Navy, 1947.

Operational Archives, U.N.H.C. "Microfilm Publication 3: Bulletins of the Intelligence Center, Pacific Ocean Areas, Joint Intelligence Center, Pacific Ocean Area and the Commander in Chief Pacific and Pacific Ocean Area 1942–1946." Edited by anonymous, 1994.

Photographs in the Still Picture Collection at the National Archives. (This photo collection was especially helpful to me in learning how the ship worked. Many of these were in Box 80-G, Numbered 99–2042. These photos tell nearly the whole story of the *Bunker Hill*, from launching at Fall River through the completion of her active service.)

Song and Service Book for Ship and Field: Army and Navy. New York: A. S. Barnes, 1942.

The United States Government. "USS *Bunker Hill* Awards." Edited by anonymous, 1945.

The United States Joint Intelligence Committee. "Japan's Secret Weapon: Suicide." 1945.

The United States Strategic Bombing Survey. "Summary Report: Pacific War." Washington, D.C.: U.S. Government Printing Office, July 1, 1946.

The United States Strategic Bombing Survey. "The Effects of Strategic Bombing on Japan's War Economy." Washington, D.C.: U.S. Government Printing Office, December 1946.

The United States Strategic Bombing Survey. "Final Reports of the United States Strategic Bombing Survey 1945–1947." 1977.

BOOKS

Appleman, Roy Edgar. *Okinawa: The Last Battle*. Washington, D.C.: Historical Division, Department of the Army, 1948.

Balch, Donald. *In the Ready Room: KAMIKAZE!*

Baldwin, Frank, et al. "The Saga of the Fighting Falcons: Marine Fighter Squadron 221," 2003. (This is an unpublished collection of memoirs from VNF-221, including specific writings of Frank Baldwin, Donald Balch, Fred Briggs, Joseph Brocia, Eugene Cameron, Dean Caswell, Warner Chapman, Blaine Imel, George Johns, and James Swett, many of whom also submitted to interviews.)

Barker, A. J. *Suicide Weapon*. London: Pan/Ballantine, 1971.

Barker, Ralph. *The Hurricats*. London: Pelham, 1978.

Bennett, Charles. *Ojai Valley's Veterans Stories: Veterans Stories of the Ojai Valley Veterans of Foreign Wars, Post 11461*. Committee Communications, 2002.

Black, Allida, et al. *The Eleanor Roosevelt Papers—Raymond Clapper*. Hyde Park, NY: Eleanor Roosevelt National Historical Site, 2003.

Brinkley, Alan. *The Unfinished Nation: A Concise History of the American People*. New York: Alfred A. Knopf, 1997.

Brokaw, Tom. *The Greatest Generation*. New York: Delta/Random House, 2001.

Bryan III, J. *Aircraft Carrier*. New York: Ballantine, 1954.

Calhoun, Raymond C. (Captain). *Typhoon: The Other Enemy*. Annapolis: Naval Institute Press, 1981.

Canterbury, C. Clapper. *Descendants*. Edited by anonymous. Cathy Canterbury, 2001.

Chihaya, M. (trans.), and Dillon Goldstein. *Fading Victory: The Diary of Admiral Matome Ugaki, 1941–1945*. Pittsburgh: University of Pittsburgh Press, 1991.

Clapper, Raymond. *Watching the World, 1934–1944*. London: Whittlesey House, 1944.

Cressman, R. J. *The Official Chronology of the US Navy in World War II*. Edited by anonymous, 2004.

Decade of Triumph: The 40s. Alexandria, VA: Time-Life Books, 1999.

Donovan, Robert J. PT 109: *John F. Kennedy in World War II*. New York: McGraw-Hill, 1961.

Edwards, Bernard. *Blood and Bushido: Japanese Atrocities at Sea, 1941–1945*. 2nd ed. (1st ed., 1991). New York: Brick Tower Press, 1997.

Faltum, Andrew. The *Essex Aircraft Carriers*. Baltimore: The Nautical and Aviation Company of America, 1996.

Ferry, Charles. *Raspberry One*. Boston: Houghton Mifflin, 1983.

Francillon, Rene J. *Japanese Aircraft of the Pacific War*. Annapolis: Naval Institute Press, 1970.

Friedman, Norman. *U.S. Aircraft Carriers: An Illustrated Design History*. Annapolis: Naval Institute Press, 1983. (Friedman was probably the most helpful author for me in learning the workings of the guns used aboard the *Bunker Hill*, and especially of the design of the ship and the compromises made necessary in the design and construction of the Essex Class, as well as the specific layout and vulnerabilities of the *Bunker Hill*.)

Greer, Captain Marshal R., USN (director). *The USS* Bunker Hill, *November 1943–November 1944: The Record of a Carrier's Combat Action Against the Axis Nations in the Pacific*. Chicago & Dixon: Rogers Printing Co., 1945.

A Guide to the Reports of the United States Strategic Bombing Survey. London: Royal Historical Society, 1981.

Hoyt, Edwin P. *The Carrier War*. New York: Avon, 1987.

———. *The Kamikazes*. New Jersey: Buford, 1999.

———. *The Last Kamikaze: The Story of Admiral Matome Ugaki*. Westport, CT: Praeger, 1993.

———. *Leyte Gulf*. New York: Avon, 1972.

———. *McCampbell's Heroes: The Story of the U.S. Navy's Most Celebrated Carrier Fighters of the Pacific War*. New York: Van Nostrand Reinhold, 1983.

———. *The Men of* Gambier Bay. New York: Avon, 1981.

Ichinose, Tomoji. *Theories and Practices of Mixed Economy Systems: A Comparative Look at the Japanese Experience*. Tokyo: Research Institute of Public Management, 1996.

Inoguchi, Rikihei, and Tadashi Nakajima. *Divine Wind: Japan's Kamikaze Force in World War II*. Annapolis: United States Naval Institute, 1958. (A seminal work on the IJN kamikazes, edited by Roger Pineau, who interviewed surviving Japanese kamikaze leadership, including Rikihei Inoguchi, as part of the Strategic Bombing Survey, and who pieced together the story of Japan's initiation of kamikaze tactics. Those parts of my book dealing with Admiral Onishi and the first kamikazes in the Philippines are based almost entirely on the narratives contained in this book.)

Johnston, Stanley. *Queen of the Flat-Tops*. New York: E. P. Dutton, 1942.

Jones, Ken, and Hubert Kelley, Jr. *Admiral Arleigh (31-Knot) Burke: The Story of a Fighting Sailor*. Philadelphia: Chilton, 1962.

Kahn, E. J. *The Stragglers*. New York: Random House, 1962.

Lamont-Brown, Raymond. *Kamikaze: Japan's Suicide Samurai*. London: Arms and Armour Press. 1977.

Lord, Walter. *A Night to Remember*. New York: Holt, Rinehart Winston, 1955.

MacArthur, Douglas. *Reminiscences*. New York: McGraw-Hill, 1964.

Maloney, Tom. *U.S. Navy War Photographs—Pearl Harbor to Tokyo Bay*. New York: Bonanza, 1984

Maraini, Fosco. *Meeting with Japan*, 2nd ed. New York: Viking, 1969.

Markey, Morris. *Well Done! An Aircraft Carrier in Battle Action*. New York: D. Appleton-Century, 1950.

Matsunaga, Ichiro, Kan Sagahara, and Gordon J. Van Wylen. *Encounter at Sea and a Heroic Lifeboat Journey*. Troy: Sabre, 1994.

Mayer, S. L., ed. *The Rise and Fall of Imperial Japan: 1894–1945*. New York: Military Press, 1984.

Millot, Bernard. Lowell Blair, trans. *Divine Thunder; The Life and Death of the Kamikazes*. New York: McCall, 1971.

Nagare, Masayuki. *The Life of a Samurai Artist*. New York: Weatherhill, 1994.

Nagatsuka, Ryuji. Nina Rootes, trans. *I Was a Kamikaze: The Knights of the Divine Wind*. London: Abelard-Schuman, 1972.

Naito, Hatsuho. *Thunder Gods: The Kamikaze Pilots Tell Their Story*. New York: Kodansha International, 1989. (This book was gathered together by a fraternal organization of Ohka pilots who did not fly their last mission. It contains numerous accounts of life at Kanoya, the bombed-out schoolhouse where Kiyoshi spent his last days, and even Kiyoshi's last morning at the base.)

Nichols, David, ed. *Ernie's War: The Best of Ernie Pyle's World War II Dispatches.* New York: Random House, 1986.

Office of the Chief of Naval Operations. *U.S. Naval Aviation in the Pacific.* United States Navy, 1947.

Office of the Chief of Naval Operations, Naval History Division. *United States Naval Chronology: World War II.* Washington, D.C.: U.S. Government Printing Office, 1955.

Ofstie, R. A. *The Campaigns of the Pacific War: United States Strategic Bombing Survey* (Pacific)—Naval Analysis Division. Washington, D.C.: U.S. Government Printing Office, 1946.

Olds, Robert. *Helldiver Squadron: The Story of Carrier Bombing Squadron 17 with Task Force 58.* New York: Dodd, Mead, 1944.

Omura, Bunji. *The Last Genro—Rince Saionji: The Man Who Westernized Japan.* Philadelphia: J. B. Lippincott, 1938.

O'Neill, Richard. *Suicide Squads: WWII—Axis and Allied Special Task Weapons of World War II: Their Development and Their Missions.* New York: St. Martin's Press, 1982.

Overy, Richard. *Why the Allies Won.* New York: W. W. Norton, 1995.

Pawlowski, Gareth L. *Flat Tops and Fledglings: A History of American Aircraft Carriers.* New York: Castle, 1971.

Phillips, Christopher. *Steichen at War.* New York: Portland House, 1981.

Pinguet, Maurice. *Voluntary Death in Japan.* Cambridge, MA: Polity Press, 1993.

Polman, Norman. *Aircraft Carriers: A Graphic History of Carrier Aviation and Its Influence on World Events.* Garden City: Doubleday, 1969.

Popp, Wilbert P. "Beads." *The Survival of a WWII Navy Fighter Pilot.* (This unpublished recollection of "Beads" Popp covers in great detail his time aboard the *Bunker Hill* and training at Alameda with Air Group 84. It was enormously helpful in laying out a basic timeline for the ship and her crew, as well as giving very specific information about the day-to-day activities of airmen aboard the ship and their combat experiences. Popp supplemented this written record with several interviews that were both illuminating and fun.)

Raven, Alan. *Essex-Class Carriers.* Annapolis: Naval Institute Press, 1988. (Much of my description of the architecture and design of the *Bunker Hill* is based on Raven's book.)

Reynolds, Clark G. *The Fast Carriers: The Forging of an Air Navy.* Annapolis: Naval Institute Press, 1982. (The absolutely essential, detailed history of the carrier task force.)

Roberts, John. *The Aircraft Carrier* Intrepid. Annapolis: Naval Institute Press, 1982.

Sakai, Saburo, with Martha Caidin and Fred Saito. *SAMURAI!* New York: Doubleday, 1957.

Sakamoto, Kerri. *One Hundred Million Hearts.* New York: Alfred A. Knopf, 2003.

Schafer, Ronald. *Wings of Judgment: American Bombing in World War II.* New York: Oxford University Press, 1985.

Sears, Stephen W. *Carrier War in the Pacific.* New York: American Heritage, 1966.

Seward, Jack. *Hara-Kiri: Japanese Historical Suicide.* Rutland: Charles E. Tuttle, 1969.

Shimizu, Tsukasa. *Waseda University: A Photographic History of 100 Years (1882–1982).* Tokyo: Waseda University, 1982.

Sides, Hampton. *Ghost Soldiers.* New York: Doubleday, 2001.

Sledge, E. B. *With the Old Breed—At Peleliu and Okinawa.* New York: Oxford Unversity Press, 1990.

Smith, Martin Cruz. *December 6.* New York: Simon & Schuster, 2002.

Smith, Michael C. *Essex Class Carriers in Action.* Carrollton, TX: Squadron Signal Publications, date unknown. (This simple book was an excellent supplement to Friedman's and Raven's design histories.)

Smith, Peter C. *The History of Dive Bombing.* Annapolis: The Nautical Aviation Publishing Company, 1982.

Spector, Ronald H. *Eagle Against the Sun: The American War with Japan.* New York: Free Press, 1985.

Spurr, Russell. *A Glorious Way to Die: The Kamikaze Mission of the Battleship* Yamato, *April 1945.* New York: Newmarket, 1981.

St. John, Philip A. *USS* Essex *CV/CVA/CVS-9.* Kentucky: Turner, 1999.

Stanton, Doug. *In Harm's Way: The Sinking of the USS* Indianapolis *and the Extraordinary Story of Its Survivors.* New York: Henry Holt, 2001.

Steichen, Edward, ed. *U.S. Navy War Photographs: Pearl Harbor to Tokyo Harbor.* New York: US Camera.

Tillman, Barrett. *Helldiver Units in World War II.* London: Osprey, 1997.

Toland, John. *The Rising Sun: The Decline and Fall of the Japanese Empire, 1936–1945.* New York: Random House, 1970.

Treanor, Tom. *One Damn Thing After Another.* Garden City: Double-day, Doran, 1944.

Tsunoda, Ryusaku, Wm. Theodore de Bary, and Donald Keene, eds. *Sources of Japanese Tradition,* Volumes I and II. New York: Columbia University Press, 1958.

Turnbull, S. R. *The Samurai: A Military History.* New York: Mac-millan, 1977.

Turnbull, Stephen. *The Samurai Sourcebook.* London: Arms and Armour Press, 1998.

Udoff, Irv. *The* Bunker Hill *Story.* Paducah, KY. Turner, 1994. (This Turner publication was created by Irv Udoff, who edited the *Bunker Hill*'s ship's newspaper, *The Monument.* After the war, Udoff pieced together a series of interviews with crewmem-bers, plus their own recollections, to create a sort of unofficial history of the *Bunker Hill.* The book includes excerpts from the ship's log. Udoff made the documents on which he based his book available to me, and I am grateful for his generosity).

Uhnuki-Tierney, Emiko. *Kamikaze, Cherry Blossoms, and National-isms: The Militarization of Aesthetics in Japanese History.* Chi-cago: University of Chicago Press, 2002.

The United States Government Printing Office. *Handbook of Japa-nese Explosive Ordnance.* Washington D. C.: U.S. Government Printing Office, 1945.

United States Navy. *The Bluejacket's Manual, Eleventh Edition.* Annapolis: United States Naval Institute, 1943.

United States Navy. *The Bluejacket's Manual, Twelfth Edition.* Anna-polis: United States Naval Institute, 1944.

Vanneman, B. "Who We Are—September 2003 The Planet News-letter—Sierra Club—Lloyd Tupling." *The Planet Newsletter*, edited by anonymous, Sierra Club, 2003.

Warner, Denis, Peggy Warner, and Sadao Seno. *The Sacred Warriors: Japan's Suicide Legions.* Cincinnati: Van Nostrand Reinhold, 1982.

White, William Lindsay. *They Were Expendable.* New York: Harcourt, Brace, 1942.

Winton, John. *War in the Pacific: Pearl Harbor to Tokyo Bay.* New York: Mayflower, 1978.

Woodward, C. Vann. *The Battle for Leyte Gulf.* New York: Ballantine, 1947.

Yokuta, Yutaka, and Joseph D. Harrington. *The Kaiten Weapon.* New York: Ballantine, 1962.

Yoshimura, Akira. *One Man's Justice.* San Diego: Harvest Harcourt, 1978.

ACADEMIC PUBLICATIONS

A great deal of work has been done by modern academics, including psychiatrists and psychologists, studying the modern phenomenon of suicide bombings, which, while different in many ways from the practice of Japan's kamikaze pilots, still informs their experience. Following are the psychological studies I found most helpful.

"Countering Suicide Terrorism: An International Conference." The International Policy Institute for Counter-Terrorism at the Interdisciplinary Center Herzliya Conference, February 20–23, 2000.

Dale, Stephen Frederic. "Religious Suicide in Islamic Asia: Anticolonial Terrorism in India, Indonesia, and the Philippines." *Journal of Conflict Resolution*, date unknown.

Gordon, Harvey. "The 'Suicide' Bomber: Is It a Psychiatric Phenomenon?" *Psychiatric Bulletin*, No. 26, 2002.

Kushner, Harvey W. "Suicide Bombers: Business as Usual." *Studies in Conflict and Terrorism*, No. 19, 1996.

Luft, Gal. "The Palestinian H-Bomb: Terror's Winning Strategy." *Foreign Affairs*, 2002.

Rapoport, David C. "Fear and Trembling: Terrorism in Three Religious Traditions." *American Political Science Review*, No. 78, 1984.

Taylor, Maxwell, and Helen Ryan. "Fanatics, Political Suicide and Terrorism." *Terrorism*, 1988.

NEWSPAPERS, MAGAZINES, AND JOURNALS

Adams, Steve. "Memorial Day Observances; Marine Killed in Vietnam Is Honored." *Patriot Ledger*, May 26, 1998.

"Add Three Stars to Your Ribbons." *The Monument*, No. 2, 1944.

Ash, Timothy Garton. "Is There a Good Terrorist?" *New York Review of Books*, Vol. XL VIII, 2001.

"Aviation Celebration." *New Hampshire Sunday News*, September 23, 2001.

"Aviator Faced Danger Many Times but Came Home." *Orlando Sentinel*, 1999.

"Beaverton High School." *The Hummer*, 1977.

Bergstein, Brian. "WWII Relics Returned; Suicide Pilot's Effects Found in Kansas Garage." Associated Press, San Francisco, March 30, 2001.

Bermann, R. B. "*Bunker Hill* Now in Bremerton Yard." *Seattle Post-Intelligencer*, June 27, 1945.

"Bombed Out—After Seeing Action at Iwo Jima." *Baltimore News-Post*, August 1945.

Brown, Matthew. "Veterans with Bond Meet 50 Years Later." *Hartford Courant*. November 11, 1995.

"*Bunker Hill* Lives Through Fiery Ordeal." Associated Press, June 28, 1945.

"*Bunker Hill* Makes Her Last Cruise." Associated Press, date unknown.

Burke, Rear Admiral A. A. "Character" (speech—1952), Washington, D.C., Navy Yard.

Burke, Arleigh A. "Arleigh A. Burke—Transcribed Narratives." 2003. (These narratives, an oral history by Arleigh Burke still stored at the U.S. Naval Historical Center at the Washington, D.C., Navy Yard, are a brillant first-person record of Burke's service and his time aboard the *Bunker Hill*).

Burrows, Leo H. "Rebel Leader, Hostilities Have Ceased." *Naval History*, July/August, 1995.

"Carrier Hit by Suicide Planes, Toll 656." *New York Daily Mirror*, June 28, 1945.

"Carrier Smash Horrible Sight." I.N.S., date unknown.

Casey, Gene R. "373 Navy Men Died as Jap Planes Made Carrier *Bunker Hill* a Torch." *Boston Daily Globe*, 1945.

"Casualties Total 656." Associated Press, June 27, 1945.

"Chaplain Fought Flames for 11 Hours." *Boston Globe*, date unknown.

Clapper, Raymond. "Their Skipper." Date unknown.

"Commodore Seitz Dead in Honolulu: Military Governor of Marshall Islands Was Wartime Chief of Carrier *Bunker Hill*." *New York Times*, 1947.

"Cool Heroism Saves the Ship." *New York Daily Mirror*, June 28, 1945.

"Daughter of Air Hero Awarded Medals by Navy." Date unknown.

"Design Histories of United States Warships of World War II, the Essex Class (Part 1)." *Warship International*, 1999.

Dudley, Kristine. "Purple Heart Recipient Writes About Fateful Day." *Tulsa World*, 2000.

Dunne, John Gregory. "The Okinawa Nightmare." *New York Review of Books*, Vol. 48, 2001.

Edwards, Greg. "2 Recall Their Final, Terrible Day on U.S.S. *Bunker Hill*." *Roanoke Times and World News*, May 29, 1995.

Egelko, Bob. "Kamikaze Pilot's Keepsakes Finally Find Way to His Family." *San Diego Union Tribune*, 2001.

Epstein, Aaron. "Former Justice White Dies at 84." *Baltimore Sun*, April 16, 2002.

"Famed *Bunker Hill* Reaches Seattle." *Seattle Post-Intelligencer*, October 24, 1945.

"Flyers in Truk Raid Pass Thru Chicago." *Chicago Daily Tribune*, 1944.

"Fremont Youths Enter Service." Periodical and date unknown.

Gault, Owen, and Robert Olds. "Start Engines: The Saga of the *Bunker Hill*." *Air Classics*, date unknown.

"Gilberto. Frank Gilberto." *Hartford Courant*, September 17, 1997.

Goldin, D. "Raymond Clapper." Edited by anonymous, *Radio Gold Index*, 2004.

"Harold Posey on Leave from Navy." Date unknown.

"Harold Posey Spending 30-Day Leave in States." Date unknown.

Houle, Barbara. "King of the Castle." *Telegram & Gazette*. May 13, 1998.

Imel, Blaine. "Purple Heart Recipient Writes About Fateful Day." *Your Community World*, January 5, 2000.

"Income Tax Returns." *The Monument*, No. 1, 1943.

"Irvin Udoff Attached to Carrier." *The Guide*, October 25, 1945.

"Jap Bombs Kill 373 on Big U.S. Carrier." *Seattle Post-Intelligencer*, 1945.

"Japs Blast Flagship Carrier; 373 Die." *Daily News*, 1945.

"Japanese Suicide Planes Scored Two Direct Bomb Hits on the Carrier *Bunker Hill*." Associated Press, June 27, 1945.

"Kamikaze's Items Returned." Associated Press, date unknown.

Kapur, N. "Cato and His Heirs: Roman Ideas of Suicide." Edited by anonymous, 2000.

———. "Divine Winds and Ancient Heroes: Reconstructing Kamikaze Ideology." Edited by anonymous, 2002. *Roanoke Times and World News*.

"Knot Burke Dead at 94." United Press International, January 1, 1996.

"Local Boys Safe on Carrier." *Daily Evening Item*, 1945.

"Local Vet Honored with 7 Medals." *The Herald*, 1995.

Manson, Frank A. "'Get the *Yamato*!' The Sinking of Japan's Last Super-Battleship." *Sea Classics*, No. 30, 1997.

"Mitscher's Carrier Blasted; 392 Lost." *Los Angeles Examiner*, 1945.

Mozai, Torao. "The Lost Fleet of Kublai Khan." *National Geographic*. No. 162, 1982.

Narvis, Marion. "Flier Who Helped Sink Her Says *Yamato* Was Help-
    ful." *Honolulu Star-Bulletin*, 1945.

"1945: The Year in Pictures, May 9–September 2." *Life*, June 5, 1995.

Nolte, Carl. "Doing His Duty." *San Francisco Chronicle,* March 29,
    2001.

"Notes from the *Globe*." *Boston Daily Globe*. June 28, 1945.

"Obituary of Commander Charles Owen." *The Daily Telegraph*,
    October 24, 2001.

Orr, Jack. "The Holiday Express: U.S.S. *Bunker Hill*'s Run to Glory."
    Date unknown.

"Over Japan." *Recognition Journal*.

Owen, Joseph. "WWII Sub Officer, Torpedoed Officer Collaborate
    on Book." *Pacific Stars and Stripes*, 1996.

"Posey Boys Met in South Pacific Port." Date unknown.

Powers, Thomas. "The Trouble with the CIA." *New York Review of
    Books*, Vol. 49, No. 1, 2002.

Public Information Office. "Captain of USS *Bunker Hill* Stresses
    Need of Speedy Repair of Battle Damage." Edited by anony-
    mous, 1945.

"Relics Return to Kamikaze's Family." *Dallas Morning News*, 2001.

Reynolds, H. K. "392 Die on Huge Carrier *Bunker Hill*." *Daily Record*,
    1945.

Riley, Pat. "Reunion Brings Rejoicing, Remorse." *The Enterprise*, 1989.

Rodman, Robert. "Psychoanalysis in the Twenty-first Century: A
    Moment of Reflection." University of São Paolo, April 6, 2002.

Sanders, Jacquin. "50 Years Ago—Okinawa—The Last Battlefield."
    St. Petersburg Times, April 2, 1995.

Sasaki, M. "Who Became Kamikaze Pilots, and How Did They Feel
    Towards Their Suicide Mission?" *Concord Review*, 1997.

Skacan, Edmund. "Editorial: Letters to the Editor—'Mercy Is a War-
    time Virtue.'" *Pittsburgh Post-Gazette*, November 5, 2001.

Staff writer. "Raymond Clapper." *New York Times*, 1944.

Staff writer. "Obituary—Mark R. Clapper." *Daily Star Online*, 2003.

Stokes, C. Ray. *Bunker Hill*'s Airmen Brought Down 100 Jap Planes
    Before Carrier Put Out of Action." *Lewiston Evening Journal*,
    1945.

Stork, Joe. "Erased in a Moment: Suicide Bombing Attacks Against Israeli Civilians." Publication unknown, 2002.

"Survivors in Rites Aboard *Bunker Hill*." Date unknown.

"Swords into Ploughshares." *News from Hope College*, 1994.

"The German People." *Life*, 1945.

Tuppling, Lloyd. "Aboard Vice Admiral Marc A. Mitscher's Flagship." United Press International, date unknown.

"373 Killed! 264 Wounded!" Associated Press Wire Photos, June 27, 1945.

"373 Killed, 263 Wounded, and 19 Lost." *Seattle Times*, 1945.

"2 Jap Fliers Take 656 Toll on Carrier." *Boston Herald*, 1945.

"Two Posey Boys in the Navy." Date unknown.

Udoff, Irving. "The Sailor Behind the Photo." *Proceedings*, May 1995.

———. "We've Been Hit!" *The Guide*, date unknown.

———. "With the Armed Forces: News and Gossip of Marylanders in U.S. Services. *The Guide*, 1945.

"U.S. Carrier Blasted!" *Los Angeles Times*, 1945.

VanOrman, Bill. "The Battle for the *Bunker Hill*," 43–65.

———. "The Holiday Express & The Battle for the *Bunker Hill*." *Sea Classics*, No. 6, 1973.

Vogel, Steve. "For Navajos, an Award of Gratitude." *Washington Post*, 2001.

Walker, Dana Sue. "Architect Imel Honored with OU Professorship." *Tulsa World*, June 14, 1999.

Walker, Tom. "Wartime Reading." *News-Journal*, 2004.

"Walker Knapp Home from Sea with Five Battle Stars." Date unknown.

Weinberg, Steven. "Can Missile Defense Work?" *New York Review of Books*, Vol. 49, 2002.

Whitely, Peyton. "Slow Death for a Carrier." *New York Times*, date unknown.

Wilson, Col. Randy. "The Final Stepping Stones." *United States Naval Institute: History*, June 1995.

Woll, Lt.(jg) Martin P. "Kamikaze." *Wings of Gold*, 1997.

———. "Kamikaze." *Foundation*, Spring 1997.

———. "Breeches-Buoy: AKA Bosun's Chair." *Fox Tales*, July 2002.

"World War II Warlord Remembers Air Battles with Japanese." Department of Defense, February 14, 1997.

Yoshida, Mitsuru. "The End of the *Yamato*." *United States Naval Institute Proceedings*, No. 78, 1952.

WEB REFERENCES

Note: those pages marked with ** cannot be found at the time of printing, but in most cases the root web exists.

Accident-Report.com: Military Aviation Incident Reports.
http://www.accident-report.com/

Albright, Steven. "Squadron History." Tailhook Magazine.
http://warlords.hobbyvista.com/history.htm

American Aircraft of World War II.
http://www.daveswarbirds.com/uplanes/

Anonymous. "Tactics Used by the 56th FG."
http://www.56thfightergroup.org/tac.html

Boeing Company: History.
http://www.boeing.com/history/

Bunker Hill Discussion Deck.
http://jollyroger.com/zz/ymilitaryd/BUNKERHILLhall/cas/2.html

**http://www.chinfo.navy.mil/navpalib/allhands/ah0197/rankrate
.html

**http://www.chinfo.navy.mil/navpalib/organization/org-top.html

Clancey, Patrick. "About Me." 2006.
http://ftp 1.us.proftpd.org/hyperwar/clancey.html
Patrick Clancey's contribution to the Web as a useful database is nonpareil.

DANFS Online: Aircraft Carriers.
http://www.hazegray.org/danfs/carriers/

Federation of American Scientists: Introductory Military Equipment Tutorials.
http://www.fas.org/man/dod-101/sys/dumb/index.html

**http://www.finerartmodels.com/yorktown_0002_26.htm

Flight Journal Magazine.
http://www.flightjournal.com

High Iron Illustrations—Col. James Swett.
http://www.highironillustrations.com/rogues/james_swett.html

**http://www.hilssborowi.com/MARC_A~1.html

HullNumber.com Listing: USS *Bunker Hill* CV-17.
http://www.hullnumber.com/CV-17

Imperial Japanese Navy Page.
http://www.combinedfleet.com

Index of hyperwar/USN/ships.
http://ibilio.org/hyperwar/USN/ships

Kinney, Orus. "Secret Nazi Smart Bombs in WWII."
http://www.kilroywashere.org/003-Pages/03-OrusKinney.html

Links: World War II in the Air & at Sea.
http://www.teacheroz.com/WWIIAirSea.htm

List of War Journalists.
http://www.spartacus.schoolnet.co.uk/2WWreporters.htm

**http://www.mediacen.navy.mil/pubs/allhands/nov98/Novpg40.htm

McKnight, Jack. "Weary." Diary. March 1945.
http://www.sinclair.edu/sec/his103/diary/103d01n.htm

Military.com Unit Page for USS *Bunker Hill*.
http://unitpages.military.com/unitpages/unit.do?id=20019

ModelShipbuilding.com: Essex Class Carriers from the 1950's to the 1980's.
http://www.modelshipbuilding.com/essexclass.htm

National Park Service: Raymond Clapper Biography.
http://www.nps.gov/archive/elro/glossary/clapper-raymond.htm

Naval Historical Center Online Library of Selected Images: USS
    Bunker Hill.
http://www.history.navy.mil/photos/sh-usn/usnsh-b/cv17.htm

NavSource Online: Aircraft Carrier Photo Archive for the USS
    Bunker Hill (CV-17).
http://www.navsource.org/archives/02/17.htm

**http://www.northgrum.com/news/rev_mag/review08_02_3.html

Navy History: Personal Experiences on the USS *Bunker Hill.*
http://www.multied.com/NAVY/stories/bunkerhill.html

Royal Marshall Islands Embassy: Nuclear Issues Links.
http://www.rmiembassyus.org/Nuclear%20Issues.htm

**http://www.stanford.edu/~nickpk/writings/Kamikaze.html

**http://www.stanford.edu/~nickpk/writings/Romansuicide.html

Schoenherr, Steven. "Ernie Pyle." Revised 2007.
http://history.sandiego.edu/gen/ww2Timeline/erniepyle.html

Sasaki, Mako. "Who Became Kamikaze Pilots, and How Did They
    Feel Towards Their Suicide Mission?"
http://www.tcr.org/kamikaze.html

SciFiJapan.com Review: *Eiji Tsuburaya: Master of Monsters.*
http://www.scifijapan.com/articles/2008/01/06/review-eiji
    -tsuburaya-master-of-monsters/

SteelNavy.com: USS *Bunker Hill.*
http://www.steelnavy.com/BunkerHillPM.htm

TotalNavy.com: Online Resource for all things that are Navy!
http://www.totalnavy.com/

United States Military Enlisted Rank Insignia.
http://www.defenselink.mil/specials/insignias/enlisted.html

United States Navy *All Hands* Magazine Archive.
http://www.navy.mil/allhands.asp

United States Navy Memorial Online.
http://www.lonesailor.org/

United States Navy Organization.
http://www.navy.mil/navydata/orgnization/org-top.asp

University of Chicago Chronicle Archive. "Biographical Study
    Unveils Some of Justice Byron White's Mystery."
http://chronicle.unchicago.edu/981029/hutchinson.shtml

University of Montana School of Journalism, Veterans History Proj-
    ect: Allen Houston and Jack Weidenfeller.
http://www.umt.edu/journalism/veterans_history_project/jacobs
    .html

Unknown author. "Obituary: Byron White."
http://www.guardian.co.uk/news/2002/apr/18/guardianobituaries

USS Enterprise CV6 – Site Map – Sources and Credits.
http://www.cv6.org/site/reference.htm

Virginia Fights: World War II.
http://www.vahistory.org/WWII/index.php

Virginia Fights: World War II – Image Archive.
http://www.vcdh.virginia.edu/vahistory/WWII/image_archive/
    image_archive.php?location=92&page=image_archive

VectorSite.Net: Writings in the Public Domain.
http://www.vectorsite.net/

Warbird Alley: Privately-owned, vintage, ex-military aircraft.
http://www.warbirdalley.com

Warbird Resource Group: Mitsubishi J2M Raiden (Thunderbolt).
http://www.warbirdsresourcegroup.org/IJARG/j2mraiden.html

Whittington, Herschel. "Destined to Fly." *Dispatch*, Vol. 21, No. 3,
    Fall 1996.

http://rwebs.net/dispatch/output.asp?ArticleID=40

Wikipedia entry: USS *Bunker Hill*.
http://en.wikipedia. org/wiki/USS_Bunker_Hill_(CV-17)

**http://www1.itnet.com.pl/~wojmos/KAMIKAZE

Wilbur, Ted. "The First Flight Across the Atlantic." From *The Smith-sonian,* 1969.
http://history.sandiego.edu/gen/ww2Timeline/firstflight.html

Wilson, Randy. "The Final Stepping Stones." *Dispatch*, Vol. 20, No. 1, Spring 1995.
http://rwebs.net/dispatch/output.asp?ArticleID=48

MUSEUMS

Chiran Tokko Heiwa Kaikan
(Peace Museum for Kamikaze
   Pilots)
17881 Kori Chiran-Cho
Kawanabe-Gun
Kagoshima, Japan

Harvard Map Collection
Harvard College Library
Cambridge, Massachusetts
   02138

Kanoya Peace Museum
JMSDF Base, Kanoya
Kagoshima Prefecture
Kyushu, Japan

The Manuscript Reading Room
The Library of Congress
101 Independence Avenue SE
Room LM 101
James Madison Memorial Bldg.
Washington, D.C. 20540-4680

The National Institute for
   Defense Studies
Department of Military History

2-2-1 Nakameguro, Meguro-ku
Tokyo, Japan 153-8648

Naval Historical Center
805 Kidder Breese Street SE
Washington Navy Yard, DC
   20374-5060

Togo Shrine,
Harajuku
Tokyo, Japan

The United States Navy Memorial
701 Pennsylvania Avenue NW
Washington, D.C. 20004

The U.S. National Archives and
   Records Administration
   (NARA)
8601 Adelphi Road
College Park, MD 20740-6001

Yasukuni Jinia Yushukan
3-1-1-Kudan-Kita
Chiyoda-Ku
Tokyo, Japan

INDEX

Page numbers in italics refer to illustrations.

Adams, John Quincy, 13
adrenaline, 291, 306, 383–84, 395
Air Aft, 295
Air Combat Intelligence (ACI) unit, 79
Air Department, 78–79, 83
Air Group 17, 71, 75
Air Group 84, 71, 74, 75, 134–37,
  189–90, 236, 253
  Yamato and, 202–11
Air Plot, 78–79
Akatonbo biplanes, 95–96
Ako, 257–58
Akutan Island, 105
Alameda, 134, *169*, 173
Alaska, USS, 137, 429
Albacore (U.S. submarine), 112
Aleutian Islands, 20, 36, 39, 42, 105,
  116
altitude chamber, 72–73
aluminum, *133, 321*, 323, *323*, 335, 402,
  411, 449
Amamioshima, 213
American Century, 7
ammunition, 59, 192, 241, 277, 278*n*,
  349*n*
  May 11 attacks and, 301, 316, 317,
    346, 362, 365, 367, 402
  stewardsmates and, 172–73
  weight of, 56, 61
Anderson, Maxwell, 46
Androso, E. V., 155*n*
antiaircraft guns (AA), 54, 61, 102, 152,
  159, 203, 214, 227, 240, 427
  May 11 attacks and, 290, 294, 295,
    304–5, 309–10, *310, 312*, 317, 365
  Yamato and, 205–8
Archerfish (U.S. submarine), 134*n*
Arizona, USS, 21
armored hatches, 57, 367, 371
Army, Japanese, *see* Imperial Japanese
  Army
Army, U.S., 2*n*, 21, 41, 42, 100, 105, 114,
  212, 223
  in Aitape, 116*n*
  in Leyte, 120

in Okinawa, 198, 226, 231*n*, 241, 268,
  329, 436
in Philippines, 34, 35
Army Air Force, U.S., 131, 212, 216
Arnold, Henry "Hap," 443
Aruga, Kosaku, 211
ASP (anti-submarine patrol), 149
Astoria, USS, 253*n*
Atlantic Fleet, 434
atomic bomb, 420, 443, 460
Attu, 42, 116
Australia, 37, 42, 44, 211
  British in, 16, 34
  MacArthur evacuated to, 35
Avengers, *see* TBF Avenger torpedo
  bombers
avgas, 342
axes, 349, 359, *359*, 364
Ayama, Takeo, 96

B-17s, 44
B-25 medium bombers, 2*n*, 223, 243
B-29 Superfortress bombers, 104, 130,
  164, 179
  best use for, 212
  Kyushu bombed by, 176, 200, 216,
    220, 221, 223, 225, 238, 239, 243
  Okinawa reconnaissance flights of, 178
  suicide attacks and, 118*n*–19*n*
  in Tokyo raids, 128, 195–96
Baba, Mitsutaka, 268
Bacon, J. Waite "Slabo," 149–50, 271,
  273, 450
  May 11 attacks and, 304, 343–45, 355,
    406
Bakely (Tom Martin's friend), 307, 383*n*
Balch, Don, 74
Balfour, Douglas, 320–21
Bali, 34
Balikpapan, 34
Ball, George, 19*n*
Banko, 189
Basie, Count, 210
Bataan, USS, 214, 253
Bataan Death March, 36

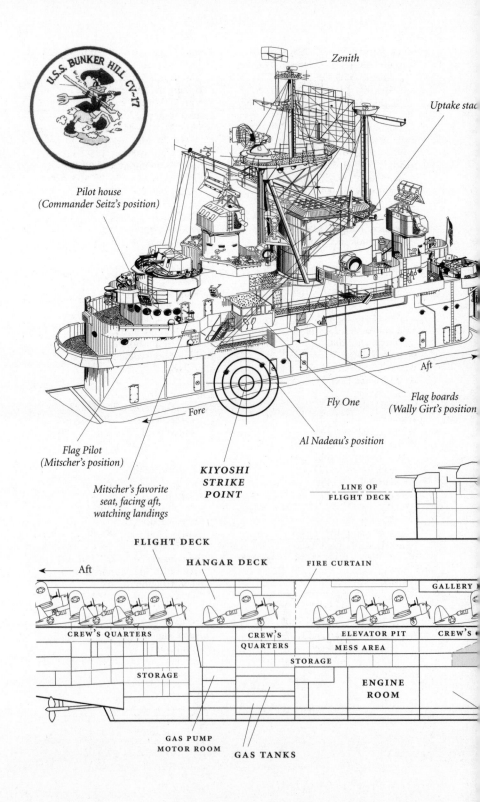

U.S.S. BUNKER HILL CV-17

Zenith

Uptake stac[k]

Pilot house
(Commander Seitz's position)

Aft

Fly One

Flag boards
(Wally Girt's position)

Fore

Al Nadeau's position

Flag Pilot
(Mitscher's position)

KIYOSHI
STRIKE
POINT

Mitscher's favorite
seat, facing aft,
watching landings

LINE OF
FLIGHT DECK

FLIGHT DECK

HANGAR DECK

FIRE CURTAIN

Aft

GALLERY

CREW'S QUARTERS

CREW'S
QUARTERS

ELEVATOR PIT

CREW'S

MESS AREA

STORAGE

STORAGE

ENGINE
ROOM

GAS PUMP
MOTOR ROOM

GAS TANKS

THE USS *BUNKER HILL*
Essex-Class Aircraft Carrier

Built by Bethlehem Steel Corp., Fore River, Quincy, Mass.

Launched Dec. 7, 1942
Commissioned May 24, 1943
Decommissioned Jan. 9, 1947

Dimensions (max.): 872' × 147.5'
Displacement: 27,100 tons standard; 36,380 tons full load
Speed: 32.7 knots

SOURCE: RAVEN, *ESSEX-CLASS CARRIERS*

(Inset to left shows port-side view of bridge structure)

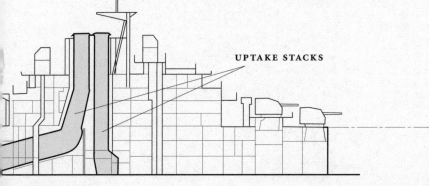

UPTAKE STACKS

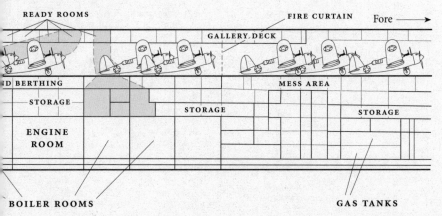

READY ROOMS

FIRE CURTAIN   Fore ⟶

GALLERY DECK

BERTHING

MESS AREA

STORAGE

STORAGE

STORAGE

ENGINE ROOM

BOILER ROOMS

GAS TANKS